KILIM

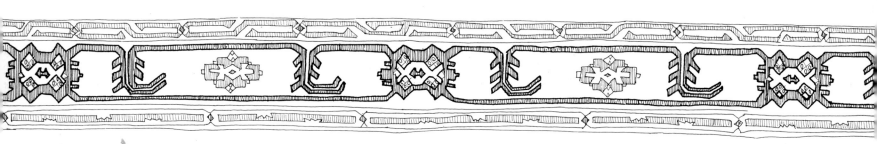

ALASTAIR HULL AND JOSÉ LUCZYC-WYHOWSKA

KILIM

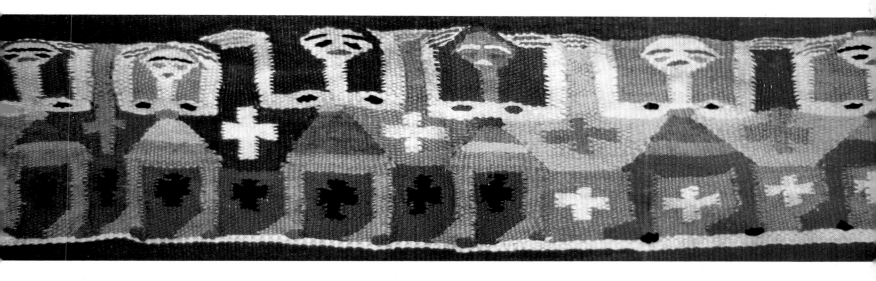

The Complete Guide

History • Pattern • Technique • Identification

INTRODUCTION BY NICHOLAS BARNARD

With 649 illustrations, 394 in colour and 18 maps

Line drawings by Miranda MacSwiney

Thames & Hudson

Page 1:

1 *A Daghestan border design.*

Details, p.2:

2 *A panel from a Kazakh* lakai *from north Afghanistan. The black hook design is typical of Central Asian kilims, and the eight-pointed star is the most popular Turkic motif, found in flatweaves of all Turkic people. (See* 516*)*

3 *The hand of Fatima, or perhaps part of a whimsical motif to mark the positions for the worshipper's hands either side of the niche, on a Balouch prayer mat from Afghanistan.*

4 *This kilim from Kuba in the Caucasus depicts a woman brandishing a hammer and sickle.*

5 *Part of a camel train, woven in dovetailing technique, from Gafsa in Tunisia.*

6 *The design brocaded into this Turkoman kilim is similar to that found on Central Asian purdah* textiles.

7 Adana *zili*
The weft-wrapping technique used in this kilim from Adana, in Anatolia, covers three warps in a horizontal direction.

Page 3:

8 *Human figures are depicted, possibly performing a ceremonial dance, on this kilim from Gafsa in Tunisia.*

Page 4:

9 *Bands of typically Turkic running motifs.*

Page 5:

10 *A Turkoman tent band from Central Asia.*

Page 6:

11 *The* bastidi gul, *a distinctive motif repeated on most Yomut Turkoman kilims from Central Asia.*

Throughout this book, the illustrations have been arranged in a sequence that runs from left to right and from top to bottom. The boxed descriptions of kilim types that appear in chapters 4–7 are intended to be a general guide to identification, and do not attempt to summarize the characteristics of every example from a particular flatweaving tribe or region.

First published in the United Kingdom in 1993 by
Thames & Hudson Ltd, 181A High Holborn, London WC1V 7QX

www.thamesandhudson.com

© 1993 Thames & Hudson Ltd, London

First paperback edition 2000
Reprinted 2008

British Library Cataloguing-in-Publication Data
A catalogue record for this book is available from the British Library

ISBN 978-0-500-28221-2

Printed and bound in Singapore by C.S. Graphics

Contents

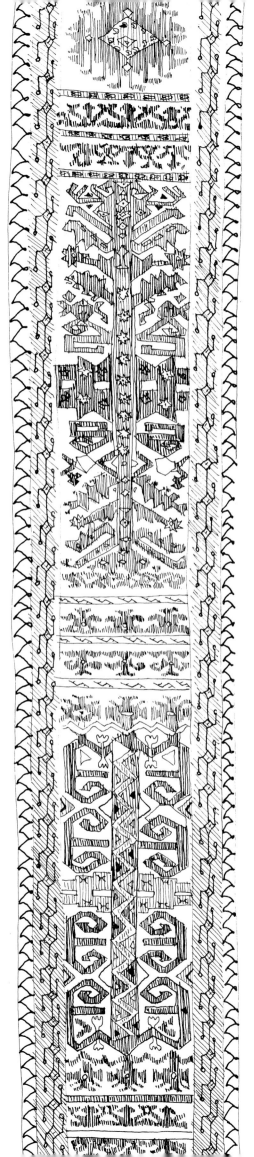

Chapter One

Introduction

12   *The kilim bazaar of Maimana in north Afghanistan. Only lengthy negotiations will secure a deal, and once struck it must be honoured.*

THROUGHOUT HISTORY, PEOPLE HAVE INSULATED THEMSELVES AGAINST THE climatic variations of their homelands by weaving cloth for clothing, rugs and all manner of covers and trappings. Textile production has evolved over thousands of years from the simplest methods of finger-plaiting and the interlacing of animal and vegetable fibres to the complexities of computer-controlled power-loom weaving, and with it textiles themselves have developed from the most basic items of utility into the most elaborate artifacts of prestige, paraded purely for their decorative beauty or as symbols of group identity.

The flatweaving of floor-rugs and trappings is practised in many communities spread over the globe. In North America the Navajo weave rugs and blankets, while in Mexico the blankets and covers known as *sarapes* are made, and the weavers of Peru, Bolivia and Ecuador are well known for their woollen rugs. Europe has its own long-established rug-weaving tradition; collectors of textiles will be familiar, for example, with the flatweaves of Scandinavia, Romania, Poland, Hungary and Greece, but may be surprised to learn that many of the traditional European flatweaving practices in fact take their origin from the nomadic groups and mountain village people of North Africa and Central and Western Asia.

Migrating over the steppes and the mountains, leading their goats and sheep, or ekeing out an existence in the remote fastness of a desert range, the nomads and villagers have successfully combined the qualities of utility, portability and ornamentation within their textiles. Their flatwoven blankets, rugs and trappings have provided protection against the fierce heat, the bitter cold, the snow and the rain. Tents are kept dry and secure, and the earth floor is spread with rugs and bedding blankets of sheep's wool. From such modest needs has developed a flatweaving culture without equal. The fruits of these simple nomadic and village looms we now know as kilims.

Almost all the weavers of the many and varied tribes and groups featured in this book are united by their Muslim faith. Although the flatweaving of rugs pre-dates the coming of Mohammed, the Islamic religion has given nomads and villagers a system of existence that, far from suppressing the believers' artistry, has unleashed a flood of creativity in their arts and crafts. Islam is an all-embracing religion which has amalgamated well with the lifestyles and traditions of the people and the skills and practices of their pre-Muslim past. The sophistication of the decorative arts of the Muslim world is reflected in the colours and the patterns of the kilims reproduced in the pages that follow. Yet most of the textiles illustrated here are not commissioned or even inspired by the wealthy court hierarchy for which the Ottoman, Safavid and Mameluke empires are known. On the contrary, they represent the work and wealth of communities living humble lives in harsh conditions.

The process of weaving was developed in various regions of the world at different times. There are many historical references to weaving and the nature and quality of cloth; the Iliad, amongst other works of classical literature, and the Bible are perhaps the most obvious examples, and early Egyptian tomb paintings depict vivid scenes of weavers at work. The finds from within the sarcophagi of the Nile region chart the development of weaving from plain to simple banded patterning through to slitweave work by about 1000 BC. The domestication and selective breeding of the sheep, goat, horse and camel ensured the ready

availability of wool and hair, and both plant and animal kingdoms provided a wealth of dyestuffs. From an early period certain regions and groups became known for their specialist rearing of breeds of sheep or goats, and dyers assumed almost shamanistic status for their preparation of colours of legendary brilliance. The trade in the raw materials of cloth production over the last five hundred years has been truly international; fine fleeces and wool from the Caucasus and dyestuffs such as indigo blue from the Indian subcontinent and Tyrian purple from the eastern and southern Mediterranean were luxury trading commodities highly valued throughout the Near East and Asia.

The history of the weaving processes of disparate groups will never be known. Textiles rot and disintegrate after a relatively short period unless preserved under extraordinary conditions. Similarly, wooden or bone weaving tools, such as combs and spindles, timber looms and accessories, will also have disintegrated, leaving only stone or metal implements to provide evidence of textile manufacture. The small quantity of cloth that has been exhumed, however, has proved to be of superlative quality, technical sophistication and creative ingenuity. Ancient textiles have been discovered in near-immaculate condition in the desert tombs of South America and the frozen crypts of Pazyryk in the Siberian Altai. The textile remains of Pazyryk provide an array of fascinating

13   *A Western trader concludes a deal with a wealthy Armenian kilim dealer. Hanging to the left of this Anatolian shop is a large kilim from Sivas or Malatya, and above the door a collection of Kars yastiks. The Senna kilims displayed either side of the door are easily recognizable.*

14 *A western Anatolian shepherd wearing a felt cloak decorated by star motifs that often appear on kilims. These cloaks provide a practical and effective shield against the elements.*

15 Erzurum
(1.43 × 1.25 m, 4'8" × 4')
The weaver of this kilim from Erzurum, Anatolia, has purposefully created 'lazy lines' for visual impact by completing small areas instead of weaving right across the central area of red ground. The date of 1279 (1862) is woven into the apex of the prayer arch.

Opposite:
16 Erzurum
(1.86 × 1.48 m, 6'1" × 4'10")
The intricate design of this nineteenth-century kilim is woven in slitweave, and its detailed patterning is characteristic of most Erzurum prayer kilims. The seven points where the body of the devotee touches the kilim are well defined: the places for the hands are on the red ground; the large hexagonal motifs positioning the forehead and knees, and the triangular emblems for the feet are contained within the blue/green field.

artifacts for oriental rug historians: a near-complete knotted rug survives, embellished with figurative motifs, as well as sundry flatweaves and felts, all dating from the fifth and fourth centuries BC. The rug's construction of woven and knotted yarn would have demanded a superior level of technological expertise together with a more settled lifestyle than that required for the relatively simple act of flatweaving alone. We can therefore be certain that flatweaving in this region pre-dates these remains, but we shall never know by how many millennia. Neither are we likely to discover how widespread were these ancient flatweaving skills. Other fragments of flatweaves have been unearthed in southern Siberia, as well as in northern Mongolia. The Anatolian isthmus has also yielded up textile remains; textiles dated to the seventh century BC have been found in Phrygia, and although it proved impossible to preserve them, they were initially recognizable as flatweaves. Excavations at Dorak have also provided evidence of flatweaving and tools used in the weaving process have come to light during archaeological digs all over Anatolia. Taking into consideration how advanced the Anatolians were,

17 *In the dyers' district of Marrakesh, skeins of recently dyed wool are strung on lines across the streets to dry.*

even in the sixth century BC, there is every reason to surmise that they would have known how to weave so basic a textile as a kilim; furthermore their communal lifestyle would have engendered the exchange of ideas and experimentation with different techniques conducive to the development of new weaving processes.

Excavations at Fostat, near Cairo, have provided a wealth of new evidence. Thousands of textile fragments have been exhumed that have dated from the seventh to the eleventh century and earlier. These finds were so copious that most museums the world over hold samples. Many of these are of local Coptic origin, and have proved to be tapestry decorations from vestments for clothing the dead. The Coptic weavers' skill in depicting the movement of animals and the detail of plantlife within the limitations of the flatweave technique is astounding. There is no doubt that such expertise must have been relished and nurtured by the invading Arabs of AD 641, and that this legacy of weaving skills inspired the succeeding Muslim empires of the region.

The Islamic empires of the Seljuks, Ottomans, Mongols, Safavids, Mamelukes and Berbers were great patrons of the textile arts. These groups ruled the lands from the Mediterranean shores to Cathay between the seventh and eighteenth centuries and established a network of trade that extended from the Atlantic coast to the South China Sea; many of their enlightened rulers established workshops and gathered dyers and weavers from all over Asia to satisfy the affluent desires of the court and the ruling elite. This thousand-year period proved to be a golden era in the history of Islamic decorative textiles, during which time the weavers at their encampment and village looms were influenced by court fashions and were beholden to the demands of suzerainty from their rulers. From this era comes one of the earliest surviving Anatolian flatweaves: a weft-wrapped rug which is thought to be Ottoman in origin. Such courtly styles are evident, even today, in the floral work of the weavers of Senna (modern Sanandaj) in Iran.

Many more kilim fragments have survived from the eighteenth and nineteenth centuries, but unfortunately it has proved impossible to be exact in ascertaining either their date or place of origin. Certainly, aside from the ancient weaves from the frozen tombs of Central Asia, and until the eighteenth and the nineteenth centuries, when kilim fragments, and even complete rugs, became more widely available, the evidence of the flatweaving styles of the past is focused firmly on the finds in Egypt and Anatolia.

As the wealthy townspeople of the Islamic empires sought out the finest textiles and weavers both within their own lands and abroad, the villagers and nomads continued to weave the traditional knotted and flatwoven rugs and trappings that provided both the essentials and the comforts for basic existence. These peoples, particularly the nomads, had little else but the natural environment to provide them with all the elements necessary for weaving. Harvesting the wool and hair from their animals, synthesizing the dyes from whatever source was available and building the coarsely hewn looms from bushes and trees, the villagers and nomads have produced an astonishing array of rugs and trappings over the centuries. Kilims served as rugs, and the flatweave process facilitated the production of strong and colourful bags to contain personal possessions, straps to tie the bags on to the animals during migration, bands to secure the tents when erected and large sacks for the transportation of food and clothing. Tent walls for the division of the men's and women's areas were also often made from kilims.

1 Morocco 2 Algeria 3 Tunisia
4 Spain 5 Libya 6 Egypt
7 Atlantic Ocean 8 Mediterranean Sea
9 Tennsift 10 High Atlas
11 Saharan Atlas

Tribal Movement and Migration in North Africa, 10th–16th Century

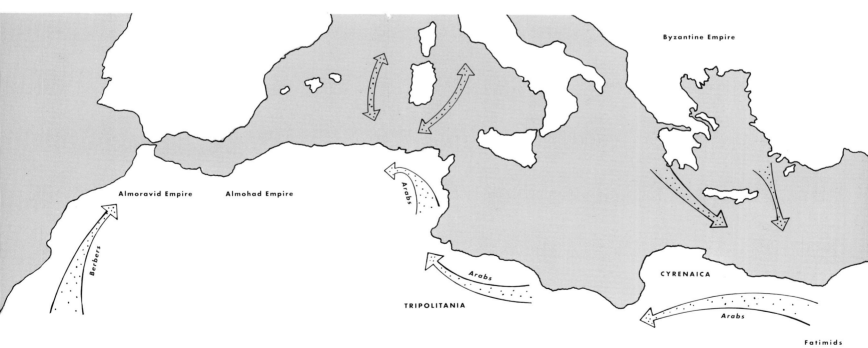

18 Shahsavan of Mogan
(1.14 × 0.61 m, 3′9″ × 2′)
A classic, old and very beautiful khorjin *donkey bag from Iran. The central star motif in green, reflected in each corner of the central panel, is often found. The running motif on a white ground is derived from a complex dragon image.*

19 Shahsavan
(2.47 × 2.01 m, 8′1″ × 6′7″)
A caravan of one hundred camels, charmingly depicted by the Shahsavan tribe of Iran. Note the dog-like creatures climbing up the camels' legs. Woven in plainweave and weft wrapping in two pieces and joined, this naturally dyed horse cover of the late nineteenth century is constructed with different coloured warps across the centre.

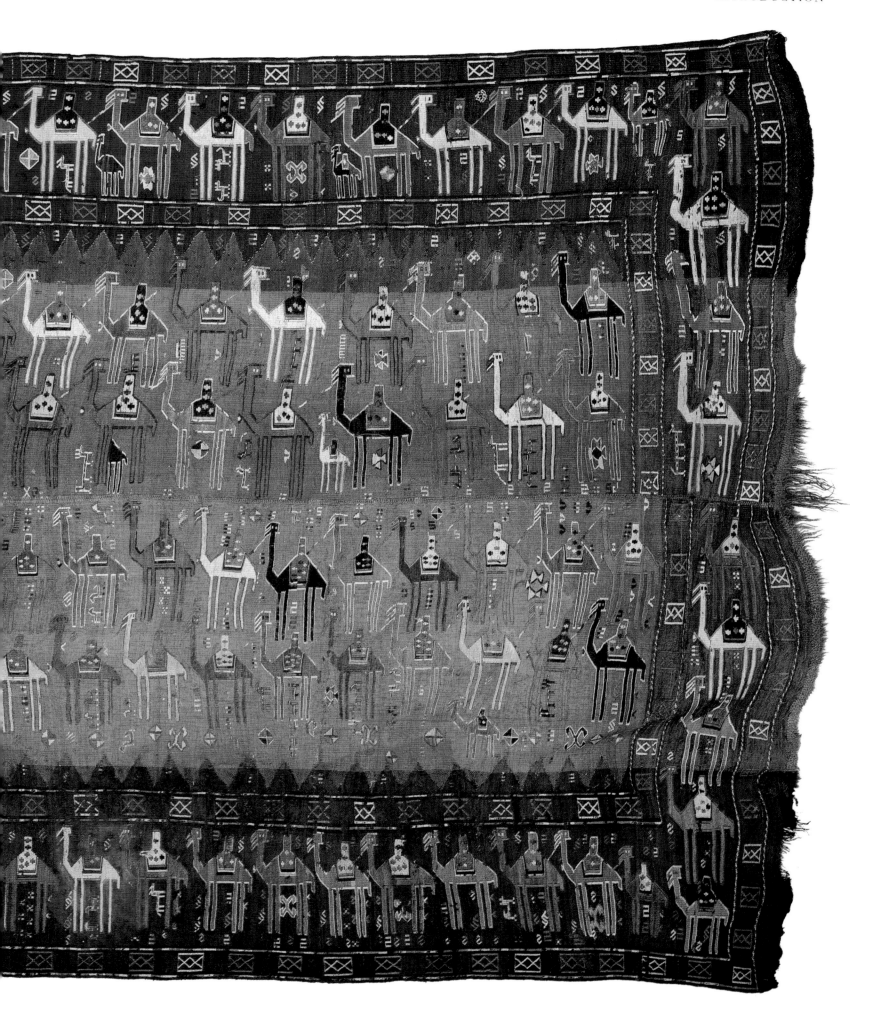

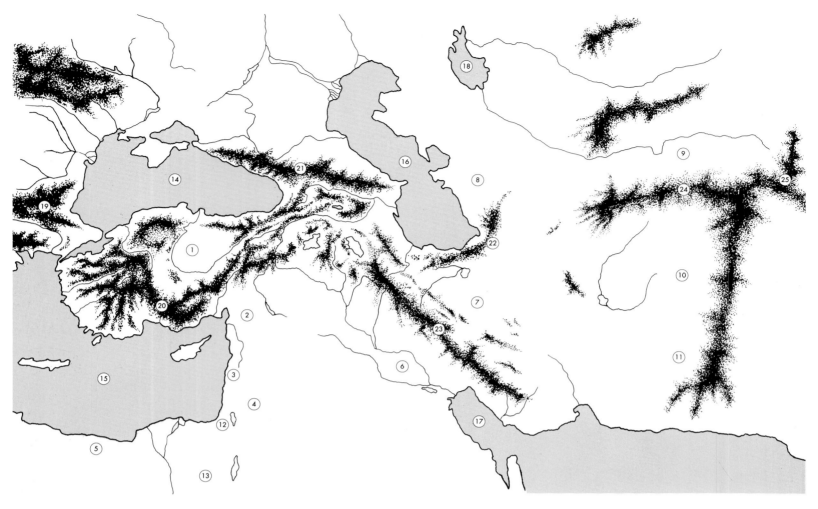

1 Anatolia   2 Syria   3 Lebanon
4 Jordan   5 Egypt   6 Iraq
7 Persia (Iran)   8 Turkestan
9 Uzbekistan   10 Afghanistan
11 Balouchistan   12 Palestine
13 Arabia   14 Black Sea
15 Mediterranean Sea   16 Caspian Sea
17 Persian Gulf   18 Aral Sea
19 Balkan Mountains
20 Taurus Mountains   21 The Caucasus
22 Elburz Mountains
23 Zagros Mountains   24 Hindu Kush
25 Karakorum Mountains

Kilims were used as door flaps, covers for food in preparation, eating cloths and prayer rugs. Guests would be treated to a fine array of the best flatweaves as a display of their hosts' status and hospitality; as the main room of a Muslim house contains little in the way of furniture, the host and guest would sit or recline on the floor, resting against a *balisht* floor cushion or rolls of bedding. In the summer months rugs would be spread outside in a shaded yard or on the flat roofs of the houses in the evening, to provide a comfortable refuge from the heat. Much the same arrangement exists in the tents of the nomads, who keep kilims neatly in bags both to save space and for ease of transportation. As well as providing comfort, kilims, together with jewelry, clothing, tent furnishings and animal trappings, expressed the identity of the village or nomadic group and served, along with the knotted rugs, precious metals and animals, as a form of family wealth. At a time of crisis, or of need for a commodity that can neither be made nor gathered, any of these possessions could be bartered or exchanged for currency to use in the markets of the local market town.

Most importantly, the production of kilims has remained an integral part of a young woman's, and her family's, opportunity to improve their standing through marriage, for not only does her weaving provide a useful source of wealth for her husband and his group, but it has also always formed a major part of the bride's dowry. Then, as now, the arrangement of marriage by the elders of the family was vitally important, and involved much more than the union of two people. A girl would be betrothed at an early age, becoming an instrument of liaison between two families and so creating possible financial, commercial and political benefit to at least the groom's family, if not to both parties concerned. The exchange of

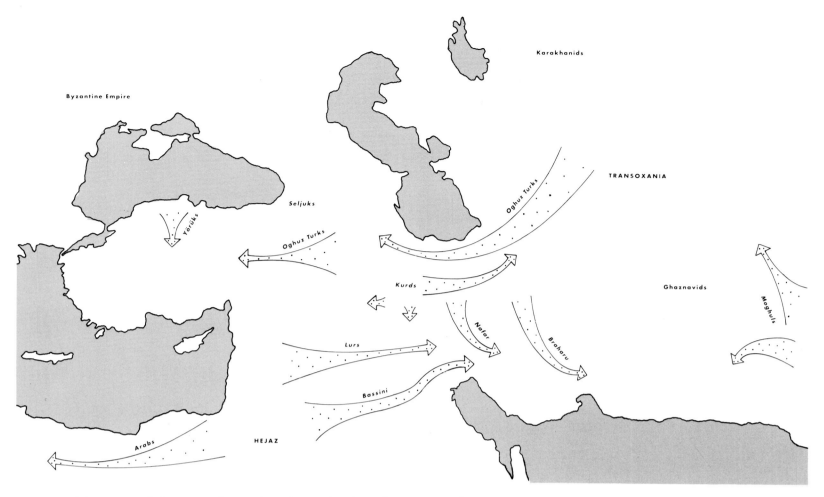

Tribal Movement and Migration in Central Asia, 10th–16th Century

wealth was made by way of rugs, jewelry, animals and money, and the granting of grazing, water and irrigation rights. Therefore, the weaving of kilims was an important skill to be mastered by a young bride, learned from her mother and other women of the family. Created with a sense of pride, duty and love, every article would contain symbols of the family's traditions and tribal identity and totems of superstition, good luck and fertility, spiced with the personal inspiration of the future bride, whose youthful exuberance would be held in check by the mores and tenets of a conservative Muslim society. Such standards and codes, the laws of Islam and time-honoured tribal traditions, have not quashed the vitality of tribal creativity, but have in fact provided a structured framework, a set of rules and guidelines, within which the imaginative potential and skills of the weaver may be disciplined. The constraints on self-expression have also ensured the continuity of tribal compositions, patterns and designs from generation to generation, and it is these elements, when combined with the zealous desire to create a dowry of quantity and quality, that explain why so many kilims have been so painstakingly crafted over the centuries without a prospect of real commercial gain.

The art of weaving has always been a predominantly female preserve, and continues to form part of a woman's daily round of duties in the household or encampment. Rather than weaving continuously, she is more likely to start and stop as she wishes. Certainly the seasonal agrarian cycle will dictate the pattern of weaving activity. For the nomads, the sojourn at a summer camp high in the mountains is the time most conducive to intensive work on a ground loom. For the villagers, however, such summer months are a busy period of crop tending

20 *Hazara women and children work together on ground looms in the privacy of the compound of a traditional Muslim house. This photograph was taken by the renowned traveller and writer, Wilfred Thesiger, on his journey through central Afghanistan in 1954.*

and harvesting for all the family, and so winter is the most productive weaving season. In most of the sedentary communities, kilim-weaving is very much a cottage industry and is performed as a pastime rather than as a main occupation. It is often a communal activity, so that two or three women may work on a large kilim simultaneously.

Kilim-weaving has also provided an opportunity for alms-giving, prescribed by the Koran. Kilims, donated by both the rich and poor of the community, not only provide colourful decoration for the mosque floor, they also serve as a many-layered, warm and comfortable ground for prayer and prostration. In Anatolia particularly, the prevalence of alms-giving has ensured that, at least until recently, the mosques have functioned as a depository of flatweave and knotted-rug local history.

Towards the end of the nineteenth century the demands of international trade began to exert increasing pressure on the largely self-sufficient lifestyle of the nomads and villagers. Faced with the forced settlement of the 'unruly' wanderers in the interests of the state, and the flooding of the marketplace with cheap textiles, yarns and dyestuffs, the rural peoples were disenfranchised from their independent existence. Once settled, a tribe had to survive by trade or barter, which meant that many skills apparently irrelevant to village or town life were abandoned. In this way the weaving of tent bands and decorations as well as some sacks and bags has been the first element of traditional textile production to suffer in the face of the absorption of the group into modern society.

Settled tribes have generally continued to produce kilims, however, which are predominantly for home use or local consumption. Although some tribes have indeed ceased weaving altogether, other groups or villages have become well known for their creation of new rugs, and of late have increased their output. There is no doubt that the composition of the kilims has been dramatically affected. Tribal intermarriage has become more common, hastening the amalgamation of cultural styles and confusing the heritage of the 'traditional' arts. These changes have often been accompanied by a decline in craftsmanship, particularly evident in the appearance of brash colours which stems from the introduction of synthetic dyes from Europe in the late nineteenth century. The disintegration of weaving and dyeing standards has not, however, been uniform, but has spread slowly from the cities to the towns, villages and eventually to the rural areas so that until relatively recently some of the nomadic groups of North Africa, Anatolia, Iran and Afghanistan were still weaving with the raw materials and styles of their ancestors. There are occasions when the fusion of designs and styles of different tribes, or the use of modern dyestuffs and design influences from the West, has resulted in the creation of highly individual kilims.

The collecting of kilims by Westerners is a recent enthusiasm. Whereas the exotic and luxurious chararacter of the knotted carpet had ensured its desirability by the church and elite even before the sixteenth century, flatwoven rugs were ignored or regarded as the inferior work of the peasantry, and used by the colonials as dog blankets, picnic rugs and wrapping for bales of knotted carpets. The collecting of flatweaves was the exclusive preserve of textile specialists, enlightened travellers and expatriates with an interest in tribal Islamic art. It was only in the the 1950s and 1960s, in the aftermath of the introduction of rapid mass transportation and the institution of aid programmes by worthy agencies, that large numbers of Westerners first awoke to the allure of flatweaves. The primary focus of attention in the West was concentrated on the colourful and powerfully patterned textiles of the Anatolian groups and tribespeople from southern Iran.

At first kilims were, for the most part, appreciated by Westerners for their graphic qualities, and hung on the wall; indeed, it was the bold and intensely coloured patterning of nomadic kilims such as those of the Qashqai that first attracted collectors and travellers. These large and powerfully dramatic works were displayed by specialist textile galleries in the Western World, initiating, along with the enthusiastic demands of emancipated tourists and the perspicacity of certain interior designers, a general awareness of the kilim as an unusual floor rug or hanging. By the middle of the 1980s the kilim had gained credibility throughout the furnishing market of the Western nations, so that new Turkish flatweaves may now be found within oriental carpet galleries, furniture and department stores alike. People have now started to use kilims in very imaginative ways. The old, traditional and rare kilims, because of their historic value and visual interest, are usually only displayed in museums or kept in private collections. Other kilims with decorative and practical appeal have been used as upholstery, cushion covers and curtains, as well as material for fashion accessories, including handbags, wallets, belts, hats, shoes, suitcases and briefcases, and as covers for books and even tennis rackets, along with other uses dreamt up by imaginative designers. Kilims certainly provide the versatility required for the designer market, as their endless wealth of patterns and unusual

21 *A Qashqai camel girth.*

colour combinations offer fresh inspiration to all. Kilim designs and colours have also had a big impact on the clothing and textile industry, which has borrowed their ancient compositions and recreated them so that both pre-Islamic and Islamic tribal designs appear on printed and woven fabric throughout the Western World. Photographs of kilims, seen in their entirety or as details, now appear on greeting cards, postcards and wrapping paper.

Ironically, now the inherent artistry of flatweaving is widely recognized, the output of the traditional forms of flatweave is on the wane. The market desire is for the 'old' kilim, and yet the 'naive', 'pre-industrial' and 'pre-Western-commercial' lifestyle that ensured the copious weaving of the 'traditional' flatwoven rug is no more and is not likely to come again. And so the old kilims have been collected with zeal, with predictable results: prices have soared the world over as the supply of such kilims, which was never large to begin with, has virtually dried up, and dealers' methods of procuring these items have become more unscrupulous. In Anatolia, for instance, when the Western demand for kilims was first established, old kilims were bought or exchanged from the homes of individual tribespeople; when this supply dwindled, the mosques were targeted. The many thousands of kilims donated to mosques as alms have proved irresistible to the traders or their agents, who would approach the senior local cleric, the *iman*, and attempt, by fair means or foul, to part him from his existing collection – offering new replacement kilims and carpets in exchange. Slowly, the kilims have disappeared from the mosques of Anatolia, and virtually no old indigenous examples remain.

It is hardly surprising, therefore, that the weavers themselves, especially within Anatolia and Iran, have not only been continuing to produce their own 'village' rugs, but have begun to produce kilims that replicate the compositions and colours of the past – with varying degrees of success and, therefore, value. The village production of kilims has continued, but the standard of weaving has declined and the use of natural dyes or traditional combinations of dyes is much less frequent. The village weavers of today do not have the time or inclination to weave a quality kilim, for the faster the weaver can finish her work, the sooner she can sell it and buy a refrigerator or television set for her home. In one village, with

22 *A Kuba kilim woven in Azerbaijan.*

23 *Caucasian carpet and kilim dealers sitting outside their booth in a bazaar at the turn of the century. Hanging above and to the right of the booth is an enormous* jajim, *a kilim made of narrow strips of plainweave intricately embroidered and sewn together.*

no electricity supply, lived a weaver who had bought a refrigerator, proudly placed it in the living room and filled it with all her most precious possessions!

The weaving of new kilims for commercial purposes is now a firmly established industry. The character of these modern kilims is often far removed from that of new flatweaves made for the weavers' own use, but they do fill a gap in the market, and have also provided an income for the weavers. Authentic compositions are employed, but the wool is often of poor quality and the dyes are often very 'flat'. However, despite their drawbacks, these new commercial kilims have become very popular, primarily because they can be sold in the West at a competitive price. There is a wide variation in quality, which ranges from the everyday inexpensive examples to the 'replicas', woven of naturally dyed, hand-spun wool in traditional designs, which continue to be made in the authentic way.

It is clear that the motivations for kilim-weaving have changed greatly of late. Kilims made for profit and commerce in an international or tourist market have largely replaced the 'traditional' examples produced for domestic use or as part of a dowry. The marketplace may now seem enormously confusing to the potential

24   *A Turkoman tent band.*

collector, for not only are there traditional examples to be found but also a flood of recent village production, as well as new village and commercial kilims of every quality and value. Only by becoming familiar with many different kilims, old and new, from a diverse range of tribes and villages, will one be able to discern the commercial value of a piece. Whether the example is a valuable antique expressing a powerful ethnic identity, or a modern flatweave produced with great verve, using chemical dyes, the individual character and beauty of each makes the study of kilims hugely enjoyable and rewarding.

Within this book you will find a remarkable array of flatweaves from the Islamic world, from the Atlantic coast of North Africa, along the Mediterranean, through the Middle East to Central Asia (although some Muslim countries fall outside the areas of major weaving activity: Saudi Arabia and the Levant, for example, do have traditions of kilim-weaving, but not in significant quantities or variations in design). The various stages involved in gathering and processing the raw materials are charted first of all, from the fleece to the dye bath and on to the loom, after which a detailed description of the many diverse techniques of flatweaving is given. Kilim motifs and symbols are then analysed, in an attempt to determine the influence of the loom-weaving process itself, and of the beliefs, superstitions, traditions and folklore of the weavers on design compositions.

Country by country and region by region, the chapters interlink and advance geographically west to east, from North Africa to Afghanistan and Central Asia, examining the tribal origins and weaving history of the nomads, villagers and townspeople. Details of principal kilim types are given to help with recognition and identification. Colour plates demonstrate the variety and visual energy of the kilims and black and white illustrations offer a pictorial account of the lifestyle of the weavers, and show traders and dealers in the bazaar. Separate chapters are reserved for the utilitarian flatweaves, such as bags and trappings, and for a survey of recent kilim production and its future.

The final chapters of this book are for those in need of help and advice when buying, caring for and preserving kilims, and an international selection of dealers, importers and repairers can be found within the last section. Finally, for those confused or disorientated by the plethora of exotic titles and descriptions, there is a comprehensive glossary and index.

The terms used to describe flatweaves are indeed as varied as the tribal weaving groups themselves. Some of the names used to describe flatwoven rugs are *hanbel* in North Africa, *kilim* in Turkey, *palas* in the Caucasus, *gelim* in Iran and *kelim* in Afghanistan. Such has been the growth in interest in these flatweaves over the past two decades and so fruitful have proved the weaving communities of Turkey and Iran, that the term 'kilim' has now become the known term for a flatwoven rug of any origin, raw material, method of construction and patterning. Wherever possible specialist titles of artifacts such as flatwoven bags and trappings, and historical and tribal placenames in the closest equivalent English spelling, have been used. As kilims are all different sizes, the following references to dimensions apply: 'large' indicates a textile over 3 m (10') long or 1.75 m (5'6") wide; and 'medium', over 2 m (6'6") long or one metre (3'3") wide. Kilims are described as 'long' when their length is greater than two and a half times their width.

Chapter Two

Making Kilims

25 *A woman weaving a kilim on a vertical loom in Morocco ties alternate woollen warps to the heddle to separate them and form the shed. Designs very similar to the patterns she is weaving can be seen tattooed on her hands and wrists.*

THE HIGHLY INDIVIDUAL CHARACTER OF FLATWEAVES IS INTIMATELY connected with their production: the materials used for the warps and wefts, the way the yarn is spun, the choice of dye colours, the structural make-up and the method of finish. The wide variety of materials, techniques and colourings has evolved and developed in response to resources, practical needs and tribal influences. All these different components and techniques can be analysed or isolated in order to help identify the possible age and origin of a flatweave.

Materials

THROUGHOUT THE KILIM-PRODUCING COUNTRIES, THE MATERIALS USED FOR weaving – sheep's wool, the hair of the goat, camel and horse, and cotton – are all readily available close at hand. The production of kilims only became so prolific and socially important within the various ethnic cultures (as a form of wealth, an essential part of a wedding dowry and as items of practical use) because of the surfeit of these raw materials. The nomads, who in better times have flocks of many thousands of sheep, shear large quantities of wool each year. In the past their insular and self-sufficient lifestyle, in which they had little contact with trading bazaars, would have enabled the women to make many more fabrics, rugs and bags than were immediately required. The excess would have been stored, and could gain value by being exchanged for both essential utensils and contracts for land, irrigation and marriage. The value of a textile would have been determined by its comparative qualities of workmanship, materials, colour and design, and therefore, over time, the weavers would try to improve on all aspects of the finished flatweave with the available materials in order to increase the potential worth of the work.

Wool

As sheep have evolved from their prehistoric ancestors to the domesticated breeds of today, so has man's use of their wool, and the techniques and skills involved in its weaving. The prehistoric sheep had a coat of matted hair more like felt than a fleece that could be shorn, but since the domestication of sheep some ten millennia past and subsequent selective breeding and husbandry, the fleece has evolved into a long-stapled, soft fibre that can be spun. Sheep were amongst the first animals known to be domesticated by man, and care of the flock led primitive people into a pastoralist existence. Certainly wool has always been the dominant source of yarn in Central Asia and North Africa.

The characteristics of wool are quite different from hair, cotton and silk. Minute scales on the surface of the fibre 'knit' the wool together when it is felted or spun; it also has a high oil content of about forty percent, so that the cloth not only insulates but also wears well. There are two breeds of original wild sheep from which the domestic sheep has developed, the mouflon and the urial. Both have an inner coat of soft felted wool and an outer coat of longer wool.

The mouflon (*Ovis musimon*) looks like a small antelope with long twisted horns, and is still abundant in Asia. Both male and female are quite small. The mouflon can be domesticated, but is highly prized as quarry and hunted by the Qashqai in the Zagros Mountains, the Turkomen in the Hindu Kush and the Balouch tribesmen in the Palangan and Chagai Hills. The urial sheep (*Ovis vignai*) is confined in its wild state to the Elburz Mountains to the south of the Caspian Sea, and most of the domesticated breeds of sheep are descended from the ancestors of this animal.

The various pastoral groups require different qualities from their flocks, whether it be the quantity of meat, wool, and milk, or the hardiness to survive the climate, the periods of scant food and water, or the long migrations, and these requirements have been met by cross-breeding. Each tribe and region supports breeds that can be identified and named – the kermani, balouchi, rukhshani and kurdi, for example. Other types, such as the merino, native of Australia and New Zealand, have been imported for breeding from other parts of the world to increase quality and quantity. The colour of the wool can vary enormously from breed to breed, ranging from ivory white and light brown to dark reddish brown, grey and black.

A number of major types of sheep are found in Turkey. In the west, near Bursa, the merino sheep predominates, famous for its soft and long-stapled wool. In central and eastern Anatolia the dağlic, or mountain sheep, the red karaman and white karaman provide a long wool of medium quality that produces strong and thick yarn. Another breed, the kivicik sheep, also found in central and eastern Anatolia, yields a curly, shorter yarn.

Domestic sheep are either fat-tailed, long-tailed or fat-rumped. Fat-tailed sheep are found all over Central and Near Asia as well as North Africa. The wool that has for many years made the famous carpets and kilims of the Caucasus so coveted comes from this breed, which is highly valued by the Qashqai for its ability to migrate long distances. The awassi is much favoured in Israel, south-west Iran, Iraq and north-eastern Arabia. The karaqul sheep produces a dual fleece consisting of two types of wool growing simultaneously; its inner fleece is well known for the tight curls of 'Persian Lamb', used by milliners and coat makers, whereas the outer fleece is long-stapled and hard-wearing and is much used in carpet and kilim-weaving in north Afghanistan. The tail can develop to an enormous size, some 13 to 18 kg (30 to 40 lbs) and the fats deposited in the tail that sustain the sheep in times of shortage of water and food also provide nourishment for the pastoralists. Long-tailed sheep are found in the eastern parts of Afghanistan and Balouchistan, in parts of Arabia near the Persian Gulf, Syria and the Lebanon and in North Africa. The fat-rumped variety, named for the large projection of fat over the loins and rear of the animal, are found in the northern parts of Central Asia and in North Africa. This breed is favoured by the Turkomen as it can travel long distances in harsh conditions whilst retaining its ability to produce milk, and maintaining its bodyweight.

The quality of wool from any breed depends on the climate and pasture. The famous fleeces from Khorassan have derived their lustrous shine, softness and excellent dye-taking qualities from the equable climate and lush grazing lands, as well as from the attention given over centuries to sheep breeding for carpet wool. In the hot, sandy desert areas, the wool is much harsher.

26 *Shorn fleeces must be left in the sun to dry. The flat roofs in the outskirts of Konya, in Anatolia, provide an ideal location.*

Shearing Shearing is done by hand and takes place once or twice a year, initially when the coldest winter weather is over, in April or May, or – as with the Qashqai and the Bakhtiari – when the flocks have been moved to the summer pastures. In warmer coastal areas, such as North Africa, Arabia and southern Iran, shearing can take place as early as March, whereas in the mountainous areas with a continental climate, such as parts of eastern Turkey, north-east Iran and Afghanistan, as late as June. Some tribes shear the short summer fleece in the late summer or early autumn. The amount of wool produced by one sheep varies from about one to 3 kg (2 to 6 lbs), and the fleeces are washed either on the hoof by driving the whole flock through a stream, or after shearing. In the areas where the best quality wool is sought, care is taken over all the processes of preparing the yarn. The wool is repeatedly washed and scoured until it is clean and the natural oil content is as desired. For cleansing, soft water is the ideal, and good streams and pools are jealously guarded by families over generations. Their rights of use are as important as access to irrigation water, and comprise an integral part of dowry exchange. Chemical compounds such as potash, carbonate of soda and other alkalis (including plant materials) are sometimes added to the water to help remove dirt and the superfluous fats and oils.

The washing process is important not only to remove the dirt from the fleece, but also to prepare the wool for dyeing. Certain dyes are taken up more successfully and produce a fine sheen and lustre if the wool is washed very lightly in soft water. The wool is then sorted by colour and graded by quality, so that the coarse and rough hairs are separated from the soft fleece taken from the shoulders, chest and underside of the sheep. Commercialization and the inevitable lowering of standards in quality production today result in less care being taken in the

process of sorting. There is now much mixing of wool from different shearing seasons, and the factors will include in the batch the wool taken from the carcasses of slaughtered animals.

The next process is known as carding, and aligns the fibres. The most common carding tool is a block of wood with rows of metal spikes, embedded in the ground; the wool is pulled through the spikes repeatedly until all the fibres lie in the same direction and the longer fibres are separated from the shorter. Some groups have traditionally used 'butter pat' carders – two spiked boards held in the hands – but these tools make the work a slow process. In Central Asia, the string of a bow is used to fluff and align the fibres of both wool and cotton.

Spinning Spinning is a very laborious and seemingly never-ending task, usually done by all the community; only the Qashqai look upon spinning as solely women's work. Not all wool used in the carpet and kilim business is hand-spun, for there is an economic advantage in buying machine-spun wool. Nevertheless, it is far from suitable; machine-spun wool is fine and frizzy, the staples are broken short and much of the elastic and flexible character of the wool has been lost. The most common method of hand-spinning is with a drop spindle, for which the simplest whorl can be a stone or piece of clay, but a vertical wooden or metal spindle driven through a whorl in the form of a notched square or disk is most often seen. Alternatively, simple crossed pieces of wood are used. These are often decorated with carved patterns, both for personalization and as talismans for good luck. The 'thigh' spindle, made of a long wooden stick, is flat in the middle with blunt points and notches at the ends; such a tool is used by the older members of Balouch tribes as well as the Kirghiz and Kurds in east Turkey.

27 *At a wool factory in Uşak, western Anatolia, three women engage in the endless task of separating the light from the darker wool, in preparation for spinning.*

28 *Wool fibres have to be aligned after shearing and washing before spinning can begin. Here, in Mhadia in Tunisia, two boards with nails are used as combs to card the wool.*

33   *In the southern Iranian province of Kerman, a woman of Turkic origin works at a spinning wheel. Crudely made from wood, a wheel of this design is used by sedentary people in south and east Iran and Balouchistan. In skilled hands, yarn can be produced more quickly on a wheel than on a drop spindle.*

With practice spinning becomes an almost automatic task, and it is common to see shepherds spinning while watching their flocks. Women and girls spin in their leisure hours, while minding the babies, or even when riding on camels to fresh pastures during the summer migration. The wool rove – a bundle of fibres drawn from the washed fleece – is wrapped round the left arm and teased into alignment and proper thickness using the thumb and forefinger of the right hand. A short length of twisted wool is attached to the whorl, the left hand is lifted, and a slight spin on the spindle sets the process in motion. As long as the wool is teased out from the rove, the spindle turns automatically to spin and wind the wool. With experience, a strong, pliable and even thread can be spun, and when the spindle reaches the ground, the spun thread is wound round the shaft below the whorl, and so the whole process starts again. A full spindle is unwound, stretched and wound into a ball weighing up to 2 kg (5 lbs). Individual threads have a twist that corresponds to the direction in which the spindle has been spun, either in a clockwise direction giving a 'Z' twist, or anti-clockwise to create an 'S' twist. The natural turn of the spindle for right-handed people is clockwise, and so yarn with a 'Z' twist is the more common. Workshop and factory yarns, as they are spun using machines, may have an 'S' twist. Two or more threads may be spun together to obtain a plied yarn that is much stronger than the individual thread (which is likely to untwist after spinning). The direction of the spin of plied wool is opposite to that of the threads, so a 'Z'-spun thread is plied in an anticlockwise direction. The yarn is therefore balanced through the combination of the two opposing twists, so it is less likely to unravel and break. Unplied yarn is used only where fineness of thread is more important than strength, and is therefore very rarely used either as the warp or weft of flatweaves.

Yarn is classified first by the direction of the twist, then by the number of threads in the ply, and lastly by the direction of the twist of the ply, so that 'Z2S', for example, would indicate the common ply of two 'Z'-twist yarns with an 'S' twist. A combination of Z3S is often found in old Caucasian weavings. Cotton yarn is normally spun in a higher ply, such as Z4S or Z8S, to give the strength needed for long warps.

Opposite:

29   *A Tunisian girl is drawing a fleece through a comb of long metal teeth and spinning it directly on to her spindle. The device is home-made, and is designed to speed up the process of carding and spinning.*

30   *This Tunisian girl sets her whorl spinning. The task of spinning is undertaken by the whole family, and is most time-consuming.*

31   *A man in traditional everyday garb spins yarn, using a drop spindle, in the sunshine outside his house in Aleppo.*

32   *An elderly Persian man spinning wool. Round his left arm is wrapped the rove of unspun wool, from which he teases a strand on to the drop spindle, spinning it until it reaches the ground. The yarn is then wound round the spindle under the wooden cross of the whorl.*

Hair

Goat, camel and horse hair are also used in flatweaving, but in limited quantities. Goat hair, taken from close to the animal's skin, has a silky sheen, and is used as warp yarn in some bags and horse covers; it is also sometimes found spun into sheep's wool to give a soft fringe on the warps of a kilim. The long, tough outer hair of the goat is used to make hard-wearing selvedges and as a warp material for some Central Asian nomadic weavings. Camel hair is extremely durable and is a better insulator than wool. The Bactrian two-humped camel of Central Asia moults a considerable amount of hair, which, along with hair shorn from the neck and throat, is used sparingly in nomadic flatweaving in Afghanistan, Balouchistan and east Iran. Camel-coloured wool, found both as warp and weft, is often mistaken for camel hair. Some hair is plucked from the single-humped dromedary camel of North Africa and Arabia during the moulting season and used as reinforcement and strengthening for functional flatweaves. Horse hair taken from the mane and tail is used as decorative tassels and fringes. Such hair is particularly popular with the horse-loving Uzbeks, Kazakhs and Turkomen of north Afghanistan, and is used by the Shahsavan and Qashqai as an additional ornament on horse blankets and trappings.

Cotton

Cotton grows wild in most of the fertile valleys of Central Asia and North Africa, and has been cultivated commercially and collectively by sedentary farmers in large quantities for most of this century. Cotton is used primarily as a ground material, and has numerous advantages over wool. It is in plentiful supply, is strong, does not change or lose shape and can be spun into relatively thin strands for fine weaving. Although used primarily for warps, it is often used for highlighting designs and patterns, for, unlike white wool which turns cream or ivory with age, cotton retains its original brightness. Cotton does, however, mat together and never holds dye with the lustre and sheen of wool.

Other Materials

Silk kilims were once produced in Aleppo, Syria, and in the Safavid period they were made in Senna workshops for the fashions and ephemeral desires of the Persian court, yet nowadays silk is rarely used for flatweaving, except in the Kayseri region of Anatolia. Occasionally silk can be found as a supplementary weft decoration in bags and trappings, particularly on a dowry piece. More unusual materials are very popular with certain tribes and groups; metal threads, artificial fibres in lurid colours, beads, shells and coins are items of rarity and thus fascination to nomadic people, who shop in a small bazaar perhaps once a year. The attraction of such fripperies for the nomads only serves to highlight the differences in culture and wealth between their world and the West.

34 *A Turkoman tent band.*

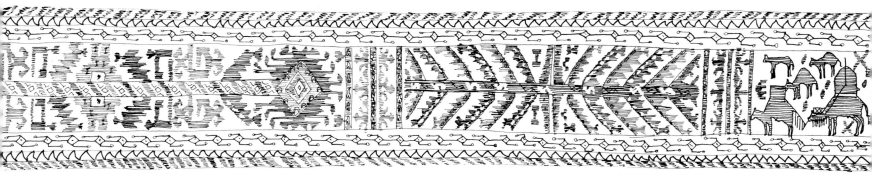

Dyes

COLOUR HAS AN INEXORABLE ATTRACTION: BY ITS VERY NATURE IT IS THE FIRST thing that catches the eye. The tones and combinations of colours found on a kilim are amongst the most important elements of its character, and highlight the design. Colour is created by many different dyestuffs, and the most attractive hues and tones are made from natural elements. Obtaining colours from natural dyestuffs is never predictable; recipes are personal and never precise, and the many variable factors, such as soil type, vagaries of climate and the particular fixing agent, or mordant, used, all affect the end result. It is because of such unknown quantities that the whole process of dyeing was often accompanied by a proliferation of superstitious rituals believed to help procure the desired shade.

Harmonious use of colour determines the overall effect, and the nomadic and village weavers often possess a truly creative and imaginative flair as far as colour is concerned. It is interesting to note that sometimes their inclusion of an unusual or 'unexpected' colour can add the necessary contrast to make the total combination of colours work, although such a ploy can also have a contrary effect at times.

There is wide difference in colour choice from one country to another, and the preference of the nomadic and village weavers is, in general, very different to that of the consumer in the West. Certainly the dazzling colours preferred by the weavers look quite different in the bright and harsh light of the plains and mountains where they live. Lack of outside influence to some extent dictates that the nomads derive their inspiration from the brilliance of nature itself.

Many Westerners think of red and blue as being the colours most typical of oriental rugs, and are puzzled by the predominance of red, as they generally find it not to their liking. Red, orange, yellow and brown are all warm tones, and since rugs provided insulation, it is possible that such colours were used to enhance this purpose. What is certain, however, is that the colouring of most rugs and kilims was largely dictated by the dyestuffs available, and the choice of colour within this range was the weaver's alone. Also, to a certain degree, cost was another instrumental factor, as deep colours obtained from natural dyes were more difficult and expensive to procure.

Relationship of Colours

The relationship and placement of colours are instrumental in creating a balance of colour and design. Depending on the adjoining colour, a tone can appear more potent or be subdued. The primary colours are red, yellow and blue, secondary colours are violet, orange and green, and the tertiary colours are red/brown, yellow/brown and blue/green. Colours opposite each other in the spectrum combine harmoniously, as can be seen when blue is juxtaposed with red/orange/yellow, red with yellow/green/blue and yellow with blue/violet/red. Tertiary colours are not as strong as primary and secondary colours because they are colour compounds. For maximum impact, strong primary and secondary colours should be used in a composition, and to soften the effect, the introduction of tertiary colours is necessary. In kilims the relationship of colours is, obviously, vital to the composition not only for a harmonious effect but also for illustrating

35 *A Cappadocian village housewife turns her skills to dyeing with locally available natural dyestuffs. Her enclosed backyard is clean and tidy and no animals are allowed to disrupt her activities.*

the patterns and designs. If, for example, a kilim has a dark blue background and the main pattern is woven in reds and yellows, the field will tend to 'disappear' and the eye will be drawn to the pattern alone. By contrast, if the field colour is red and the main pattern is blue and yellow, the appearance of the kilim will be more 'solid', because the eye will 'see' the red as much as it will see the design.

History

Dyed textiles date back to at least the twenty-fifth century BC, as excavations from Egyptian tombs have proved. During the era of the Phoenician and Roman empires, there arose a considerable demand amongst the nobility for 'Tyrian purple', a colour named after the shellfish beds lying off the coast of Tyre. This exotic colour was obtained from the mucous gland of a certain murex whelk, and whole villages on the eastern and southern coasts of the Mediterranean were solely engaged in the production of the purple dye. Within the community, the dyer was an esteemed tradesman, easily identified by his colour-stained hands and his habit of sporting a piece of dyed cloth behind his ear. The supply of bright and fast coloured cloth was dependent on the trade from Cathay and the Indian subcontinent, where mordant dyeing is an ancient craft. Such skills have spread to Europe by way of Persia and Turkey in the last five hundred years.

Of the synthetic dyes, the first was purple, obtained from a chemical procedure using aniline (derived from coal tar) by a chemistry student, William Henry Perkin, at his home laboratory in London in 1856. Aniline purple, later known as mauve, was instantly successful and so Perkin, using the same method – oxidizing aniline – went on to produce fuchsin, a crimson or magenta colour, and then blues and greens. By 1868 German chemists had synthesized alizarin, which is the main colourant contained in the natural vegetable colour source madder, to produce colours that range from violet to yellow in the spectrum. This was the first time a natural dye substance was prepared by chemical means. In the 1870s azo dyes appeared, having previously been discovered in 1858 by a German, Johann Peter Griess. Azo dyes come in all colours and need no mordant.

Colour created from natural elements lasts much longer and is far superior to chemical dyes for other reasons. With exposure to light all colour fades, but natural dyes fade or mellow leaving lighter tones that are just as beautiful, if not more so, than the original colour. They are also more compatible and harmonious with one another. By contrast, chemical colours are easy to use and can produce excellent results, but have certain drawbacks, in that they can look hard or garish; some fade very quickly, and others fade unevenly leaving blotches.

One of the key reasons why natural colours look better than chemical colours is because they are not 'pure' colour: a natural red, for example, will include some blue and yellow, whereas a chemical red will only contain red pigment. Natural colour is inherently more muted than chemical colour, which looks very stark, and so if chemical colours are used while the desired effect is for the 'natural' look, it will be necessary to mix a variety of colours in imitation of nature.

Abrash A sudden change in the tone of a colour that does not relate to any change in the design of a rug is called 'abrash'. This variation is caused by the weaver using small batches of yarn, each dyed separately. The varying temperature and immersion time of each dyeing results in a different intensity and tone of colour. This also occurs if a hank of wool is tied too tightly when immersed, so that the dye cannot easily penetrate the fibres in the centre of the bound areas. It is not, however, considered a sign of poor workmanship; indeed, abrash adds considerably to the character and life in the design of a rug and usually indicates a nomadic or village origin. Deliberate attempts at creating abrash are not always successful, and sometimes result in a distinctly striped effect, often seen in modern kilims when little attention has been given to dyeing the wool.

Dating and Attribution of Kilims

Colour is helpful, to a certain degree, in dating kilims, as chemical dyes only became available in more isolated regions considerably later than the first decade of their introduction. But it seems that even science itself cannot determine an exact date of manufacture, for the carbon testing of textiles in general, including kilims, has proved to be very inaccurate. The age of ancient kilims can only ever be closely estimated by taking into account all the known facts relating to its origin, where and when it was found or bought, and its design, structure, condition and coloration. When dating kilims made during the nineteenth century, certain facts may be useful to know. The colour fuchsin became widely available in quantity in 1863, so that any kilim containing fuchsin was woven subsequent to that date. Fuchsin fades to a very light grey and so, by gently paring open the grey fibres to their centre, the bright original colour may be revealed. If cochineal is present, the kilim was probably woven in the latter half of the nineteenth century, for large-scale cochineal production in the Canaries at that time resulted in the availability of cheaper cochineal. Previously the kilim weavers would not have been able to afford so costly a dyestuff. With the advent of the yet cheaper fuchsin, the use of cochineal in turn was supplanted.

Colours can also indicate the region of a kilim's origin. Before the cheap and easily transportable chemical dyes were available, the weavers either had to use whatever dyestuff was indigenous to their habitat or alternatively purchase yarn dyed elsewhere at a premium price. In some regions, natural dyestuffs such as madder are so copious and inexpensive that even with the advent of chemical dyes, the weavers continue to produce kilims in colours that have a long-established tradition of use.

Dyestuffs, Pigments and Mordants

Dyestuffs are soluble in water, but pigments are not, as they consist of organic matter. Mordants (from the Latin *mordere*, 'to bite') are used to treat the yarn so that it will accept the colourant. They can also be used to improve the colour and make it fast. The shade will vary depending on the mordant used.

Natural colourants fall into three categories, according to the techniques for using them – mordant dyes, vat dyes and direct dyes.

Mordant Dyes This is the largest category. Without a mordant these dyes cannot penetrate the fibre, or can do so only slightly, and the fixing action of a mordant is essential if the dye is to take. Mordants may be used before, during or subsequent to dyeing. When they are used both before and after the dyeing process, the resultant colour will be stronger. The mordant alum (potassium aluminium sulphate) is most commonly used as it gives the brightest colours.

36 *Madder (Rubia tinctorum)*

Vat Dyes   The most important of these is indigo. Vat dyes are not soluble in water, but can be brewed in an alkaline liquid in a sealed container, or vat, to produce a liquor in which the dye is present as a colourless salt. Urine is often used to make the indigo brew, so the liquor is yellow. It is diluted for dyeing and no blue colour appears until the yarn is removed from the dyebath. Contact with air reverses the original brewing reaction, precipitating indigo onto the fibres.

Direct Dyes   As the name suggests, direct dyes colour the fibre without a mordant or vatting. Walnut husks and leaves provide direct dyes that produce various shades of brown.

Natural dye colours are derived from the following elements:

REDS:

	Source		Colour
Madder	*Rubia tinctorum*	Root	Reds/various
Cochineal	*Dactylopius coccus cacti*	Insect	Blue/red
Lac	*Laccifer lacca*	Insect	Pink
Kermes	*Kermes ilicis*	Insect	Red
Safflower	*Carthamus tinctorius*	Flower head	Red/yellow
Cudbear	*Roccella tinctoria*	Lichen	Red

Madder is indigenous to, and was also cultivated in, many rug-weaving countries, and its main constituents are alizarin and pseudopurpurin. Red is also derived from other plants, berries and flowers, such as poppies (producing dark red), cherry skins, some rose roots (crimson), and tulip petals (maroon). The bark of the jujube tree (*Ziziphus nummlaria*) and rhamnus (*Rhamnus persicus*) also provide red, as do the roots of rhubarb (*Rheum*).

Cochineal is a red pigment, analysed as potassium salt of carmine acid, and is found in the fat cells of the female of the insect *Dactylopius coccus*, which lives on various types of cacti in Mexico and Central America. These insects must be dried and powdered in a very great quantity to produce the dye. The female of the insect *Kermes ilicis*, which lives on the kermes oak (*Quercus coccifera*) in parts of the Mediterranean and North Africa, produces kermesic acid when dried and powdered. Laccaic acid comes from female lac insects (*Laccifer lacca*), and is a resinous deposit found on the surface of the insect and on the trees in which it lives, in South-East Asia. These dyes have always been expensive as many thousands of insects have to be collected to provide small amounts of pigment.

BLUES:

	Source		Colour
Indigo	*Indigofera tinctoria*	Leaves	Blue
Indigo (Dyer's Woad)	*Isatis tinctoria*	Leaves	Blue
Indigo Sulphonic Acid		Indigo and sulphuric acid	Blue/green

Indigo has been in use for many centuries, and the plants of the genus *Indigofera* produce a much stronger dye than those of the *Isatis* (woad) family; however,

37 *Safflower (Carthamus tinctorius)*

dyer's woad is much more easily cultivated and therefore more widely used than *Indigofera*, which needs a tropical climate. *Isatis tinctoria* grows up to approximately 1.50 m (5′) in height and can be harvested three times a year, whereupon the leaves are dried and kept for two months before use. Indigo sulphonic acid is a derivative of indigo, made from the combination of indigo and sulphuric acid, and there is evidence to show that this dye was used as early as the sixteenth century, although it was not recognized scientifically until the eighteenth century.

YELLOWS:

	Source		Colour
Spurge	*Euphorbia*	All, save root	Yellow
Onion	*Allium cepa*	Skin	Yellow/ brownish yellow
St John's Wort	*Hypericum empetrifolium*	All, save roots	Yellow
Tanners' Sumach	*Rhus coriaria*	Leaves	Yellow/ brown/black
Buckthorn	*Rhamnus petiolaris*	Berries	Intense yellow
Dyer's Camomile	*Anthemis tinctoria*	Flowers	Yellow
Wild Camomile	*Anthemis chia*	Flowers	Yellow
Camomile	*Matricaria chamomilla*	Flowers	Yellow
Saffron	*Crocus sativus*	Stigma	Yellow/orange
Dyer's Weed	*Reseda luteola*	All, save roots	Bright yellow
Sage	*Salvia triloba*	Stem, leaves	Yellow
Dyer's Sumach	*Cotinus coggygria*	Wood	Yellow/orange
Bastard Hemp	*Datisca cannabina*	All	Brilliant yellow

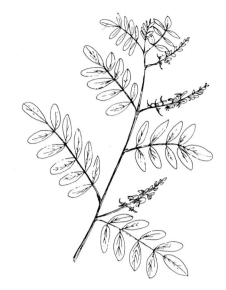

38 *Indigo (*Indigofera tinctoria*)*

A number of these plants yield more than one type of yellow dye. Quercetin is frequently the main constituent, and is found in spurge, onion, St John's wort, tanner's sumach, buckthorn, camomile and dyer's camomile. It is also found in bastard hemp, although it is the datiscetin that produces the brilliant yellow colour that results from combining the dye with an alum mordant. Apigenin is found in camomile, wild camomile and dyer's weed. Camomile and dyer's weed also contain luteolin. Fisetin is present in dyer's sumach and crocin in saffron. Centaury roots, turmeric, artemisia and the leaves of daphne are also occasionally used to produce yellow dye. With the exception of madder, it is the plants yielding yellow dyes that are more readily available than any other primary colourants used in the dyeing process. It is very difficult to identify the different yellows used, as many of the same dye-yielding plants grow throughout the flatweaving regions.

ORANGES:

Orange is made by combining red and yellow dyes; madder, not cochineal, is used for the red colourant. Various yellow dyes are used. Quercetin produces a very bright orange, apigenin less brilliant, and luteolin results in a reddish orange. Grass roots and the bark of plum trees also serve. The dried and pulverized leaves of henna are popular not only for dyeing wool but also for decorating the human body and hair.

39 *Dyer's Weed (*Reseda luteola*)*

40 *The dye-bath. Here the wool is being dyed with walnut husks, which yield shades of brown varying in relation to the length of time the wool remains in the bath and the quantity of husks used.*

PURPLES:
Purple or violet is made by combining red and blue. The woollen yarn is first dyed with indigo and then by either madder or cochineal. The purple found in most Anatolian kilims contains no indigo, but is derived instead from two madder dyes using an iron mordant.

GREENS:
Green is produced by mixing yellow and blue. The various yellow dyes combined with indigo or indigo sulphonic acid result in differing tones of green. Pistachio and olive leaves produce a light green, although leaves often yield a yellowish green. With indigo, the yellow dyes are usually quercetin and luteolin, whereas with indigo sulphonic acid, buckthorn berries are used.

BROWNS:
Brown is most often derived from walnut husks. These make a direct dye which is easy to use. Natural brown wool is also abundant.

BLACKS:
Black is achieved by combining plants with a tannin content with iron. This introduction of iron and the processing necessary damages the wool, so that it tends to corrode with time. Plant sources of tannin are the knobbly oak (of the *Quercus* family), oak apples, tanner's sumach, and the skin of the pomegranate (*Punica granatum*).

WHITES:
Cotton is used to achieve a pure white, and natural wool yields an ivory white.

Because of the regional variation of soil, dye plants from different areas will produce different results. There are, therefore, a multitude of possible colour permutations. The time required for colouring the wool, the mordants, and the water used will also affect the end colour. One dyebath will produce different results from another.

Modern Use of Natural Colours

In most of the rug-weaving countries, natural dyestuffs had been almost entirely replaced by chemical dyes by the end of the last century, yet criticism of the poor results achieved with the synthetic dyes has led to a reassessment of the art of natural dyeing. Through the introduction of synthetic dye techniques that are more suited to woollen yarn and the availability of the most modern dyes, good colouring has been achieved, but nothing will replace the beauty of natural dyeing, and so it is no wonder that there has been a recent return to the practice of this ancient skill. The leaders in this field were the Turkish carpet-makers of the Dobag project. This group was created near Canakkale for the weaving of knotted rugs using hand-spun wool and natural colours. Inspired by their commercial success, other weavers, including makers of kilims, are returning to the traditional methods, and not only in Anatolia but in Iran as well. The lengthy processes of preparing and dyeing the wool, and the grade of wool that must be used to ensure the dye will take, mean that the kilim is more expensive, but it will last and still look beautiful in many years' time. A number of dyestuffs marketed as 'natural' by their producers, however, are probably chemical counterparts; the chemical composition of indigo, for instance, is identical to the naturally derived dye. Nevertheless, it is heartening that many of the dyeplants found in kilim-weaving countries are still growing and available for use. Indeed, a dye cauldron steaming over an open fire in the back yard of a village house is a reassuring sight. Hanks of hand-spun wool are immersed into the dye pot and emerge a glowing red, brilliant blue or golden yellow. The art of natural dyeing is not obsolete after all.

Wool Preparation and Dyeing

Scouring

Scouring is the first step in the preparation of wool. Every 10 kg (22 lbs) of wool requires 365 litres (80 gallons) of water, to which soap is added and stirred while it is heated to simmering temperature. The wool is immersed in the simmering water for forty-five minutes. It is then removed, cooled and rinsed until all the soap has gone, strained of the excess water and mordanted straight away, or else left to dry.

Mordanting

Alum (potassium aluminium sulphate) is the most widely used mordant for dyeing with natural dyes. Chrome (potassium dichromate), copper sulphate, copperas (iron or ferrous sulphate), tannin (tannic acid) and tin (stannous chloride) are also used.

Pre-dyeing   One kilo (2 lb) of dry wool requires 27 litres (6 gallons) of water. The mordant is placed in warm water and stirred until dissolved. The wool is added and simmered for one hour, and then cooled, rinsed, dyed or dried. Clearer colours are obtained by mordanting before dyeing.

While Dyeing   Proportions are as above. The mordant is either dissolved in the dyebath or separately and added. The wet, scoured wool is immersed and simmered for thirty minutes. Then 285 g (10 oz) of tartaric acid and a generous cup of dye salts are dissolved in 1.25 litres (2¼ pints) of water and added to the dyebath. These facilitate the action of the mordant. The wool is simmered for another half hour, cooled in the liquid thoroughly rinsed and hung out to dry. It is less trouble to mordant while dyeing, but the colour may not be as good.

Post-dyeing   The process for mordanting pre-dyeing is followed. The wool is then dyed, rinsed, and returned to the original mordant solution, simmered for thirty minutes, removed, rinsed and dried. This fixes the colour. If a different tone of colour is required, half the original amount of mordant to fresh water is dissolved, the wool added and simmered for thirty minutes or until the desired colour change has occurred, then it is removed, rinsed and dried.

Colour Run   If a colour bleeds into another, it means that the dye has not been properly fixed, or mordanted. Colour run may also be caused by a less-than-thorough rinsing of the wool after dyeing, so that an excess of dye is left. There are few successful chemical recipes for removing colour run. The best solution is to leave the kilim exposed to sunlight over a period of time, although the sun-bleaching process will also fade the fast colours. A preparation of seven parts natural yoghurt and one part commercial colour remover can also yield reasonable results. Bleach is effective on cotton, but turns wool yellow.

Mordanting Recipes

Alum   For one kilo of wool, 180 g (6 oz) of alum in 27 litres (6 gallons) of water is mixed and stirred until dissolved. The wet, scoured wool is added, and simmered for one hour. When it has been cooled and rinsed, the wool is ready for dyeing.

Copper Sulphate   115 g (4 oz) is sufficient for one kilo of wool. This is simmered for an hour, or less if lighter tones are needed. If very dark colours are required, the amount of mordant is increased. Good for dyeing shades of green.

Chrome   The process for pre-dyeing is followed. Two heaped tablespoons of chrome is enough for one kilo of wool. The chrome is dissolved, then the wool is added, simmered for forty-five minutes, cooled in the liquid and rinsed. The dyepot should be kept covered, as chrome is sensitive to light and different tones may result from what is required. Likewise, dyed wool is invariably dried in the shade.

Copperas   45–60 g ($1\frac{1}{2}$–2 oz) per one kilo of wool is dissolved before the wool is immersed and simmered for thirty minutes. $8\frac{1}{4}$ tablespoons tartaric acid and a generous cup of dye salts dissolved beforehand in a litre of water, are added and simmered for a further thirty minutes. The wool is then cooled in the liquid and rinsed. Copperas is corrosive, and kilims may show wear as a result.

Tin   One kilo of wool requires $4\frac{1}{4}$ teaspoons tin, dissolved completely in the dye bath before the wool is immersed. The heat is increased slowly over one hour to simmering point, and then kept there for one hour; the wool is then cooled in the liquid and rinsed.

Dye Recipes

Dye recipes have always been kept as closely guarded secrets by their creators, handed down over the generations, and because of this they are not always precise. The following, for example, is the recipe of an Indian dyer from Tabriz (quoted in W.A. Hawley's *Oriental Rugs: Antique and Modern*):

> Birbul's Blue: Take cinnabar, indigo and alum, grind and sift lighter than light dust of the high hills, soak for ten hours, keep stirring it, put in the wool and soak for many hours. Boil for three hours, wash in kurd water, water in which kurds and whey have been well beaten up, leave for three hours, then wash again and beat in water.

Indigo with Urine   The proportion needed is double the weight in grammes of powdered indigo to litres of urine. Indigo is stirred little by little into urine fermented for ten to fourteen days outside at a temperature of at least 24°C (75°F) in a sealed container. After another ten to fourteen days outside in the sun, with daily stirring, the indigo should have dissolved and the liquid can be used for dyeing. One generous quarter litre of the liquid added to 25 litres ($5\frac{1}{2}$ gallons) of water will dye one kilo of wool.

Cochineal   It takes approximately a quarter of a million *Coccus cacti* insects immersed in boiling water, removed, cooled, dried and powdered to make one kilo of dye. One kilo of cochineal is added to warm water until it has the consistency of milk. Then 280 g (10 oz) tartaric acid and a heaped cup of dye salts, are stirred in and the mixture left for twelve hours, with occasional stirring, during which time it expands and thickens. The mixture is then added to 35 litres ($7\frac{1}{2}$ gallons) of warm water, all lumps are removed, and it is heated and simmered for fifteen minutes. Wool that has been previously mordanted with tin should then be added and simmered for thirty to thirty-five minutes, cooled and rinsed until the water runs clear, and hung in a shady place until dry. This process yields a bright red colour which is fast. The dyebath may be re-used until the colour has disappeared.

Madder Root with Chrome Mordant   One kilo of wool requires the same weight of madder root, $8\frac{1}{4}$ tablespoons of tartaric acid and one cup of dye salts. The wool is scoured and mordanted with chrome. The madder roots are cut into 2 cm ($\frac{3}{4}''$) chips, covered with 33 litres ($7\frac{1}{4}$ gallons) of water and soaked for twelve hours until the roots absorb the water and swell a little. After soaking, $4\frac{1}{2}$ litres (one gallon) of water are added and boiled for forty-five minutes, cooled and the roots removed. The damp wool is added to the dye bath and simmered for half an hour; less time is necessary if lighter shades are required. A solution of tartaric acid and dye salts in one litre ($1\frac{3}{4}$ pints) of water is added to the dye bath, simmered for a further half hour, after which time the wool is cooled and rinsed, wrung out and left to dry in the shade.

Safflower with Alum Mordant   One kilo of wool requires the same weight of dried powdered safflower blossoms, $8\frac{1}{4}$ tablespoons tartaric of acid and one cup of dye salts. The safflower is placed in a thin cotton sack tied at the neck, in a dye bath, covered with 33 litres ($7\frac{1}{4}$ gallons) water and boiled for two hours and then removed. Scoured wool mordanted with alum is added and simmered for half an hour, and a solution of tartaric and dye salts in one litre of water is added, and simmered for a further thirty minutes. The wool is cooled, rinsed, wrung out and left to dry in a shady place.

41   *A Turkoman tent band.*

42 *Anatolian village weavers stretch the warps before attaching them to the loom. Pre-strung warps such as these save a great deal of time, and are often used in new kilim production.*

Weaving

The Loom

The use of a loom to interlace two sets of threads, the lengthwise warps and widthwise wefts, distinguishes weaving from other methods of producing textiles, such as knitting, knotting and crochet. All the looms used for the manufacture of kilims are extremely simple, yet the simplicity of the loom has little to do with the type of weave produced. Indeed, many intricate weaves have been created on very basic looms. More complex looms generally serve to increase the speed of output and reduce the physical workload.

The oldest illustration of a ground loom is on the side of an Egyptian bowl of *c.* 4000 BC, but most probably the loom developed with the earliest civilizations. Loom-weaving may well have followed on from the creation of reed or plant fibre mats, which were made by loosely interlacing fibres without any means of keeping them under tension or in parallel order. Traditionally, weaving has been women's work, with grandmother, mother and daughter working side by side, chatting, teaching and passing on stories, traditions and techniques. In some tribes or groups the men have assisted, especially with the setting up of the loom and stringing the warp threads. More recently men, and especially boys, have become involved in commercial weaving.

There are two types of loom, the ground loom, which is the most basic form, where the work is carried out horizontally on the ground, and the semi-permanent vertical loom, where the weaver usually sits working on a bench or the floor facing the weave held in a vertical position. The ground loom is used extensively and traditionally throughout all the kilim-weaving areas. The nomadic people, such as the Qashqai and Balouch, use the ground loom because of its portability. It may easily be unpegged from the ground, rolled up and packed on to an animal for migration, and re-erected when the troupe reaches the summer or winter quarters. Such dismantling does, however, disturb the tension of the fabric and may lead to an uneven selvedge or weave. The difficulty of maintaining the correct tension across the weave whilst it is in a horizontal position has meant that only narrow strips, up to about one metre (3′6″) in length can successfully be woven on the ground loom. Large kilims can be made by sewing two identical halves together, or joining a series of very narrow bands at their selvedges.

Every tribe or region has a different design of loom and modifications to the apparatus and variations in tools can even be found in neighbouring villages. The looms used by the Berbers in North Africa, some Yörüks in Anatolia, the Qashqai in Iran and the Balouch in Afghanistan, have a horizontal beam at each end, firmly anchored by posts driven into the ground. The warps are tensioned between these in figures of eight, and are sometimes dampened to increase the tension. Additional tension is achieved by driving the end beams further apart.

Another ground-loom design, particularly favoured by the Turkomen and Kurds, has additional side beams that are notched over and bolted to the end beams, thus forming a rigid rectangular frame. The end beams are firmly anchored to the ground with pegs, and the warps are tensioned by a tourniquet of twisted rope or a screw bolt. This whole frame may then be raised on piles of stones.

The looms are constructed with local timber, and a common variety is the very fast-growing poplar, more recently the eucalyptus. In some areas where there is a shortage of timber, the beams must be purchased in the local bazaar. The loom is usually made by the men of the family or group, otherwise it is made up professionally, although crudely, by a local carpenter.

No heddles are needed to create the shed – the space between alternate sets of warp threads – for weft-faced plainweave or for patterning techniques such as slitweave and dovetailing. The weaver lifts every alternate warp by hand and inserts the wefts underneath from a ball, or crude stick shuttle loaded with coloured wool. For long stretches of work a shed stick is used to divide the warps. To convert a ground loom for weaving brocaded fabrics, a heddle rod of smooth wood is attached to alternate warps, usually with cotton or wool string loops. A tripod of three poles is erected over the loom to which the heddle rod is attached by a rope. When the rope is pulled a shed is opened. A rod is inserted into the shed so that when the rope is released the alternate set of warp threads is depressed, creating a counter-shed. Up to three rods, creating shed and counter-shed at intervals, can be used for more complex brocading work. The width of the weave is kept constant and under tension by string loops sewn into the selvedge that are then tensioned by twisting. The weaver sits cross-legged on the finished work, moving the tripod and heddle rod ahead of her as the work progresses.

The vertical loom is a more permanent structure and is usually found in villages and towns. On such a loom all sizes of rugs can be woven, from small prayer mats or bags up to the largest of kilims (about 7.5 × 3 m, 25 × 10′). The construction of anything greater in size is impeded by the dimensions of the working room and the fact that kilims made any larger seldom lie flat because of the difficulty of maintaining the tension of the warps and wefts. The construction of a vertical loom is similar to that of a flat loom. To support the structure vertically, the end warp beams are inserted into slots hewn into upright posts, or into some suitable part of the weaving room, such as the roof joists. The weaver sits on a raised bench

43 *Although the weaver knows this design well, it still requires considerable concentration to reproduce it correctly, placing all the colours in the right sequence.*

44 *A photograph of the completed design reminds the weaver of the pattern and arrangement of colours. The weft wrapping at the apex of the upper triangles is worked from the reverse side.*

45   *A Tunisian mother, her daughter at her side, weaves a simple bag for transporting goods on a mule. Very crude materials and tools are used.*

to work, and adjusts and maintains warp tension by wedges or more sophisticated screw mechanisms. Both types of loom can be developed to accommodate continuous warps, so that kilims may be twice the height or length of the loom. Finished areas can be pulled round to lie behind the work in progress.

The roller beam loom is most commonly used in Turkey and north Afghanistan to make very large kilims. On such a loom the finished flatweave is wound on to the bottom warp beam, as the unwoven warps are unrolled from the top beam. In this way the weaver is always working at the same height although producing very long kilims. The looms are usually located in a room, often very small and dark, in a house in the village or town, and in the prolific weaving areas where such work has traditionally been the main occupation and source of income, every house may have a loom. The Turkomen are known to set up a *yurt* – a round felt-covered tent – to weave in, within the boundaries of their houses.

Tools

The tools of the weaver are crude, being either home-made or purchased in the local bazaar. Combs made either entirely from wood, or from a rough piece of wood with long metal teeth are used to beat the wefts down and to regulate the spacing of the warps. Those with long handles are used as levers to adjust the tension of the warps or wefts. Battens and heddle rods are of smooth polished wood, and are often very old and worn. The shuttle, if used, is a simple stick with notches at each end to hold the weft thread. Scissors and knives are made by a local smith or bought from itinerant tinkers.

Weaving Techniques

The interlacing of strands to create a textile evolved from the simplest finger-plaiting to the fixing of warps on a loom making possible the efficient and rapid construction of tightly woven cloth. By weaving a balanced structure of weft and warp in undyed natural wool, a simple plain-coloured textile is produced. Basic stripes of different shades of natural wool may be achieved by combing down the shaded wefts to obscure the warps. The sophistication of woven cloth progressed with the gradual evolution of loom construction as well as with the processes of spinning, dyeing and weaving itself. Seeking to express themselves more adroitly, the weavers learned to pattern the textile with a greater range and complexity of compositions, designs and motifs. This was possible through the development of weaving techniques that allowed for the creation of blocks of colour that could be built in a vertical plane along the warps as well as in a horizontal plane, across the wefts.

The possibilities open to the weaver for free expression in flatweaving are limited, however, by the techniques of weaving; this is in contrast to the more versatile work of the knotted-carpet makers. As the pattern on a knotted pile carpet is made up of coloured wool tied round the hidden warp threads, and forms no part of the structure, each knot may be a different colour. In this way free-flowing compositions taking any form can be drawn. Not so with flatweaving, for the disciplines of integrating colour changes into the structure limit the variety and dimension of the patterns that can be drawn. The weaving technique used, therefore, has a direct and conclusive influence on the patterning of the rug.

The essential aim of any flatweaver is to create patterning with the wool threads that are exposed on the face of the rug by alternating and varying the colours of the threads, whilst at the same time maintaining both structure and rigidity. Generations of weavers have developed techniques to produce effects of texture and colour change within the technical strictures of flatweaving, from curvilinear weave that facilitates the drawing of more realistic representations of motifs and symbols, through to the complex weft wrapping techniques and extra weft inserts resulting in textural changes and intricate patterning.

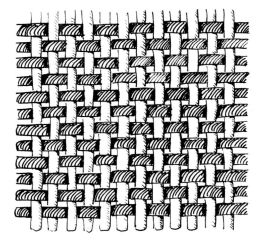

46 *Balanced plainweave*

Balanced Plainweave

This is the simplest form of weaving. The warp and weft are interlaced over and under each other, and if they are of about the same thickness and pliability, both will show equally on the face and the reverse of the weave. Because both the warp and weft are seen, and are usually of the same colour, this is generally a non-decorative type of weave, which is difficult to mix with other decorative techniques. When the warp and the weft are of different colours the effect is speckled, or tweeded. Balanced plainweave is sometimes used on the undecorated kilim end panels to both flatweaves and knotted pile rugs, and often on the reverse side of bags.

Weft-faced Plainweave

When the number of wefts is greater than the number of warps, the warp threads will be concealed, especially if the wefts are beaten down close together. The colour of the weave is therefore determined by the colour of the wefts, and so the

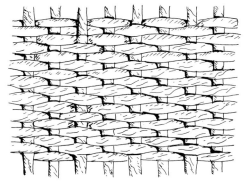

47 *Weft-faced plainweave*

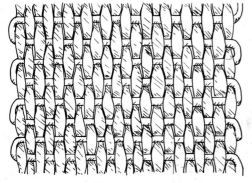

48 *Warp-faced plainweave.*

49 *Twill*

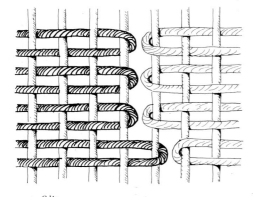

50 *Slitweave*

51 *The apex of the prayer arch is completed. This kilim features an Elmadağ prayer design (the rest of the pattern is visible through the warps), although it was woven in Konya.*

warps may be monochrome or undyed. This technique is used extensively in flatweaving, from Morocco on the Atlantic coast through to Afghanistan in Central Asia, and is seen as horizontal bands of single colour appearing on the non-decorated areas of bags, such as the reverse, and on kilim end panels. Many flatweaves from the High Atlas Mountains of Morocco consist of bands of plain weft-faced weave between bands of knotted pile decoration.

Warp-faced Plainweave

This weave is the opposite of the above. The greater the number of warp threads in comparison to weft threads, and the closer they are pushed together, the more the warp will conceal the weft. This type of weave has been developed by certain groups of flatweavers into a more complex form that allows for the inclusion of colour patterning in both the twill and warp-faced techniques.

Twill

Twill weave differs from weft-faced and warp-faced plainweave in that it involves a more complex method of separating and dividing the threads during weaving. This requires a more complex loom construction. Syrian weavers are thought to have been among the first to have added an extra shaft to the two-shaft horizontal loom, thus making possible the simplest twill weave. The Chinese, however, are known to have exported silk textiles in twill weave to the West as early as 1500 BC, so it is possible that the Syrian weavers used the wool and cotton available to them to copy the technique from a silk shawl imported from Cathay. Twill weaves may be either warp-faced or weft-faced and the most common is of a '2:2' structure, where both the warps and wefts interlace over two and under two, producing a diagonal direction to the weave. Herringbone, zig-zag and lozenge patterning can be produced in the weave through different methods of floating and grouping the wefts and warps. The twill technique is also used as a finishing on kilims, bags and tent bands.

Slitweave

This is the commonest of all flatweaving techniques, and until about twenty years ago a slitwoven structure was considered the only defining aspect of a kilim. With the exception of the North African Berbers, all flatweaving peoples use slitweave extensively as the basis for floor rugs, covers and bags. Coloured wefts are used to create blocks of colour, rather than simple horizontal bands of colour. The weft is returned round the last warp in its colour area and the weft of the adjoining colour is later returned around the adjacent warp, thus leaving a vertical slit between the boundaries of the two colours. The weaver works on one colour block, beating the wefts down hard, before moving on to the next colour, and subsequently building up the pattern of the textile. Obviously the vertical slit cannot be too long, or the structure of the rug will be weakened, and so the slits are offset diagonally or are crenellated in short lengths, usually to a maximum of just over a centimetre (half an inch) long. The resulting patterns produced by this technique are geometric and diagonal, and therefore diamonds and triangles, or distinctive stepped crenellations, are common. There are two advantages to slitweave: it ensures that the rug can be completely reversible with the same weave and pattern on both sides, and it also produces a clear, sharp definition to the boundaries of

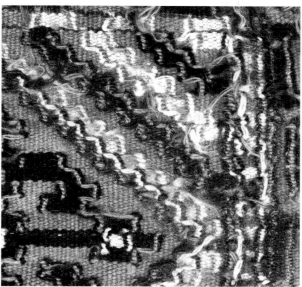

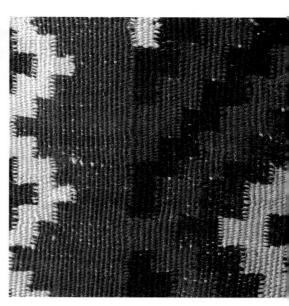

52, 53   *Details of the face and reverse of a section of double-interlock weave. Its firm texture and sharp colour definition are evident on the face. This weave is not reversible, for ridges are formed along the back by the interlocking of the wefts. (Uzbek Tartari, Afghanistan)*

54   *Dovetail is the simple interlocking of the wefts on a single warp, as they return to their colour block. The weave is reversible, but the definition of the colour is blurred at the edges. (Lurs)*

each colour block by separating the colours by a divide. Slitweave can also be used in large areas of single colour, to enable the weaver to work in stages on small parts of the colour area and so divide the work with diagonal lines of slitweave, known as 'lazy lines'.

Dovetailing or Single-interlock Weave

This is similar to slitweave, except that the wefts at the edge of each colour block share the same warp. There is therefore no slit or gap left between the colours, so it is possible to delineate patterns vertically without having to step or crenellate the weave to maintain the structure. The interlocking of the two colours does, however, leave a blurred division between them, and because the wefts are doubled up on one warp, the weave cannot be as tight and dense as with other techniques. Kilims are woven in this technique in all the weaving areas with the exception of Anatolia and North Africa, where it is used only occasonally.

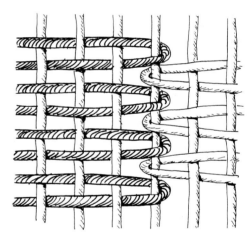

55   *Dovetailing, or single-interlock weave*

Double-interlock Weave

This is another weaving technique that can be used to join blocks of colour vertically down the rug. Here, however, the junction between the colours is not formed on a common warp, for the wefts interlock with each other between the warps: in its simplest form, one weft loops through the adjacent weft to turn back into the weave of its colour block, and this is known as an interlocking weft. 'Double interlocking' describes the looping of each weft to interlock with two adjacent wefts. By this method, a very crisp outline is created between the colours, and the structure remains strong, without the disadvantages of slits or the doubling up of wefts on one warp, as with dovetailing. The resulting rug is, however, not reversible, as a ridge of interlocks is formed on the back. This weaving technique is most commonly found on Bakhtiari, Luri and Turkoman weavings.

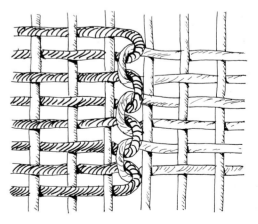

56   *Double-interlock weave*

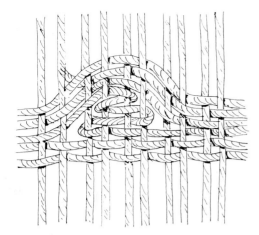

57   *Extra weft inserts*

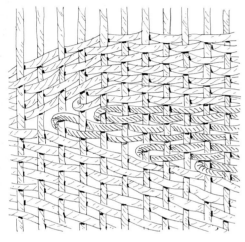

58   *Curved wefts*

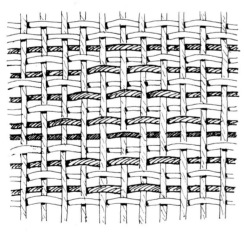

59   *Weft-faced patterning*

60, 61   *Weft-faced patterning produces narrow bands of intricate weave. Small repeating patterns show on the face of the weave; the weft threads 'float' on the reverse when not forming part of the pattern. (Balouch Malaki)*

Extra Weft Inserts and Curved Wefts

Normally the weft is passed over and under the warps at right angles to them. However, by beating down on the wefts unevenly, or by using wool spun to a different thickness, the weft can move out of line and lie at an angle. This 'fault' is corrected by the insertion of a wedge of extra wefts, and this technique can also be used decoratively by deliberately curving the wefts and inserting extra wefts to exaggerate the curve. A masterful weaver can create curvilinear shapes by altering the density and closeness of the wefts and inserting small areas of extra wefts, and thus draw realistic zoomorphic and floral forms, waves and even complete circles. Great skill is needed to produce a weave that is flat despite the variation in tension and density, and usually only the finest of spun fibres can be used for this purpose. This method of weaving is found in all flatweaves as a corrective to the line of the wefts, and on occasion as an idiosyncratic design element, but it is used most extensively by the Kurdish weavers of Senna in Iran, who have developed it into a sophisticated way of drawing flowing patterns and representational motifs that are characteristic of their kilims.

Weft-faced Patterning

This technique of weaving used to produce patterning by colour change is fundamentally different from that of slitweave, dovetailing and interlocking, where the colours are worked in blocks and patterns are made by changing the colour blocks. In weft-faced patterning, coloured wefts are woven so that they only show on the front face of the weave when they are needed for part of a pattern that involves two or more colours. When the weft is not being used on the face of the weave it floats freely on the back of the fabric. The face and back of the textile therefore look completely different and are often a reverse image of one another. Weft-faced patterning can also be achieved by interlacing two colours in a complex twill weave, where, for example, one weft is worked over three and under one, the adjacent weft over one under one, and so on. This produces a reversible fabric with the colours of the pattern mirrored on the back. Weft-faced patterning is used decoratively in flatweaves from all areas, but is used most extensively by the Balouch as the main structural technique of their rugs, and by the weavers in north-west Afghanistan, north-east Iran and North Africa.

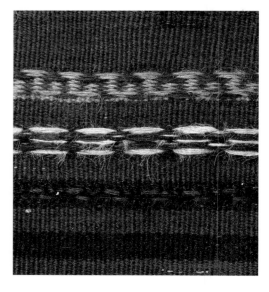

Warp-faced Patterning

With this technique, the warps are used to create the pattern in different colours and the wefts remain hidden. It is a relatively difficult technique to master, and fabric can only be woven up to a maximum of 38 cm (15″) in width – usually no more than 10 cm (4″) to 15 cm (6″). It is impossible to maintain the correct tension in the warp and weft if such strips are woven greater than a certain width. The warp is stretched on the loom and the various coloured strands required for the patterning set in the correct order. The weft is interwoven but remains concealed, whilst the warp shows on the surface of the fabric when required for the patterning, floating loose on the reverse when not required. As with weft-faced patterning, this technique is not reversible unless it is worked in a complex twill weave. To make a floor rug, animal blanket or household cover, equal lengths of the weave are cut and sewn together along their selvedges. Then the cut edges are bound and stitched. This stripweave technique, commonly called *ghudjeri* in Afghanistan and *jajim* in Iran, is used in all the kilim-producing areas, although most frequently in the Shahsavan areas of north-west Iran and by the Uzbeks of north Afghanistan. It is usually used for weaving binding-bands for securing loads on pack animals and tent bands used as supports and guy ropes for the nomads' tents. *Jajim* strips are also made up into floor and bedding coverings, and blankets or saddle covers for the horse and camel.

Supplementary Wefts

The structure of a fabric is classified as 'simple' when composed of only one set each of warp and weft elements, and as 'compound' when there is more than one set of either or both. Additional warps and wefts, added to a simple weave, which in itself serves as a complete 'foundation' or 'ground', are by their very nature supplementary. Other more complex compound structures, however, have at least two sets of one type of element, either warp or weft, which are complementary to each other.

62, 63   *Details of the face and reverse of warp-faced patterning from a* ghudjeri *from north Afghanistan. The weaving technique is the same as for* jajim, *where the warps can be seen 'floating' along the back when not used for the colour patterning. (Uzbek)*

Weft-float patterning is a way of decorating a simple weave with supplementary wefts. The coloured extra-weft threads are woven into the fabric to create either a scattered motif, or a continuous pattern across the rug from selvedge to selvedge. These weft floats can be of different lengths and skip over or under any number of warps, and one of the characteristics of this supplementary weave is that the back has a pattern resembling the face but in negative. It is often mistakenly thought that the extra wefts from which the pattern is formed are embroidered into the piece after the ground weave is finished, yet they are interlaced as the work progresses. Since the extra yarn is generally thicker than the warp and the weft, a raised or couched pattern forms. This technique is used in all areas, from Morocco to Afghanistan, but extensively in Turkey. There it is called *çiçim*, a term thought to have derived from a combination of the Turkish word *çiçi*, meaning 'small and delightful', and the first person possessive suffix 'im'. Supplementary wefts can also be floated on the face of a fabric, held down by single interlacing under the warp at intervals to produce the patterning. Such work is frequently found decorating plainweave and *jajim* on Shahsavan bags, and forming small scattered ornamental motifs on weavings from most areas.

There are other supplementary weaves that are similar in appearance to the floating weft and warp techniques described above, but they have two or more

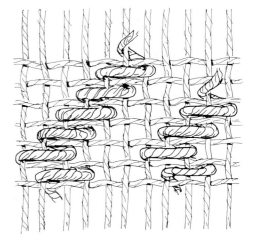

64   *Supplementary weft patterning*

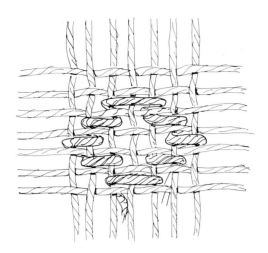

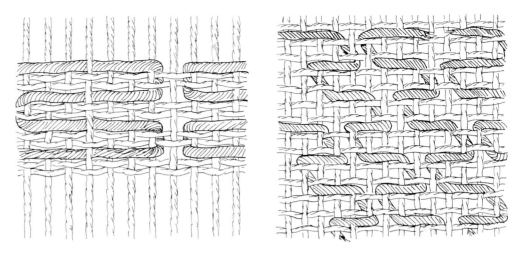

65 *Supplementary weft patterning forming a single motif*

66, 67 *Vertical and horizontal* zili *supplementary weft patterning*

complementary sets of warps or wefts used in equal proportions in the structure of the weave. No set dominates by being the foundation or the design, and although the appearance on the face can be the same as a floating technique, on the back of the fabric the colours and patterns are the same but reversed and reciprocal.

There is a supplementary-weft technique that, like weft-faced patterning, is also a float weave. Called *zili*, a Turkish word meaning 'small bells or chimes', it is a method used exclusively in Turkey. On the surface of the rug it resembles a cording which always runs parallel with the warps. Extra wefts are wrapped round the warps in a common ratio of 2:1, 3:1, or 5:1, with the longer float in thick-spun wool on the face of the rug. Two or three rows of hidden ground weft are shot between each row of floating weft and the surface is completely covered with float over two, three or five warps, with each colour turning back in its own colour block; contours may be created only with the same 'floating two, three or five' system. One or more warps are visible where the set has been split between each surface float. In contrast to *çiçim*, *zili* is an easy technique for weaving horizontal and vertical lines. The weaving of diagonals is a good deal more complicated and can only be done by offsetting the weft floats with a single warp. The plain ground of most *çiçim* and *zili* can be distinguished by its colour, a characteristic raspberry red, dark grey or white, depending on the area of origin. (If the ground is left plain without supplementary patterning it is called *tzoul*, a simple striped woven fabric used for waggon covers and the backs of saddlebags.)

Weft Wrapping

The principle of this weaving technique is that the weft is wrapped around the warp in a variety of complex mathematical combinations, which gives the weaver the ability to draw free-flowing designs with interesting textures and directions in the weave. The technique has mistakenly been named *soumak* and *suzani*. *Suzani* is a Persian word for 'needlework', and although the finished work does sometimes look as if it is embroidered on a finished fabric, this is not the case, as the wefts are woven in as the work progresses and form part of the structure. The term *soumak* is said to have derived from the Caucasian town, Shemakha, also known as Soumak, and once the capital of the khanate of Shirvan but now in the province of Azerbaijan, where very fine weft-wrapped rugs have been woven for centuries.

68 *Weft wrapping, countered on a 4:2 ratio, produces a herring-bone effect in the weave. The ratio and counter has to be changed in detailed patterning, giving the weave a complex and varied appearance. (Kazakh* lakai)

The use of the technique can be traced back to at least 2000 BC, the date of some famous weft-wrapped linen fragments found in Switzerland. Other early remnants of textiles woven in the weft-wrap technique originate from Peru, Egypt and from Persia. At the beginning of the twentieth century the first rug connoisseurs erroneously believed that this structure of weaving was exclusive to Shemakha, and published it accordingly, so that the word became an eponym. In fact the weft-wrapping technique is not only found extensively in the Caucasus and north-west Iran, it is widely used by the Bakhtiari, Luri, Balouch and Aimaq tribes and the Iraqi Kurds, and is common to most of the other weavers of kilim-producing areas. The word *soumak* is confusingly common in Iran, being the name of a shrub which produces a sour-tasting seed used in cooking, as well as the name of a district in Luristan. It is, however, never used by the weavers to describe the weft-wrapping technique.

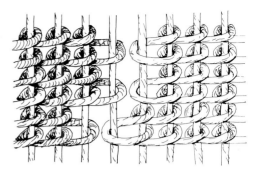

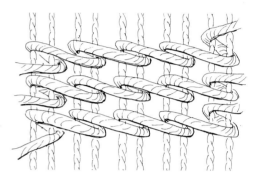

69, 70 *Plain weft wrapping*

Plain Weft Wrapping

There are no extra woven wefts in this most basic but little used form of the technique. The wefts are discontinuous across the fabric, building up blocks of colour separated by short gaps, as in slitweaving. Because there is no continuous horizontal, or lateral, structure, the wefts cannot wrap the warps in a ratio greater than two over and one under without a loss of structural integrity.

Compound Weft Wrapping

In contrast to plain weft-wrapping work, this compound weft-wrapping technique has a ground weft woven in between the rows of wrapped weft to lend additional strength and join the colours where they meet. There are many combinations of wraps that will significantly alter the appearance of the finished fabric. For example, by wrapping over four and under two (4:2), a different finish in both texture and design to a combination of 3:2 is created. Likewise the number of ground wefts, whether they are single or in pairs, alters the appearance of the textile: these characteristics can help identify a kilim's place of origin. The Lurs, for instance, often weave a 4:2 combination with two separate ground wefts between each wrapped weft, thus revealing the ground wefts and separating the wrapped wefts into narrow contours across the rug.

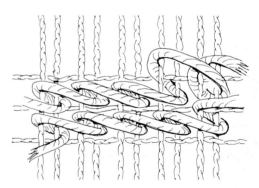

The direction of the weft wrapping also makes a significant difference to the structure and appearance of the finished product. The weft may be worked horizontally, vertically or diagonally and the rows of wrapping may all lie in the same direction, or countered, in opposite directions in alternate rows. The first produces no special textural pattern, while the second results in a textural herringbone effect. Various permutations are possible, but horizontal weft wrapping is seen most frequently, in either the plain or herringbone form. The backs of these weaves differ from the face because of the lengths of the weft visible (the 'grains'), and because the wrapping passes two warps on the face and only one on the reverse (2:1), or four warps on the face and two on the back as in the case of 4:2 weave. This can be reversed so that the short weft wrappings are on the face, giving a vertical ribbed appearance to the fabric. The combinations can be elaborated yet further with an extra encirclement of the warp, either advancing across the rug on the face after each extra loop, or advancing on the back giving yet another different texture. Alternating weft wrapping also uses a 2:1 or 4:2

71, 72 *Compound weft wrapping and (below) reverse*

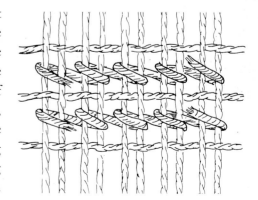

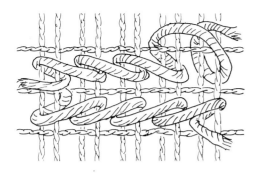

73 *Compound weft wrapping worked in a herringbone pattern*

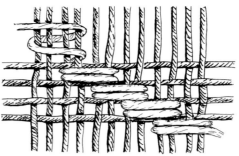

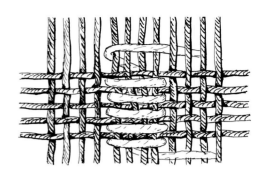

74, 75 *Diagonal and vertical compound weft wrapping*

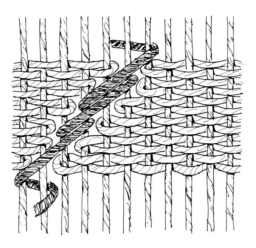

76 *Wrapping with a coloured weft*

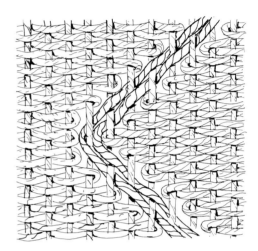

77 *Contour bands of curved weft*

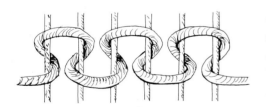

78 *Alternating weft wrapping*

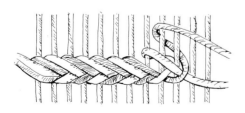

79 *Wrapping in two colours*

ratio, but the wrapping of the weft over the warp threads occurs first from the face and then from the back, resulting in two parallel lines across the fabric. Two contrasting colours can be used, for example, to produce a herringbone and barber-pole design as an ornament or finish to the edge of a textile. Here two strands of different colours are wrapped round alternate warps in a 4:2 ratio crossing over and under each other on the face.

Vertical weft wrapping is usually used as a long vertical line between colours in a pattern or motif, and to separate the borders of extra weft wrapped textiles from the field. The simplest form is a progression of equal ratio wrappings, 1:1, 2:2 and 4:4 up the warps, but it can be alternated with a long wrapping over four warps between two short wrappings over two warps. Diagonal weft wrapping is most commonly used to weave contour bands. Contour bands are produced by a weft wrapping technique to cover and reinforce the slits, or gaps, left in slitweave. Contrasting coloured threads are wrapped round the wefts between the blocks of colour, outlining each area, and this technique is commonly used throughout Turkey, and is found on some Persian kilims, particularly from Bijar and Garmsar. It is a useful and quick way of raising the quality of a rug by closing loose gaps between the colours, and adds a richness by outlining the pattern and motifs. Further elaboration may be achieved with an extra encirclement of the warps.

Yet another of the seemingly never-ending variations in this complex form of weaving uses a knot in the form of a half hitch in the sequence of, for instance, a 2:4

ratio. This is a far more difficult technique to master and is only known to be practised in the Caucasus and north-west Iran, although some Aimaq or Balouch weavings that have yet to be analysed conclusively may be partly woven in this manner.

Weft Twining

Twining is not weaving in the strict definition of the word, but rugs can be made from weft and warp twining, and weft twining in combination with other weaving techniques is an important part of rug weaving. The process of twining does not need a loom and so may well pre-date weaving as a method of producing fabric. The technique, which is also used in basket making, is used extensively by primitive societies, and in modern industry in the manufacture of machinery drive-belts using advanced synthetic fibres. Weft twining is an 'ornamental extra' particularly common on weavings from Iran and Afghanistan, and is used to decorate the end panels of plainweave as well as to draw a textural line between patterned bands on the field of a rug. Strictly a simple form of weft wrapping, it can be categorized separately as it is most frequently used on rugs woven in techniques other than weft wrapping. The technique is worked as follows: two pairs of weft threads, usually in two colours and thickly spun, are twisted round the warps, one starting at the back, the other at the front, and meet between them. They may be twisted clockwise or anti-clockwise, producing a barber-pole pattern, or as in countered weft twining, twisted in opposite directions around the warp, thus creating a herringbone appearance.

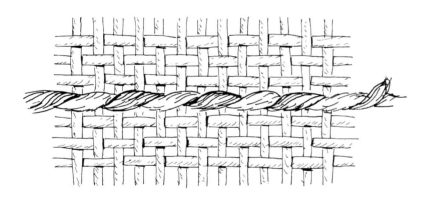

80 *Weft twining*

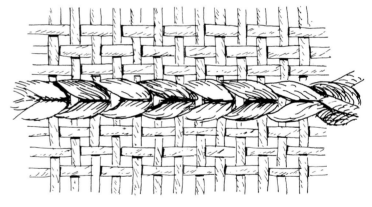

81 *Countered weft twining*

Tablet Weaving or Card Weaving

Tablet weaving is a method by which narrow bands of textile may be produced. The basis of the weave and the tools used are different from all the techniques described above; the warp and weft do not cross each other at right angles but are worked in a spiral or twining manner, with pairs of warps or wefts worked together and holding to each other. Square-shaped stiff cardboard or leather pieces are used to twist two colours in two sets of warps over and under each other, resulting in a narrow band of intricate and tight weaving with the pattern exactly reversed in opposite colours on the back. This intricate method of weaving is used all over the world to create tent bands and straps, which in many cultures are a homemade decorative alternative to industrially produced rope.

Finishes

THE FINISHING OF A FLATWEAVE – WHETHER IT IS A KILIM, A COVER, A BAG OR ANY other decorative or utilitarian textile – is an important feature that may add to its durability, its quality and appearance, as well as giving a clear guide to its origin and age. The way the ends of discontinuous wefts are tied off, the type of reinforcement and the colours used on the selvedge, the treatment and decoration of end panels, the method used to tie the fringes and the presence of any extra ornaments all add to the completeness of the finished flatweave.

Selvedges

The selvedges of a rug have to stand up to a great deal of hard wear, and unlike the selvedge of a fabric that is cut and sewn, that of a flatweave is usually made on the loom, and is finished as the work proceeds, with the exception of the rugs, certain bags and the coverings woven in the warp-faced patterning technique. It is the skill of the weaver in keeping an even tension as the weave progresses that determines the straightness of the selvedges. Many kilims have edges that curve and waver and sometimes a rug may vary by as much as a foot in width from end to end. Such variations are often the result of the use of simple and often crude equipment that may also, in the case of nomadic groups, have to be dismantled and re-erected many times during the weaving of one textile. The consequent irregularities in the weave can be enjoyed as charming idiosyncrasies.

The simplest selvedge is made by returning the weft round a single warp. All kilims have some form of reinforcement at the edge and the strength and complexity of the reinforcement usually relates to the texture, density and thickness of the kilim. A plied yarn is often used for the outside warps, found as single strands on thin and light covers, but more commonly gathered into pairs or multiples by extra-wrapping the ground weft. This is the selvedge finish used with plainweave, slitweave and interlock techniques, and is particularly associated with the kilims from Turkey and the smaller Uzbek weavings from north Afghanistan. Additional reinforcement may be created by parallel-wrapping the edge with an extra yarn, which may be in a single colour but is usually of naturally monochrome wool or goat hair. This parallel wrapping may also be oversewn with coloured yarn as a decoration, padding it out to a thick cable of wool on the edges, with contrasting colours making a barber-pole design, a technique employed by the Qashqai and other tribes from southern Iran. Extra cord reinforcement is worked by using the ground weft only (without any extra weft wrapping) usually binding from one to six warp cords, the outer ones being plied, doubled or tripled. There are no changes in the structure of the weave, only in the number of threads used, so instead of the ground weft being worked in a ratio of 1:1, it becomes 2:2, 3:3 and so forth. Extra weft wrapping can be worked into the cord reinforcement in wool of a contrasting colour. The larger, heavier kilims often have extra cord-reinforced edges, especially those from Veramin and Garmsar in north-central Iran, and Labijar in Afghanistan.

When the patterning is created with the floating weft technique, the floats usually stop short of the edge, which is finished with the ground weft extra-wrapping the gathered edge warps, and these can also be parallel-wrapped. Weft

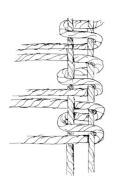
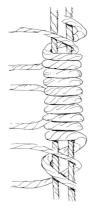

82 *Side finishing with ground weft threads*

83 *Parallel wrapping*

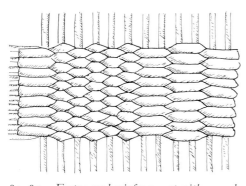
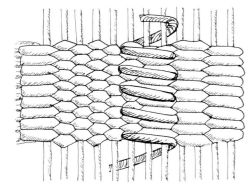

84, 85 *Extra cord reinforcement with ground weft, and (below) with a vertical line of extra weft*

wrapping work also stops short of the edge of the rug and is finished with the ground weft. In this way the work both looks neater and will lie flatter.

End Finishes

The end panels at the top and bottom of the face of a weave, outside the patterning or border, are not strictly essential to the structure, design or appearance of the rug, but do provide clues as to its age, quality and origin. Not all kilims have end panels, and certainly in the more recent work the patterning starts and finishes right at the fringe. As they are usually not part of the patterning or designs of the rug, the end panels can appear as a separate element and are usually worked in a different technique and in different colours from the main field and borders. As a general rule the weave of these panels is weft-faced, either plain or in simple bands of colour. On Anatolian kilims narrow plain end panels are often decorated with small designs in weft-float patterning that may reflect the motifs found scattered within the field. This is also a distinguishing feature of Yomut Turkoman kilims, whereas on many Persian kilims the end panels are longer, stretching up to 30 cm (about a foot) from the patterning to the fringes, and those from southern Iran are often decorated with narrow bands of supplementary weft. Bands of colour blocks in slitweave reflecting the patterning on the field, but on a smaller scale, are also characteristic of Persian as well as north Afghan kilims.

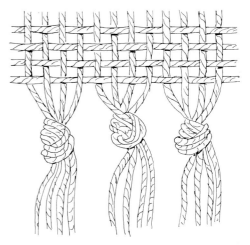

86 *Knotted fringe*

Tassels and Fringes

When a flatweave is taken off the loom, the wefts must be prevented from unravelling and the warp ends from fraying.

Simple Fringes If the plainweave of the end panels, either balanced or weft-faced, is well beaten down, the warp threads can be left loose without any additional work. The twist in the warps will, however, unravel and eventually fray with wear. In some cases the fringe is cut off and the ends turned under to the back of the rug and oversewn.

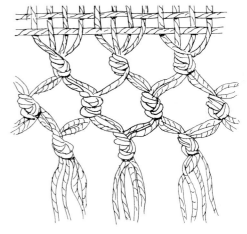

87 *Net fringe*

Knotted Fringes Here the warp threads are divided into groups and knotted together close to the last wefts. If the fringe warps are long, they can be knotted again at their very ends, a characteristic of some Anatolian and Kurdish kilims.

Net Fringes Again, the warp threads are grouped and knotted against the last wefts. Half of each group of threads is then knotted with half of the adjacent group and this can be repeated to the end of the warps. This technique is used by many kilim-weaving communities.

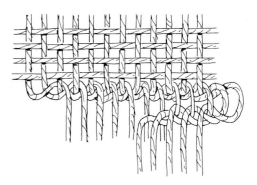

88 *Loop and chain fringe*

Loop and Chain Fringes Each warp thread is looped over and under two adjacent threads, returning at the edge and continuing, to make three or more rows. The ends of the warps are twisted together in groups of three or more and knotted together with a half-hitch for extra security.

Plaited Fringes Groups of warp threads are plaited into flat bands. The minimum number of warps in a group is three, the maximum about twelve, which produces a plait about 3 cm (one inch) wide. Such fringes are often finished with a

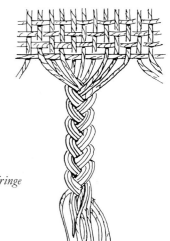

89 *Plaited fringe*

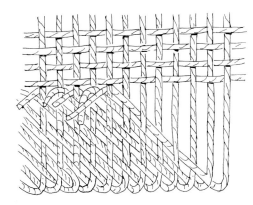

90 *Diagonally plaited fringe*

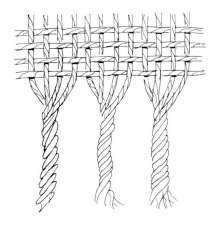

91 *Warp-loop fringe, cut at the bottom end when taken off the loom, then twisted*

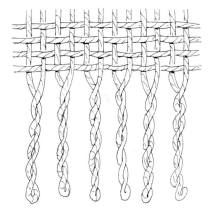

92 *Warp-loop fringe*

strand of coloured wool or cotton twisted round their ends to prevent the plait from unravelling. The plaits can also be joined in parts near to their ends and tied with a coloured thread to make a tassel. Yet another combination is sometimes found where the warps are worked into three rows of loop and chain and then divided into groups for plaiting.

Diagonally Plaited Fringes   This fringing is usually done with cotton warps, and has the appearance of weft-faced weave or a twill. The warps, which have to be long, are woven over and under diagonally from a point away from the end of the weft back towards the last weft. The structure is similar to plainweave without the weft, as the warps act as wefts for part of the time and the final ends appear on the back of the rug, at the inside edge of the finished plaiting.

Returned and Interwoven Fringes   If the weave of the end panel is loose, the warp ends can be looped back upon themselves and interwoven in the weave of the end panel. More often than not the warps are looped over each other, or knotted with a half hitch to form a cabled ridge before being interwoven. This method of fringing can only be used if the colour of the wefts in the end panel is the same colour as the warps.

Warp Loop Fringes   When the loom is first strung, the warp threads can be looped over the end beam in a continuous thread and not knotted on to it. When the weaving is finished, the end beam can be slid out from the warps, leaving them in long loops which may be twisted together. The presence of such a fringe indicates which end the weaver began, as the warps are looped over the breast beam, the bar closest to the worker. The other end has to be fringed by another method.

Other Ornamentation

Other forms of ornamentation are sometimes found on kilims and bags. Small areas of knotted pile work are incorporated into flatweaves, frequently as a symbol or totem in textiles that have a symbolic function – prayer rugs, and ritual or festive textiles such as *soufreh* (eating cloths) or dowry rugs. Small tufts of knotted work are often added to the field of long *soufreh* used by the Kurds of Khorassan at wedding feasts. Bunches of coloured wool are added to the edges of kilims by the Qashqai as a talisman for good luck, and the Turks sew a blue ceramic bead, a *bonçuk*, to certain weavings as a protection against the evil eye. Purely for decoration, the Balouch will sometimes weave a row of looped or knotted work between bands of floating weft weave, which lends the flatweave additional texture.

Bags, in all their functional and traditional shapes, are adorned with tassels, fringes, beads and shells by all groups of weavers. Some extra ornaments are added simply for traditional reasons, although their original significance is long forgotten. One example of this is the three additional tassels that usually hang from salt bags or bags for medicinal earth. Other ornaments are applied for individual reasons such as the personalization of a vanity or sewing bag.

Chapter Three

Motifs and Symbolism

93   *A prayer motif on a kilim from Sinan, Anatolia*

Structure and Geometry
Belief and Superstition
Tradition and Folklore

94 *The peacock motif – a symbol of good luck – is found on weft-wrapped textiles of the Bakhtiari, Shahsavan and Taimani people of Iran.*

95 *A flower and bud motif, or perhaps a garden motif, used by the Balouch of Afghanistan.*

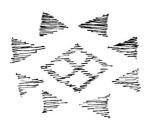

96 *The basic flower motif, woven in different forms by the Afshar, Turkomen and Balouch.*

97 *A flower and bud motif. This Shahsavan motif from Iran is also found in the border design of large kilims from Afghanistan.*

THE BUSINESS OF INTERPRETING DESIGNS ON ORIENTAL CARPETS, RUGS AND kilims has presented Western collectors with perplexing problems. In an attempt to follow a logical procedure of investigation into the meaning locked within the bewildering and chaotic array of predominantly geometric compositions, the motifs and symbols have been analysed and catalogued according to their most recognizable and common characteristics. Western enthusiasts have succumbed to a tendency to relate every motif to some mystical totem or natural form, and to see images in patterns that bear no actual relationship to the environment within which the rug was created. In this way, rug merchants, collectors and academics have gradually instituted a confident language of interpretive understanding which would seem to satisfy their desire to make sense of the unknown.

Many merchants will acquire a stock of woven goods from a third party rather than directly from the weaver or the weaver's tribe or folk, and will then, from the warm and dusty confines of their bazaar booth, concoct stories about the provenance and symbolism of a rug and its woven motifs, imbuing it with tales of mystical allure that the buyer will want to hear and retell. The resulting 'history' of the flatweave is largely embellished combinations of fact, hearsay and myth that will often become accepted as true and accurate. Ultimately, therefore, not only does the ethnographic significance of the designs and motifs have to be decoded, but also the bazaar stories themselves.

What is certain, however, is that the traditions that determine the use of motifs and patterns in the flatweaves have a colourful oral ancestry, wherein the names for a pattern or motif have been communicated verbally from mother to daughter and from weaver to weaver over the generations. Until recently there has been no literacy, and no convenient means of drawing a cartoon of a rug or part of a pattern, so the teaching of traditional tribal designs and motifs has been conducted by word of mouth over the half-completed weave on the loom, and the associated mythology and symbolism related in fireside story-telling. Given the many different languages and dialects of the flatweaving countries, it is not surprising that there are so many different names for the same pattern and motif. Any system of entirely verbal instruction is, by its very nature, subject to change and distortion, and interpretations and meanings will be altered and misunderstood over the ages. In recent years much of the strength and continuity of the oral tradition of tribal folklore and history has been lost, defeated by education, commercialization, urbanization and general loss of tribal identity.

Western academics, dealers and enthusiasts have made much of the available evidence concerning the derivation and development of motifs and symbols. Granted that many of their conclusions are indeed thought-provoking, it is nonetheless wise to be cautious before embracing any one particular theory. Academic interest was first of all focused on the history of the pile carpets of the Safavid and Ottoman master weavers, in which precision, quality of materials and, above all, time taken to produce these urban- and court-style carpets was of paramount importance. But over the last twenty years new scholarly enquiry has centred around tribal rugs, their ethnic origins, and the symbolism of the motifs used. It is becoming increasingly obvious that of these tribal rugs, the kilim bears a symbolic repertoire that clearly pre-dates that of the knotted carpets. It is indeed unfortunate, however, that this scholarly curiosity has been kindled so recently, as the object of investigation is fast disappearing: the old kilims, by their very nature, use and the position they have in relation to their culture, simply wear out and are destroyed and replaced. The recent huge changes brought about by Western influence, transport and urbanization have altered the tradition of weaving beyond recognition, so not only is the subject matter for research in short supply, but the prospects of a first-hand encounter with a maker of the unsullied artifact are also slender.

A good deal of anthropological investigation has been carried out on the Turkoman peoples of Central Asia, in an attempt to fathom the intricacies of their tribal motif, the *gul*. It is the results of this research in particular that have pointed increasingly to the fact that the tradition of flatweaving holds many of the keys to the original motifs and symbols found in carpets and related textiles. This shift of academic emphasis has been accompanied by a false glorification of the peasant and the nomadic way of life in the Near East and Central Asia. In turn, this has led to the tendency to focus too closely on the symbolism of a particular motif from one small tribal group, and to the consequent attempt to apply any resulting formula or rule, either discovered or invented, to other distantly related but quite different flatweaves.

What gradually becomes clear, after all the current literature on the subject, the discussions with dealers and makers of kilims, and the images of the designs themselves have been absorbed, is that there is no direct answer or watertight paradigm that organizes and explains the development and meaning behind the patterning and motifs found in a kilim. The real explanation is less straightforward and much less clear cut, but perhaps all the more fascinating for that. It involves three connected processes: firstly, an analysis of the structure of flatweaving and the resulting limitations on pattern and geometry; then a study of the history of tribal groups, their migrations, lifestyle, religion, beliefs and superstitions; and finally a piecing together of how such cultural patterning evolved into family tradition and the folklore of settled villagers.

98   *Part of a design woven in supplementary weft technique on a Yomut Turkoman tent band from Afghanistan.*

Structure and Geometry

THERE IS NO DOUBT THAT THE VERY PROCESS OF WEAVING ITSELF LIMITS THE TYPES of patterning possible, and that the particular technique used will determine the appearance of the composition in any one kilim, from the layout of the patterns to the nature of the individual motifs. To understand the restrictions the structure imposes on the pattern and motifs in flatweaving, it is necessary to focus for a while on the evolution of loom weaving, and the predominant characteristics of each technique.

The most simple form of weaving, of course, is balanced plainweave. The colour of both warp and weft threads shows on the surface and the only patterning that can be produced is a pleasant speckled effect. If either the warps, or more usually the wefts, are beaten on to each other with a comb, only one set of the threads and their colouring is visible, and coloured stripes may be composed

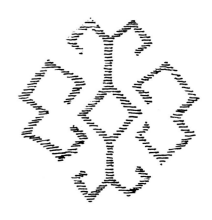

99   A bastani *motif from a Yomut Turkoman kilim woven in Herat, Afghanistan. These motifs are a distinctive characteristic of Yomut weaving.*

100 *This detail of a Kazakh kilim shows a hooked pattern similar to that found on Turkoman* gul *designs. In the centre is a panel, outlined by black and white squares, of diamond-shaped totems representing the evil eye to ward off evil, and on each side are three small squares with an hour-glass design symbolizing light and energy.*

101 *The* koçboynuzu *ram's horn design, popular with weavers throughout Anatolia, is used as part of this motif.*

across the warps or the wefts; such weft- or warp-faced banded patterning is common amongst all weaving groups and is often found used in conjunction with other techniques of decoration.

The weavers' desire to break up these stripes led to the creation of blocks of colour, most easily achieved using slitweave. Here the like-coloured threads pass back round a common warp, so that a gap or slit is left between that and the adjacent warp, forming a clear divide between the colours. In this way the colours form blocks, which may then be coordinated into patterns, rather than mere stripes. Because of the restrictions imposed by the slitwoven structure, and to keep the slits small, only triangles, diamonds, 90° and 45° angles and stepped motifs can be produced. More sophisticated and complex patterns and motifs have, however, subsequently developed, being built from these simple geometric shapes. Several facts would seem to link the nomadic tribes of Central Asia with the development of the slitweaving technique and the resulting types of patterning. The path of the Oghuz Turks – the regions they and their associated groups have inhabited and their cultural influence on other peoples – is clearly related to the areas where slitweave has evolved as the predominant kilim-weaving technique. These groups, amongst others, include the Shahsavan, Qashqai, the tribes of north Afghanistan, and the peoples of central Anatolia, all of whom weave kilims with similar patterns and motifs.

The Kazakh and Kirghiz of Afghanistan make reed screens for their *yurts* during the summer months. They give protection against the bright light and draughts, and form internal divisions across the tent and round the kitchen area. These reed screens are decorated with coloured but unspun wool in stepped geometric patterns, which are so similar to many Turkic kilim patterns that some historical connection must exist. It is, of course, possible that the patterning and colours used on the reed screen were originally forms of tribal insignia, heraldic motifs similar to the patterning on the felt roofs of the tents and akin to the traditional Turkoman-style *gul* found on bags used to identify a tribe whilst on migration. Certainly the Aimaq people from Firozkohi still decorate their summer reed screens with painted motifs similar to the original flowing designs found in felt.

A graduation from reed screens to woven woollen kilims most likely ensued when the Turkic nomads migrated across the Iranian plateau to Anatolia, and found that the slender, hard stems of steppe grass used to make reed screens were no longer available. They would have consequently had to adapt to making flatweaves using the same traditional patterning of geometrical shapes with the wool from their sheep. It is also possible that these screen motifs acted as an intermediate stage between the atavistic and ancient motifs found on felts, drawn with curvilinear and flowing lines that are easy to achieve with felted and appliquéd material, and the geometric motifs found on kilims today.

From the basic technique of slitweave were engendered more complex forms of weaving and patterning. Single- and double-interlock techniques are the obvious progeny of slitweave. Quite how the very much more complicated techniques such as weft and warp wrapping evolved will always be open to conjecture; the development of such work may well have been pioneered by the enclaves of tribal groups scattered over Near and Central Asia. These tribal groups, who have been very much isolated from outside influences for centuries, include the Bakhtiari,

102 *The field of this kilim is scattered with motifs, symbols, totems and patterns. Some are easily distinguished as representations of the weaver's natural environment, and some are traditional and ancient motifs such as the eight-pointed star. Many other motifs are still used but have lost their original meaning. These are named variously, by the weaver for convenience, by the bazaar dealer as a sales gimmick, or by Western enthusiasts in their attempts to decipher a meaning. (Qashqai)*

the Lurs and some of the Balouch, who all weave using the more complex techniques that facilitate the incorporation of a much greater range of patterns and motifs.

Reciprocal designs and a balance of positive and negative in both colour and pattern can provide either satisfying harmony and completeness or contrast and bifurcation in composition. This parallels an eastern Sufi and general Islamic concept of the ever-present duality found in life and nature: black and white, winter and summer, life and death, good and evil. In *Sufi: Expression of the Mystic Quest*, Laleh Bakhtiari writes: 'The polarization which is expressed in geometry through static and dynamic forms corresponds exactly to the inseparable pairs of complementary spiritual stations between which the seeker constantly moves: contraction/expansion, gathering/separation, sobriety/intoxication, annihilation/subsistence, presence/absence.' These Sufi philosophies are not only seen in Islamic art, architecture and calligraphy but also in the design elements in tribal flatweaves. The closely related concept of the space around a pattern or motif forming either a valid pattern or shape in itself, or an extension or negative image of the pattern, is widely used in the design repertoire of the weaver. From the division of a single unit by colour contrast, a pattern can evolve, and a motif appear by revolving, reversing or mirroring the pattern. The motif becomes more complex when linked to an adjoining motif or pattern and the space between is perceived as part of the design.

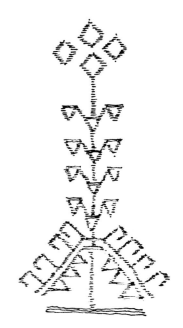

103 *A Balouch 'chain' motif, wrongly thought to represent a religious flagellation chain.*

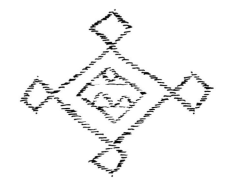

104 *An eye motif from a Balouch flatweave.*

105 *This powerful central motif dominates the design of a Qazvin kilim from Iran.*

The twentieth century has seen the dilution of the weavers' traditional attitudes to kilim patterning, so that of late there has been much mixing and reinterpreting of the meaning and origin of motifs. Commercialization, urban production and the weaving of kilim patterns in environments remote from the oral traditions and nomadic lifestyle whence they came have resulted in the oversimplification, change of scale, and even change of position of particular motifs. This has distanced the weaver from much of the meaning of what she is weaving.

Belief and Superstition

THE LANDS OF THE FLATWEAVERS HAVE UNDERGONE, SINCE THE SEVENTH century, a unification in their beliefs that embraces both the Sunni and Shi'a sects of Islam. Prior to that time, animism and shamanism, as well as Buddhism, Judaism, Christianity and Armenian Orthodoxy, were all practised by different tribal groups. Religious belief brought the tribespeople a way of systematizing their attitude to life and so their way of expressing themselves. Each new religion either encouraged or banned the use of certain motifs or styles of representation that had formed part of the iconography of the previous faith; in this way the tenets of a new faith would partially embrace the old beliefs without difficulty and reinforce a sense of identity, which the group would then owe to the new religion.

Buddhism, Islam and Christianity have been the three main religions of the kilim-weaving world, and the symbols relating to these beliefs have been deeply engrained into the rug-weavers' creative thinking. The relationship between positive and negative form in pattern is most obviously manifest in the original Taoist yin and yang symbol; however, Sufi philosophy also embraces the belief of balance in everything. The enthusiastic building of Sufic centres in north-west Persia in the fourteenth and fifteenth centuries coincided with the development of tribal division and a new migration of people across middle and central Asia. There was a rapid development and renaissance in the arts and crafts at this time in north-west Persia, and a powerful influence on design was imposed by Sufi ideology. This influence can still be seen today in many Turkic kilim designs. The evolution of the cross may be associated with the Christian cults, and can be found on kilims originating from, or influenced by, the cultures of Armenia and the Caucasus in general. The significance of this symbol, however, is frequently misconstrued, as the cross is often used merely because it is the easiest design to draw. From Islam there have come restrictions on figurative representation, and a fascination with the recurrence of numbers; the figure five, for instance, is variously associated with the five caliphs, the hand of Fatima with five fingers, and the five pillars of Islam. Flatwoven rugs have been decorated with patterns that directly relate to the Islamic faith. Prayer rugs are always recognizable, for they contain a representation of the niche, or arch, found in the mosque wall that all pray towards, known as a *mihrab*.

When permitted, these patterns and motifs continue to keep a special place in the culture and tradition of the tribe, although motifs do tend to lose their original

106 *The significance of this distinctive motif has been lost for generations. According to popular myth, it is a representation of good luck, ensuring plentiful food through harvest and hunting. Indeed, there is an eye in the centre to ward off evil, and the hunting element of its suggested meaning may derive from the apparent arrow shape on each side. (Labijar)*

meaning over time. The superstition, symbolism and beliefs appertaining to various motifs are passed down through generations by word of mouth, being elaborated, amended and changed each time. Like other tribal customs the motif becomes part of the folklore and legends of the tribe. Its original meaning having been lost, the motif retains the name that probably relates to the original symbolism, which now serves as a descriptive title for the design.

Superstition continues to play an active role in the lives of the Muslim people. Largely a residue of pre-Islamic sensibilities, much superstitious belief happily co-exists alongside the tenets of Islam. In Turkey, an otherwise Western-minded couple will attach a *bonçuk* (a blue bead that protects against the evil eye) to the cot of their baby; the origin of this amulet may have been forgotten, but its use continues. A new car is daubed with the blood of a specially sacrificed chicken. On the opening of a new business or shop, the slaughter of a sheep is necessary to bring good luck; this is done even in the main tourist shopping street in Istanbul, and when it is visited for the first time some money must be thrown into the premises, as if to sow the seeds from which the harvest will grow. These superstitions play a role in the folklore of the community in a manner equivalent to the Western belief that walking under a ladder will bring bad luck, or in the talismanic properties of the horseshoe.

Other superstitious Turkish customs include ear docking. The country dogs, known as *kangal*, protect the flock against wolves; it is customary to cut off their ears when they are puppies and feed them to them, which is supposed to make the dogs strong, and protective of the sheep. Handkerchiefs are popular presents. A girl will give a handkerchief to her admirer when he goes to do military service, with these words: 'Take this handkerchief and dry your tears with it when you think of me.' The Black Sea villagers will attach bottles to the roofs of their houses to denote how many daughters are available for marriage, and when a daughter finally weds, the father shoots down a bottle!

The Berbers believe the protective and mystical properties embodied in textiles are more important than their complex social uses and decorative qualities. The Berbers are one of the few remaining animistic cultures in all Africa, and while Islam prohibits representational motifs, the Berber universe – a realm dominated by the forces of the sun, moon, stars, plants, and animals – forms part of their artistic vocabulary. Their motifs, patterns and designs work on three levels, as family or tribal standards, as talismans to ward off evil and bring good luck, and as an expression of the weaver's aesthetic sensibilities. One of the most popular designs used to avert the evil eye is a central red medallion (usually seen on capes), with wavy lines depicting energy flowing to and from the talisman. During the entire process of weaving, from the spinning of the yarn to the finishing of the work, an awareness of the spirit world prevails, so that apotropaic designs are carved on tools such as combs and spinning whorls. The Berbers believe that a correctly made textile will have power to protect not only the weaver and her family, but also the weave itself.

In an attempt to understand the development of flatwoven and knotted rug motifs, many rug dealers and scholars have evolved their own, often very personal and certainly idiosyncratic theories. No matter how implausible or insubstantiated, some of the following concepts do hold elements of worth, although one should constantly bear in mind this truism of the rug specialist, Jon Thompson:

107–9 *Tree of life motifs found on Daghestan kilims.*

110 *This figure of a man is woven into the border of a Qazvin kilim, and probably depicts the Kurdish weaver's husband or groom. It is common for large kilims from this area of Iran to have representations of human and animal figures.*

112 *Most animals drawn with horns are intended to represent goats. These heavily stylized motifs are otherwise difficult to identify.*

111 *A weaver from Bijar, Iran, has woven a representation of herself on the left-hand side of her dowry kilim. (Her groom is depicted on the opposite side.)*

113 *A camel motif, woven into the field of a Shahsavan kilim from Iran.*

'There is a danger in the mind of forging a link that it hopes exists, without sufficient evidence to substantiate the reality of the link.' It is also likely that the significance of folkloric designs and motifs has been vastly overestimated and complicated by Western interpretation. Animal heads are certainly seen to be one of the most important kilim designs, a view strongly championed by one James Opie. Working from the designs, motifs and symbols originating from the animal-headed Luristan bronzes, cast in the fifth and sixth centuries BC, Opie has attempted to determine the history and meaning of these textile motifs. This relationship between cast and woven animal-head designs was first suggested to Opie by the patterning on bags woven by the Luri and Bakhtiari tribes of south-west Iran, which showed a hook detail on a medallion resembling an animal head in profile, with two lines of colour woven to extend from each head to look like the horns of a sheep or goat, or the plumed crest of a bird. Opie discerned close similarities between these images and the decorations and shapes of bronze objects found in ancient burial sites, such as two-headed animals, horse cheek plaques, and bridle bit sets. Such animal motifs are used extensively throughout north-east Iran, the Caucasus and Central Asia. Animal mythology is deeply rooted in the culture of these regions, and the representation of the animals is still very much part of daily life.

Opie focuses his research on the legacy of folktale and mythology preserved in remote areas that are isolated from trade or invasion, particularly in the Zagros Mountains in south-west Iran, one of the least accessible backwaters of Western Asia. The Luri and Bakhtiari people are not thought to have created the animal-head motif themselves; it is believed to have originated in prehistoric times, and spread amongst the sparse populations of Western and Central Asia, who sustained long traditions of weaving. The Luri and Bakhtiari women, because of their isolation, continued to weave using these ancient motifs without outside interference or influence. In other regions where weaving was a traditional occupation, such as the Caucasus, Anatolia and Central Asia, the styles changed, sometimes rapidly, through foreign and commercial influences that have led to a simplification of designs.

The two-headed bronze animals found in Luristan are similar to votive objects from the Indo-European cultures in the Caucasus, the Central Asian steppes and

114 *The two-headed animal motif of the Shahsavan of Iran, usually found on bags woven in weft-wrapping technique.*

115 *The two-headed peacock is found in weft-wrapped flatweaves of the Shahsavan and Bakhtiari of Iran, and is also copied by weavers from other areas. It is an expression of Sufi idealism and symbolizes the reciprocal, mirrored view of the universe. (Shahsavan of Khamseh)*

116 *A row of complex star motifs on a* maffrash *chest panel from Azerbaijan.*

in Eastern Europe. Since sheep and goats were the animals closest to the nomads – their bones, skulls and horns are found in ritualistic burials – and formed the largest part of their wealth, representations of these animals were woven into their textiles, and modelled into objects for worship. There are animal motifs on the oldest known extant weaving, the Pazyryk carpet.

Another motif found in the Luristan bronzes is the 'S' shaped hook, a form that, as Opie points out, appears in the borders of rugs. Both the bronze and woven 'S' motifs have animal heads at the tips. The same image is found in Iron-Age 'two-headed dragon' motifs from ancient civilizations in Siberia, in the Celtic art of Western Europe and in early Chinese art. Also appearing in the mythological bronzes found in Luristan are ritual and divine female figures. These were found woven into weft-faced storage bags, and were cast into the bronze columns found in Luristan in the first millennium BC.

The animal-head column motif that appears in textiles is an expansion of a group of single motifs around a medallion into a chain or column along the weave. Opie suggests that this motif is of atavistic origin, not necessarily initiated in the Zagros Mountains but certainly preserved there for two thousand years or more, and later simplified and abbreviated into medallions and borders found on kilims from Anatolia, Central Asia and the Shahsavan of Iran. Often the long motif has been separated into shorter or even single elements, and the eyes and horns found woven into the original Luri and Bakhtiari weavings have been lost. Again this shows the kind of alteration and simplification that inevitably takes place.

Opie's work raises many questions: were the animal-head motifs first absorbed into textile art from the bronze three-dimensional artifacts, or did this singular archaic design develop from other sources? Did the designs spread by means of trade, or migration? Was any knowledge of their meaning passed on to later generations? Perhaps ancient designs such as the animal-head motif were transmuted by the weaver to conceal their representational nature from Islamic censorship.

A simple theory concerning popular motifs representing the elements of the natural world has been posited by the textile scholar Parvis Tanavoli, who supposes that stars and other 'nature' motifs, such as flowers and animals, developed and proliferated merely because these items featured prominently in the daily life of the weaver. The star is the most popular motif, used on all types of flatweave in differing degrees of complexity, and is based upon an eight-pointed shape in the form of two simple crosses. The motif can be developed and expanded so the negative space left inside the pattern or between two adjacent patterns is as important to the design as the motif itself; thus the shape, size and style of star can become quite complex, with hooked points, so that it looks like, and is called, a 'crab' or 'spider'. One may suppose that the evolution of the star design has been determined by the structural limitations of slitweaving, as it must be built up from stepped and crenellated diamond-shaped and triangular patterns. The so-called 'dragon' motif is based upon an 'S' shape, and has probably developed into the complex motifs and running designs found in flatweaves through to knotted pile carpets, particularly in the Caucasus, where it has been a popular design for many centuries. The 'S' motif is used extensively, especially by Turkic people, although it can be found in the weavings of all Turkish-speaking people, as well as the Balouch.

Another school of thought has concentrated on the theory of the mother goddess, and has developed from the images and remains exhumed at Çatal Hüyük in modern Turkey. This holds that the wall paintings take their origins from weaving designs, and forges links between textile patterning and architecture, pottery and calligraphy. The Neolithic religious cult at Çatal Hüyük was based upon the worship of a mother-goddess of fertility and reincarnation.

Most of the murals discovered at Çatal Hüyük were in shrines, painted directly on to plaster in layers which were repainted in yearly cycles; lesser drawings appeared on the walls of houses. These paintings depicted scenes of hunting, goddesses giving birth and vultures stripping flesh; they were mostly geometric in form, and painted in colours of ochre, red, yellow, brown, black and grey. The paintings rapidly disintegrated upon exposure to light, but James Mellaart, the archaeologist in charge of the dig, proposed a theory based upon sketches of the originals. He claimed that the designs 'imitated kilims, easily recognized by their intricate ornament, their stitched borders and many colours'. Mellaart offers two pieces of evidence to support his theories. In the more important shrines there were peg holes which he presumed were for kilims hung to be copied in paint, and some of the wall paintings imitated a woven border, which would make no sense on a painting unless a kilim provided a model from which the image was copied. There has, however, been no evidence to date to suggest that kilim weaving was practised at Çatal Hüyük, for no flatweaving tools have been found.

117, 118 *These star motifs of the Shahsavan from Iran have developed into complex geometric patterns with hooked points.*

119 *A star motif made up from diamonds and triangles, from a kilim woven by the Shahsavan of Iran.*

120 *The simple eight-pointed star.*

121 *A Balouch motif, probably representing running water.*

The key motifs in the paintings that could be associated with kilims are the *elibelinde*, the mother goddess, a symbolic figure of life and birth that can be traced back to Neolithic cult imagery; a bull's head, similar to *koçboynuzu*, the ram's horn, a male symbol of fertility; and the zig-zag running water motif, *su yolu*, a protective motif.

The ancient symbology found in the paintings may never be sufficiently deciphered to explain the mythology of the ancient cults. Even though it may have no direct connection with flatweaving other than perhaps a common distant ancestry, there is without doubt a strong folkloric tradition in Anatolian kilims that incorporates many of these motifs.

Tradition and Folklore

THE NOMADIC AND VILLAGE LIFESTYLE OF THE PEOPLES OF THE FLATWEAVING countries has changed little over centuries, and whereas the urban centres have developed artistically and culturally, the nomadic and village weavers have remained close to nature. Their cycle of life is simple, and their history has been told by one generation to the next, sung in songs by the family elders, and by shamen's recitations which may last for nights on end. One Kirghiz shaman was famed for his recitation of 300,000 verses of the *Manas* – the principal Kirghiz story. This and others have been incorporated into the symbology of their kilims, for they have no other means of recording history visually.

For nomads there are few possessions, and their heritage is represented by their tents, animals, cooking pots, few clothes and rugs, and their tribal traditions, beliefs and superstitions, which have until recently remained the same for hundreds of years. With the settlement of people into villages and the change from a transhumant to a settled agrarian lifestyle, the original tribal traditions that related closely to migration dissipated and evolved into village folklore. The changes were slow and subtle, and the role of women as the weavers in these societies had a profound influence on this folklore. The secret language of beliefs, potions, signs and skills – of which kilim motifs are part – is handed down from mother to daughter. The ancestral tales remained but were overlaid with more recent stories and superstitions. The desires and aspirations of the settled village people became more immediate, and as wealth accumulated with the possession of goods and land, so the need for continuity and the wish for good fortune and fertility increased. Kilims functioned as a form of visual communication, an expression of the hopes and wishes of the weaver in the form of motifs and symbolic talismans. These symbols can be scattered at random over the field of a kilim, or disguised in repetitive motifs that form the essential patterning of borders and design. They can be found on the flatwoven textiles of the Berbers of Morocco, in the scattered motifs on Qashqai kilims, and in the interlocking and repetitive patterns on Shahsavan and Balouch weavings. It is Anatolian kilims, however, that are most famous for their symbols and patterns with folkloric meanings, and these may be summarized as follows:

122 *The ibrik jug or ewer is among a number of motifs representing domestic items that are found woven in rugs as an indication of their importance in the daily life of the weaver.*

123 *A reciprocal design that is a product of the technical restrictions of slitweave.*

124 Su yolu *running water motif from an Anatolian kilim.*

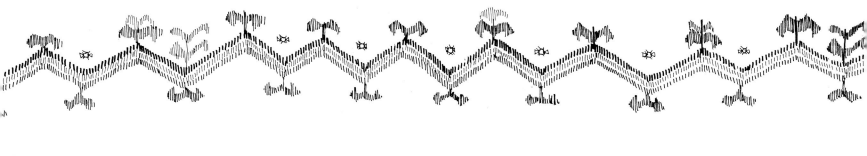

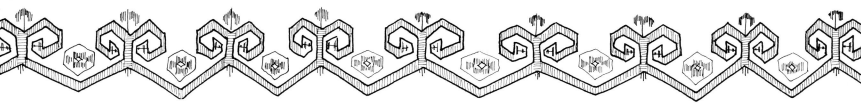

125 Elibelinde *and* su yolu *motifs combined in an Anatolian design.*

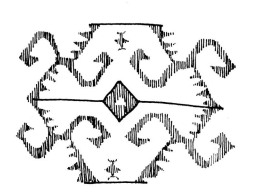

Birth Motifs

Elibelinde – Anthropomorphic goddess figure   Appearing often in an easily recognizable form, sometimes with a child depicted in the womb. The symbol of life/birth and the desire for the birth of a child. This *elibelinde* motif appears in single form and mirror image, in both fields and borders.

126–9 Elibelinde *motifs. The motif at centre left depicts the mother goddess with a child in her womb, and at far right the motif appears as a mirrored image.*

67

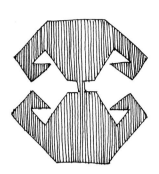

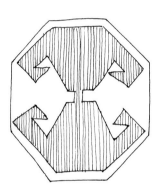

130–2 Koçboynuzu *ram's horn motifs*

Koçboynuzu – Ram's Horn   The eternal strength of the ram's horn depicts masculinity, male fertility, power and heroism. In weaving this motif the woman is hoping that her husband will be strong in every aspect and that his strength will last the test of time. The ram's horn motif is thought to be derived from a spiral which indicates eternity.

Bereket   The combination of the previous two motifs together forms this motif, which symbolizes fertility. Multi-seeded fruits and crops also signify fertility.

Insan – Human figure   Used to suggest the expectation of a child; also for remembrance.

Life Motifs

Sacbagi – Hair band; **Kupe** – Earrings   These signify the weaver's desire to marry. The hair band is a wedding ornament, whilst the earring is a frequent wedding gift.

Bukagi – Animal fetter or hobble   This symbol denotes the union of a family. However, it may also represent the result of the union, birth.

Sandikli – Chest   The *sandikli* represents the trousseau of a bride, within which she will keep very private possessions reserved for her wedding night. From the time a girl is very young she will prepare for her marriage, weaving rugs, bags and kilims of every description, embroidering handkerchiefs, scarves, belts and clothing, and making fine undergarments, pouches and smaller bags to contain her belongings. These possessions will not be used before her marriage, and the trousseau itself is stored in beautifully woven bags, such as the *maffrash* woven exclusively for this purpose by the Caucasian and Shahsavan people.

Yin-yang   The wish for a harmonious balance of relationship between man and woman.

Yildiz – Star   Generally expresses happiness. Because of weaving technicalities and limitations, Anatolian kilims often have eight pointed stars.

Protection of Life Motifs

Su yolu – Running water   Without water there is no life, so this is a very important motif that is often found incorporated into border designs and represents life itself.

Pitrak – Burdock, a prolific plant which produces pronged burrs that stick to everything. It is said to protect against the evil eye. These burrs are often found in the fringes of kilims that have been sun-faded in the fields.

El, Parmak or Tarak – Hand, finger and comb   This is also used as a fertility symbol, representing the Hand of Mother Fatima. The comb signifies the desire to be married, and to protect the union and offspring from the evil eye.

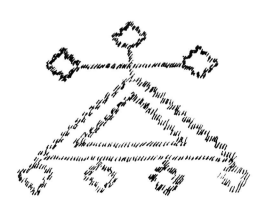

133 Tarak *comb or* saçbaği *hair band motif*

134   *Azerbaijani eight-pointed star motifs with central crosses.*

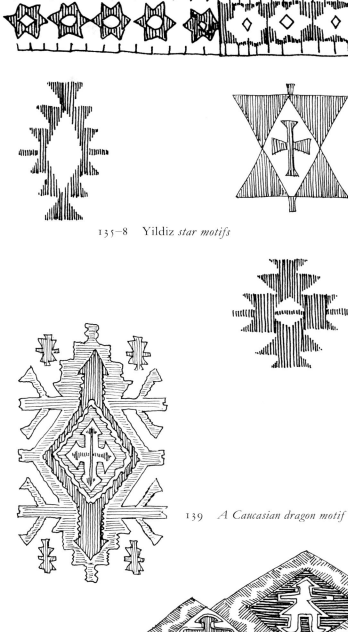

135–8   Yildiz *star motifs*

139   *A Caucasian dragon motif*

140, 143–4
Insan *human figure motifs*

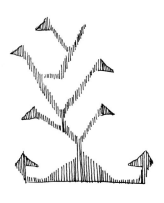

141   Kupe *earring motif*

142   Bukagi *animal fetter motif*

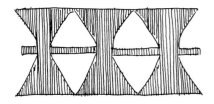

145 Nazarlik *evil eye motif*

146 Ejder *dragon motifs*

147 Kurt agzi, kurt izi *wolf track or wolf mouth motif*

Muska or **Nazarlik** – Amulet or evil eye In Anatolian superstition, a look can kill, injure and bring misfortune. Because the human eye is the source of the evil glance, the best prevention is also an eye. Evil eyes counteract the effect of the evil look and protect people against it. Blue beads are the most common talismans for this purpose, but other items are also protective, such as silver, gold and other metals, wild mustard, garlic, turtle and other shells. *Muska* is a written charm generally carried in triangular cases also believed to have the magical and religious power to protect. Since the power of the evil look is still feared, many of the motifs found in kilims protect against it, and considering their totemic patterns, some ancient kilims may well have been woven specifically for this purpose.

Nazarlik – Evil eye This charm is still used as a wall hanging and exists in various forms, often made from felt covered with fabric, adorned with shells, buttons, coins and medals, old electrical parts, central mirrors, scraps of kilim and carpets. Shapes are very variable – oval, round, pear shaped. Some have woven strips hanging from the base and tufts of wool protruding from the main body. They are sometimes made from painted ceramic shapes and glass, or from chick peas strung in a triangular form suspended from a thin piece of wood; strips of fabric and wool add colour.

Göz – Evil eye This often appears as a diamond shape, although squares and triangles are also used.

Haç – Cross A very ancient motif, dating to pre-Christian times, that also protects against the evil look, as the cruciform shape reduces its power.

Çengel – Hook Again a motif with the power to protect against the evil look.

Yilan – Snake Symbol of happiness and fertility.

Ejder – Dragon The dragon is master of the air and water, keeper of the tree of life and guardian of the secrets of the universe. A fertility symbol, the dragon was a very popular design in Caucasian rugs and kilims – particularly in Vishapagorg carpets. They also appear in kilims and weft-wrapped flatweaves – known by the name of 'dragon *soumaks*' or *zili*. Smaller dragon motifs appear as border and filler decorations.

Akrep – Scorpion In using this motif, the weaver is protecting herself from this venomous creature.

Kurt Agzi or **Kurt Izi** – Wolf's mouth or wolf's track A protective motif against wolves and other wild animals. As nomadic people were cattle and sheep breeders, wild animals were a significant and constant threat.

Afterlife Motifs

Kuş – Bird It is said that when the birds on the tree of life fly away, the soul is going to heaven. The vulture symbolizes death as it signifies the soul of the dead. This motif has more meanings than perhaps any other since the bird is also the

148, 149 Çengel *hook motifs*

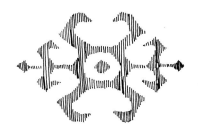

150, 152 Yildiz *star motifs*

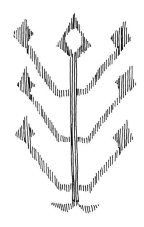

151 Akrep *scorpion motif*

153 Kuş *bird motifs from an Anatolian kilim within a horizontal band design*

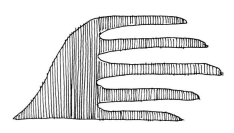 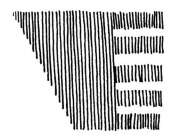

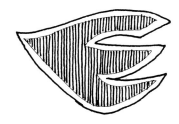 

154–7 *Bird motifs*

158 Hayat ağaci *tree of life motif*

159 *This Moroccan Berber motif is used as a talisman to disperse evil. The six directions of the Berber universe are represented by the four points of the compass and by the dimensions above and below.*

bringer of good tidings, of happiness, joy and love. It stands also for power and strength.

Hayat Ağaci – Tree of Life   Symbol of immortality. Man cannot eat the fruit of the tree of eternal life, but hopes for life after death by depicting it. Monotheistic religions frequently use this symbol and it is interesting to note that kilims with the design, when hung in a village home, are often hung upside down. This practice illustrates the fact that it is believed that the roots of the tree are in heaven, the source of all power, which is then transposed to earth by way of the branches.

Aside from the diverse motifs and symbols, a variety of flatweaves contain easily recognizable visual messages, often written in the Arabic alphabet and numerals of North Africa, Iran, Afghanistan and Central Asia. The script reads right to left, and very often indicates the name of the weaver, and in some cases the patron for whom the kilim is made. The wording may include, especially on prayer rugs, a short religious message such as 'Alla Akbar' (Allah is Great). In the Caucasus the Russian alphabet is used, and in Turkey, the Roman alphabet.

The dates woven in kilims by Christian Armenians, who occupied most of the Caucasus, eastern Anatolia and parts of western Persia, are usually those of the Gregorian calendar. Most other dates, especially if written in Arabic numerals, are probably those of the Muslim calendar, which may be translated to the Gregorian by dividing the date written by 33 (the Muslim year is approximately 1/33, or 11 days, shorter than the Gregorian year) and subtracting the result from the original date. To this figure should be added 622, the year of Mohammed's flight from Mecca to Medina and the start of the Muslim calendar.

Persian weavers have been influenced by traditional and atavistic motifs until well into this century. Despite the many political pressures to transmigrate and dissolve tribal groups, the diverse patterns have been maintained. The Turkic motifs, especially the eight-pointed star, are the easiest to recognize as having common ancestry. Nevertheless, there is little folkloric tradition associated with the various common motifs, though some are considered talismans to protect against evil and provide good luck.

Further east in Afghanistan, a country with great traditions of story telling, it is again curious that there is little folklore associated directly with motifs on flatweaves. The kilims from north Afghanistan, for example, are purely geometrical. The Turkomen from Labijar, however, include talismanic symbols of good luck and fortune in their kilim designs. The link here is to successful hunting, and its associated tales.

Balouch weavings hide many variations of traditional designs and motifs in their dark and sombre appearance. Many of these designs are clearly representational and must surely be attached to traditional tales and folklore. Without concerted fieldwork in the immediate future, such associations will be lost for ever. Meanwhile, motifs and symbols are fascinating, but by no means the most fascinating aspects of the study and enjoyment of kilims.

Chapter Four

North Africa

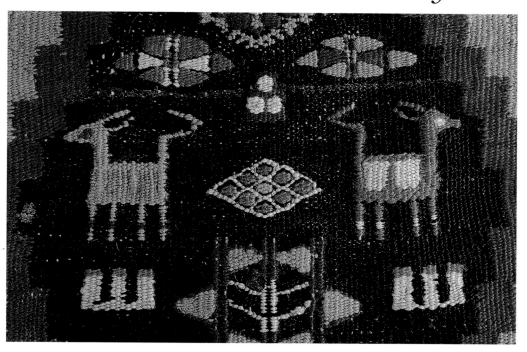

160   *The gazelles depicted on this kilim from Redeyef in Tunisia are copied from designs woven in nearby Gafsa. Redeyef kilims traditionally comprise only geometric motifs, such as diamonds and triangles.*
(Detail)

Morocco
Algeria
Tunisia

THE MUSLIM COUNTRIES OF TUNISIA, ALGERIA AND MOROCCO, ALONG WITH Tripolitania (western Libya), are known collectively as the Maghrib, and have been linked in culture and commerce by various foreign empires and by their indigenous tribal peoples for at least two thousand years. The short sea-crossing to Southern Europe and the caravan routes across the desert to sub-Saharan Africa have enabled successive waves of incursive cultural influences – Phoenician, Cartheginian, Roman, Vandal, Byzantine, Arab, Ottoman, Spanish and French – each to leave their mark.

North Africa was named 'Maghrib' – meaning 'the Land of the Setting Sun', or 'the West' – by the Arabs who conquered these lands between AD 670 and 700. The people of the Maghrib consist of Berbers and the Arab influx group. The word 'Berber' originates from the time of Roman rule, when the tribes were known as *barbari* – and, indeed, the Maghrib is also known as Barbary. The Berber people date back to the Palaeolithic and Neolithic periods, at which time they probably shared mixed ethnic ancestry. Although Berbers have varied social, cultural and physical characteristics, they have tribal unity of a sort, for despite the many foreign invasions, little intermingling of new blood has taken place, and a number of tribal people living in mountainous regions have even remained untouched by the coming of Islam. The rest of the population, however, has come under the cultural and religious influence of the Arabs, and are known as Arabic Berbers. A very strong code of propriety exists between all people, which stems from the amalgamation of the Islamic faith with the patriarchal mores of Berber society, and this religious behavioural code has helped the Berbers in dealing with the political superiority of the Arabs.

To this day the traditional textile production within the Maghrib is still practised by the mainly settled Berber tribespeople, whose previous migratory pastoralism from alpine to lowland habitats has ensured the continued weaving of woollen and goat-hair capes, tent cloth and floor coverings that provide insulation from the extremes of heat and cold. Whereas the climate in the coastal regions does not fall below freezing, the mountainous areas are very cold in winter. The Sahara Desert forms the southern boundary of the region.

History

The Maghrib's terrain has had, of course, much to do with its trading and settlement patterns; most of the northern coastline is rocky, with few natural harbours, the rivers afford no waterways, and the mountains run parallel to the coast, with the highest peaks of the Atlas range in Morocco. Habitation was therefore confined to the plains between the mountains and to the south on the fringes of the Sahara Desert, which was criss-crossed with trade routes from an early period.

There is evidence of a Neolithic civilization in the Maghrib in the sixth and fifth millennia BC, whose lifestyle was pastoral and agrarian rather than hunter-gathering. Little change occurred until the arrival of the Phoenician traders in the first millennium BC, and by *c.* 500 BC Carthaginian supremacy had prevailed; the Carthaginians, however, were a predominantly seafaring group who did not penetrate the interior. The Berbers supplied them with troops, and were also

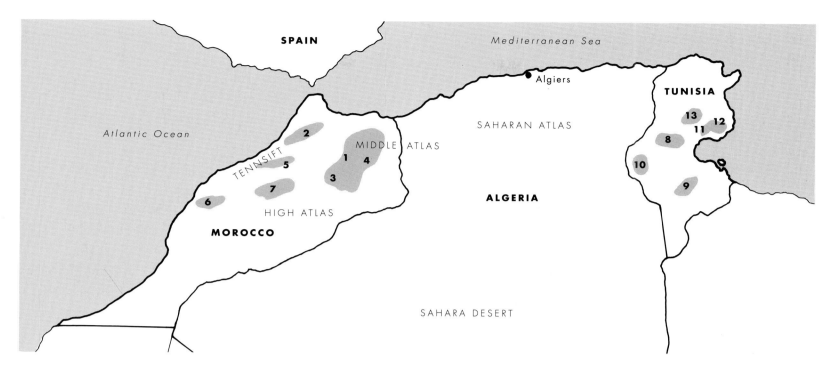

forced to pay tributes, yet the Carthaginians did benefit the Berbers by introducing more progressive agricultural techniques. The long-lasting Punic Wars (261–146 BC) eventually saw the fall of Carthage to the Romans, and under Roman rule agriculture prospered; indeed, the Maghrib came to be appreciated as the 'bread basket' of the Empire. In AD 429 the Germanic Vandals invaded, succeeded in AD 533 by the Byzantines, who met with much Berber resistance. By the seventh century the Arab invasion slowly spread across North Africa, bringing the Islamic faith, to which most of the Berbers were converted, albeit only very slowly. This invasion also brought Bedouin Arabs, further groups of whom arrived and settled in the eleventh and twelfth centuries. The Arabs did not, however, manage to confine the Berbers within eastern political control and these new rulers were also beset with Berber unrest.

From the mid-seventh century three important kingdoms emerged, the Idrissids based in Fez, the Rustamids in Tahart, and the Aghlabids in Kairouan; the latter were designated the task of promoting Islam by the caliph of Baghdad. The Fatimids, Berbers of Kabylie region, were the only prominent Shi'a tribe of the time, whose leader aspired to become caliph of Islam. His attempts at invading Egypt – a suitable vantage point for the realization of his ambition – were abortive, but his successor met with greater fortune, founding Cairo in 972. In the meantime, the Fatimids had left the Berber Zirid and Hammamid tribes in charge of their territories but, despite religious pressure, these groups openly returned to Sunnism to flout the Fatimids. Egypt launched an invasion of the Maghrib in retaliation, headed by the Beni Hilal and Beni Sulaim, and most of the region, bar a few coastal cities, was captured and reduced to rubble.

By 1069 the Almoravid dynasty had been formed by Yahia Ibn Ibrahim, a Berber chief. Ibn Yasim, a Moroccan scholar who had accompanied him on his return from Mecca, was given the task of pushing the desert tribes towards greater Islamic commitment. The Almoravids made Marrakesh their capital, and towards the end of the eleventh century they had extended their empire across the sea.

Tribes and Weaving Districts of the Maghrib
TRIBES:
1 Beni M'Tir   2 Zemmour   3 Beni M'Guild   4 Beni Ouarain   5 Zaiane
6 Oulad Bou Sbaa/Chiadma
WEAVING DISTRICTS:
7 Glaoua   8 Gafsa   9 Matmata
10 Redeyef   11 Oudref   12 El Jem
13 Sidi Bou Zid

161, 162   Zemmour/Zaer
(2.84 × 1.53 m, 9′3″ × 5′)
The rhomboid medallions forming the central pattern are not normally seen in Moroccan flatweaves, although the elements comprising the pattern are typical, and the banded ends are characteristic of Zemmour weavings. This kilim, bought in Meknes in the early 1980s, is very finely woven and is far more substantial than more modern examples. (Detail 161)

163, 164   Zemmour
(2.56 × 1.54 m, 8'4" × 5')
The banded composition is typical of
Zemmour kilims, and the weaver has
demonstrated her skill by creating a variety
of patterns and motifs. This piece is very
finely woven in weft-faced patterning
technique on natural dark brown wool
warps. Curiously, one minute motif in the
second yellow band from the lower end is
part-woven in indigo-dyed wool.
(Detail 163)

The Almoravid dynasty was popular, abolishing taxes unsanctioned by the Koran. They went on to conquer the Christians in Spain, but they themselves were later overthrown, along with the rest of the Maghrib and Andalusia, by the succeeding dynasty, the Almohads, led by Abd el Moumen. The Almohad dynasty was founded by Mohammed Ibn Tumart who, doubting Almoravid integrity, pioneered a new group under whose rule the entire Maghrib became a single Berber kingdom for the only time. Towards the end of the thirteenth century the Almohad kingdom was split into three in order to control anarchistic uprisings. In Morocco the forceful Marinids ruled, eastern Algeria was controlled by the Abd el Wadids, and in Tunisia the Hafsids lasted as a reigning group until the fifteenth century, when Tunisia became the scene of bitter fighting between the Spanish and the Ottoman Turks.

Under Marinid rule Morocco prospered and developed culturally. Many mosques and theological schools were built at this time, and the capital city of Fez flourished. At the end of the sixteenth century the Sa'dis, coming from the Draa Oasis, conquered Morocco and established their capital at Marrakesh, which then became a corrupt city under their rule. They plundered Timbuctoo and took a vast fortune of gold as well as many slaves.

Early on in the fifteenth century the Ottomans found themselves embroiled within the Maghrib region. After the Turkish pirate Barbarossa and his brother Aruj were granted permission to remain in Tunisia by the Hafsid sultan, Aruj moved on to capture Algiers, but was killed when the city was regained by the Spanish. Barbarossa turned to the Ottomans for help; they gladly responded with six thousand troops and proclaimed him governor. For the next few years there were endless power struggles between the Turks and the Spaniards, but the Ottoman Empire never reached Morocco.

In 1830 the French invaded Algeria, and Tunisia was made their protectorate in 1881, Morocco in 1912. Independence followed soon after the Second World War, Morocco and Tunisia gaining freedom in 1956 and Algeria some six years later after a ghastly war of insurrection.

The Mix of Peoples

The seventh-century Arab invasion brought many changes to the Berbers of the Maghrib. Of greatest significance was the introduction of Islam. The Berbers adapted to it in their own way, and their old tribal customs and traditions remain strong to this day. Certainly the urban dwellers have embraced the faith in a more orthodox fashion than the nomadic tribes.

Family units and tribes are still a very important part of the structure of Berber life. Whole villages were originally composed of close relatives, some of whom would share the same house, and the various tribes had vastly differing customs and beliefs, yet all incorporated Islam into their traditions. To begin with, there was little intermarriage between Berbers and the Arabs, but in time this has changed. By the tenth century, when the Arabs were still the minority race in the Maghrib, many Berber nomads were settling, or looking for good fertile land in the plains and mountain plateaux. A contingent of nomads still remained, however, most of whom travelled the desert lands with caravans of camels.

In times of conflict, the tribes would gather together as many households as possible from neighbouring areas, even though they comprised different tribes, uniting under one leader. Every tribal unit believed it had a communal ancestor with the neighbouring unit, and used the name of this sometimes fictional forebear as the name of the tribe. The various tribes needed living space and grazing for their flocks, and land belonged to the tribe, rather than to individuals. In general, within an area of about fifteen square kilometres (six square miles), two to three hundred households would comprise the tribe, governed by family chieftains who were responsible for maintaining order as well as paying taxes and distributing any profits. The more nomadic units operated within the same structure, but were of much smaller size, with perhaps ten or so families in one tribe.

This tribal structure worked very well, for the people were democratic by tradition, and there was a deep distrust of personal power. What was important to the Berbers was to maintain their freedom and independent lifestyle. Should a neighbouring chieftain become overbearing in some way, the units would call upon others of the same tribe to settle the dispute by arbitration. Because of this system of self-government, armed and bloody conflicts were very rare. The Berber way of life and tribal structure ensured a peaceful and stable existence. It was only later in the days of the Berber empires that the power struggles of the great dynasties became commonplace, and the well-ordered lifestyle of the people changed.

The first Spanish immigrants came to the Maghrib during the fifteenth century, during and after the Christian reconquest of Iberia, and these new settlers were a mixture of Arab, Berber and Iberian descent. By now the Arabs were having a disastrous effect on Berber status, for they had infiltrated every channel of power and comprised the bulk of the sultans' armies. They did as they wished, and started to unsettle the sedentary Berbers, who slowly amalgamated with the Arabs, adopting a nomadic lifestyle. This, naturally, had a catastrophic effect on food production, which had been the mainstay of the Maghrib's economy, as the farming communities left their fertile lands and joined with the Arabs; only the mountainous areas remained unaffected. The ruling dynasties attempted to control the proliferating nomads, but their efforts in this failing economy weakened their power, and they were easily overcome. When the Maghrib split into three, endless conflicts ensued and the whole of the region suffered from the pressure of wars. No real development took place until the arrival of the French in Algiers in 1830 and their attempts to extend their influence.

During the early part of the twentieth century the Sultan Abd al-Aziz made attempts to modernize Morocco, introducing new land taxation, but this created great confusion and tribal unrest, as officials did not understand how to implement and administer such a levy. The Sultan had also ingratiated and surrounded himself with Europeans at court; consequently, in 1907, he was ousted by his brother, who chastized him for his departure from Islam, and set himself up in Fez. Despite the terms laid down by the Algeciras Conference of 1906, by which France and Spain were to police the country while respecting the new Sultan's authority, he also was unable to control the people, from whom he came under siege, and had to turn to the French for greater assistance. And so the Treaty of Fez was signed in 1912, making Morocco a French Protectorate.

165   *Tarfaft*
Woven in the Middle Atlas as tent sides, these kilims are typical of the Zemmour. (Detail)

In 1930 the Berber Decree was introduced, which was a bid by the French to use the differences between Arabs and Berbers to acquire a balance in the government, although up to that time the Berbers had slowly accepted Arab customs and traditions without any pressure to do so. This decree, which stated that Berbers were exempt from Muslim law, sparked a huge Arab nationalist uprising backed by other Muslim countries, and consequently had to be modified.

The demographic constituents of the Maghrib came from across the desert as well as from the Mediterranean. The Saharan trade with West Africa resulted in the slow growth of black groups in the southern parts of the region, and the trans-Saharan routes allowed for a cross-fertilization of influences, ideas, artistic motivation and religious belief. There were also a number of Jewish people in residence until the mass emigration to Israel in 1948. Until the 1970s Moroccan people were permitted to emigrate to Europe, and this tended to relieve some of the social and economic pressures associated with the population explosion which had taken place within the whole region.

Weaving Traditions

There are regional differences in the names used for flatweaves within the Maghrib itself. North African textiles are also known by other names that refer specifically to their use, which again varies from tribe to tribe. To avoid confusion, the term 'kilim' is used instead throughout this chapter. Some of these regional names and uses are as follows:

Morocco

Hanbel	Large, rectangular	Blanket/rug
Aherbel	Large, rectangular	Blanket/rug

Tunisia

Mergoum	Small, medium and large, rectangular	Wall hanging/rug
Klim-mergoum	Small, medium and large, rectangular	Wall hanging/rug
Klim	Small, medium and large, rectangular; small, square	Wall hanging/rug/saddle rug
Bost	Small, square	Saddle rug
Usada	Small, rectangular	Cushion

Algeria

Hamel	Long, narrow	Tent partition
Melgout	Medium, rectangular	Rug/tent partition

Both Arab and Berber people weave, but their kilims are very different in character, composition and technique. Although the Berber people have probably been weaving for as many centuries as their Central Asian counterparts, there is no great museum collection of Berber tribal kilims, and although late nineteenth-century and early twentieth-century examples are in evidence, little interest has been shown in these artifacts. If not for a group of enthusiasts who collect, trade

166   *Detail of 169.*

167, 168   Sidi Bou Zid
(2.64 × 1.85 m, 8'6" × 6')
*Many of the motifs seen here, such as the crosses,
stars and diamond-shaped medallions, come from
knotted-pile Hamama rugs, which in turn are
Anatolian in inspiration. Other motifs are
imaginative and varied, and include motor
vehicles depicted in red and green, a red camel,
two people and two hands. The brown
background has mainly been woven in blocks,
instead of continuing across the area, which
together with the* abrash *creates an interesting
effect. (Detail 168)*

and write about these weavings, and for an exhibition of Moroccan kilims, 'From
the Far West: Carpets and Textiles of Morocco', at the Textile Museum in
Washington DC in the spring of 1981, with its accompanying book, they would
probably have received even less public attention.

Berber flatweaves provide furnishings for houses and tents, bags for storage,
tent bands, saddle covers and items of clothing. Their kilims are primarily
intended for domestic use and are less sophisticated than those from other
countries, which may partly explain the lack of outside interest. Another
contributing factor is that North African weavings are, in general, considered by
traders and collectors not to be as significant as other tribal kilims and carpets
despite their free-flowing designs and vibrant colours.

It is doubtful that this view will change with time, as use of colour and variety of composition in North African flatweaves are less diverse than in their Asian counterparts. They are also of a more blanket-like structure, with the exception of some older examples, and it is perhaps for these reasons as well that they have less market appeal. The advantage of their general unpopularity is, however, that old and interesting rugs can still become available for a reasonable price, although not in any quantity.

Before the Arab invasion in the seventh century the Berbers were a well-organized, mainly sedentary people supporting themselves by agriculture and animal husbandry. Trade routes across the Sahara were well established by then, and as it is quite certain that they were weaving at this time, they were possibly trading woven goods for other commodities. The North African kilim has been in demand both in urban and rural households as far back as we can trace their history. Villagers make flatweaves to the design and colour of their choice, and if they have sufficient for their own needs, the surplus will be sold with great ease, for townspeople will buy them for their homes.

Many designs woven into the kilims are derived from tribal *wasms* (Arabic for 'brand' or 'distinguishing mark'), which are also seen tattooed or painted in henna on the faces, necks, hands and feet of the tribeswomen. Such tattooing is now frowned upon, but painted henna wears off after a short while. The *wasms* are also used by the nomads as a means of identifying their animals, personal possessions and arms, and frequently appear on kilims as individual motifs as well as being repeated to form the pattern. These designs, motifs and tribal symbols are passed from one generation to the next, a mother teaching the required skills to her daughter while she is still quite young so that she will be able to weave her own dowry kilims.

With the exception of the slitweave practised by the rural Arabs of southern Morocco, the predominant techniques of the region are plainweave and weft-faced patterning, produced on horizontal and vertical looms. Knotted pile is often incorporated into kilims as individual motifs, bands or borders. North African weavers are skilled at their craft and weave both kilims and carpets, depending either on trading requirements or on their own personal need. Wool is nowadays purchased ready-spun and dyed for weaving. As in other Muslim countries weaving is practised by women at home, a specialization reinforced by the religious restriction on the movement of women. Weaving is, however, considered a prestigious and respectable occupation.

Many Berber tribes were initiated into Sufism, and this mystic Islamic order seemed to tally well with the basic traditions of tribal people, not only in North Africa but also in many other countries that were converted by the call of Allah. Certainly in Tunisia, the whole process of kilim-weaving had to be carried out according to the rules of superstitious conviction, as kilims and carpets were supposed to have magical qualities. Preparation of wool and dyeing could only be done on certain days, as these were considered fortuitous; others were unlucky and to be avoided. Superstitious belief also extends to the raw materials themselves, as wool is supposed to contain many virtues, and a tuft of wool attached to animal trappings as well as to clothing acts as a talisman.

Most motifs are small and often triangular, diamond-shaped or zig-zag in form. Stepped medallions are also found, as are human figures and animals. Motifs and symbols derived from tribal *wasms* are usually extended into a pattern. Certain motifs assuredly have folkloric significance, but in general the designs that have been passed down from the previous generation, or copied from another kilim or design seen in the mosque, are purely decorative geometric compositions. Any folkloric significance will in any case vary from tribe to tribe, as one weaver will call a particular motif by one name while to another it will represent something completely different. There is a great similarity between some of the motifs found throughout the Maghrib, although there are those that only appear in certain regions. Sequins are often woven into the kilim as added decoration, as well as tufts and long strands of wool.

North African kilims are composed entirely of geometric designs, which are often used in a banded format. Some tribes weave kilims with a mix of plainweave and decorated weft-faced patterning bands. The widths of the plain bands vary, and sometimes a single band separates the decorated ones; other compositions feature diamond shapes arranged in a diagonal fashion on the main field, often with heavily decorated borders. In some kilims of banded composition, within the bands themselves the motifs are encased inside squares or oblongs, which are formed by the edges of the band and by vertical motifs within the band, separating areas of colour.

There are also many weavings made purely of a banded composition with alternating stripes of random width and contrasting colour, which have either small areas of design or no design at all. Other compositions based on the banded format have decorated vertical stripes, resulting in the visual division of the flatweave into segments. Some patterns are freer in composition, with floating medallions and small motifs scattered over the field of the kilim.

The design of the flatweave is ultimately the creation of the weaver's imagination tailored to the size of the kilim she is weaving. A good weaver will be able to make a kilim which has no repetition of pattern within the bands; it is also important that these striped textiles convey the impression of colour and pattern movement, otherwise the kilim will look static and lifeless.

Originally only natural dyes were used in the making of flatweaves, and the Tennsift region in Morocco was renowned for its production of madder, but with the introduction of cheap and easy-to-use chemical dyes, most twentieth-century kilims have been made with synthetic colours. Many kilims feature terracotta, orange, red and brown as the principal colours, with the designs highlighted in white. The kilims of the High Atlas Mountains are often woven with natural ivory and black wool, and tribes from other areas also weave kilims in natural white wool, with small bands of decoration in red. Dark blue and green are used by the Beni M'Guild and the Beni M'Tir tribes of the Middle Atlas. With the advent of chemical dyes, however, lurid colours such as bright pink and orange have proved to be very popular and are found decorating the field of what is otherwise a very 'traditional' composition of designs and colours. The bright white of cotton is frequently used as the principal colour for designs and motifs, and this contrasts well against the reddish-brown of the field.

The North African kilim, used by wealthy and poor alike, is the most essential furnishing accessory of both urban and rural households and tents. Kilims serve as floor rugs, wall decorations, bedding covers, eating cloths, containers for animal fodder and bags for possessions, tent sides, bands, clothing such as women's

169 Zemmour
(3.32 × 1.64 m, 11′ × 5′3″)
The banded patterning of this Zemmour kilim features tribal designs characteristic of these Middle Atlas people. Their kilims frequently have a red ground with the pattern depicted in white cotton, and are woven in weft-faced patterning and plainweave. (Detail 166)

170 Gafsa
Kilims woven in this region have many designs, some of which are depicted in square or rectangular forms. The flag motifs seen here are rare and may be commemorative symbols. (Detail)

Above and opposite:
171, 172 Gafsa
(2.98 × 1.86 m, 9′9″ × 6′)
Contemporary kilims such as this flatweave from Gafsa region are made purely for sale in government-controlled co-operatives. They are of blanket weight and are loosely woven in dovetailing technique. The glaring colours fade rapidly with exposure to natural light. The weaver of this kilim has drawn her design with humour, even including two camels at the lower end. (Detail 171)

shawls and cloaks for men, saddle covers and animal trappings. All these items are for both daily and festive use. Many of the flatweaves have dual functions; some floor kilims, for example, will also be used as blankets or wrappers. In many rural houses, kilims will only be spread out on the floor when visitors come, or when eating.

The most important kilims that are woven in the Middle Atlas are those with sequins incorporated into the composition, as the tribal women prepare these for their weddings. They are afterwards hung in the house or tent to reflect the light of the stars, and on the woman's death are used as covers for the corpse in the procession to the burial place. As this usually takes place at dusk, the body is spirited away up the mountain with the sequins glittering in the moonlight.

Although most kilims are woven for domestic use, some are made for foreign trade. Recently, weaving co-operatives have been set up in many of the larger towns; these mainly produce knotted rugs, but kilims are also made in this manner in countries such as Tunisia. Most Moroccan kilims are of a tribal composition, and woven by the village people who attend the weekly souks, which offer the seller a good marketplace and the buyer a good choice of merchandise. Here, many of the town dealers will buy kilims, unless they acquire them directly from a weaver or her intermediary visiting their shops.

Buying kilims in North Africa is not easy. Much bargaining is necessary, and unless one is aware of the true value of a kilim, a deal struck for even half the original asking price may well be far above the 'real' value of the article. The inevitable glasses of mint tea are part of the rituals of hospitality offered to a prospective purchaser, and it is hard to extract oneself from a dealer's shop without being sold something, and virtually impossible to escape having a 'guide' in any of the cities, all of whom are paid a commission on any subsequent sale. Such techniques are common in many countries.

Morocco

MOROCCO IS PRINCIPALLY INHABITED BY BERBERS, DESPITE THE NUMBER OF foreign groups who have invaded and settled over the centuries. The Berber language consists of many different tribal dialects, so that pronunciation varies very greatly from region to region, even though the grammar and vocabulary are similar. The Berbers have no written language of their own, and use Arabic script.

Morocco is the only country of the Maghrib that was never conquered by the Ottoman Empire. The main external cultural influences remain those stemming from the Arab invasion of the seventh century and the French occupation of more recent years. Before the Arab invasion, a stable economy existed based on agriculture, but with subsequent religious and political upheavals the country suffered much unrest and destabilization. Today it benefits from a good tourist industry, and is recovering from centuries of weak governments who had done little to improve the economy or standards of living. The main religion of the people is Sunni.

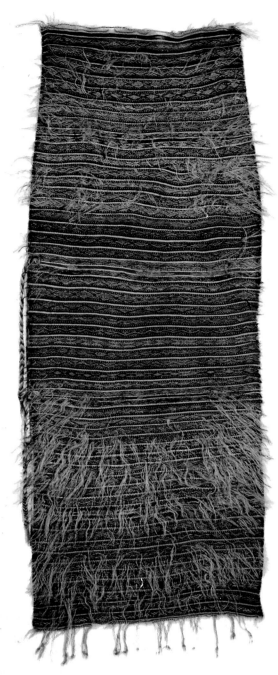

173   Beni Ouarain or Beni M'Guild *cape*
(2.43 × 0.99 m, 8′ × 3′3″)
*This Tahddun flatweave from the Middle Atlas
was made for use as a woman's cape or shawl,
with the long strands of wool adding a different
textural effect.*

Morocco has the largest population of Berbers in the Maghrib, with approximately six hundred different tribes, some of whom are still semi-nomadic and whose main occupation is farming, both in the mountains and on the plains. A few true nomads are to be found within and around the Sahara Desert; these are the 'Blue Men', so called because the indigo of their clothes rubs off on to their skin. The Berber way of life has, however, changed, as many have moved to the cities, but as they retain their tribal connections, the pace of life in Morocco moves more slowly than in many other countries. In mountainous areas, new changes and influences are felt yet more slowly.

The weavers of kilims are women, who are governed by the strict codes of practice laid down by their Muslim faith. Young girls are not allowed out by themselves, and in the mountains they are usually married by the time they are fourteen or fifteen, after which they spend their time looking after children, keeping house and caring for domestic animals, cooking and preparing food. The women are totally under the control of their husbands, who dictate what they can or cannot do, yet despite all they have a peaceful demeanour and are very welcoming to visitors. It is never any trouble to prepare a special dish of tagine and couscous, which is served on large platters and eaten with the hands. Of great significance is their work at the loom. Weaving is considered a prestigious occupation, particularly as it can be done at home in the family environment. The bags that the men carry with them to market are given great attention, as these are seen by all, and if the bag is particularly well woven and beautiful, it gives the husband a better standing in the community.

Rural women have somewhat more freedom than their urban counterparts, but it is still mainly the men who conduct the business transactions. If a woman wishes to sell her kilim, she may sometimes have to enlist the help of an intermediary, a man who is known to her, to fix the price payable on the sale of her rug. The weekly souks are the main selling-place for rural merchandise; these are colourful and wonderfully atmospheric. The kilims are either folded in pyramidical shapes or piled up, and poultry is often kept for sale alongside. The souks also sell camels, horses and sheep, animal products, such as sheep or goat stomachs blown up with air and dried, to serve as water bottles, rush mats that are part straw, part wool, and other commodities such as salt and sugar. The smell of meat cooking over charcoal mingles with the more potent aromas of animals, and the air is filled with the noise of frantic bargaining.

The Berbers

The main kilim-weaving tribe of the coastal strip is the Zemmour. Inland live the tribes of the Middle Atlas, the Beni M'Guild, Beni M'Tir, Beni Ouarain and the Zaiane. Most Berber kilims are a mixture of plainweave and weft-faced patterning; however, bands or single motifs in knotted pile are often included, as Berbers are adept weavers and can complete a rug in whatever technique is most appropriate to its intended use. Some kilims retain long strands of wool left on the reverse of the patterned bands, which are purposely woven in this manner so that they are reversible, and provide extra insulation when used as a blanket. This method of weaving is extremely difficult, as the weaver works from the back of the kilim, which is a mass of different-coloured threads, creating from these the pattern that is viewed from the front. The vertical loom is used for the construction of most kilims, bags and other weavings, the horizontal loom for weaving tent bands and animal straps.

A different type of rug is woven in the Middle Atlas, which is known as an *agrtil*, or, in French, a *tapis de terre*, meaning literally a 'carpet for the earth'. These are woven on wool warps with the main area of weft being comprised of dwarf palm leaves, and the decoration in weft-faced patterning woven in wool. These *agrtil* have the same tribal designs as other kilims, and are generally woven in bright red wool which contrasts well with the sand colour of the palm leaves. The rugs are used in the tents as a ground cover upon which kilims are laid, and the loose ends of the palm leaves on the underside of these rugs act as good insulation when spread on the earth floor. The *agrtil* are found only in rural areas, and sold in the weekly souks.

Beni Ouarain 173

DESIGN	Field: Finely drawn and detailed geometric patterns arranged in bands, interspersed with plain narrow stripes
SIZE AND SHAPE	Medium and rectangular/Small
MATERIALS	Wool, cotton, silk
STRUCTURE	Weft-faced patterning, plainweave
COLOURS	Contrasting light and dark palette
FRINGE	Plain
SELVEDGE	Plain
Remarks	Many capes woven

Beni M'Tir 174

DESIGN	Field: Composite diamond patterns Borders: Narrow/None
SIZE AND SHAPE	Generally long and narrow
MATERIALS	Wool, some cotton
STRUCTURE	Weft-faced patterning
COLOURS	Varied dull to medium palette
FRINGE	Knotted/Twisted
SELVEDGE	Plain
Remarks	Similar in design and colouring to Beni M'Guild

174 Beni M'Tir
The diamond grid pattern is characteristic of these kilims, but the weaver has included some unusual motifs: a teapot, a sugar bowl, and an oblong divided motif that may represent cups, a tray, or a flag. (Detail)

175, 176 Zemmour *agrtil*
(1.52 × 0.98 m, 5′ × 3′2″)
Made for the floor of tents, agrtil *(also known as* tapis de terre, *meaning 'carpets for the earth') are woven from a combination of wool and palm fronds. Modern versions have the excess fronds left loose on the underside for added insulation. They are woven by Zemmour women in the Middle Atlas, and are sold at the weekly souks at Khenifra and Khemisset.
(Detail 175)*

177   *A prospective buyer peruses* agrtil *at the souk in Khemisset. These palm-frond mats are decorated with wool in traditional Berber designs.*

Glaoua

178

DESIGN	Field: Banded composition of plain and decorated stripes Borders: None
SIZE AND SHAPE	Large and rectangular
MATERIALS	Wool
STRUCTURE	Weft-faced patterning, plainweave
COLOURS	Black, white, small areas of coloured decoration
FRINGE	Plain
SELVEDGE	Plain
Remarks	Many pile rugs woven

Zaiane

179

DESIGN	Field: Composite diamond patterns, as overall decoration or arranged in wide bands, separated by plain narrow stripes
SIZE AND SHAPE	Long and narrow/Medium and rectangular/Small
MATERIALS	Wool, cotton
STRUCTURE	Weft-faced patterning, plainweave
COLOURS	Mostly dark palette of red, blue, some white
FRINGE	Plain/Knotted
SELVEDGE	Plain
Remarks	Shawls are also woven with natural white wool ground that are more similar to Zemmour designs

The Zemmour weave kilims of a banded composition, with lines of small geometric designs running across the field. Designs are made up of diamond shapes, triangles, crosses and zig-zags, all arranged within bands across the kilim, while other bands are left free of patterning. If borders are present, they generally tend to be heavily decorated and often feature a repeat in vertical lines of the design within the field of the kilim. Some kilims, such as those of the Beni M'Guild, have an all-over design composed of diamond shapes with a narrow side border and skirt. Zaiane kilims are usually decorated over the whole field of the kilim. Wool, cotton and silk are in common use, and this century has seen the introduction of synthetic materials.

Most Berber kilims, in particular the work of the Zemmour, feature red, white, black, orange, green and yellow. Blue is not so frequently used apart from occasional appearances in Beni M'Guild and Zaiane kilims. High Atlas Glaoui kilims woven in the Glaoua region are black and white, with minute areas of colour.

178 Glaoua
(3.34 × 1.52 m, 11′ × 5′)
This kilim woven in the High Atlas Mountains is principally black and white. This is archetypal of both flatweaves and knotted carpets from the area, as is the addition of small amounts of coloured patterning, often achieved with henna. These flatweaves are usually woven in plainweave and weft-faced patterning. Carpets from this area have similar patterns, although knotted pile is used to form the designs.

179 Zaiane
(3.20 × 1.76 m, 10′6″ × 5′9″)
The central panel with the medallion, and the zig-zag bands, are similar in design to the knotted carpets woven in this area.

180 Zemmour
(1.68 × 1.09 m, 5'6" × 3'6")
*This kilim is typical of Berber weaving from the
Middle Atlas, although human figures are not
regularly depicted. It is woven in plainweave
with the design in weft-faced patterning, and its
chemical colours have been toned down with
exposure to the sun.*

181 Beni M'Guild
*Beni M'Guild kilims are mainly woven as
blankets, although they can be used as floor rugs.
They have a unique design format, often
featuring compartmented squares arranged
within horizontal bands. The Beni M'Guild are
one of the few tribes who use blue or black as a
predominant colour, combined with reds and
white cotton. (Detail)*

Zemmour	164, 169, 180
DESIGN	Field: Small geometric patterns arranged in banded format interspersed with plain stripes Borders: Usually none
SIZE AND SHAPE	Mainly large and rectangular/Small
MATERIALS	Wool, cotton, silk, synthetics
STRUCTURE	Weft-faced patterning, plainweave
COLOURS	Red ground, white cotton, some other colours
FRINGE	Plain/Knotted
SELVEDGE	Plain
REMARKS	Saddle rugs, bags, some cushions and straw rugs also made

Beni M'Guild 181

DESIGN	Field: Heavy overall decoration/Areas of intense patterning forming compartments that are filled with plain stripes Borders: Narrow
SIZE AND SHAPE	Large and rectangular
MATERIALS	Wool, cotton
STRUCTURE	Weft-faced patterning, plainweave
COLOURS	Dark palette of blue, black, red, some white, yellow
FRINGE	Plain/Knotted
SELVEDGE	Plain, with thicker outside warps
Remarks	Dark colouring is characteristic of Beni M'Guild kilims

The Rural Arabs

The main groups of rural Arabs consist of the Oulad Bou Sbaa and the Chiadma, found in the southern part of Morocco in the Tennsift River region. Their presence in the area dates from the time of the Arab invasions, the first of which was during the Marinid dynasty (1269–1472), the second at the beginning of the sixteenth century by the Sa'di people. During the first invasion, Abu Yusuf, leader of the Marinids, captured Marrakesh from the ruling Almohads with the help of various Arab tribes, of whom the Oulad Bou Sbaa were later rewarded with land. It is also possible that the Chiadma came to this region at about the same time, as they were established before the arrival of the Sa'dis. Rural Arabs have kept their own customs; there has been little intermixing with the indigens, a fact that is reflected in their weaving, which is quite distinct from that of the Berbers. Most of the people speak only Arabic, with exception of the Oulad Bou Sbaa, who speak Berber as well.

The Oulad Bou Sbaa and Chiadma tribes weave kilims mainly in the slitweave technique, which is more in keeping with Arabic nomadic groups found in Tunisia and the other kilim-weaving countries. Slitweave is referred to in the Tennsift region as *saideh*, which is also the name of a particular type of Chiadma kilim, and translates as 'happy'; certainly, these kilims contain cheerful colours,

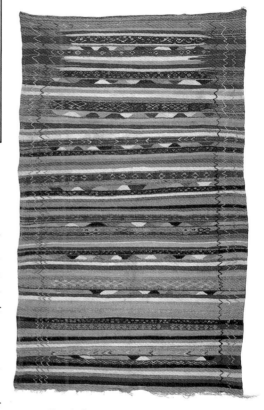

182 Boujade
(3.58 × 1.96 m, 11′10″ × 6′4″)
Boujade kilims usually feature geometric designs in a banded format. The zig-zag pattern seen here is typical of both kilims and carpets woven by the Oulad Bou Sbaa.

183 *Detail of 185.*

184 Oulad Bou Sbaa
(3.66 × 1.94 m, 12′ × 6′4″)
The kilims of the Oulad Bou Sbaa, who are rural Arabs inhabiting the Tennsift River region, are completely different from Berber rugs and textiles, and are usually woven in slitweave. Their colouring is principally red, once derived from madder that grew in abundance along the banks of the Tennsift River.

185 Chiadma
(1.42 × 0.53 m, 4′6″ × 1′8″)
The larger motifs of this mixed-technique kilim are woven in knotted pile. This piece was originally made as a bag or most probably a cushion, as the decoration is elaborate. The zig-zag motif often appears in both Chiadma and Oulad Bou Sbaa weavings. (Detail 183)

Oulad Bou Sbaa 184

DESIGN	Field: Principally banded compositions, some with organized patterns and repetitive motifs/Little decoration and a much freer format Borders: Organized patterns and repetitive motifs
SIZE AND SHAPE	Large and rectangular
MATERIALS	Wool
STRUCTURE	Slitweave, plainweave, occasional knotted pile
COLOURS	Hot palette of red, orange, yellow, blue, white, green, some black
FRINGE	Plain
SELVEDGE	Plain
Remarks	One of the few Moroccan tribes who use slitweave

Chiadma 185

DESIGN	Field: Bands of varying widths with geometric patterns Borders: Usually none
SIZE AND SHAPE	Long and narrow
MATERIALS	Wool
STRUCTURE	Slitweave, plainweave, some knotted pile
COLOURS	Bright and garish palette of red, pink, green, orange
FRINGE	Plain
SELVEDGE	Plain
Remarks	Designs and motifs used are similar to those of Anatolia and Iran/Bags and cushions woven

mainly bright pink, orange and red. Designs and motifs resemble those found in Asia Minor, and are very different to Berber weavings. *Wasms* are used as single motifs, and also form designs. Before the advent of chemical dyes, natural madder red was found in the weavings from this region. Nowadays all the colours are produced by chemical dyes.

Algeria

ALGERIAN KILIMS ARE VERY SIMILAR IN CONSTRUCTION AND DESIGN TO KILIMS from Tunisia. This is most probably a result of the fact that the people are mainly Berbers, whose weaving traditions have remained unchanged for many centuries, although their dialects vary from region to region, and kilims are identified by different names. A *melgout* is a kilim which is used as a rug or tent partition. These are woven in plainweave, with bands of weft-faced patterning in contrasting colours, in a similar manner to Zemmour kilims of the Middle Atlas, and are rectangular in shape.

A *hamel*, also used as a tent partition, is longer than the *melgout*. Its composition comprises a broad band woven in weft-faced patterning, with a horizontal stripe woven in the same technique, mixed with further bands of plain colour. The main field ground is worked in plainweave and is often red in colour. The *usada*, or cushion, is woven in the same technique as the above but with varying colours. There are many other textiles woven in flatweave techniques, and these are used principally as items of clothing, including women's shawls and capes for men. Weaving is done both on horizontal and vertical looms and, with the exception of the natural wool tones, the colours used are derived from chemical dyes.

Tunisia

AS WITH THE OTHER COUNTRIES OF THE MAGHRIB, TUNISIA'S INDIGENOUS population is comprised of Berber tribes. Their land was invaded by Phoenicians, Romans, Byzantines, Vandals, Spanish Moors, Arabs and Turks, and trade routes spread in from the east by land, bringing new culture and agricultural techniques. The Tyrian merchants occupied the North African coastal settlements along the Mediterranean and Atlantic, one of which developed into the city state of Carthage. This new civilization enjoyed supremacy over the west Mediterranean for six hundred years. As the Phoenicians plied their trade on the seas they showed little interest in the interior of the country, and so their occupation of the Maghrib left little cultural influence.

Tunisia was the starting point for the Arab invasions of the seventh, eleventh and twelfth centuries. As elsewhere, Arabic culture, tradition and the Muslim

186 *Detail of* 188.

187 *Detail of* 189.

religion have had a great impact on the Berber people, and the Islamic faith remains strong to this day. The rural populace was not much influenced by the Arab way of life in the beginning, and it was only the invading nomadic and Bedouin tribes, sent from Egypt after the Fatimids had conquered Cairo, that drove the Berbers, who had adopted the Muslim faith, to the mountains. There, in turn, they spread the word of Islam to others, and so Tunisia became an Arabic country. As early as the eighth century, Kairouan became a renowned centre for the weaving of silk, cotton and linen fabrics, and it was at this time that the souks were built. Later, when Tunis became the capital, this and the other towns of the land formed the nucleus for specialized craft production, including the weaving of rugs and kilims.

There is no documentary evidence that marks the beginning of weaving in Tunisia, but it is quite probable that the Berber people had been weaving long before the cultural influences of other groups took root. Organized co-operatives for the production of woven goods and other artifacts have long existed in this country. Co-operative weaving lacks the individual expression that is part of the charm of kilims and adds so much to their character, for within the workshops the quality is controlled and spontaneity removed from the textile's creation. Since the independence of Tunisia, ending French rule, the country has rapidly changed, so that with industrialization and the importation of mass-produced goods the skills of the weaver are fast disappearing, and nowadays there is little tribal production of kilims.

Flatweaves are mainly made using the dovetailing, weft-faced patterning and plainweave techniques, usually with wool, yet recently mercerized cotton (posing as silk) and synthetic materials have found their way into these kilims. Goat and camel hair are also used, and the animals are shorn in late spring when their hair is long. Cotton is another common component, and although it is now mainly imported, it was once cultivated.

Colours are now chemically produced, whereas in the past natural dyestuffs and pigments were prepared with much care and ritual. Some sources of natural dyes were indigenous, and were cultivated, such as madder, which grows in the south. Other plants such as centaury, daphne, and artemisia, all of which produce yellow tones, were readily available. Indigo was also grown in Tunisia at one time, and of course henna is prolific and much cultivated. Red pigment comes from the dried female insect, *Kermes ilicis*, which lives on a type of oak tree found in northern Tunisia, and pomegranate peel and the bark of the wild jujube tree are used for brown tones. Other dyestuffs were imported, and were thus expensive, so that with the advent of cheap chemical dyes, which were easily used, the often costly natural dyes were abandoned. Dyeing with natural colours did not always provide the desired result, as dye recipes were handed down from mother to daughter, father to son, closely guarded in an oral tradition in which the measures remembered were imprecise, as was the time necessary to achieve the colour required. The typical dyepot would be a copper container which was heated over an open fire. It is no wonder that many rituals and superstitious beliefs accompanied the whole process of dyeing.

The motifs incorporated into the compositions and designs of Tunisian kilims are said to represent many things, including items in daily use such as lanterns, combs, storage pots, shoes and jewelry, and tile patterning was probably copied

188 Gafsa
(0.60 × 1.33 m, 2′ × 4′4″)
*Gafsa flatweaves are distinctive in character.
The designs are usually arranged in rows, and
depict animals and geometric patterns
comprising squares, triangles and diamonds.
Kilims such as this are not used as floor
coverings as they are not strong enough, but have
been made as blankets or covers, principally for
commercial purposes, for several centuries.
(Detail 186)*

from those seen in the mosque. Food – beans, cakes, bread and fish – animals, such as camels or gazelles, and pests, like snakes and scorpions, as well as the *wasms*, or tribal motifs, are all represented. Apart from the animal and human forms, which are figurative, all these motifs are symbolized. Nowadays, however, within the confines of co-operative workshops, the weavers just copy whatever pattern is given to them.

Regional Weaving

Gafsa   Kilims from this region are woven in dovetailing technique, and often feature figurative designs such as rows of camels or people, interspaced with geometric designs and bands of plainweave in contrasting colours. There are also kilims that are composed of chequerboard medallions, and zig-zag patterned borders. These are normally very brightly coloured, although the dyes used fade rapidly on exposure to natural light. Their texture, although tightly woven, is blanket-like, hence they are not strong enough for constant floor use. Most kilims are woven by women in this region and are specially made for commercial purposes.

189   Sidi Bou Zid
(2.68 × 1.57 m, 9′ × 5′)
*The zig-zag pattern of the border is
characteristic of Tunisian kilims, as is the
chequered effect of the medallions; it is possible
that this kilim may have been woven in Algeria,
however, as the field pattern is atypical of most
known Tunisian designs. This kilim has been
created with skill and humour. The abrash
effect of the red gives it an added dimension, with
the medallions appearing to 'float' on the dark
background. (Detail 187)*

Sidi Bou Zid   These kilims have a more open design composition than examples from Redeyef and Oudref regions, and are more likely to have been made for private use. Designs are woven in plainweave and dovetailing technique, and often feature floating medallions on a plain ground. Motifs are often copied from knotted pile rugs that show Anatolian influence. Modern artifacts are incorporated into the designs and these combine with traditional patterns to make an interesting mixture. Borders of Sidi Bou Zid kilims usually have a repetitive geometric design.

Redeyef   Weft-faced patterning and plainweave technique are used, and this method of construction allows detailed designs to be made. The designs are primarily of banded construction, which allows the inclusion of compartments to make the pattern more interesting. Many design elements have been copied from Gafsa region.

190   Gafsa *hûli*
(3.42 × 1.52 m, 11'3" × 5')
A hûli, *or* houli, *is a flatwoven textile made as a blanket. It is, in fact, sufficiently strong to use on the floor, but as it is not intended for this, its texture is softer and more supple than a rug, and not as durable. These zig-zag and chequered designs are typical of the work of the Gafsa region. (Detail 195)*

Gafsa
8, 172, 188, 190

DESIGN	Field: Chequered floating medallions/Pictorial scenes of camel trains and human figures Borders: Some zig-zag patterning
SIZE AND SHAPE	Medium and rectangular/Small
MATERIALS	Wool
STRUCTURE	Plainweave, dovetail
COLOURS	Bright and varied palette
FRINGE	Plain
SELVEDGE	Plain
Remarks	Nowadays most kilims woven for the tourist trade

Sidi Bou Zid
167, 189

DESIGN	Field: Floating medallions on plain ground Borders: Zig-zag patterns often used
SIZE AND SHAPE	Mainly medium and rectangular
MATERIALS	Wool
STRUCTURE	Plainweave, dovetail
COLOURS	Bright and varied palette
FRINGE	Plain
SELVEDGE	Plain
Remarks	Motifs are similar to those found in knotted carpets

Redeyef
160, 193

DESIGN	Field: Heavily decorated with small geometric patterning, sometimes with central compartments
SIZE AND SHAPE	Medium and rectangular
MATERIALS	Wool, cotton
STRUCTURE	Weft-faced patterning, plainweave
COLOURS	Hot palette of red, orange, yellow, black, white
FRINGE	Plain
SELVEDGE	Plain
Remarks	Many designs (including animals) have been copied from Gafsa region

Oudref

191

DESIGN	Field: Small geometric patterns Borders: Small geometric patterns
SIZE AND SHAPE	Medium and rectangular/Small
MATERIALS	Wool, cotton
STRUCTURE	Weft-faced patterning, plainweave
COLOURS	Varied palette with white cotton
FRINGE	Plain
SELVEDGE	Plain
Remarks	'Tight' and cluttered designs/Renowned for saddle blankets

El Jem

194

DESIGN	Field: Small geometric patterns, mostly in banded and compartment format Borders: None
SIZE AND SHAPE	Medium and rectangular/Small
MATERIALS	Wool, cotton
STRUCTURE	Weft-faced patterning, plainweave
COLOURS	Rust ground with pattern depicted in white cotton
FRINGE	Plain
SELVEDGE	Plain, with thicker outside warps
Remarks	Many shawls woven/Tie-dyeing is also practised

Matmata

192

DESIGN	Field: Small brocaded geometric patterning, mostly arranged in banded format
SIZE AND SHAPE	Medium and rectangular/Small
MATERIALS	Wool, cotton
STRUCTURE	Weft-faced patterning, plainweave
COLOURS	Varied palette
FRINGE	Plain
SELVEDGE	Plain
Remarks	Blankets and saddle rugs are woven here

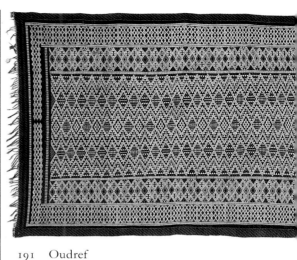

191   Oudref
(1.86 × 1.24 m, 6' × 4')
This type of rug is locally known as a klim. *It usually features small, intricate designs decorating the entire surface of the piece, borders included, woven in weft-faced patterning. Oudref is an oasis town, and has long been renowned for its weaving traditions.*

192   Matmata
(2.44 × 1.26 m, 8' × 4')
Matmata is a troglodyte town, and its subterranean dwellings, which are grouped around a central courtyard, have proved a popular tourist attraction. It has been suggested that the weaver included the fish pattern on the borders to register her feeling of being like a fish in a bowl, on permanent display to tourists, for Matmata itself has no connection with any sea or river. Small repetitive designs are often seen in Tunisian kilims.

193 Redeyef
(2.89 × 1.54 m, 9′6″ × 5′)
Redeyef kilims are woven by people of Libyan descent who settled in the area after the start of phosphate mining in south-west Tunisia in 1912. They integrated their weaving customs with those of nearby Gafsa, and many of the kilims they wove were intended for sale. This kilim has been constructed using plainweave and dovetailing, with the border woven in weft-faced patterning. The paired diamonds are said to represent the shoes of a cadi, a Mohammedan judge.

194 El Jem *mouchtiya*
(2.69 × 1.23 m, 8′10″ × 4′)
Flatweaves such as this are made as capes or shawls, but mouchtiya *can only be worn by married women. This piece was woven in the area of El Jem by Berbers. The black colour is dyed before weaving, but the rest is dyed rust red afterwards. The main design is woven in white cotton, which is not affected by dyeing. It is not easy to weave a pattern in natural white wool and cotton, and the weaver must be skilled in her work to accomplish the desired effect successfully.*

195 *Detail of 190.*

Oudref The motifs used are often of an elongated diamond shape which is repeated in a smaller form as a border pattern. The overall effect of these kilims is busy and cluttered, with insufficient surrounding space for the design to be clearly legible. The white cotton decoration in weft-faced patterning lightens these kilims, however. Oudref is renowned for its textiles, particularly saddle blankets. These were highly prized by tribal horsemen and are called *bost*.

El Jem Flatweaves from here are first woven then subsequently dyed rust red; the white cotton patterning does not take the dye, so the design only emerges after dyeing. Any darker colours are woven with dyed wool, but the weaver works mainly with natural coloured wool and cotton; this process makes it more difficult to predict the end result of the work. Tie-dyeing is also practised. Small pebbles are tightly tied into a pocket of the fabric before dyeing, which results in circles of lighter colour, considered desirable by the weaver. Many shawls are woven here, such as the *mouchtiya*, which is worn by a woman only after seven days have elapsed since her marriage. Large blankets are also woven; these are known as *wazra*.

Matmata The banded design format of most Matmata kilims is popular in many regions, and many of the patterns found in these flatweaves are copied from Tripolitania and Oudref. Matmata kilims are woven in weft-faced patterning and plainweave and have small elongated diamond motifs, triangles, zig-zags and fish motifs arranged in rows of varying widths, interspersed with bands of plain colours. The colours are generally varied. Saddle rugs, rugs and blankets are all woven; apart from the saddle rugs, these have a range of names dictated by the size and intensity of design elements.

Chapter Five

Anatolia

196   *This zig-zag pattern, on a kilim from Aydin, can be interpreted as a* su yolu *water of life motif. Double ram's horn designs are used as a filler pattern. A similar pattern is also woven around Konya generally with fewer scattered field motifs. (Detail)*

The Turkish Kurds · The Iraqi Kurds · The Caucasian Turks
The Black Sea Coast and Northern Anatolia
Thrace · Aegean Anatolia · Western Anatolia
Mediterranean Anatolia · Konya and Konya Region
The Taurus Yörüks · Aleppo

197 *A* hayat ağaci *tree of life design adapted to form a running border.*

Turkey is divided between Europe and Asia by the Bosphorus straits, and its Asian lands are known as Anatolia, formerly Asia Minor. Anatolia is also known as Anadolu, which translates from Turkish *ana*, meaning 'mother', and *dolu*, 'full', giving the sense of the 'fertile mother' or 'earth'. Although both the names of Anatolia and Turkey are in use today, Anatolia, or Anadolu, is used to mean from, or of, the land, or the countryside.

Reaching out from the Orient and Central Asia to Europe, this isthmus has formed a bridge between the two continents for thousands of years. The flux of foreign cultures crossing the land has been wonderfully varied. Through ancient times the Iranians, Greeks and Romans were followed by the Byzantines and Turks, each leaving a legacy of diverse and potent influences, archaeological remains and architecture that delight the visitor to this welcoming and fast-changing country.

The mix of indigenous Kurds, Assyrians, Armenians, Greeks, Yörük and Turkic peoples, coupled with cultural and religious influences from the Orient as well as the Mediterranean, has assured Anatolian kilim production of a fertile and dynamic tradition which still thrives to this day. A land of varied climate, wherein the southern coastal regions remain temperate all year round while the north-east experiences long, hard winters with short summers, Anatolia has an equally varied landscape that ranges from continental flatlands to desert scrub and high alpine wildernesses, all bounded by a seemingly never-ending coastline. Predominantly fertile, Anatolia is home to a majority of Sunni Muslim villagers for whom agriculture is the mainstay of daily life. Hordes of nomads known as Yörük (from the Turkic verb *yürümek*, to walk) and Turkomen once crossed these lands. Now these groups are often either semi-nomadic or sedentary, bringing to the villages yet more variations in tradition and lore. Even though the Turkish Empire is now no more, Anatolia itself remains a vast country which has much to offer, not least a long heritage of kilim-weaving.

As in most flatweaving cultures, techniques and designs have been handed down from generation to generation. What sets Anatolian flatweave production apart, however, is the diversity and richness of its designs as well as the variety and brightness of its palette. This inspirational and ever-modifying legacy continues to develop as a result of lively interaction between peoples and ideas, influences and personal creativity. Indeed, unlike the kilim culture of Central Asia, Iran and North Africa, where weaves are governed, restricted and inspired, more or less, within a tribal environment, that of Anatolia has been embellished by its rich folkloric tradition and diversity of foreign influence.

History

The earliest archaeological evidence so far discovered indicates that by 7000 BC, basic agriculture had developed and the breeding of animals had started in the Fertile Crescent of Iraqi Kurdistan, northern Syria, the Levant, and the coastal plain of Cilicia in Anatolia, although food production possibly developed here as early as ten thousand years ago. Excavations at Hacilar, which was first inhabited around that time, revealed that people were by then living in mud-brick houses with plastered walls, but were not yet making pottery. Hacilar was subsequently

198   *A Fethiye kilim.*

reinhabited at the end of the Neolithic period by a far more developed people with
a better organized social structure and a strong artistic culture. Çatal Hüyük, near
Konya, was a remarkable Neolithic small town, of great fascination to
archaeologists, which was occupied from the early seventh to the mid-sixth
millennium BC. This site has yielded much information about life at that time.
Each house was similarly constructed, with rectangular rooms of sun-dried brick
and plastered walls; and access to the lower storey was by a wooden ladder or
staircase to the flat roof, the upper storeys of the houses being only partially
covered. The people of Çatal Hüyük still hunted wild animals for food, and appear
to have had a strong religious cult, as many murals were found that would appear
to be shrines. These were painted on plaster, and the plaster renewed and new
murals applied in a yearly cycle. They depicted hunting scenes, goddesses –
sometimes in the act of giving birth, bulls' heads, and vultures eating the flesh of
the dead – motifs that bear strong resemblance to designs found in kilims woven
many centuries later (see Chapter Three, p. 65). It is possible that weaving was
practised, although no concrete evidence has, to date, substantiated this. Figures
of humans and animals made from clay and plaster were unearthed at the site, as
well as plain pottery. Many tools, sometimes ornately decorated, as well as
weapons, wooden utensils and other paraphernalia of a cultured society also
contribute to our knowledge of the people of Çatal Hüyük. The settlement used to
lie on the banks of a river where crops were grown. Overall, this advanced society
appears to be unique, and its discovery has played an important part in the study of
the development of mankind.

The indigenous Anatolians emerged from the Neolithic into the Chalcolithic
age a well-developed people in social and cultural organization; they lived in
houses, practised agriculture, kept livestock, made pottery and baskets, tools and
weapons, and sculpted and painted for religious and cult purposes. Little wonder,
then, that when the Hittites, who were an Indo-European people, arrived in 1900

199 Erzurum
(1.65 × 1.28 m, 5′5″ × 4′2″)
The blue/green colouring of this kilim, woven in slitweave on natural brown wool warps, is typical of prayer kilims from Erzurum in the north-east, although the white ground surrounding the niche is less so. The motif in the red border is frequently used in kilims from this region, and a very similar motif regularly appears in Caucasian rugs.

200 Aydin
(1.59 × 1.02 m, 5′2″ × 3′4″)
The wide borders of this kilim from Aydin in Aegean Anatolia are filled with movement, contrasting totally with the static central panel; its weaver created it with skill, but the composition is bizarre. The colouring is very appealing, featuring the red ground often found in Aydin kilims.

Captions for 201–4 on page 104.

BC and found such a civilized land, they took over and developed Anatolia into a powerful nation, building their capital at Hattusas (modern Boğazkale), and capturing Syria from the Egyptians.

After the Trojan War of the late thirteenth century BC, the Lydians and Phrygians invaded west and central Anatolia from 1200 to 700 BC, whereas the east of the land came under the control of the Armenian Urartu kingdom. Subsequently the states of Achaea, Ionia, Aeolia and Doria were formed, heralding the beginning of Greek civilization in Anatolia. From 1200 BC to AD 1070 parts of Anatolia came under Persian, Hellenistic, Roman and Byzantine influence and control, the most infamous period being that of Alexander the Great in the fourth century BC. The first invasion of Seljuk Turks into Anatolia took place in AD 1071, and seven years later the first Seljuk emirate was established at Nicaea. The Seljuk sultanate was itself established at Konya in 1097. In 1202 the Fourth Crusade ravaged Constantinople leaving the Byzantines much weakened. Groups of the Oghuz tribe escaping from the Mongols quickly took advantage of this, resulting in the founding of the Ottoman Empire in 1288, and so beginning a story of Ottoman rule that was to include both periods of great glory and long-drawn-out decline.

At first, the Ottoman Empire grew steadily, despite setbacks, and reached its peak in the sixteenth century under the rule of Sultan Suleyman the Magnificent. Although subsequent rulers were less competent, the strength of the Empire

Page 103:

201, 202   Konya
(4.52 × 1.44 m, 13'8" × 4'9")
Woven in plainweave, this striped nineteenth-century kilim relies entirely on colour for effect. Its creator has excelled in her sense of balance and combination. Note the minute patterns occurring along the narrow brown bands.
(Detail 202)

203, 204   Konya
(3.53 × 1.69 m, 11'7" × 5'6")
The design of this kilim is similar to 206 and 305, and it is interesting to compare how the varied arrangement of the pattern and the colours used can greatly alter the effect. This nineteenth-century kilim is a lovely example of the design both in colouring and form; the variety of small motifs used bears testimony to the weaver's imagination and artistry.
(Detail 203)

continued until the end of the seventeenth century, after which stagnation and unrest set the tone for several hundred years. The gradual disintegration of the Empire was closely watched by European powers, all wanting to gain control of Ottoman territories, especially after Greece gained its independence in 1830. In the aftermath of the First World War, national pride was at first shattered by the invasion in 1919 of the formerly subject Greeks. During the Turkish War of Independence (1920–22), however, the Ottoman general Mustapha Kemal managed to turn the tide of the advancing Greeks and became a national hero. After the abolition of the sultanate and the end of the Ottoman Empire, a republic was founded in 1923, under the leadership of Kemal, later known as Kemal Ataturk. His successful reforms brought widespread changes and laid the foundations of modern Turkey. The subsequent history of the country has been punctuated by unresolved conflicts between democracy and authoritarianism, modernization and tradition, but also – and most recently – energetic attempts to forge European economic and cultural links.

Indigenous Peoples

The Kurds

Of Aryan descent, the Kurds are thought to have inhabited eastern Anatolia since about 2000 BC. They are a very independent group, and because of the inaccessibility of their mountain habitat little outside influence has penetrated their culture aside from the Islamic faith brought by Arabs in the seventh century AD. The Kurds have fought as mercenaries, however, both for the Turks and the Persians, and later against the Russians.

It was not until 1880 that these traditional people united together to form a national movement, which came about directly as a result of their being enlisted to fight various wars for different countries. By the early part of this century, however, newly established political borders restricted tribal movement and the tribes began to split up. Since 1924 suppression and genocide have been the overtures of their host nation states; the closure of mosques and the bans on Kurdish national dress and ceremonies seem inconsequential by comparison with the frequent and enforced mass-exodus of the people from one refuge to another. As a consequence, the Kurdish peoples have now been thoroughly splintered, some residing in Iran and Iraq while others were moved to different parts of Turkey, basically to diversify and weaken any strongholds or concentrated areas where Kurds congregated.

Invasion and Influx

The Yörüks

The word *yörük* encompasses all nomadic peoples and has no definite ethnic association. The Yörüks of Anatolia are Ural-Altai people, related to Mongols and Samoyeds as well as Hungarian and Finnish peoples. They first emerged in the sixth century AD and eventually came to occupy a large territory stretching from Hungary to China. Famous for their migratory lifestyle, they were a warrior

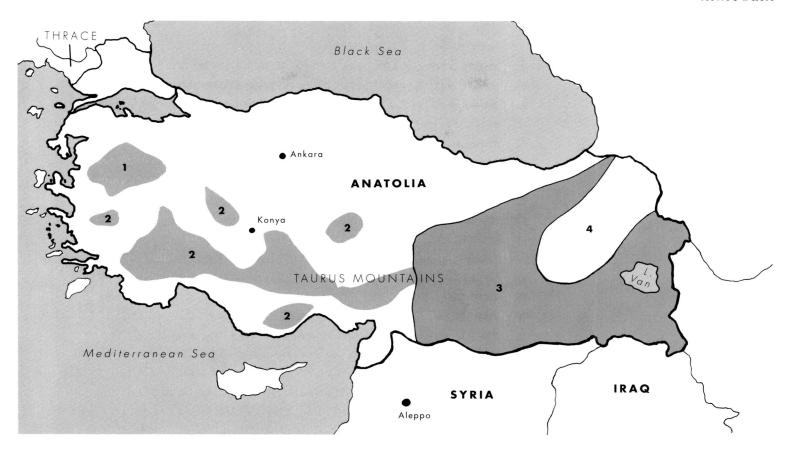

THRACE

Black Sea

Ankara

ANATOLIA

Konya

1

2

2

2

2

2

TAURUS MOUNTAINS

3

4

L. Van

Mediterranean Sea

SYRIA

Aleppo

IRAQ

Tribal Regions of Anatolia
1 Yüncü Yörüks   2 Taurus Yörüks
3 Turkish Kurds   4 Caucasian Turks

nation much respected for good horsemanship and archery, and although they had their own language, their history was recorded by the sedentary people with whom they came into contact. Converting to Islam, the Yörüks became known as 'Turkomen' in the ninth century. The waves of Mongol hordes eventually drove them westward, where they first settled in the Pontic Mountains, then in the Taurus Mountains, for there the climate was more to their liking and somewhat similar to that of Central Asia. As nomads they continued to pursue their customary migration between summer and winter pastures, and in some regions this still continues.

The Oghuz Seljuks

The Oghuz Turkomen people first started arriving in Anatolia in small groups from Mongolia and the Asian Steppes. They became known as the Seljuks, after the leader of the Kinik tribe, Selçuk Bey, whose grandson, Tugrul Bey, founded the Seljuk state. Other divisions of Oghuz came from Azerbaijan in a disorganized migration of tribespeople. By overcoming the Byzantines at the Battle of Manzikert in 1071 they were able to advance into Byzantine territory where they acted as mercenaries in localized power struggles, but essentially the Seljuks were *gazis*, or religious warriors, fighting for the cause of Islam. Turkey benefited greatly from Seljuk rule, coming to be considered a rich country by its neighbours as cultural and learning centres were established, and later in the twelfth century Konya became its capital. Fragmentation of the state and the attacks of the Mongols created the Seljuk downfall in the thirteenth century.

The Oghuz Ottomans

This group was a division of the Oghuz, initially known as the Kayi tribe and later called Ottomans after their leader Osman (Uthman in Arabic). Osman was the founder of both a dynasty and an empire which lasted from the thirteenth century until the end of the First World War. The Ottomans, again, were warriors for the Islamic faith, who fought against both the Mongols and the Byzantines. From the thirteenth to the fifteenth century there was continual territorial expansion, which encompassed Anatolia, Syria, Bulgaria and the Balkan Peninsula, resulting in the repossession and reorganization of the Seljuk territories. Anatolia was then lost to the Mongols under Tamerlane, and thereafter only slowly regained as further territory came under Ottoman rule. The empire grew and reached its peak during the sixteenth century under the control of Suleyman I, who encouraged both cultural and artistic endeavour as well as the acquisition of yet more territories.

By the sixteenth and seventeenth centuries the population of Anatolia had greatly increased and survival in the villages became difficult, so that large numbers of the landless and unemployed moved to the larger cities, only to increase the strain on food supplies there. Those who remained in the villages formed rebel groups known as *celâlis*, who took what they desired from the remaining farmers and traders. The *celâlis* grew in power and soon came to control the food supply and tax revenues destined for the cities and armies, acting quite outside government ruling. As a consequence, the army began to disintegrate and many soldiers joined the rebels, seeing a lawless life as a rich and easy source of income. The main body of the army remained strong enough, however, to curb the most serious revolts. By the seventeenth century the government started a reform programme, compelling the villagers to return to the land to increase productivity, and industry and trade were encouraged as the corruption and dissention were stamped out. The many reforms that took place included a reorganization of the structure of power, the secularization of justice and the modernization of the army.

Nevertheless, the social stagnation of the culture could not in the end be halted; as a consequence there was widespread disintegration, and loss of territory occurred during the eighteenth and nineteenth centuries. At this time, when the Ottoman Empire itself was busily preoccupied with internal problems, it failed to realize that many of the nations of Western Europe were rapidly developing, and becoming increasingly powerful, until the nineteenth century. Such was the cultural turpitude of the Empire that some of the ruling classes took up a more 'Western' style of living, building large residences and holding garden parties. The growing of tulips, which had become very popular in Europe by the sixteenth century, demonstrated yet further the desire for European ways, becoming a craze adopted by all; this era was known as the 'tulip period'.

Tribal Relationships

The tribal groups of Anatolia were, in general, small bands of people who mainly inhabited the mountainous areas as nomads, and were organized by their powerful chiefs. Far removed from urban society and politics, they lived independently and survived by their own enterprise. Their nomadic existence meant that during migration they invariably came into contact with other groups and settlements, enabling a communication of tribal customs to take place. These people wove a great variety of kilims, bags and trappings, both out of necessity and as a luxury.

205   *A Kağizman prayer kilim.*

Special tribal emblems, or *damga*, were incorporated into their designs, and these have subsequently provided scholars with a means of tracing tribal movements, which were often far-reaching.

Religion has played an important role in the history of nomadic life, and it was partly through contact with the dervishes that superstition and mysticism remained integral to tribal belief even after their conversion to Islam. The different groups interpreted the dervish teachings in their own ways, which led to new Sufic circles being formed, and the further evolution of tribal beliefs. The diversity of these circles, together with their varied origins, customs and weaving traditions, has ensured that certain kilim designs are unique to their native region. However, continuous tribal movement and population expansion has also meant that some similar tribal practices and, consequently, kilim motifs, are sometimes found in areas quite remote from each other.

For the past four centuries successive governments have forcibly tried to settle, relocate and fragment such tribal groups, and yet after a short time in a new site the tribes would often return to where they considered their homelands to be. This would commonly lead to conflict, as on their return the group might discover that another had taken over the rights to its grazing pastures. Some groups settled in

206 Konya
(3.81 × 1.60 m, 12′6″ × 5′2″)
Both the size of the extending arms on the white cotton ground and the crowded hooked medallions give a rigid appearance to this kilim. Its dark tones, contrasting against the white, define the pattern well but the overall impression is stark. The cluttered design improves a little when viewed horizontally.

the cities and became immured by their urban lifestyle; naturally they were looked down upon by their nomadic counterparts, although nowadays it is the nomads who are considered inferior.

There can be no doubt that the nomadic way of life is now rapidly disappearing in Turkey. Although the nomads were given special status by Ataturk, as he considered that they exemplified Turkish culture in its most traditional form, twentieth-century government pressure, along with the compulsory payments for land tenancy and village growth, has proved terminally damaging. Aside from political settlement, the need to move to and from the summer pastures has itself lessened with more efficient production of food and deep drilling for a regular supply of water. Combined with this is the fact that as the population has grown so rapidly in some areas, the available summer grazing would not in any case sustain the extra flocks and herds.

Weaving Traditions

To date, it has been impossible to establish just when the weaving of kilims first began in Anatolia, and it is likely to remain so. As kilims were purely functional and had no real commercial value, few surviving examples pre-date the seventeenth century, for a kilim would have been used until disintegration. There are extant examples of seventeenth-century court kilims and eighteenth-century nomadic and village kilims, and nineteenth-century flatweaves are relatively common. Of the latter, the quantities in market circulation are rapidly decreasing, for many are now secure in private collections. Weaving at that time was certainly prolific, yet by the early part of the twentieth century it was in decline and in some regions had already become extinct.

Traditionally the majority of the population of Anatolia – approximately eighty per cent – were villagers who lived a life of self-sufficiency, and although within the state political and legal system, they had to pay taxes, they had little else to do with the government. Most of the settlements were fairly small, and upheld their own system of social, political and economic affairs. Many villagers owned their land, and as ownership was often determined by family rights rather than by legality, many sometimes violent disputes erupted.

Like the nomadic people, the villagers weave kilims for domestic use, to make their lives both more comfortable and more colourful. Existence is otherwise harsh. Most villages have no paving on their streets, and in winter rain and snow turn the earth into a muddy quagmire; until recently they had no electricity or running water either. Sheep-rearing is an age-old occupation. The animals are shorn twice a year, and the wool is either used by their owner or sold to a local wool factory or trader. Many villagers will spin, dye and weave the wool from their small flock into a kilim that will subsequently be sold. Bags and *çuval* (sacks) are still woven for the storage of possessions and animal fodder.

Anatolian villagers continue to live close to nature, as they have done for centuries, so that in addition to the lack of amenities, in many villages animals still wander in and out of the houses at will. The main room of a typical primitive village house has a wood-burning stove, which doubles up as a heater in winter, a loom, some cooking utensils, a mass of storage sacks and little else. The arts and crafts of such a primitive lifestyle hold no interest for more sophisticated urban people, and kilims have remained unappreciated and largely undiscovered within Anatolia itself for many centuries. Indeed, there are still many modern Turkish city-dwellers who are completely uninterested in their tribal past, and would never want to own any tribal artifact connecting them with their ancestors.

Until recently, Anatolian kilims continued to be woven by women and girls as dowry pieces and commemorative textiles for certain rites of passage such as birth, death and circumcision, all of which are important in the Islamic faith. The woman's role is to look after children, prepare and cook food, maintain the house, gather crops in summer, and be generally compliant with her husband's wishes. Although she has no rights as such, she presides over her household, and quite apart from any religious restriction barring her from activities outside the home, she would be too proud to seek work elsewhere. In the past, her only avenue of personal creative expression was craftwork, weaving and embroidery. In this way village and nomadic women were much freer than their urban counterparts, and so during the winter months, when keeping warm inside was a necessity, they had time to make things for the home, kilims included.

Kilims were used as covers for the floor, as doorway and window curtains, prayer rugs and, occasionally, eating cloths. They were also made into every size of bag for storage and transportation, as well as serving as trappings to decorate the animals. Aside from domestic use, the flatweaves were made for donation to the mosque, and more recently for trade. Kilims, given their light weight, were also woven in the summer months specifically as covers for seating. In the traditional Anatolian village house the salon is furnished with banquettes that also double up as beds for visitors. It is for these that many large Anatolian kilims are made, in a long and narrow format that is perfect for the back and seat of a banquette. A wealthy family may perhaps exchange kilims for carpets that afford more comfort in the wintertime.

Large kilims are woven as walls for tents, where the slitweave technique allows for the free circulation of air. Kilims are also used as hangings in the mosque to separate the men from the women, and on the floor for praying on. According to Islamic faith, prayer must be conducted five times daily, and many small kilims, light and easy to carry, are woven as prayer rugs. The wide variety of storage sacks serves a dual purpose, as decorative containers for possessions and also as floor cushions, in both the tents and village houses.

Amongst the most notable aspects of the majority of Anatolian kilims are their wonderful colours and the clever interrelationship constructed between them. Indeed, a glowing, vibrant and bold use of colour is the 'traditional' characteristic of Anatolian kilims. Colour is used as an integral part of the creation of spatial effects, forming the positive and negative areas of the composition, and highlighting one or other shape created by the colour field.

Originally, dyes were obtained from natural sources such as flowers, vegetables, the leaves and roots of plants, bark, acorns, nuts, and even volcanic mud. Natural dyestuffs can produce spectacular colours, which are in every way superior to their chemically produced counterparts, and which improve (to Western taste) with the passage of time. Although in general Anatolian kilims incorporate a wide variety of colours, some kilims may use many colours and different hues of colour whereas others may have only three. Both can be equally

207 Malatya
(3.64 × 1.72 m, 11′11″ × 5′7″)
Woven in two halves, the design of this kilim aligns perfectly, not an easy accomplishment. It was bought late at night in the half light of a dusty basement in Central Anatolia, the white cotton radiating through the gloom, and is another example of a flatweave that should be viewed horizontally.

effective, as long as the colours are set in harmony. Many old, naturally dyed kilims may display a pleasing mellowness and softness of character, depending on how much exposure to light they have had. At the time when the kilims were woven, however, the colours would have been generally darker and more severe – the effect probably originally desired by the weaver, just as loud and brash colours seem to appeal to the villagers of today.

To achieve the time-worn effect so beloved by the Western consumer, the practice of sun-fading both kilims and carpets is widespread, reducing the harsh colours to a more acceptable palette; sun-fading is less damaging to the wool than heavy chemical washing, which is customary for carpets. All colours fade with exposure to natural light, and natural colours remain much stronger than some chemical dyes which will tone down in a space of weeks. During the summer months, therefore, particularly in the south of Anatolia, near Antalya, once the harvest is finished, the farmers spread kilims and carpets on the bare ground; the acres of rugs stretching across the fields create a spectacular sight.

208   *The end border motif is typical of Konya kilims.*

The identification of kilim types is a problematic business that perplexes the market worldwide. Because of the incredible number of different kilim designs prevalent – especially within Anatolia, and often within one small area – and the lack of documentation on kilim-weaving, it is difficult to be entirely accurate about the attribution of kilims. Further confusion is added by dealers who ascribe localities inaccurately since these can often become the recognized 'provenance' of a rug. Such misleading information conceals and protects the dealer's source, and so lessens the competition from other merchants and collectors. The prospective purchaser would be well advised to rely as far as possible on the colour, pattern, weave, size and materials of a rug for clues as to its true origin. One of the interesting properties of natural dyes – as opposed to chemical dyes – is that they are composed of many different hues; the 'pure' colour of chemical dyes is much flatter and therefore much more harsh. This affects the balance and harmony of colours used, and consequently the appearance of the kilim. The use of colour, to a certain extent, can indicate the provenance of a rug, and the type of dye colour is also helpful in dating a kilim.

A kilim's patterns and designs are other important factors in the unravelling of the provenance puzzle, although such visual clues can, on occasions, be misleading, as designs travel far and their traditional use dies hard. Although compositions, patterns and designs are handed down the generations, certain tribal characteristics are mixed with new innovations, and woven in different areas. A girl from Malatya, for example, may marry and move to Sivas. Her weaving will follow the pattern of a Malatya composition, yet she will be using materials available in Sivas. The resulting kilim, therefore, will be labelled as Sivas, although the composition will have originated elsewhere.

The Turkish Kurds of Eastern Anatolia

Kurdish weaving continues here today on a small scale, and as it is principally a cottage industry, the Kurds' well-known sense of originality and vital expression has remained intact, although weaving in some areas such as Kars and Malatya is now more commercially orientated. Kurdish kilims are, generally speaking, decorated with patterning over the whole surface; slitweave and weft-wrapping techniques are employed, and the use of dark colours is prevalent. Kurds have always been involved in the rug trade, collecting flatweaves from the villages and selling them in the bazaars of larger towns, and many people in the kilim and carpet business in Istanbul are originally from Malatya, of Turkish and Kurdish descent. The changing of borders and the frequent conflicts in the region have led to a haphazard mixing of cultural influences. The Iraqi Kurdish kilims are often classified and sold as Van kilims, and some designs have been so influenced by the Caucasian groups that it is at times difficult to tell on which side of the political border a kilim was woven. By comparison with the rest of Anatolia, these Kurdish areas have remained fairly isolated from the modern world and its commercial influences since the First World War.

Van

Van lies on the south-east side of Lake Van, which is the largest water mass in Anatolia, and the second largest in the Middle East. Lake Van is a salt-water lake with little natural life bar the darekh, a type of carp which has adapted itself to a saline environment. Close to modern Van and near the Rock of Van, where ruins show cuneiform inscriptions dating from the seventh and eighth centuries BC, lies Tooshpa, which was the capital of the Urartian kingdom of the seventeenth to the thirteenth century BC. Van enjoyed prosperity under the Armenian Bagratid dynasty during the eighth century AD, before the town was taken over by Seljuk Turks in the eleventh century and subsequently came under Ottoman rule in the fifteenth century. Old Van was destroyed by the Ottomans when occupied by Russia between 1915 and 1917. The new Van city was built a short distance away, and forms an important market centre for the Kurdish tribes. The Hartushi tribe resides in this area, as well as across the border close by in Iraq. Hartushi kilims are of the slitweave variety. Similarly the once nomadic Herki tribe are to be found here as well as in Iraq. The Herki weave kilims in weft-wrapping technique.

Kilims continue to be woven in Van, although not on a scale sufficient for commercial and export purposes. The wool and the quality of the weaving is good, yet their colours lack the intensity to mimic older pieces successfully. Van is now very much on the tourist path, and one should be cautious of buying kilims here. They are a good deal cheaper in Istanbul.

Van kilims are easily recognizable by their compositions and coloration. The central designs are often in paired hooked diamond-shaped medallions. A second design features smaller medallions and hooked motifs in horizontal rows, and this type generally have vertical bands of contrasting ground colour. Another variety has horizontal bands, the wider of which are filled with small hexagonal motifs. Sometimes this format has plain-coloured wide bands, with the design in the smaller bands. Borders are always narrow, and often have a zig-zag pattern or hook design.

210 Van
(2.58 × 1.75 m, 8′5″ × 5′8″)
The basic format of pairs of hooked or crenellated medallions is characteristic of Van kilims. Made in two halves, these flatweaves often have a distorted pattern and sides of unequal lengths, although this does not detract from the powerful design and rich colours of this particular example. The green in the centre of the medallions is unusual for Van kilims, whose predominant colours are deep reds and blues.

211 Van
This elibelinde *motif is used in mirror image. (Detail)*

212 Van
The çengel *hook motif is often set within a lozenge shape on Van kilims. (Detail of 213)*

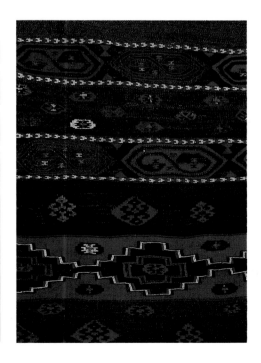

Van

210, 213−14

DESIGN	Field: Large hooked or crenellated medallions repeated down the field Borders: Narrow
SIZE AND SHAPE	Mainly medium
MATERIALS	Medium to thick wool, metallic thread
STRUCTURE	Slitweave (narrow slits), made in two halves
COLOURS	Dark palette of blue, red, brown, white
FRINGE	Plaited, often with long tassels
SELVEDGE	Plain, with thicker outside warps
Remarks	Easily recognizable because of similar designs, colouring and texture

213 Van
(2.54 × 1.72 m, 8'3" × 5'7")
This kilim probably originates from south of Hakkari, near, or over, the Iraq border. There are many similarities between kilims woven in Iraq and south-eastern Anatolia, and most are just attributed to Van. This example is finely woven in slitweave, with long silky warps forming the plaiting and fringe.

214 Van
(2.83 × 1.57 m, 9'3" × 5'1")
The fringes of this kilim, probably woven in the Hakkari area, or possibly in Iraq, were originally plaited, which had resulted in the corners of the kilim being drawn in and curling. The plait has subsequently been unravelled, and the warps knotted and trimmed.

Colours are generally dark – reds and blues, with some white. Small amounts of orange, green and pink have appeared of late. The use of metallic thread is very popular in this area, but fortunately it loses its brilliance with age and is only noticeable on close inspection.

Van kilims are made with thick wool warps and so are generally very strong and tightly woven. The ends of the kilim are often plaited with long fringes, but although this provides a decorative finish it can result in a runkling rug, as the warps are drawn unevenly into the plait. The warps are often of differing colours and slitweave is the predominant technique.

Gaziantep

This town lies in south-eastern Turkey, close by the Syrian border and the Euphrates River. Previously called Aintab and then Antep by Ottomans, Gaziantep acquired its present name after it fell to the French in April 1920, having been defended by the nationalists for ten months. This stupendous effort was recognized by the Turkish Grand National Assembly, who gave the city the prefix title of Gazi, meaning 'Defender of the Faith'. Kilim-weaving has long since ceased in this area. Gaziantep designs have horizontal bands of differing colours with three diamond-shaped serrated emblems joined together to form the main pattern, often filled with star motifs, which also decorate other areas of the kilim. These intricate designs are often highlighted with white cotton for additional effect. Borders are narrow with reciprocal designs or repeated motifs, and the fringes can be plaited or knotted. The colouring is normally dark, often with a predominance of red. Both large rectangular kilims (made in two halves) and small kilims are constructed in slitweave from finely spun wool.

215 Gaziantep
(1.50 × 1.00 m, 4'11" × 3'3")
The end border or skirt design is cleverly drawn, incorporating both elibelinde *and* akrep *motifs.*

216 Gaziantep
(3.20 × 1.70 m, 10'5" × 5'6")
The six-pointed star decorating this kilim is known as the 'Seal of Solomon', although it has been used since Phrygian times.

Gaziantep

215–16

DESIGN	Field: Horizontal bands and geometric emblems Borders: Narrow with reciprocal designs or repeated motifs
SIZE AND SHAPE	Large and rectangular/Small
MATERIALS	Medium and fine wool, cotton
STRUCTURE	Slitweave, made in two halves
COLOURS	Dark to medium palette of red, blue, green, white cotton, brown, white
FRINGE	Plaited/Knotted/Plain
SELVEDGE	Plain
Remarks	Star motifs also prevalent, often filled with yin/yang design representing harmony

217   Sivas/Malatya
Glowing colours used in perfect harmony, together with an unusual design, combine to make a very attractive kilim. (Detail)

Sivas	219–20, 222
DESIGN	Field: Large central medallions/*Saf*/Prayer arches Borders: Often leaf and vine pattern
SIZE AND SHAPE	Long and rectangular/Small
MATERIALS	Fine wool
STRUCTURE	Slitweave, plainweave weft wrapping
COLOURS	Bright red, light and medium green, orange, some blue, brown, black, white
FRINGE	Webbed/Knotted/Plaited
SELVEDGE	Plain
Remarks	Some *çiçims* woven

Sivas

In the third century, Sivas was a Roman city known as Sebastea, the capital of Armenia Minor. Flourishing under Byzantine rule, Sivas reached a peak of prosperity under the Seljuks, only to be plundered in the fourteenth century by Tamerlane, as it was an important venue on the Persian and Iraqi trade routes. The Sivas region is inhabited by Turkish and Kurdish people, and until the genocide wrought by the Turks early this century, many Armenians dwelt there as well. Sivas gained a certain fame as the site for the Sivas Congress of September 1919, convened by Mustafa Kemal, which, together with the Erzurum meeting in the July, formulated the subsequent revolution and way to the War of Independence. The surrounding area is mainly agricultural, and Sivas itself is now a modern town with a railway station, which has helped to restore some of its former economic importance.

Many prayer arch kilims come from here, as well as small kilims, and large kilims woven in two halves. The designs of the large medallion kilims are very similar to those of Malatya area, featuring large oblong central medallions, with many varied smaller filler motifs such as stars or wolf tracks. *Saf* kilims are multiple prayer-arch flatweaves. This pattern is either made in a unidirectional form, or can be double-ended. Both versions are woven here. The borders of the large kilims, particularly the medallion kilims, feature repeat hooked motifs in a single main border, whereas the smaller kilims often have multiple borders with differing motifs. Colours are of a lighter hue than other Kurdish weavings, particularly the reds and greens. The standard of weaving varies a great deal, and is mainly slitweave. The wool is of good quality, but of variable fineness. Some *çiçims* are woven in the Sivas area, and also small prayer kilims and runners.

Some kilims that are attributed to Sivas are actually woven in Şarkisla, a town further south-west, and these are in fact very different in character and weave, although the design compositions are fairly similar, consisting of rows of floating medallions that are usually of a hexagonal or hooked diamond form filling the field. These kilims often feature a red ground ornamented with browns, black, orange and grey (faded aniline blue or purple), with two or three main borders. In

218   Sivas
(1.52 × 0.98 m, 4′11″ × 3′2″)
This nineteenth-century kilim has quite a primitive feel, for the pattern has not been well drawn, yet it is redeemed by its fine weave, soft colours and barber-pole effect segmenting the field motif – curiously absent from the white area. The leaf and vine motif is often used as a border design.

219   Sivas
(3.64 × 1.76 m, 11′11″ × 5′9″)
*This example is typical of large kilims from
this area. The design is very similar to Malatya
medallion kilims, and is only distinguishable by
its lighter colours. Kilims of this size were often
made as seating covers, with the pattern designed
to be viewed horizontally.*

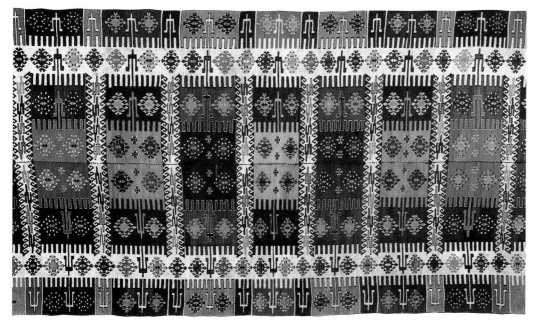

220   Sivas
(3.84 × 1.92 m, 12′7″ × 6′3″)
*Although woven quite recently, this design has
been used for centuries. The weaver has
completed her work with a skill rarely seen in
kilims made within the last few decades.*

221   Sivas/Malatya
(3.53 × 1.76 m, 11′6″ × 5′9″)
*The design of this kilim suggests that it
originates from Sivas, but its colouring is more
typical of Kurdish Malatya kilims. Viewed
horizontally, the motifs adjoining the border and
those that form the medallion can be seen as an
elibelinde mother-goddess design repeated in
expanded rows. Considering that the design is
woven vertically, the weaver has calculated it
with skill.*

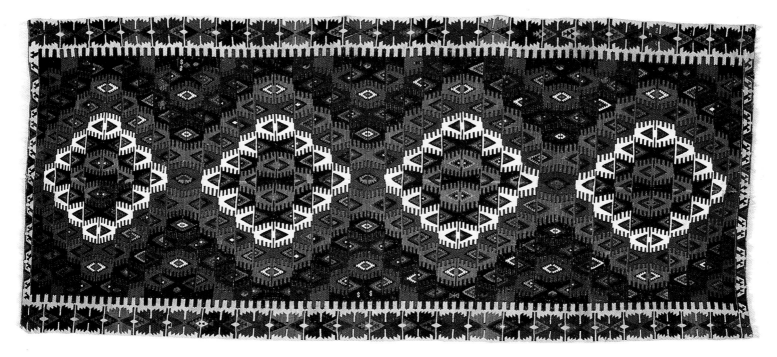

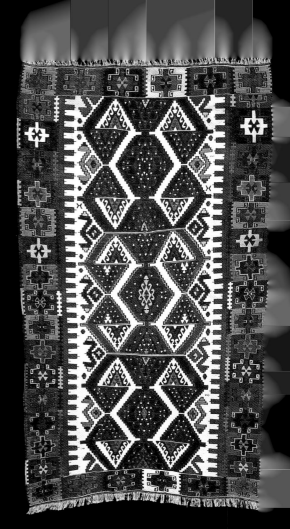

the older kilims, blue, black and sometimes green and yellow medallions occur, again on a red ground. Şarkisla kilims are, on the whole, loosely woven in slitweave and generally of a coarse texture, although sometimes the wool used for the warps is soft and silky. Many very large kilims come from this region. Some medium sizes are found, but very few small kilims.

Malatya

Malatya is a town built on one main street that continues for a number of miles. It is situated in the Tohmasuyu River basin which is encircled by the high peaks of the eastern Taurus Mountains. This is a fertile agricultural region, particularly for apricots, and has been a prolific weaving area for many years. The modern town was established in 1838; old Malatya, which is close by, was once an important city in Armenia Minor. In Roman times it was important as a garrison town on the eastern frontier, and the settlement came under Ottoman rule in the early fifteenth century. Considering the number of kilims woven in this region there is a surprising lack of diversity in design, especially in the larger kilims; this is possibly a direct result of the Kurdish tribal tradition of weaving only one type of design. Small prayer rugs are more varied, and often have great character and individuality. The quality of the kilims now woven in the region is deteriorating, and production for commercial purposes is slowly spreading into the villages.

Large kilims generally feature three or four central medallions, while the smaller variety are usually decorated with one in the centre. Some of these kilims have been referred to as 'Rashwan' weavings. The Rashwan were a Kurdish tribe who settled in parts of central and eastern Anatolia. These kilims are not easy to weave, for the designs are complicated and the filler motifs plentiful; indeed, their value has probably been underestimated by the market.

Another variety of medallion kilim is also found in a smaller size, and features a hexagonally shaped medallion with arms or hooks extending from the sides. This is used as a central motif arranged in a vertical line for smaller kilims, and for larger sizes it is repeated in rows down the field. Such a motif is also found in Aksaray and Aleppo kilims, which have a lighter colour palette.

Banded kilims are borderless, and patterned with both narrow and wide alternating stripes. These are decorated with small motifs, often in supplementary weft-wrapping technique, and separated either by smaller patterned bands or by a plain colour. Large sizes are made in two halves. As in other Kurdish weavings, a dark colour palette of red, blue, brown, and some green is used that contrasts with

Opposite:

222 Sivas
(2.16 × 1.54 m, 7′ × 5′)
This kilim bears a wealth of interesting motifs, the most noticeable of which being the five tree-like shapes that appear on the white ground and above the central emblem. It would appear that the weaver was experimenting with different motifs, for the reciprocal design at the top end of the green centre is hooked while at the bottom it culminates in a pronged design.

223 Malatya
(2.18 × 1.21 m, 7′2″ × 4′)
This nineteenth-century kilim is very similar to 225, although here the use of white cotton accentuates the pattern. The border motif is derived from a family crest or sign, originally of the Oghuz tribe. The light brown sections appear to have been rewoven.

224 Sivas
(2.28 × 1.92 m, 7′ × 6′4″)
Distinctly Kurdish motifs such as the comb or hour-glass are evident on this kilim, woven in the mid-nineteenth century. The form of hooked prayer arch depicted here is also seen in Erzurum kilims, and is often used in saf, *multiple prayer-arch, compositions.*

225 Malatya
(1.97 × 1.03 m, 6′5″ × 3′4″)
This kilim has a characteristically Kurdish look – dark, rich colours and an asymmetric lower end. Note the small star with extending arms, enclosing the yin-yang symbol of harmony.

226 Malatya
(2.84 × 0.80 m, 9′4″ × 2′7″)
The positive/negative effect of the hexagonal and hour-glass motifs leads to shifts in dominance from one to the other. The decorated bands are woven in slitweave, the narrow bands in plainweave, and the small 'S' motifs in supplementary weft wrapping.

227   Malatya (above)
(1.68 × 1.07 m, 5′6″ × 3′6″)
Woven by the Drican tribe from the north-west of Malatya. The dark colour palette and ornate decoration are characteristic of Kurdish kilims from the Malatya area.

229   Malatya (left)
(1.21 × 0.81 m, 3′11″ × 2′7″)
A delightful kilim with a well-balanced design. The care that has gone into the making of this kilim suggests that it may have been woven as a dowry piece. Note the bonçuk *bead at the bottom of the red area, a symbol for good luck.*

228   Malatya (above)
(2.89 × 1.87 m, 9′5″ × 6′1″)
This typical example of a Malatya medallion kilim was woven in the nineteenth century, most probably as a seating cover. The eight-armed motifs around the medallions resemble the sign of the Bagduz family, of Oghuz origin.

The distinct zig-zag pattern in the narrow bands of this kilim is said to represent birds. According to folkloric interpretation, the bird is not only a symbol of death, it is also the bringer of good news, happiness, and love.

undyed wool or bright white cotton. The wool is of good quality and lustrous, and sometimes very finely spun. Weaving techniques vary a great deal; some kilims incorporate both plainweave and supplementary weft wrapping, although slitweave is predominantly used. The fringes of Malatya kilims are sometimes plaited. Many different sizes are found – large kilims, generally woven in two halves, small kilims, *yastiks* (cushions) and *çuval* (sacks).

231 Sinan
(1.65 × 0.89 m, 5'4" × 2'10")
Kurdish kilims are often irregular in shape, as is this example. The wavy lines at either end represent running water, which symbolizes the wish for life.

Malatya	207, 223, 225–6, 228, 230, 565, 569, 592
DESIGN	Field: Banded/Central medallions Borders: Banded kilims have none
SIZE AND SHAPE	Large and rectangular/Small
MATERIALS	Fine wool with silky texture, cotton
STRUCTURE	Slitweave, plainweave, supplementary weft wrapping
COLOURS	Dark brown, red, blue, green, brown, black, white
FRINGE	Knotted/Plaited/Plain
SELVEDGE	Plain
Remarks	Large sizes are made in two halves

Sinan Sinan kilims are woven near Malatya, and are mainly of a small size. The designs are varied, often comprising small motifs, and some have prayer arches. The weaving is of good quality – slitweave is normally used, although some *çuval* are made in weft-wrapping technique. Colouring is characteristically Kurdish, of dark red, blue, and black, with white cotton and undyed wool used as a contrast. Metallic thread is also popular.

232 Iraqi
Most probably woven by the Surchi tribe, this kilim is made in bands of plainweave and weft-wrapping technique, without borders. The design shows both Persian and Turkish Kurd influences. Dark colours predominate, and the quality of wool is generally good. (Detail)

Opposite, above:

233 Kağizman
(3.69 × 1.23 m, 12'1" × 4')
The interior patterns of these medallions are also found in Kuba kilims woven in the Caucasus. Viewed horizontally, the motif resembles an elibelinde mother-goddess design, although when this pattern occurs on Caucasian rugs, it is regarded as merely decorative.

234 Kağizman
(3.28 × 1.74 m, 10'9" × 5'8")
The dark, rich colouring and inner border motif indicate a kilim of Kurdish origin, though the medallion composition and the remains of plaited fringes show Caucasian influence. The main border motif also appears on Erzurum kilims and in Caucasian rugs. The short yellow lines in the centre of some of the medallions help define the pattern and give it an added depth.

The Iraqi Kurds

These Kurds are mainly concentrated within a mountainous region of north and north-east Iraq. Originally a Central Asian people, the Kurds are Sunni Muslims, retaining their national Kurdish identity and resistant to change in whatever country they reside. Characteristics of Kurdish kilims include a weft-wrapping technique that leaves long floating wefts on the reverse of the kilim, and ends that are often plaited with long fringes. The main kilim-weaving tribes include the Herki, Dizai, Yazidi and Surchi. Of these, the Herkis were the most prolific weavers, making flatweaves in weft-wrapping technique. Their kilims are generally woven in two pieces and joined. Designs are very variable and colours include dark reds, browns and blues, with a little white. More modern kilims feature small amounts of pink and orange.

The Dizai are now mainly settled. They weave a few bags and trappings, and their slitwoven kilims are not dissimilar to the banded kilims from Malatya. The Yazidi from the north of Mosul make both slitweave and supplementary weft-wrapped kilims, and their designs are arranged usually in horizontal bands; the slitweave variety resemble those made near Van in the Hakkari region of Turkey. The kilims of the Surchi are similar to those of the Herki, except that the designs tend to be a little larger. Iraqi Kurdish kilims do not appear with great frequency in the markets, save for some Herki pieces, and no doubt with the upheavals following the Gulf War, even fewer kilims will appear in the future.

Iraqi Kurd	232
DESIGN	Field: Paired medallions/Banded format
SIZE AND SHAPE	Medium/Few large/Some small
MATERIALS	Medium to thick wool
STRUCTURE	Slitweave, plainweave, weft-wrapping
COLOURS	Dark palette of brown, red, blue, green, some white
FRINGE	Plaited, with long tassels/Plain
SELVEDGE	Plain, with thicker outer warps
Remarks	Similar to eastern Anatolian kilms

The Caucasian Turks of North-East Anatolia

Kilims from this area have a different look to those of their Turkish Kurd neighbours, for part of their design content is Caucasian in origin – the Kars/Kağizman kilims, for example, are strongly influenced by Caucasian design. This area has also produced many prayer-arch kilims, the majority of which display an Erzurum/Byburt – Kurdish influence. Many prayer-arch kilims were woven in the nineteenth century in the Erzurum/Byburt area. Erzurum is a frontier town, a

235   Kağizman (below left)
(1.86 × 1.79 m, 6'1" × 5'10")
*This border motif can also be found in Erzurum
kilims, whereas the tree designs on the green
ground appear in a format that is more similar
to those of regions further west, such as Obruk.
The central tree of life with birds on its
branches is reminiscent of Thracian kilims.*

236   Kars (below right)
(1.69 × 1.12 m, 5'6" × 3'8")
*Woven in slitweave on natural brown warps,
with lazy lines in the central panel, this kilim is
unusual in that it depicts star motifs as a plain
form without further decoration. The zig-zag
pattern in the outside border, although
simplified, bears some relation to the border
designs found in Caucasian kilims, particularly
from the Kuba area.*

bulwark of Turkish defence first against the Persians and then the Russians. The only area in this region still producing kilims is Kars, although many carpets continue to be woven.

Kars and Kağizman

The old sector and newer southern districts of Kars are joined by a bridge built by the Seljuk Turks over the Kars Cayi River. The town was occupied by an independent Armenian group during the ninth and tenth centuries AD, by the Seljuks from the eleventh to the thirteenth century and by the Mongols for part of the thirteenth century. Incorporated into the Ottoman Empire in the early fifteenth century, the town saw many further rulers from the eighteenth century onwards, being invaded firstly by Iran, then by the Russians before being returned to Turkey in 1918. Despite suffering severe winters, the surrounding area is used for arable farming and raising livestock, and is well known for its cheese production.

Kilims woven since 1950 are distinctive for their natural brown wool warps and for their dull colouring of browns, oranges and pinks, as well as for their long and narrow shape. Because of their impractical size, many have ended up being made into fashion accessories in the West. Designs are geometric, and are woven in slitweave with thick warps that result in coarsely woven rugs with long fringes. Many *çuval* and *yastiks* are woven in Kars region. The older kilims from this area are usually attributed to Kağizman and are very different to the later weavings of Kars, as they were closer woven and used mainly natural dyes.

Kars and Kağizman kilims often feature geometric medallions, some of which are similar to Caucasian designs. Prayer kilims were also woven, although less so in recent years, and generally of a larger size than most. A pale blue ground is sometimes favoured for the niche itself. Kağizman kilims have a dark and rich palette of browns, reds, blues, green and yellow; prayer kilims are generally lighter in tone.

237 Kağizman
(1.33 × 1.18 m, 4'4" × 3'10")
Loosely woven in slitweave on natural brown wool warps, this kilim has been created with great artistry. The pattern features a double prayer niche. The lower one creates a 'floating' effect. The zig-zag motifs represent water, the source of life.

Kars and Kağizman	233–4, 236, 572
DESIGN	Field: All-over interconnecting medallions/Medallions as central theme/Prayer kilims Borders: Varied in number and complexity of pattern
SIZE AND SHAPE	Long and rectangular, often narrow/Small
MATERIALS	Thick, mainly natural brown wool warps
STRUCTURE	Loose slitweave
COLOURS	Older kilims have dark and varied palette/Recent kilims feature brown, pink, orange, white
FRINGE	Twisted/Plaited/Plain, often left long
SELVEDGE	Plain, with thicker outside warps
Remarks	Recently woven Kars kilims have dull colouring and are of impractical size/Many *yastiks* made

Erzurum

Erzurum was once a key frontier town, used to defend Anatolia against many invasions, and was also an important point on the caravan route between Anatolia and Iran. Settlement began at an early date, but the town only gained prominence during the fifth century A D as a Byzantine fortress, which fell to the Arabs in the seventh century, and was subsequently fought for by the Byzantines, Arabs and Armenians until the Seljuk occupation of the late tenth century. An Ottoman town in the fifteenth century, it was taken by Russia in 1829, 1878, and between 1916 and 1918. From 1923 it was incorporated into Turkey.

The climate is very severe in this mountainous region. In winter there is much snow, and the temperature averages −9°C (16°F), and in summer it seldom exceeds 20°C (68°F); as weaving is primarily a cold-weather occupation, it comes as no surprise to learn that many kilims were woven here. This town is particularly renowned for its prayer kilims, which are generally of a larger size than those from other regions of Anatolia, and more often than not have a green, or blue/green, field in the prayer arch. Few larger kilims were woven in this region. As there are a great number of Kurdish people in Erzurum and the surrounding area many kurdish design characteristics are evident in the flatweaves, such as the wolf track or wolf mouth motif used as border designs. The tree of life motif also often forms one of the multiple borders characteristic of Erzurum kilims.

Many prayer kilims were woven featuring the tree of life motif in the prayer arch and a double-ended prayer design can occasionally be found. Kars is another area where such compositions were sometimes woven. Byburt is a town situated close to Erzurum, but which never had the same strategic significance. Erzurum and Byburt kilims are very similar in design and colouring, and both are often dated. Some Byburt kilims, however, have a plant and flower motif that is not seen on Erzurum kilims. The colours are predominantly warm tones of green, blue/green, yellow, ochre, apricot, brown, and red – overall of a lighter palette than is found on other Kurdish weavings. They are made in medium to fine slitweave, a little on the loose side, and natural brown wool is often used for warps.

238 Erzurum
(1.53 × 1.27 m, 5′ × 4′1″)
The central design can be seen either as a tree of life or as an earring motif. It is surrounded by a plethora of small filler motifs resulting in a crowded pattern which is confusing to the eye. The use of white cotton adds to this effect.

Erzurum	15–16, 239, 241, 242, 644
DESIGN	Field: Prayer arches with small filler motifs Borders: Multiple/Single
SIZE AND SHAPE	Small/Medium/Some long and rectangular/Large and square
MATERIALS	Medium and fine wool for wefts, natural brown wool often used for warps
STRUCTURE	Slitweave
COLOURS	Varied dark to medium palette
FRINGE	Plain/Knotted/Twisted
SELVEDGE	Plain
REMARKS	Tree of life and wolf track motifs often used

239 Erzurum
(1.38 × 1.24 m, 4′6″ × 4′)
The tree of life design is frequently found on prayer kilims, both as a central motif and as border decoration, as it is here. The drawing of the patterns and the irregular shape of this nineteenth-century example indicates that it was probably one of the weaver's earlier attempts.

240 Erzurum (1.48 × 1.26 m, 4′10″ × 4′1″)
*Yellow main borders are typical of Erzurum prayer kilims, but the dark
ground colour of this early twentieth-century example is less characteristic.
Prayer niches are normally either blue/green or red in colour.*

241 Erzurum (1.63 × 1.21 m, 5′4″ × 3′11″)
*The abrash in the greenish-blue central panel adds depth to the plain ground.
The small ewer motifs are said to represent the desire to have children, or
could mean that the weaver was pregnant whilst working on this kilim.*

242 Erzurum (3.84 × 1.53 m, 12′7″ × 5′)
An interesting version of a prayer kilim, with niches at either end of the main field. Except in saf *kilims, double-ended prayer niches are not often seen.
Another anomaly is the change of ground colour in the centre, and an apricot border replaces the usual yellow colouring. Note the individual motif, which
appears in the main border at the top left-hand corner where the pattern indents.*

Turkish Karabağs These flatweaves, decorated with geometrized floral patterns, are not traditionally woven anywhere else in Anatolia. The designs are influenced by floral Caucasian kilims, some from the Karabakh area, and this is presumably how the name of Karabağ originated. They have been woven around Erzurum for approximately the last forty years, and some were used as wall hangings – many of the larger sizes still retain their loops. The kilims have dark backgrounds, either of black or deep brown, and their flowers are coloured in reds, pinks and orange with borders that are usually light beige or white. The warps in the older pieces are often of natural dark wool and more modern examples are seen with cotton warps. The sizes found are often long and narrow. Slitweaving is predominant, and a small quantity of these decorative kilims is now produced for the export market in more manageable sizes.

243 Karabağ
(2.35 × 1.62 m, 7'8" × 5'3")
The dark ground colour is characteristic of Karabağ kilims, as are the red and pink flowers.

Turkish Karabağs		243
DESIGN	Field: Floral patterns Borders: Floral patterns	
SIZE AND SHAPE	Mainly long and rectangular/Some medium	
MATERIALS	Thick wool/Cotton sometimes used for warps	
STRUCTURE	Slitweave	
COLOURS	Dark brown, grey and black natural wool used for field, bright orange, red and pink flowers, with light-coloured borders	
FRINGE	Plain/Plaited/Twisted	
SELVEDGE	Plain	
Remarks	In Anatolia, the tradition of weaving floral patterns is only found in the east	

The Black Sea Coast and Northern Anatolia

Çorum and Çankiri

Çorum is situated on an ancient Anatolian trade route, in a region that was at one time part of the Hittite Empire. Tombs dating to 3000 BC have been excavated at nearby Alacahöyük, just one of the many important archaeological sites in the vicinity. This town was at one time famous for spinning and weaving, as well as for the production of copper and leather goods. Çankiri, once called Gangra, was the capital of Paphlagonia, and its Great Mosque was designed in the fifteenth century by Sinan, court architect to Suleyman the Magnificent. The salt mines dating back to Byzantine times are still in operation. Although weaving is no longer practised around Çankiri, the Çorum region produces some very long narrow runners, on which some designs are similar to eastern Anatolian and Kurdish patterns such as the comb (or its mirror-image hour-glass) motif.

244 Karabağ
(1.57 × 1.12 m, 5'1" × 3'8")
Woven in slitweave on cotton warps, this kilim features a geometrized floral pattern of Caucasian influence. Note the bonçuk *beads at the apex of the prayer arch.*

Colours are usually reds, blues, green, yellow, brown and black. This region also produces some long kilims woven in two halves, which feature a compartment format made of narrow oblongs of different colours.

245   Çorum/Çankiri
(4.27 × 1.52 m, 14′ × 4′11″)
The differences in the border patterns are so pronounced that this kilim, probably woven as a seating cover, would almost seem to be the work of two different weavers; it is only the more decorated side that has any degree of regularity. The primitive drawing of the motifs adds interest to a static and compartmented design format.

Çorum and Çankiri		245
DESIGN	Field: Compartmented kilims with small geometric filler motifs, comb or hour-glass pattern often used Borders: Multiple/Single	
SIZE AND SHAPE	Large and rectangular	
MATERIALS	Medium and fine wool, occasionally cotton	
STRUCTURE	Slitweave, made in two halves	
COLOURS	Bright and varied palette	
FRINGE	Plain/Knotted	
SELVEDGE	Plain	
Remarks	Recent weavings include many long narrow runners	

Elmadağ		251
DESIGN	Field: Banded format/Prayer kilims with small divided hexagonal motifs Borders: Patterns similar to bird motifs at ends	
SIZE AND SHAPE	Large and rectangular/Small	
MATERIALS	Medium and fine wool, cotton used for effect	
STRUCTURE	Slitweave	
COLOURS	Dark palette with contrasting white cotton	
FRINGE	Plain/Knotted	
SELVEDGE	Plain	
Remarks	Prayer designs feature a small floating arch	

Elmadağ

Elmadağ ('the Apple Mountain') is another region where kilim-weaving has long ceased. The composition of Elmadağ kilims is based on crenellated diamond-shaped medallions arranged in varying formats, sometimes found repeated as large central patterns. They are also used as smaller motifs in banded form separated by narrow stripes featuring chevron motifs. The main end border pattern, similar to a bird motif, is a marked characteristic of Elmadağ kilims, appearing in both large and small varieties. A type of prayer-arch kilim also comes from Elmadağ, which has a field decorated with small hexagonal motifs. The kilims are woven in slitweave of fine and medium quality wool, in reds, blues, green, apricot and black, with small amounts of white cotton.

Sivrihisar

Sivrihisar is situated halfway between Ankara and Afyon. The name translates from Turkish as 'the Pinnacled Castle', which may be a reference to the Roman or Hellenistic ruins nearby. Perhaps the most notable of the Sivrihisar compositions is the so-called multiple prayer niche, stacked vertically. This is known as *bacali*, or the 'chimney' design, and may have been inspired by the local ruins. Its prayer niches vary in number from three to as many as fourteen. Another motif that is often found in Sivrihisar kilims in varying compositions is the *elibelinde* mother-goddess motif, generally used in mirror-image form. The small rugs, prayer kilims and large flatweaves produced here are of medium to fine slitweave, in blues, reds, pinks, purple, green, yellow and brown.

Sivrihisar	247, 249
DESIGN	Field: *Elibelinde* motif often used in mirror-image form in differing patterns/*Bacali* or 'chimney' prayer niche motif, sometimes as many as fourteen, vertically stacked
SIZE AND SHAPE	Large and rectangular/Medium/Small
MATERIALS	Medium and fine wool, cotton often used for effect
STRUCTURE	Slitweave, large kilims mostly made in two halves
COLOURS	Varied and often bright palette
FRINGE	Plain/Knotted
SELVEDGE	Plain
Remarks	Designs usually well drawn

Manastir	250, 253
DESIGN	Field: Floating prayer arches and small geometric motifs placed at random/Interconnecting serrated diamond-shaped medallions
SIZE AND SHAPE	Mainly small/Some large and rectangular
MATERIALS	Fine wool/Cotton often used for warps
STRUCTURE	Slitweave
COLOURS	Bright palette
FRINGE	Plain/Knotted
SELVEDGE	Plain
Remarks	Designs are different to other Anatolian kilims because of Balkan influence

Page 130:

246 Çankiri
(4.30 × 1.74 m, 14′1″ × 5′8″)
This kilim has a very unusual design. The intricate pattern has been woven with great care, the weaver frequently alternating the colours for full effect.

247 Sivrihisar
(3.38 × 1.89 m, 11′ × 6′2″)
The regular proportions of both the central pattern and border design suggest that the weaver of this kilim knew this composition by heart. Her use of white cotton and light colours freshens the overall effect.

248 Çankiri
(1.54 × 0.90 m, 5′ × 2′11″)
For a contemporary weaving, the pattern has been well drawn and the work is even and flat, although the wool is rather coarse. The design used is traditional.

249 Sivrihisar
(1.67 × 0.99 m, 5′5″ × 3′2″)
These bacali *have a more angular feel to them than most. The eccentric arrangement of the small cross and yin-yang motifs is very attractive.*

250 Manastir
(1.82 × 0.98 m, 5′11″ × 3′2″)
The floating prayer arch is frequently found on kilims with a yellow ground and red or pink borders. The star motif in the red borders is another regular feature, as are the triangular forms.

Page 131:

251 Elmadağ
(3.88 × 1.48 m, 12′8″ × 4′10″)
The repeated surrounds of the diamond-shaped medallions give the effect of an ever-expanding design, adding movement to the arrangement. The border motif is typical, although the overall colour palette is lighter than usual.

252 Çankiri
(1.57 × 1.26 m, 5′12″ × 4′2″)
The square shape and formation of the design suggest that this kilim was made as an eating cloth. Its colour combination identifies it as Çankiri, although the motifs used both in the centre and border are frequently seen in kilims from Konya and Sivrihisar.

253 Manastir
(1.81 × 1.22 m, 5′11″ × 4′)
This serrated medallion design woven on cotton warps is characteristic of the region, as are the bright and contrasting colours.

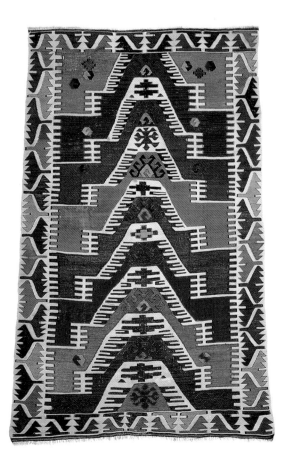

Captions for 246–253 on page 129.

254 Manastir
(4.00 × 2.02 m, 13′1″ × 6′7″)
*This kilim consists of three strips joined
together. The sections align almost perfectly.*

255 Keles
(1.48 × 0.79 m, 4′10″ × 2′7″)
*Woven in the Uludağ Mountains, this small
kilim features an unusual prayer design.*

Manastir

Manastir kilims are very different to other Anatolian flatweaves as they were woven by Balkan expatriates who settled in Mihalıççik area. The region is particularly well known for its prayer kilims, which have a floating prayer niche on a yellow or black ground with a red or pink surround. The field of these kilims is sparsely decorated with star motifs, and the skirts are the only areas which have further adornment. Another compositional style features a serrated diamond-shape which is repeated over the whole field of the kilim. These kilims are generally brightly coloured with reds, pinks, blues, yellow, green and black, and are of slitweave on thin cotton or very fine wool warps, producing fine quality weaving. Small sizes predominate, but large kilims can occasionally also be found.

Keles

Keles, situated near Bursa in the Uludağ Mountains, produces kilims similar to others woven in the Anatolian mountain regions. These are generally of a small size, of fairly coarse slitweave, in reds, blues and browns, often decorated with tufts of wool (supposed to bring luck to the weaver and owner of the kilim) or with small details woven in the knotted technique. The small kilims are commonly woven in a prayer design format; the larger sizes, however, do not follow any particular design composition. Most kilims from Keles are full of character and charm, even though they are not finely made.

Keles	255
DESIGN	Field: Prayer arches/Varied
SIZE AND SHAPE	Mostly small/Some medium and rectangular
MATERIALS	Thick wool, sometimes coarse
STRUCTURE	Loose slitweave, some details in weft-wrapping technique
COLOURS	Dull palette of brown, red, some yellow, blue
FRINGE	Knotted/Plain
SELVEDGE	Plain, with thicker outside warps
Remarks	Tufts of knotted pile often found as extra decoration

Thrace

Thrace today comprises the region which is bordered by Macedonia to the west, Bulgaria and the Black Sea to the north, with the Aegean Sea forming the southern perimeter. Its eastern side incorporates the European part of Turkey. The countryside features mountainous basins and deep river valleys, and its people are descended from Indo-Europeans, good warriors who were requisitioned by both the Romans and Macedonians. Despite their simple village lifestyle, their culture was advanced, particularly in poetry and music.

The Balkan Peninsula, the centre of the earliest European civilization, was first inhabited from about 200,000 to 100,000 BC, and excavations have revealed Neanderthal and Palaeolithic remains. In the middle of the fifth century BC the first Thracian state was established in the Maritsa valley, which was ruled by the Odrysian King, Teres. According to Thucydides, the Athenian historian, this nation became most prosperous, and lasted until the fourth century BC. Philip II of Macedon, father of Alexander the Great, then unified all territories from southern Thrace to Albania, thus beginning the Macedonian Empire. From the middle of the thirteenth century Thrace came under Ottoman rule, which continued until the nineteenth century.

During the twentieth century the lifestyle and ethnic character of the people have become more uniform as a direct result of wars and forced migrations. The Muslim Turkish residents in Thrace were exempt from forced repatriation in 1923, but many subsequently left because of worsening relations between Turkey and Greece. Now the land is mainly inhabited by Greeks, and the Greek language has superseded Turkish even in the Muslim schools. Most Thracian Muslims are of Turkish descent, and the other ethnic groups include the Pomaks, who are Muslims speaking a Bulgarian dialect, and some settled gypsies who speak Romany and Turkish. The region primarily trades in tobacco, wine and animal products, and there is a yearly wine festival at Alexandroupolis. The coastal region is famous for oyster farming and eel fishing.

Archaeological evidence of weaving in this region dates back to the Neolithic era – excavations have unearthed loom weights, spindle whorls, and the impressions of woven mats. Kilims from this region are known as Thracian or Şarkoy kilims, even though Şarkoy is geographically within modern Turkey. The name Şarkoy is also used for kilims woven farther north in Bulgaria.

256 Şarkoy
(2.19 × 1.58 m, 7′2″ × 5′2″)
Known as 'Pirot', this kilim was probably woven in Bulgaria. The border motif is unusually reminiscent of Anatolian saf designs, whereas the central pattern is quite typical of the area.

Şarkoy

257–9

DESIGN	Field: Tree of life pattern prevalent Borders: Bird motifs/Leaf and vine pattern/Small prayer arches
SIZE AND SHAPE	Large and square/Medium/Small
MATERIALS	Very fine wool
STRUCTURE	Very fine slitweave, curvilinear weaving
COLOURS	Dark palette of red, blue, green, some yellow, white
FRINGE	Plain
SELVEDGE	Plain
Remarks	Dark colouring and fine weave is typical

Şarkoy

Şarkoy kilims are very finely woven in slitweave in a variety of sizes and are made in one piece. Many feature the tree of life composition that is often used in a multitude of repeats on large kilims, and singly on smaller sizes. Birds also regularly appear either as filler motifs, border designs or depicted sitting on the

257 Şarkoy
(3.79 × 2.74 m, 12′5″ × 8′11″)
A deep blue/red colour was virtually always used as a background for kilims woven in this pattern, but in recently woven kilims this red has been replaced by a harsh, brighter tone. Although the main design has remained constant, the border motifs may vary, featuring charmingly drawn birds on this kilim.

258 Şarkoy
(3.38 × 2.77 m, 11′1″ × 9′)
The main pattern of this nineteenth-century kilim is made up of trees of life, a format often used for large sizes. When the birds who sit on the branches of the tree fly away, the soul goes to heaven. The birds appear to be ready to fly at any time, indicating the transience of life. The border motif also represents birds.

259 Şarkoy
(1.51 × 1.02 m, 4′11″ × 3′4″)
These Thracian flatweaves have a very distinctive character and most of the designs follow certain formats – many prayer kilims, for instance, feature the tree of life design. This example was woven in the second half of the nineteenth century.

branches of the tree. Other motifs include stylized leaves, either on the tree of life or incorporated into a leaf and vine border pattern. Trees, birds and leaves are also found enclosed by small prayer arches arranged in rows down the field of the kilim, or sometimes as a border pattern. Prayer arch kilims were also woven, as well as some designs with hooked diamond-shaped medallions. Şarkoy motifs are very stylized, although figurative, and often resemble modern-day computer graphics. Colours are dark red, blues, greens, with a little yellow and white. More modern kilims tend to feature a harsh bright red, black and white, although the weaving is still very fine. One type of Bulgarian Şarkoy kilim has serrated medallion patterns and a colour palette of brown, beige or yellow, dark and light blue. Again, many sizes are woven in one piece, and these are of a squarer shape than most Anatolian kilims.

Aegean Anatolia

Yüncü Yörük	263
DESIGN	Field: Ram's horn motif/Interlocking designs Borders: Simple
SIZE AND SHAPE	Large and medium rectangular/Many *çuval*
MATERIALS	Medium to fine wool/some *çuval* have very finely spun wool
STRUCTURE	Slitweave/*Çuval* woven in plainweave, supplementary weft-wrapping
COLOURS	Dark madder red, indigo blue, some green, white
FRINGE	Knotted/Twisted/Plain
SELVEDGE	Plain, with thicker outside warps
Remarks	Bold but simple patterning and dark colouring characteristic

The Yüncü Yörüks

Western Anatolian tribes from the Yüncü region were registered in Ottoman times as *yörüks* and still describe themselves as such. *Yörük* translates as 'we who roam', even though they have been settled in the area for many years. The name *yörük* became a symbol of Turkish belief in the nomadic existence, and the word *göçebe* is used to describe the fully nomadic tribes, *yerli* the more settled or semi-

260   Yüncü Yörük
(4.17 × 1.58 m, 13′6″ × 5′2″)
Limited use of colour, predominantly dark reds and blues and occasionally some green, is typical of these kilims. This one features an unusual amount of white, which also decorates the thin bands woven in weft-wrapping technique. White outlining gives the bands of medallions a lacy appearance.

261   Balikesir (left)
(2.54 × 1.87 m, 8′3″ × 6′2″)
It is still possible to find good quality fine wool spun by hand in this region, as has been used in this kilim. Recently woven kilims from this area usually have uncomplicated designs and large areas of plain ground. It is one of the few places in Anatolia where medium sizes are woven.

262   Balikesir (right)
(2.54 × 1.87 m, 8′3″ × 6′2″)
An example of an almost 'empty' kilim, bar the central medallion, possibly woven as an eating cloth. It is interesting to see how the weaver has joined the medallion to the border by way of a line of abrash, *in a manner that suggests an umbilical cord. The red and dark blue are typical colours for this region.*

263 Yüncü Yörük
(2.24 × 1.65 m, 7′3″ × 5′5″)
Sheep are of central importance in the life of a nomad, and are duly acknowledged in weaving designs by way of the ram's horn motif, which often appears in Yüncü kilims. Also typical is the motif extending from the border, which frequently forms the main design in a reciprocal pattern. Kilims like this nineteenth-century example seldom appear in the marketplace, as they have been sought after for many years.

nomadic peoples. Old Yüncü kilims are very distinctive and have been collected for many years; very few now appear on the market, although some fine *çuval* are still to be found. The designs feature a tree or pole with extending hooked arms known as the ram's horn motif. Yüncü kilims are generally not as long as many Anatolian kilims, are squarer in shape, and mostly made in one piece. They are coloured with madder reds and indigo blues, with some occasional dark green and a little white. Kilims are generally made in slitweave with medium to fine lustrous wool. Many *çuval* made by Yörüks have a decorated banded front and a striped back, and are woven in plainweave and supplementary weft-wrapping technique.

Balikesir

Previously known as Palaeokastron, this site has been inhabited for over five thousand years. In the fourteenth century Balikesir was an important town of the Karasi Emirate, afterwards incorporated into the Ottoman Empire. The area is now known for its production of cotton, flour, leather and rugs. Nowadays, Balikesir is, ironically, a modern town with not much to offer. There is some new kilim production, which uses good hand-spun wool and occasionally natural dyes. These kilims are woven for the export market, but not mass-produced as in the Uşak and Denizli areas.

Balikesir	262
DESIGN	Field: 'Empty'/Sparsely decorated Borders: Plain, often of a colour contrasting with the field
SIZE AND SHAPE	Medium and square/Small
MATERIALS	Medium and fine wool
STRUCTURE	Slitweave, plainweave, supplementary weft wrapping
COLOURS	Red, blue, some pink, green
FRINGE	Knotted/Plain
SELVEDGE	Plain
Remarks	Many 'empty' kilims and *çuval* woven

Balikesir is one of the few regions that weave 'empty' field kilims, generally of a dark red with a small plain border and a wider skirt in dark blue; variations can feature a floating central medallion and some decoration on the skirt. Other compositions include different arrangements of medallions – for example, a main central serrated medallion with medallions of the same type filling the field, bordered with a contrasting colour. Skirts are decorated with a variety of motifs. Colours are the 'traditional' Yüncü tones of dark reds and blues, as well as terracotta, lighter reds, pink, and green.

The rugs are woven in slitweave or plainweave, usually in one piece. The *çuval* are made with bands of weft-wrapped design and plainweave. Some striped kilims are woven – sometimes with narrow lines of supplementary-weft-wrapping technique arranged along the bands. Medium and small kilims, as well as *çuval*, *yastiks* and *heybe* (donkey bags), are made.

Bergama	264, 267, 574
DESIGN	Field: Small patterns in rows, hand of Fatima motif Borders: Small and decorated
SIZE AND SHAPE	Medium and square/Small
MATERIALS	Medium and fine wool
STRUCTURE	Slitweave, plainweave, supplementary weft wrapping
COLOURS	Red, blue, green, some yellow
FRINGE	Plain/Knotted/Plaited
SELVEDGE	Plain, with thicker outside warps
Remarks	Many *çuval*, and *çiçim* and *zili* technique rugs woven

264 Bergama
(1.97 × 1.10 m, 6′5″ × 3′7″)
Very distinctive, and typically Bergama, this late nineteenth-century design has been widely copied by weavers of new kilims. In Anatolian folklore the hand motif signifies fertility.

Bergama

Many tourists come to Bergama to see the ruins of Pergamum, an urban civilization that has existed since the Trojan era, at its height after the coming of Alexander the Great and before the Roman rule of *c.* 200–100 BC. Pergamum flourished under Eumenes II, who developed the city into a cultural and medical centre. His library nearly equalled that of Alexandria in Egypt, and was said to contain some 200,000 books. The Egyptians became afraid that scholars would flock to Pergamum and withheld stocks of papyrus from the Nile. As a result the people of Pergamum developed writing material themselves, made from animal hides – indeed the word 'parchment' takes its origin from the city's name. Subsequently, however, the Roman emperor Marcus Aurelius plundered the Pergamum library to replace books destroyed by a fire in Alexandria. Bergama today is a picturesque agricultural town, where many kilim and carpet traders' shops can be found in the main square.

Peculiar to Bergama is a design which features pairs of hand or comb motifs facing into the centre of the kilim. This format has been much copied in new kilims woven in the Uşak and Denizli areas, so that as a composition it has stood the test of time well, and now it is only the chemical colours which betray any lack of authenticity. Many weft-wrapped technique *zili* and *çiçim* rugs were woven in the Bergama area featuring a traditional cross motif surrounded by a segmented square; this design is then repeated in alternating colours and regular lines over the field of the rug. Again, although the composition continues to be woven, the colours of the new work lack the depth and lustre of their ancestors. These new flatweaves are woven near Kozak, a village close to Bergama. Many plainweave *çuval* with bands of supplementary-weft-wrapping technique are made here. Typical Bergama colours are reds, blues, greens and a little yellow. The quality of weaving is medium to fine, and slitweave is used, as well as *çiçim* and *zili* techniques.

265 Aydin
(1.61 × 0.83 m, 5′3″ × 2′8″)
Large sections at either end of this kilim have been rewoven, although the rest of the kilim has hardly been used – even the original outlining remains, usually the first part to disappear. The motif occurs in many Anatolian kilims, but the patterning is Aydin.

266　Bergama (above)
(3.05 × 1.64 m, 10′ × 5′4″)
The border motifs and serrated medallions betray the true origin of this kilim, although the main design is similar to that of the Karakeçili tribe, and contemporary Antalya Kilims.

267　Bergama (above right)
(2.58 × 1.75 m, 8′5″ × 5′8″)
A beautiful nineteenth-century example of supplementary weft-wrapping work executed using lustrous wool; this method of weaving is often used in Bergama, but few kilims are as attractively coloured. The proportions of the design are interesting: eight motifs in each band and eight bands in total. The square motif represents a chest, signifying the weaver's desire to marry.

268, 269　Aydin
(1.86 × 1.25 m, 6′1″ × 4′1″)
Woven near the village of Cine, this kilim bears the same motif as 265, a pattern normally used as a border or filler motif rather than as a main design. It is interesting to note that the white crenellated forms are missing from one side.
(Detail 268)

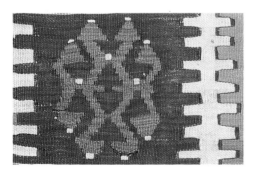

270 Bergama (top left)
(1.52 × 0.96 m, 4′11″ × 3′1″)
Woven in plainweave, with the pattern in knotted pile, this nineteenth-century mixed-technique rug is unusual for an Anatolian kilim. The red and blue colouring is extensively used in the Bergama area, as is the motif contained within the small hexagonal design.

271 Aydin (top right)
(1.58 × 1.02 m, 5′2″ × 3′4″)
Some of the motifs used here are found in other kilims from this area, although the colour palette is darker than usual, and the large area of deep indigo blue is uncommon. This nineteenth-century kilim has the overall feel of Aydin work, rather than any one particular distinguishing element. The central motif is seen in a similar form in Balikesir kilims.

272 Manisa (centre)
(3.68 × 1.54 m, 12′2″ × 5′)
A very unusual nineteenth-century kilim. The main design formation is not often seen and the light blue ground is seldom used as an overall colour. The abrash in the blue gives depth to the design, so that the motifs seem to be floating.

273 Aydin (right)
A contemporary example of an ancient design which is also woven in Konya, although the filler motifs tend to be smaller and more crowded in the Aydin version. Woven in slitweave using strong but rather coarse wool, this kilim has been sun-faded. (Detail)

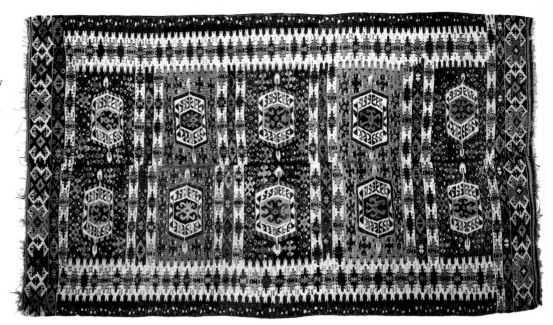

274 Aydin
(3.08 × 1.85 m, 10′1″ × 6′)
Heavily patterned designs such as this are frequently woven in the Aydin area. The hexagonal field motif is similar to those found in Çumra and Niğde, near Konya. The outer and inner borders and the field compartments feature different reciprocal formations.

Aydin

During the thirteenth century Aydin was called Guzelhisar, which translates as 'the Beautiful Castle'. Aydin's location near the Mediterranean ensured its importance as a centre for trade and for hiring mercenaries. Aydin today is an agricultural area where weaving has ceased.

As in many western Anatolian regions, a number of designs were woven, for prayer-arch kilims as well as large kilims which are made in two halves. Some of the latter feature a small squarish emblem which is repeated down the field of the kilim in vertical lines; other designs are similar to those woven in the Konya area, the main difference being that the Aydin weavings have many more infill motifs and so appear busier than the Konya varieties. A small hooked motif derived from the eight-pointed star, generally used as an infill or border motif, appears as the main pattern in some kilims from this region. Aydin kilims are made in slitweave and have a pleasing colour palette: some feature a red ground, and other colours used are reds, blues, apricot, green and brown.

275 Aydin
(3.24 × 1.78 m, 10′7″ × 5′9″)
Almost an exact replica of 273. These two kilims may have been woven in different years by the same weaver.

Aydin	196, 200, 274–5
DESIGN	Field: Overall patterns/Large central medallions/Prayer arches
SIZE AND SHAPE	Large and rectangular/Small
MATERIALS	Medium and fine wool
STRUCTURE	Slitweave, large kilims made in two halves
COLOURS	Usually bright and varied palette
FRINGE	Knotted/Plain
SELVEDGE	Plain
REMARKS	Red is sometimes used as the field colour

Western Anatolia

Uşak, Denizli and Eşme

Now one of the most important centres for new kilim manufacture (see Chapter Nine, p. 320), Uşak has been a weaving centre for a long time, and is noted for producing Anatolia's largest kilims, made in sizes up to 5.00 × 4.50 m (16′5″ × 14′ 8″). These kilims are loosely woven and generally have a large central medallion surrounded by a sizeable ground field usually of plain red, featuring decorated borders.

Uşak, together with Denizli and Eşme, has concentrated on the production of new kilims for the commercial and export market. However, there are still many kilims that are not specifically woven for trade, and these are generally made from hand-spun wool and coloured to the weaver's own taste. Such kilims are unsaleable in their original condition and have to be sun-faded for two months during the summer to tone down the bright colours, creating a more 'subdued' appearance acceptable to the export market.

276 Uşak
Uşak is one of the few areas in Anatolia that produce very large kilims, as well as vast knotted pile rugs. The large central medallion of this example, with square corner emblems and large expanses of plain ground, is typical of its kind. Border patterns vary in number, but usually have one predominant design with at least two secondary patterns. (Detail)

Uşak	276
Design	Field: Large central medallion Borders: Decorated
Size and Shape	Very large and square/Medium and square
Materials	Thick and loosely spun wool
Structure	Loose slitweave
Colours	Red ground, blue, green, yellow, mauve, black, white
Fringe	Plain/Knotted
Selvedge	Plain
Remarks	Many very large carpets and new kilims woven

Denizli	277
Design	Field: Bold serrated medallions as a central theme Borders: Reciprocal designs on large kilims
Size and Shape	Large and rectangular/Small
Materials	Medium wool, cotton often used for warps
Structure	Slitweave
Colours	Bright and varied palette
Fringe	Plain/Knotted
Selvedge	Plain
Remarks	Village and new production kilims woven

277 Denizli
(1.35 × 1.05 m, 4′5″ × 3′1″)
A contemporary kilim with an atypical design. Note the teapot in the apex of the prayer arch.

278 Eşme (below left)
(3.28 × 1.85 m, 10′9″ × 6′1″)
A well-made example of a contemporary village flatweave, in which the weaver has worked hard to create this archetypal design. The faded colours result from some weeks in the sun.

279 Eşme (below right)
(3.61 × 1.83 m, 11′10″ × 6′)
This Eşme design is common, but usually has simpler borders. Woven in about 1950, the composition has been well drawn, but its flat, chemical colours do little to enhance its appearance.

Denizli designs often consist of three or four bold serrated diamond medallions that form the central pattern of large kilims. The smaller kilims have a variety of compositions; often smaller medallions are used, and these are more compact than those found in large sizes. The borders of large kilims generally feature a reciprocal hook motif, whereas smaller sizes have single motifs such as a simplified star composed of two triangles, one inverted with a bar in the middle. Colours include red, black, green, orange, blue, purple, and yellow. The green and orange often do not fade as much as the other colours and are therefore more noticeable – not a popular feature in the West.

Large Eşme kilims often feature hexagonal medallions, either arranged in pairs or woven singly as central motifs, with smaller infill designs decorating the rest of

the field and borders. These kilims have gained great favour in the Western markets as they are woven in one piece, are not too long and narrow, and fade to soft colours. Sadly, many have ended up being made into sofas, cushions and other soft furnishings that happened to be in vogue at the time, but this is an inevitable consequence of the versatility of kilims. Small Eşme kilims are woven in a variety of designs, and copies of old Aydin and Kula prayer-arch compositions with tree of life motifs are often found. The colouring of Eşme kilims is similar to that of Denizli, but a little softer: red and pink, purple and blue that fade to grey, as well as black, orange and some yellow. Both areas use slitweave, with medium- to fine-spun wool, and cotton is often used for the warps. Eşme kilims have more detailed designs and a finer quality of weaving.

280 Eşme
(3.48 × 1.83 m, 11′5″ × 6′)
This design format is a favourite of contemporary weavers in this area. After two months in the sun the colours have faded considerably; the pale grey in the centre would originally have been a glaring blue or purple.

281 Çal
(2.94 × 1.88 m, 9′7″ × 6′2″)
This design and colouring are typical, particularly the orange, although the soft tones are achieved by sun-fading. The border patterns and other motifs are ancient kilim designs.

282   Eşme
The elibelinde *mother-goddess motif has survived many centuries. It is depicted here in a recent weaving. (Detail)*

Eşme 278–80

DESIGN	Field: Heavily decorated with small filler motifs and hexagonal medallions/Prayer arches Borders: Small filler motifs
SIZE AND SHAPE	Large and rectangular/Small
MATERIALS	Medium wool, cotton often used for warps
STRUCTURE	Slitweave
COLOURS	Initially bright palette, which fades to an overall effect of soft pinks and greys
FRINGE	Plain/Knotted
SELVEDGE	Plain
Remarks	Village kilims very popular in the West/Many new production kilims woven

Çal 281

DESIGN	Field: Large central medallion/Banded patterns Borders: Decorated
SIZE AND SHAPE	Medium and rectangular/Small
MATERIALS	Medium wool, cotton often used for warps
STRUCTURE	Slitweave
COLOURS	Warm palette of red, orange, pink, green, some yellow
FRINGE	Knotted/Plain
SELVEDGE	Plain
Remarks	Similar colouring found in all designs

Dazkiri 284

DESIGN	Field: Deeply crenellated medallions mostly in rows
SIZE AND SHAPE	Medium and rectangular/Small
MATERIALS	Medium and fine wool, cotton used for effect
STRUCTURE	Slitweave
COLOURS	Dark and medium palette
FRINGE	Knotted/Plaited/Plain
SELVEDGE	Plain
Remarks	Motifs and designs used are not unique to the region

Çal

Çal is located near Denizli, yet its kilims have their own distinctive designs and colour combinations. The most common design features a central medallion on a fairly open ground with decorated skirts. Their coloration is perhaps the most distinctive feature, for these kilims are generally found in warm to hot tones, with a lot of orange, and some red and green. Çal kilims are woven in one piece in slitweave; a few small sizes are made, but the majority are large, and rectangular in shape.

Dazkiri

Dazkiri is situated halfway between Afyon and Denizli, near Acigol Lake (which translates as 'spicy' or 'hot'). Designs from here usually feature a crenellated hexagonal-shaped medallion used in varying design formats. This type of design, also found in other areas, is not unlike the *parmakli* finger motif of the Afyon region. The shared characteristics of the kilims of this vicinity make the task of distinguishing different types more difficult, although on the whole the 'fingers' of the Dazkiri medallions are straight-ended, whereas the Afyon variety are angled. Colours are usually quite dark tones of reds, blues, and browns, but some kilims have a lighter colour palette. They are made in slitweave, of medium- and fine-spun wool.

Afyon

Afyon translates into English as 'opium'; the town was previously named Afyonkarahisar, which means 'the Dark Opium Castle'. *Haşhaş*, the opium poppy, continues to be cultivated here for pharmaceutical purposes, and it is said that once the juice has been extracted from the plants, the residue is fed to the cows, which in turn produce milk with a high fat content. This is made into the local cream, or *kaymak*, for which Afyon is renowned. Marble is quarried in this area, and cement is produced, as well as mohair and wool. Crops include wheat, barley, potatoes, and sugar beet. Everything about Afyon is bizarre, from the rock formations upon which the old fortress is built to the kilim designs themselves.

283 Afyon
(3.03 × 1.86 m, 9′11″ × 6′1″)
This kilim is woven using a variation of the parmakli *motif as the thematic medallion, with the ends of the fingers uniformly shaped, unlike those in 289. According to folkloric belief, one of the functions of the hand or finger symbol is to guard against evil.*

Afyon	283, 289
DESIGN	Field: *Parmakli* finger motifs and medallions often used Borders: Varied
SIZE AND SHAPE	Large and rectangular/Medium/Small
MATERIALS	Medium and fine wool
STRUCTURE	Slitweave/Plainweave
COLOURS	Mainly light palette of apricot, blue, green, pink and yellow/New village kilims are garish
FRINGE	Plain/Knotted
SELVEDGE	Plain
Remarks	Varied designs

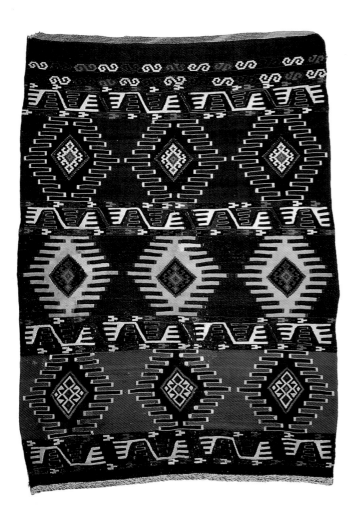

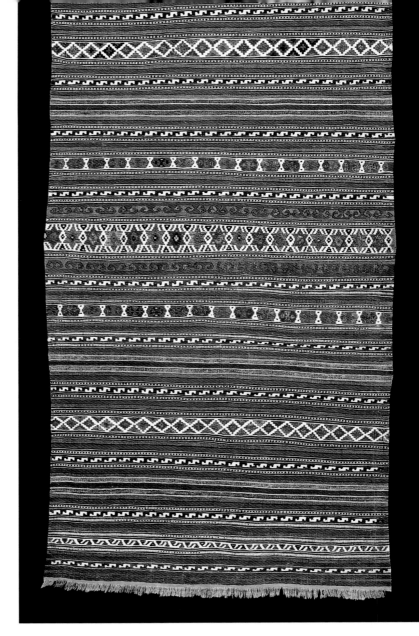

284 Dazkiri
(1.79 × 1.28 m, 5′10″ × 4′2″)
The pattern created by the medallions and plain-coloured triangular areas is found in both Persian and Caucasian kilims, and is an ancient and easily woven design format. By weaving the main motif and leaving regular spacing, the secondary motif is created. The plaited fringes are rarely seen in western Anatolian kilims.

285 Dazkiri
(2.54 × 1.12 m, 8′4″ × 3′8″)
Finely woven in plainweave and slitweave with minute details in supplementary-weft-wrapping technique, this kilim is enlivened by its light colouring and inclusion of white cotton. The central band featuring a star design with flanking rows of ram's horns depicted in green stands out from the rest.

Parmakli or finger designs are often woven in the Afyon region, and these motifs appear in different forms, sometimes decorating medallions and prayer arches, sometimes as protrusions from square or oblong shapes. This design was still being woven quite recently, but the colours used are very garish. Other compositions are woven, but do not have the strong design continuity of the *parmakli* group. Afyon kilims are often woven in light tones which include some red, apricot, pink, blues, green, and a little yellow. Slitweave technique is used, and the wool is medium- to fine-spun.

Mediterranean Anatolia

Fethiye

Located on the Mediterranean Sea, in the bay of Fethiye with the western Taurus Mountains behind, Fethiye is built on the ancient Lycian site of Telmessus. The tombs and sarcophagi there date back to the fifth and fourth centuries BC and there is also a Byzantine fortress which stands ruined on a hill nearby. An earthquake in 1958 destroyed most of the old buildings in Fethiye, and yet it is now a popular tourist location, particularly as the picturesque town of Uludeniz lies close by.

286 Fethiye (left)
(3.10 × 1.84 m, 10′ 2″ × 6′)
The same format as is seen in the end panels of 290 is used here as an all-over pattern. This variation is usually woven in dark colours, particularly in reds and blues.

288 Fethiye (below left)
(2.76 × 1.74 m, 9′ × 5′ 8″)
Heavily decorated end panels and plain centres are traditional features of Fethiye kilims: the components comprising the medallions may change, but the main form of the pattern remains constant.

289 Afyon (below right)
(2.24 × 1.69 m, 7′ 4″ × 5′ 6″)
A powerful yet uncomplicated nineteenth-century design, beautifully illustrated with contrasting colours. The parmakli, or finger pattern, is a characteristic feature of Afyon kilims.

287 Afyon (above)
(1.48 × 0.96 m, 4′ 10″ × 3′ 1″)
This prayer rug is finely woven in slitweave with a band of weft wrapping on the lower border. The soft colour palette is typical of the region.

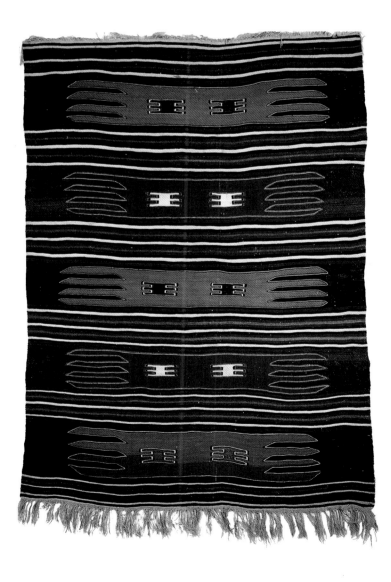

290   Fethiye
(2.83 × 1.49 m, 9′3″ × 4′11″)
The drawing of this design is precise, the quality of weaving uniform, and even the abrash *has been cleverly calculated. The use of white in the four main medallions enlarges the look of the panels.*

From Fethiye comes an unusual composition that features an 'empty' centre with busily decorated skirts. This centre is usually woven in plainweave with red or pink colours, and occasionally a small floating central medallion is included. These kilims either have no borders, or have a framing vertical line of contrasting colour, such as blue. It is possible that this format was used as a cover for coffins, like the *saf* compositions. Another popular composition is that of interconnecting hooked medallions covering the whole field, with narrow borders and skirts. Some *çiçims* are woven here that are generally of a mixture of plainweave in narrow bands of colour and stripes of *çiçim* weave. Another design, often found in supplementary weft-wrapping technique, is that of a star motif arranged in straight or diagonal rows over the main field of the kilim.

Colours include blues, reds, browns, green, orange and purple. The old kilims are woven in reds, pinks, blues, yellow, brown and a little green. Most are made in slitweave, but some *çiçim* and *zili* technique is also used. The more recent examples tend to be woven with rather coarse wool, although they are on the whole well made. Kilims that are large and rectangular are most common, although small sizes also occur.

Fethiye	286, 288, 290
DESIGN	Field: Empty/Busily interconnecting medallions Borders: Heavily decorated at ends
SIZE AND SHAPE	Medium/large and rectangular/Small
MATERIALS	Medium wool, sometimes coarse
STRUCTURE	Plainweave, slitweave, supplementary weft wrapping
COLOURS	'Empty' field kilims feature red and pink ground/Dark palette
FRINGE	Plain/Knotted/Plaited
SELVEDGE	Plain
Remarks	*Çiçims* also woven

Antalya

Founded in 200 BC by Attalus II, king of Pergamum, Antalya, then named Attaleia, has always been a bustling port. During the Crusades the town was used for the embarkation of troops on their way to Palestine, as it was a Byzantine stronghold at the time. Antalya was captured by Seljuks in the early twelfth century, and late in the fifteenth century it became part of the Ottoman Empire. There are many interesting monuments in the town such as the Hadrian Gate, a three-arched marble portal constructed to honour the visit of the famous Roman Emperor Hadrian in AD 130; an ancient tower, which was probably used as a lighthouse; a Seljuk theological college; and a mosque which dates to 1250. The Antalya Museum has a good ethnographical section which includes a Yörük tent, and room-sets from Ottoman houses as well as a village home complete with loom.

Weaving continues to be practised in the villages of the Antalya area, although the modern production is coarsely woven with garish colours that need sun-fading. The sun-fading of both kilims and carpets is the task which lies ahead of farmers in the area once the crops have been harvested, for then the rugs are laid out for approximately two months, depending on the dyes used and the degree of fading required.

The designs of recently woven kilims do not appear to bear any relation to their ancestors. The modern variety are borderless, and have elongated hexagonal shapes filling the field, or large serrated diamond shapes appearing in various formats with striped skirts. The colours are generally reds, pinks, oranges, brown, yellow, green, blue and purple fading to grey.

Antalya	291
DESIGN	Field: Small geometric motifs arranged in rows/ Interlocking hexagonal medallions Borders: Usually none
SIZE AND SHAPE	Large and rectangular/Medium/Some small
MATERIALS	Old kilims have fine wool and cotton/Modern kilims are very coarse
STRUCTURE	Slitweave
COLOURS	Light and medium palette
FRINGE	Plain/Knotted
SELVEDGE	Plain
Remarks	Recently woven village kilims need sun-fading

Adana

Situated in the fertile Çukurova plain (previously known as the Cilician plain, through which the Seyhan and Ceyhan rivers run), Adana is a busy industrial and agricultural centre. The region has always benefited from its location on the Arab and Anatolian trade route by controlling the passes through the Taurus Mountains to Syria. A Hittite settlement existed there from *c.* 1400 BC, and the land was conquered by Alexander the Great in the fourth century BC. From the late thirteenth century to the eighteenth century Adana was ruled by the Turkoman Ramazan dynasty, succeeded in turn by Ottoman rule.

Large kilims made in two halves often have medallions of various shapes – hexagonal diamonds, for example – as a main feature, whereas others have small and repetitive motifs, such as a hooked diamond shape enclosed within a hexagon, filling the main field. Single borders are usually found on both large and small kilims. The small kilims differ widely in design; amongst others, some prayer-arch kilims and some with hexagonal hooked motifs can be seen. Kilims continue to be woven in the villages of the Adana region that are made according to the weavers' taste, and as with other modern village kilims the colours need the benefit of two months' sun-fading to become saleable. The Adana region produces much cotton,

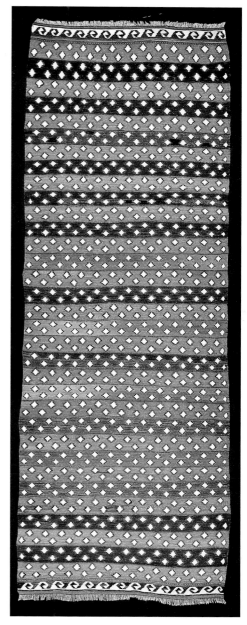

291 Antalya
(3.55 × 1.24 m, 12′2″ × 4′1″)
This design is no longer woven in the region, but a few examples survive from the nineteenth and early twentieth centuries. Nothing similar to this pattern is woven elsewhere; its simple, borderless construction is perhaps an expression of the weaver's love of open space and the elements of nature.

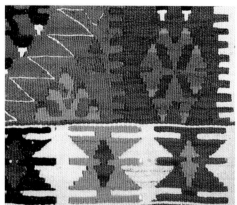

295   Adana
Simplified bird motifs are placed either side of a medallion. (Detail)

and its kilims often have cotton warps. Cotton is also used for colour contrast in both border and field, where reds, pink, orange, green, purple and blue fading to grey are also common. The older kilims are of medium- and fine-spun wool whereas the modern kilims are becoming very coarse and loosely woven. Slitweave is the prevalent weaving technique of the area.

Adana	292–4
DESIGN	Field: Varied/Small repeated motifs/Central medallions Borders: Simple and single
SIZE AND SHAPE	Large and rectangular/Small
MATERIALS	Medium and thick wool, cotton frequently used for warps as well as for effect
STRUCTURE	Slitweave, large kilims made in two halves
COLOURS	Bright palette of red, pink, orange, white
FRINGE	Knotted/Plain
SELVEDGE	Plain
Remarks	Many village kilims still woven in this area

On the far west tip of the Cilician plain, south-west of Adana and close to the Mediterranean Sea, the town of Silifke was founded in the third century BC by the Alexandran general Seleucus Nicator, who established the Seleucid dynasty that ruled Syria. Silifke is also known as the place where Emperor Frederick Barbarossa met his demise during the Third Crusade, by falling off his horse into the river! Kilims made in this region are normally small or medium in size. *Yastiks* and *çuval* are also woven in *çiçim*, *zili* and weft-wrapping techniques. The design often consists of a thin *elibelinde* mother-goddess motif repeated in different

Opposite:

292   Adana
(4.31 × 1.86 m, 14′2″ × 6′1″)
The filler hooked medallions scattered over the field are typical of recent Adana kilims, which are often woven in reds, pinks and orange, with white cotton rather than wool used to create contrast. The texture of this kilim is impressive for contemporary work, and it is evenly made, having a complementary colour balance.

293, 296   Adana
(1.77 × 1.12 m, 5′9″ × 3′8″)
Kilims such as this have been woven within the last decade in traditional designs using very bright chemical colours that must be sun-faded. The wool is often coarse and the weaving loose. (Detail 296, this page, top right)

294, 297   Adana
(1.85 × 1.13 m, 6′ × 3′8″)
A weaver has skilfully copied a traditional pattern to make a prayer kilim with a tree of life design. (Detail 297, this page, above)

colours in vertical lines – this creates an interesting three-dimensional effect. Colours used include red, brown, orange, pink, some blue and green, and white cotton.

Reyhanli

The old Reyhanli kilims are amongst the finest woven in Anatolia, and their designs are well drawn and precise. It is thought that this is mainly due to the influence of people from west Caucasia who settled in the Reyhanli area in the middle of the nineteenth century. The superb quality of these kilims suggests that they were probably woven for sale, as they are very different to other Anatolian kilims destined for personal use. Since the early part of the twentieth century weaving has ceased in the area, and the village of Reyhanli itself does not have much to offer the visitor apart from, of course, the usual warm Turkish hospitality.

Designs often feature elongated hexagonal or diamond-shaped medallions as a central theme, a composition that always has multiple borders. Another main pattern features a prayer arch, either used singly or as a repeat field motif in a smaller format. It has been said that a 'true' Reyhanli kilim must contain a leaf and vine design within its outside border, but not all kilims attributed to Reyhanli bear this motif; it does, however, often appear in at least one of the borders. Another design that was woven in this region is of a compartmented format, featuring square and oblong panels with multiple borders. This pattern is very similar to the present-day village kilims woven in the Kayseri region, although the originals were of a much finer and more detailed weave. Contrasting colours are used: dark burgundy red, terracotta, dark and medium blue, green, black, and white cotton. Natural white cotton is frequently found in Reyhanli kilims. The quality of weaving is generally very fine, the wool tightly spun, and of a lustrous silky texture. Sizes include large rectangular kilims woven in two halves, small prayer-size kilims, and occasional medium rectangular kilims, again woven in two halves.

298   Reyhanli
(1.57 × 1.16 m, 5′1″ × 3′9″)
The outside border motif is alien to kilims from this area, but the rest of the design is common. The fine slitweaving allows intricate patterns to be created in a manner that is unique amongst Anatolian flatweaves.

Reyhanli	298, 299
DESIGN	Field: Large central medallions, small repeat motifs Borders: Multiple, often with leaf and vine pattern
SIZE AND SHAPE	Large and rectangular/Small
MATERIALS	Fine and very fine wool with silky texture, occasionally cotton
STRUCTURE	Slitweave, made in two halves
COLOURS	Dark palette of red, blue, green, contrasting white cotton frequently used
FRINGE	Plain/Knotted
SELVEDGE	Plain
Remarks	Popular because of their fine weave

Konya and Konya Region

In as early as the thirteenth century Marco Polo noted, in his account of his travels to the region, that superlative rugs were to be found in the Konya area. Fortunately the art of weaving good kilims has not totally died out even today, for there are small quantities of kilims still being made with hand-spun wool and mainly natural colours. As the capacity for such production is not large and prices remain high, it is unlikely that commercialism will corrupt these enterprises.

299   Reyhanli
(1.86 × 0.98 m, 6′1″ × 3′2″)
The weaving of kilims near Reyhanli has long since ceased, and few examples remain. These are very distinctive both in their weave and their dark colour palette, often embellished with white cotton for contrast and to highlight the pattern. The design of this nineteenth-century kilim displays a Kurdish influence.

Konya	203, 206, 302, 305–6, 310, 315, 594, 640
DESIGN	Field: Very varied/Large central medallions/Heavily decorated
SIZE AND SHAPE	Large and rectangular/Medium/Small
MATERIALS	Medium and fine wool
STRUCTURE	Slitweave, plainweave, some supplementary weft wrapping, sometimes made in two halves
COLOURS	Bright and varied palette
FRINGE	Plain/Knotted
SELVEDGE	Plain, some with thicker outside warps
Remarks	Wide variation of design and colour/Good quality new kilims woven

300   Konya
An example of a contemporary Konya kilim woven in slitweave. The colouring is typical of that which is now being used, and the patterning, although well drawn, is not at all exciting. The quality of the weaving is reasonably good and even; small motifs have been added in supplementary weft wrapping. (Detail)

301 Konya
(2.15 × 0.88 m, 7' × 2'10")
The koçboynuzu, or ram's horn, motifs
decorate the inner border and ends of the prayer
arch. The outer border features a combination of
elibelinde mother-goddess and koçboynuzu
motifs that, according to Anatolian folklore,
represents both male and female fertility,
suggesting that this mid-nineteenth-century kilim
may well have been woven as a dowry piece. The
vibrant colours are created with natural dyes.

302 Konya
(1.68 × 0.86 m, 5'6" × 2'10")
By working the colours in a diagonal format, the
weaver added variety to an otherwise repetitive
pattern. Such basic grid designs depend on the
placement of colours to determine their
character, and often appear as medallion
arrangements. It appears that the brown
dyestuff used in the field of this nineteenth-
century kilim was different to that of the border,
as the field has eroded more rapidly.

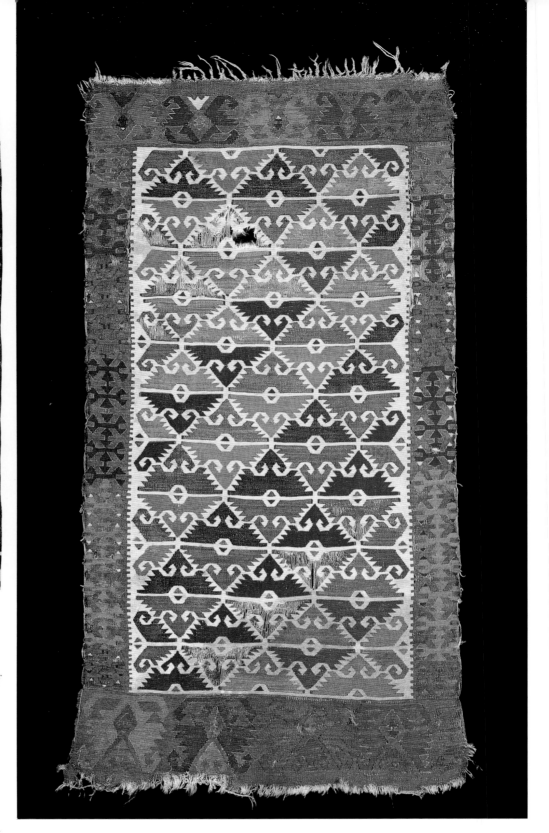

Konya

Konya, in south-central Anatolia, was the capital of the Seljuk Empire from the mid-eleventh to the thirteenth century and was in its prime during that period. Many of Konya's impressive buildings were constructed at that time by the Seljuk sultans in an architectural style reflecting Persian and Byzantine influence. Previously known as Iconium, this is one of the oldest urban centres in the world: according to Phrygian legend, Konya was the first city to rise from the waters after the great flood. Excavations here have revealed bones from the Bronze Age (*c*. 3000 BC). In the third century the town was mainly occupied by the Greeks.

303, 304 Konya
(2.82 × 1.73 m, 9'3" × 5'8")
Although designs similar to this are woven in regions such as Aydin and Sivas, its soft colouring denotes its origin. If this kilim had been woven in Aydin, the reds and browns would have been darker and more pronounced, and Sivas colouring would have featured brighter reds and greens. The border motifs at either end are also typical of Konya work. (Detail 303)

305 Konya
(3.47 × 1.24 m, 11'4" × 4')
The extending arms of the central medallions are repeated in a smaller form as the reciprocal border pattern. This design was obviously popular, as many examples exist, although not necessarily as well formulated.

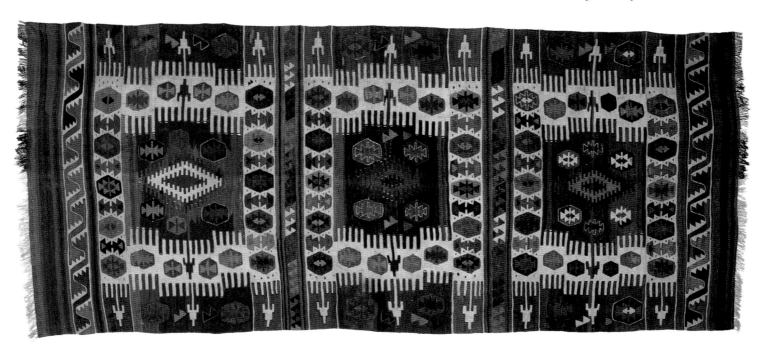

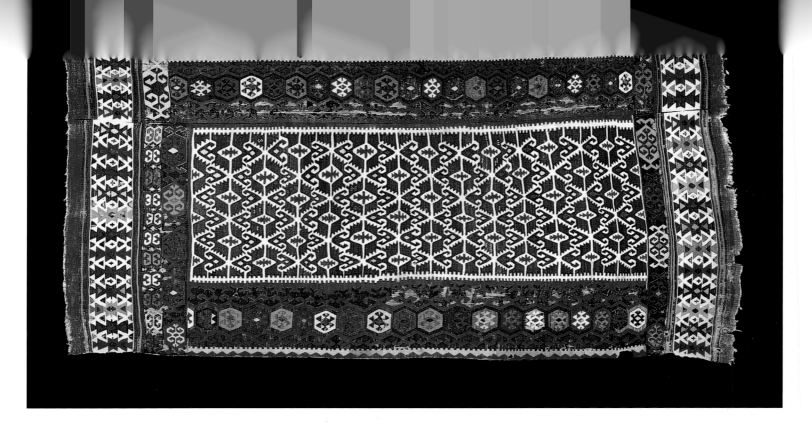

306 Konya (above)
(3.87 × 1.63 m, 12′9″ × 5′4″)
Here, the fundamental design is the same as in 302.
The kilim is woven in slitweave in two pieces. Quite
a number of Konya kilims are woven in this way with
a border, or both borders, being made separately,
whereas most other Anatolian kilims are joined in
the centre. This nineteenth-century kilim is attributed
to the Konya area, but the design is also used in
Aksaray.

Opposite:

310, 311 Konya (above left)
(3.11 × 1.80 m, 10′2″a × 5′10″)
The pattern is typical of Konya, and although the
weaving is not as fine as many kilims made in the
area, it is consequently stronger than most. Note the
small triangular motifs, which appear as two hands
clasped together. (Detail 311)

314 Konya (below)
(3.83 × 1.54 m, 12′6″ × 5′)
Small tufts of silky wool, both plain and coloured,
are scattered over the face of this kilim. The pattern
connecting the field and border is different on either
side. Note the zig-zag pattern contained within the
small dark motif on the left-hand red ground, also
found in a small motif near the centre. This is said to
represent a snake, symbolizing happiness and
fertility.

307, 308 Ereğli (above and above right)
(1.78 × 1.16 m, 5′9″ × 3′9″)
The abrash and lazy lines in the red ground
create depth and interest in expanses of plain
colour. Contemporary Ereğli kilims are
generally woven in dark colours which benefit
from sun-fading, as here. Weaving quality is
usually good, although this design is simplistic
and the inner border pattern of a leaf and vine
motif rather basic. (Detail 308)

309 Konya/Aksaray (right)
This kilim features an unusual design, generally
used in mirror image on the other side of the
weave. (Detail)

312, 313　Çumra (above and left)
(1.84 × 1.19 m, 6′ × 3′10″)
Although the hexagonal motif may have been derived from the Turkoman gul, this nineteenth-century kilim has a distinctly Anatolian appearance. The complex design has been proficiently woven in slitweave. Small details depicted in supplementary-weft-wrapping technique are still intact and show that this kilim has hardly been used. The good workmanship and careful attention to detail indicate that it was possibly woven as a dowry piece. (Detail 313)

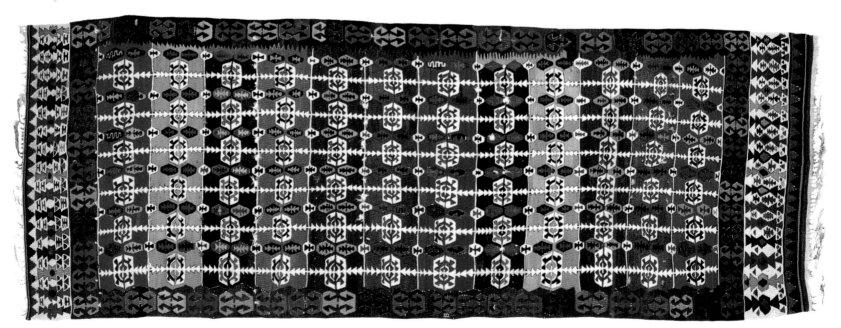

315   Konya
Known as 'Konya Muzumla', these kilims feature intricate and crowded designs. The shape produced by the white running motif is reminiscent of 'keyhole' designs found in knotted rugs. The motif on the dark brown border is often seen in Aydin kilims, whereas the reciprocal end border is similar to kilims from southern Iran. (Detail)

316   *Detail of 318.*

Konya has always been an important centre for religion, culture and trade, and also as a collection point for the many weaving centres nearby. The mystical order of the Whirling Dervishes was established in the town in the twelfth century by Mevlana Celal ad-Din ar-Rumi, an Afghan from Balkh, and a dervish festival is held in Konya during December. This festival is tolerated, but has suffered government oppression since the time of Ataturk. During Ottoman times the dervishes were powerful, but Ataturk viewed the group as contrary to the modern development of Turkey, and many monasteries have now been turned into museums. Konya continues to be a very religious place, and presently is becoming even more so.

Konya kilims feature the most varied compositions found in Anatolia, and there have been a great number of kilims made there over the centuries. Old Konya kilims still occasionally appear on the market today – but not necessarily in Konya itself. Although patterns are very diverse, they generally have much decoration covering the whole field of the kilim – a design format of large hexagonal motifs with extending hooked arms is a well-known characteristic. Again, a great variety of colours is used, most often of a lighter palette than in eastern Anatolia. Some very fine kilims have emerged, but in general the kilims are of medium-fine texture of weave, mostly made in slitweave technique with some *çiçim*. New kilims tend to be woven on thick warps. Konya kilims are made in all sizes, although there are fewer of medium size.

Ladik, Çumra and Ereğli all lie close to Konya. Ladik is best known for its carpet production. It does, however, produce kilims that often have tulip motifs incorporated into the design. Weaving in Çumra has long since ceased, but the kilims that still remain are very similar. Recent Ereğli kilims are well made with good wool, and tend towards the dark colours that greatly benefit from sun-fading.

Obruk		318–19, 321
DESIGN		Field: Prayer arches/Hooked central medallions/ *Çiçims* feature interconnecting diamond-shaped motifs Borders: Multiple/Wide/Narrow
SIZE AND SHAPE		Long narrow runners/Medium and square/Small
MATERIALS		Medium and fine wool, some cotton/Recent kilims have a hard texture although finely woven
STRUCTURE		Slitweave, weft-wrapping
COLOURS		Older kilims have a bright palette of red and blue/ Modern kilims have a dark dull palette
FRINGE		Knotted/Plain
SELVEDGE		Plain
Remarks		Tree of life frequently depicted

Obruk

This settlement has shrunk in size since the demise of the caravanserai; however, its traditionally patterned prayer kilims are known worldwide.

Obruk patterning is very easily recognized, and once seen never forgotten. It incorporates a hooked prayer arch with a tree of life situated at the apex of the niche and with two floating trees placed on either side. The tree design is often repeated in the centre of the prayer niche, sometimes alone, otherwise in pairs and triplets. The field is at times left plain and undecorated. Two or three main borders are present, with smaller, less important borders. There is another main design format that comes from Obruk, which is found in long runner-size kilims. This consists of a squarish medallion with extending arms at the four corners, and triangular protrusions filling the empty spaces — it has been said that the motif

317   Obruk
(2.12 × 1.24 m, 7′ × 4′1″)
Enough remains of this lovely nineteenth-century kilim for its glorious colouring and classic design to be properly appreciated; only the end border band with the hooked motif is missing.

318   Obruk
(1.88 × 1.32 m, 6′1″ × 4′3″)
The light border colours are unusual for Obruk prayer-arch kilims. The often-used motif within the yellow border is also seen in Konya and Aydin flatweaves. The weaver has created the feeling of movement at the bottom end of the kilim by distorting the pattern. (Detail 316)

319 Obruk (above left)
(1.57 × 1.18 m, 5'1" × 3'10")
The indented diamond-shaped motif that appears at the apex of the prayer arch, with extending arms and ram's horn motif at the top, is, according to folkloric belief, a symbol of fertility. It is an amalgamation of male and female signs: the female part is depicted as a berry or fruit loaded with seeds.

320 Obruk (above right)
(1.86 × 1.28 m, 6'1" × 4'2")
The central motif is widely used in Anatolian kilims. The beige ground is not dyed, but woven in natural camel hair, whereas the border is dyed brown, probably with walnut husks. Note the small tree of life motif, depicted in typical Obruk style at the top of the deeper blue emblem.

321 Obruk
(1.92 × 1.28 m, 6'3" × 4'2")
The positioning of the two trees of life flanking the prayer arch, the third extending from it, the shape of the niche, the white crenellated pattern separating borders and field, and the cross motif of the outer border, are all characteristic of Obruk work. Contemporary kilims are still woven in designs and colours similar to this in the Konya/Obruk area, but the modern dyes do not produce comparable results.

'neck', as Keçimuhsine *çicims*; others feature a prayer niche.

Karapınar

Particularly known for *saf* kilims, Karapınar production mostly features multiple prayer niches in a unidirectional horizontal arrangement. *Saf* kilims are believed to have many uses, for family prayer, for covering the coffins on their way to burial, and for segregating the women's section in the mosque. The basic *saf* design has changed little over the centuries, and is still being woven in the Konya area today. Different compositions retaining the basic *saf* model also exist, and sometimes the *saf* motif is used as a border decoration instead of the central emblem. Some Karapınar kilims display the same legged square with central

Keçimuhsine *Çicims*	322, 324
DESIGN	Field: Tree motif supported by angular shapes
SIZE AND SHAPE	Small and square
MATERIALS	Quite fine wool
STRUCTURE	Supplementary weft wrapping on plainweave
COLOURS	White ground, varied colours, overall light appearance
FRINGE	Knotted
SELVEDGE	Plain
REMARKS	Unique design

Keçimuhsine *Çicims*

Çicims from Keçimuhsine, a village near Konya, are particularly distinctive, featuring a motif described as a cypress tree on a white ground. This pattern is peculiar to the village, although some of the angular shapes that support the tree motif are also found in Karapınar kilims. Fine examples of these generally small *çicims* are sometimes seen hanging in a place of importance behind the desk of kilim and carpet merchants in Turkey. The white ground of these *çicims* is decorated with coloured patterning in reds, blues, browns, black, and orange, and gives a generally light appearance.

represents a mirror-image bull's head. This pattern is repeated down the field of the kilim, surrounded by one main border and small infill motifs. Old Obruk kilims are woven in reds, blues, greens, and browns. More modern kilims still feature the same traditional compositions, but the colours have become very harsh and dark, and now include orange. They are made in medium and medium-fine slitweave work, as well as in supplementary-weft-wrapping technique. Prayer kilims are generous in size, and long runners are also found.

Obruk *çicims* are found mainly with a white but sometimes with a coloured ground, and their composition is principally a small diamond-shaped medallion repeated in various scales decorating the field. *Çicims* are normally square, and the weaving lighter than slitweave. As a result, these flatweaves are used as window, door and table covers.

Karapınar kilims feature finely drawn designs, and are frequently of a prayer or saf pattern with multiple prayer arches appearing side by side. It is a design format which can easily be adapted, as is shown in this kilim, which has a prayer arch as a central theme. The border pattern also consists of a repeated saf motif, which becomes obvious when viewed horizontally.

323 Karapınar
(1.53 × 1.07 m, 5' × 3'6")

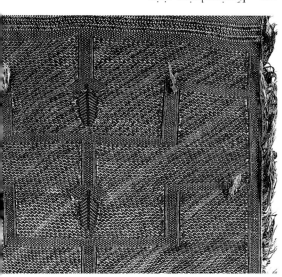

322 Keçimuhsine Çicim
The weaver has decorated the sides with strips of fabric, and tufts of the same are placed at random in the field. This custom is supposed to bring good luck. (Detail)

Aksaray

Now an agricultural town, incorporating some interesting buildings from the Seljuk period, Aksaray is known for its minaret constructed in brick in the early twelfth century, which now inclines at a curious angle and is known as the 'Turkish Tower of Pisa'. The Aksaray area has produced many fine kilims.

Aksaray cannot claim, as can other regions, very distinctive kilim compositions, and those which do appear are often composite arrangements of motifs that bear a greater association with other places, particularly Konya. Colours are, in general, of a slightly darker palette than Konya kilims. These commonly large, rectangular kilims are usually slitwoven, and in some cases the weaving is very fine, using tightly spun, shiny wool.

Niğde During the eleventh and twelfth centuries Niğde, south-east of Aksaray, became an important town controlling the mountain pass on the northern trade

Aksaray	326, 327
DESIGN	Field: Repeated geometric motifs Borders: Decorated
SIZE AND SHAPE	Large and rectangular/Small
MATERIALS	Medium and fine wool
STRUCTURE	Slitweave, with small details in weft wrapping
COLOURS	Bright and medium palette
FRINGE	Plain/Knotted
SELVEDGE	Plain

Karapınar	323, 325
DESIGN	Field: Multiple prayer arches
SIZE AND SHAPE	Large and rectangular/Small
MATERIALS	Fine wool
STRUCTURE	Slitweave
COLOURS	Light ground, design depicted in dark tones
FRINGE	Plain/Knotted
SELVEDGE	Plain
REMARKS	Çuval also made in supplementary weft wrapping technique

Colours used in this area are reds, blues, green, pink, and brown. Kilims are made in slitweave, and çuval in supplementary-weft-wrapping technique and plainweave, with wool that is usually medium to finely spun.

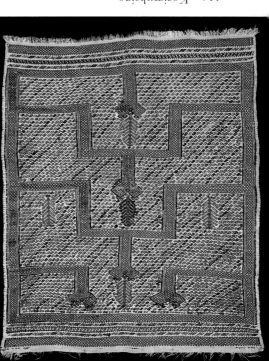

324 Keçimuhsine
(1.81 × 1.28 m, 5'11" × 4'2")
This pattern is totally unique to the area, and represents a Cyprus tree. This particular example was woven in the nineteenth century.

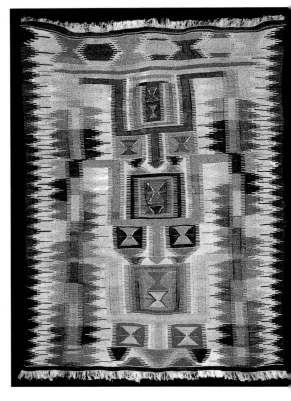

325 Karapınar
(1.51 × 1.10m, 4'11" × 3'7")
The small brown triangle in the central square represents an amulet which, according to folklore, guards against the evil eye.

328 Konya/Aksaray (above)
(1.71 × 0.87 m, 5′7″ × 2′10″)
*Finely woven in slitweave, with small details in
weft-wrapping technique, this kilim features the*
elibelinde *motif as the principal design.*

326 Aksaray (above left)
(3.67 × 1.73 m, 12′ × 5′8″)
*Each border motif has a background of a
different colour, a feature often found in older
Anatolian kilims. Particularly prominent in the
field of the kilim is the 'secondary' design,
created by the white areas.*

327 Aksaray (above centre)
(2.33 × 0.76 m, 7′7″ × 2′5″)
*This nineteenth-century kilim fragment fully
demonstrates the wonderful colours that can be
found in Anatolian kilims. The pattern is
drawn with great precision.*

329 Nevsehir (left)
(2.78 × 1.69 m, 9′1″ × 5′6″)
*The colouring of this nineteenth-century kilim is
wonderful, unusually featuring an apricot border,
and the white cotton adds distinction to both the
design and colours. Note the positive/negative
duality of the end border pattern, the
undecorated area creating another form.*

163

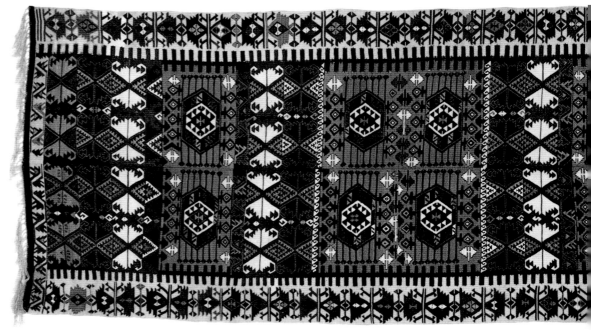

330 Niğde
(4.13 × 1.75 m, 13′6″ × 5′8″)
Probably made as a seating cover, this kilim is
finely woven from soft and silky wool. The
hexagonal motif is similar to those woven in
Çumra, and the 'Ottoman Carnation' design is
also seen in Konya and eastern Anatolian
kilims. The pattern has been well drawn, for the
two halves join symmetrically.

331 Konya/Aksaray
(1.64 × 1.18 m, 5′4″ × 3′10″)
The border motif of this slitwoven kilim and the
one contained within the hexagons are both
characteristic of Konya flatweaves. The
arrangement of the pattern is very static and
regular, which results in an uninteresting overall
effect.

link from Cilicia (now Adana) to inner Anatolia. By the early thirteenth century the town was in ruins, most likely as a result of wars between the Mongols and the Turkoman Karaman people. The surrounding area is agriculturally fertile and rich in minerals. Angora goats are bred here for mohair wool.

Niğde designs often feature hexagonal serrated motifs, possibly derived from the 'Ottoman Carnation' design, arranged in rows segmented by zig-zag vertical lines. Again these designs are influenced by nearby Konya, and are often labelled as Konya – an attribution that is not wholly incorrect, as Niğde does in fact lie within Konya province. Colours are varied, and are similar to Konya kilims. As only old kilims from Niğde are found, weaving is usually fine to very fine, and is of lustrous wool. They are either large and rectangular, or small.

Kayseri

The earliest recorded occupation of Kayseri dates back to Hellenistic times, and although there is no evidence to date, the town was probably built on an early Hittite site as there are many such settlements close by – Kanesh, the first Hittite capital, was situated north-east of Kayseri, at Kultepe. During the first century AD the town was named Caesarea by the Roman emperor Tiberius, later becoming famous as the birthplace of St Basil the Great who was one of the Church Fathers. From the thirteenth to the fifteenth century there were many changes of rulers, amongst whom were the Egyptian Mamelukes, until finally the Ottomans resumed their initial control. Kayseri was once the capital of Cappadocia, being situated at the foot of Mount Erciyes, one of the two volcanoes (the other being Melendes Daği, near Niğde) that erupted spreading hot volcanic ash over the region, which then hardened into a porous stone called tuff. Over the passage of time erosion occurred leaving strange mushroom-shaped pedestals known as 'fairy chimneys', or *peribaca*. The tuff, being soft, was also easily hollowed out for shelter, and during invasions the Cappadocians would retreat underground. Christians also found the caverns suitable for their churches, particularly during the Arab invasions of the seventh century. These churches, complete with wall paintings, and caves and other subterranean dwellings, were inhabited by the descendants of the ancient Cappadocians until early this century.

Beyond the valleys of the weird rock formations and caves of the Urgup region, the terrain changes into vast sweeps of open country, which end with the impressive snow-clad peak of Mount Erciyes, on the way to Kayseri. North-east of Kayseri are two Seljuk *hans* or caravanserais, which have been well restored. Kayseri people are known throughout Turkey as being very slick in business, and many jokes are made about them. The caravanserai in Kayseri is situated next to the bazaar, and is now used by many kilim and carpet traders. Within the thick walls there is set a small metal door, behind which is the safe where visitors could leave money and other valuables overnight.

Kayseri people still weave kilims, and many are made specifically for the export market. It is also the only region producing silk kilims, which are generally loosely worked in slitweave. Other kilims are made in natural wool colours, such as white, browns, grey and white, again in slitweave. Many compartment-type kilims are

332 Kayseri
(3.93 × 1.62 m, 12′10″ × 5′8″)
Many Kayseri kilims are loosely woven with rather coarse wool, but the wool used in this kilim is soft and silky. The main compartmented design is frequently seen in combination with various border patterns. Contemporary colouring is usually of a predominantly red and brown palette.

333 Kayseri
(3.48 × 1.75 m, 11′4″ × 5′8″)
This kilim was probably woven in about 1970, and looks more recent, but the quality of weaving is good. It has at one time been used as a wall hanging.

334   Kayseri
The border pattern is very typical of Kayseri kilims woven within the last few decades, but many of the motifs used are not necessarily characteristic of the region, and have been copied to compile the design. (Detail)

woven featuring a square emblem repeated three or four times down the field, according to length. These kilims generally have two main borders, and a plethora of small infill motifs which decorate the rest of the field. Another design format features large central medallions of varying shapes; again most of the field is decorated with small motifs. The borders vary in number, and colours are of an autumnal palette.

Kayseri	332–4
DESIGN	Field: Compartmented format/Central medallions/Small filler motifs Borders: Leaf and vine pattern often used
SIZE AND SHAPE	Large and rectangular/Small
MATERIALS	Quite thick wool, often coarse/Silk
STRUCTURE	Slitweave, often loosely constructed in two halves
COLOURS	Dull palette of brown, red, some yellow, white
FRINGE	Plain/Knotted
SELVEDGE	Plain
Remarks	Small kilims feature one section of the compartmented design

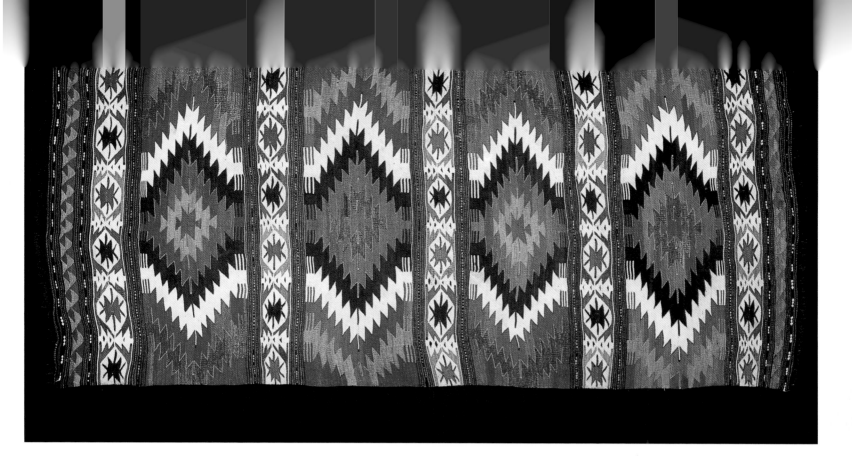

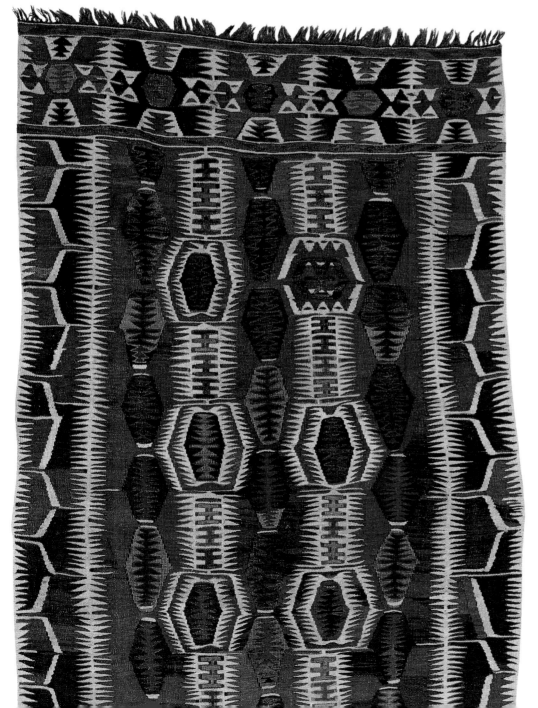

336 Mut
(2.67 × 1.23 m, 8'9" × 4')
This kilim, made in the Mut region of the Taurus Mountains, is typically Yörük, with serrated medallions prevailing over the design and creating the illusion of expansion; the same pattern with fewer medallions is also used in small kilims from this region. Similar medallions are found in Konya kilims, but the Mut variety are much bolder because of the juxtaposition of dark brown and white.

337 Mut
(2.98 × 1.75 m, 9'9" × 5'8")
The warps of this kilim are of natural brown goat hair, which provides a strong base upon which to weave such an unusual design, exclusive to this area. Small kilims are also made in the same pattern. The fingered protrusions are comparable to the parmakli *design woven in the Afyon region. The predominant colours of Mut kilims are reds, blues and brown.*

Opposite:

335 Mut
(2.86 × 1.71 m, 9'4" × 5'7")
Reciprocal border motifs are often found in Mut kilims, as are the hexagonal medallions that frequently appear as the focal point of the design. Mut is amongst the few areas in Anatolia where medium-sized flatweaves are produced. The soft colour palette, although delicate, gives rather a bland appearance to this kilim.

167

338 Mut
(3.19 × 1.82 m, 10'6" × 6')
*The design of this contemporary kilim bears
some similarity to 335, and is often seen, with
variations, in kilims from Mut. The quality of
weaving is adequate although the wool is rather
coarse. Note the snake motifs on the white
ground of some of the medallions, thought to
symbolize fertility and happiness.*

The Taurus Yörüks

The Taurus Yörüks are migratory people of Central Asian origin, who were driven westward by the Mongols as early as the tenth century. Moving in small groups in search of new pastures for their flocks, they entered Anatolia by the north-east and first settled near Samsun, then progressing due south to the Taurus Mountains. There are also Kurdish people from eastern Anatolia in this area, relocated by governments in an effort to maintain their control.

Today the Yörüks lead a semi-nomadic life. Their winter quarters in the villages are known as *kişla*, and once the harvest is gathered they move to the cooler mountain pastures with their flocks. There their tented encampments are known as *yayla*, and the ground upon which the *yurts* stand is deemed holy. Yörüks are fiercely proud of their nomadic existence, and consider it to be the only valid way of life.

The weavings of these Yörüks are strong both in design and substance, as befits the lifestyle of their makers. Goat hair is often used as warping material, and because of their transhumant existence, they weave many types of bags, mainly in weft-wrapping technique.

Mut

Kilims continue to be woven in this area today, primarily for home use. Although many find their way into the commercial market, they are not woven specifically for the export trade as Uşak or Denizli kilims are, and like other contemporary village weavings they greatly benefit from sun-fading. The warps of Mut kilims often contain goat or horse hair and are therefore bulky, and dark brown in colour, and their fringes are twisted or plaited and frequently found at only one end. The bold serrated diamond-shaped medallions found in Mut kilims are often compared with the weavings of the North American Navajo Indians, and contrasting colours such as dark brown, white and red, and a little blue and yellow, are used to full effect, highlighting this prominent design. Small kilims are woven in a similar format using predominantly natural wool tones of grey, brown and white, with small areas of dyed wool, generally in red, pink, orange or yellow.

Another composition that is frequently woven is of large hexagonal-shaped medallions arranged in pairs down the field of the kilim, with considerable areas of sparsely decorated ground, usually red or terracotta, a reciprocal border design and a narrow skirt pattern. A similar composition is also woven using hooked diamond-shaped medallions which interconnect, forming the pattern that covers the field and creates a floating effect. An unusual double prayer-arch design is occasionally found, the apex of each prayer arch joining at the centre of the kilim; these were possibly made as camel or horse covers. There are a number of different designs woven in this area, mostly using hooked, serrated or fingered medallions of varying sizes in their composition.

Older kilims generally have a more mellow colour palette of red, pink, brown, blue and yellow. More recent weavings have autumnal tones of terracotta, brown, orange, yellow and some green. Tight slitweave is used, so that the designs do not contain any long vertical slits; this, together with the thick warps and wefts, results in a substantial and hard-wearing textile.

Mut 335–8

DESIGN	Field: Bold serrated medallions/Hexagonal medallions arranged in pairs/Interconnecting hexagonal motifs
SIZE AND SHAPE	Medium and rectangular, some quite narrow/Small
MATERIALS	Coarse wool/Goat and horse hair often used for warps
STRUCTURE	Slitweave
COLOURS	Bright, also mellow palette, brown, red, pink, blue, yellow, white
FRINGE	Twisted/Plaited/Plain
SELVEDGE	Plain
Remarks	Grey and brown natural wool often used

339   Aleppo
This late nineteenth-century flatweave is similar in its dark colours to Reyhanli kilims, although it is not as striking because of its overall patterning. (Detail)

Dağ

Kilims known as *dağ*, or mountain kilims, are woven in this region, and are frequently found for sale in Konya. The designs are similar to old Obruk patterns used for long and wide runners. These feature a square medallion with large hooks at the corners that is repeated down the field, and borders are generally wide. This pattern is thought to represent a double bull's-head motif – the bull was a prominent feature of Neolithic cult religion. Usually only the head of the bull is depicted, and it is thought that this animal represented both the husband and son of the mother goddess. It is perhaps no surprise that this design has survived here, within the regions of the Taurus Mountains. This composition is used for long and narrow, medium square and small sizes, and is woven in coarse slitweave using good quality wool. Colours are red, brown, orange, green and some yellow.

340   Aleppo
(4.28 × 1.76 m, 14′ × 5′9″)
The design seen here is found in many areas of Anatolia. Its repetitiveness is alleviated by different background tones.

Aleppo 339–41

DESIGN	Field: Repeat patterning in rows/Narrow and banded Borders: Narrow and decorated
SIZE AND SHAPE	Large and rectangular/Small
MATERIALS	Fine and very fine wool/Occasionally cotton
STRUCTURE	Slitweave, large kilims made in two halves
COLOURS	Varied dark and light palette
FRINGE	Knotted/Plain
SELVEDGE	Plain
Remarks	Designs similar to Anatolian kilims

341 Aleppo
(3.89 × 1.94 m, 12′9″ × 6′4″)
*The stepped medallion with extending arms and
the end border motifs are typical of this area,
whereas the side borders and separating narrow
bands feature motifs found in many other places,
particularly Konya. Large kilims woven in two
halves were often used as portal covers, although
these were frequently longer than was necessary,
suggesting that they were not specifically woven
for this purpose.*

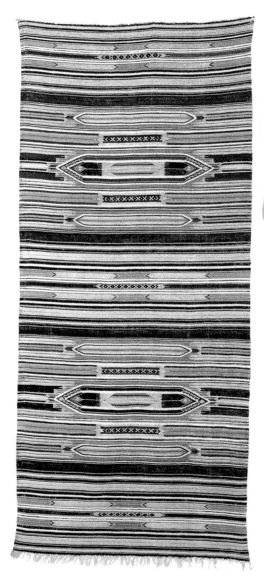

342 Aleppo
(1.76 × 0.75 m, 5′9″ × 2′5″)
*Finely drawn compositions such as this, the
format of which is similar to a saf design, were
often woven in silk as well as wool. The narrow
stripes typical of such mid-nineteenth-century
kilims are woven in plainweave with slitwoven
patterning.*

Aleppo

Although a city within present-day Syria, Aleppo was part of the Ottoman Empire from the fifteenth to the early nineteenth centuries, so its regional production of kilims, now a thing of the past, is more usually associated with Anatolian work.

Historically, Aleppo is a legendary market town on the caravan routes between Asia, Europe and the Mediterranean. Locally known as Haleb, the town prospered under Ottoman rule, and to this day continues to uphold its place as a centre for religious study and education. It also has one of the most interesting and original bazaars of the Orient.

The weaving of kilims appears to have ceased at the end of the nineteenth, or beginning of the twentieth century, as later examples are not found. Aleppo kilims are characterized by fine weaving, reciprocal patterns joining border and field designs and many similar border motifs. The main field compositions are often filled with rows of small diamond-shaped motifs with flat arms or hooks at either end. Most of the kilims woven in this region are of a large rectangular shape, made in two halves, and were once used as door and window curtains.

Another composition features a narrow striped format with *saf*-type designs. This pattern was very finely woven in silk more often than wool. The weaving technique used for Aleppo kilims is predominantly slitweave, with some plainweave. Colouring is varied, including red, blue, green, apricot, purple, brown, some yellow, and white cotton.

Chapter Six

Persia and the Caucasus

343 *A full palette of colour and bands of Turkic motifs are typical of the Shahsavan of the Hashtrud and Mogan regions. (Detail)*

PERSIA: The Kurds · The Shahsavan
The Lurs · The Bakhtiari · The Qashqai
The Khamsa · The Afshar · Regional Weaving
THE CAUCASUS

Marco Polo wrote of that vast area in south-west Asia, 'Now you must know that Persia is a very great country.' The greatness he adduced was not a reference to its geography, but to the hierarchy of its empires and the beauty of its crafts. By contrast, the Caucasus is an enigma, not only serving as a trading gateway between the East and West, but also in the steep valleys as a place of refuge and settlement. To combine Persia and the Caucasus into a single chapter is a device of geographical convenience in a region where there exists an extraordinary amalgam of tribes and a diversity and wealth of flatweaving.

Persia

It was from the eighteenth and nineteenth centuries onwards that the Western carpet collector began to adopt 'Persia' rather than 'Turkey' as the common synonym for 'oriental'. The lands of the Persians, now known again by the ancient name of Iran, proved to be a rich repository of fine and large carpets, woven with precious raw materials such as silk, patterned in a sophisticated and decorative manner and further enhanced by a fashionable colour palette. Commissioned for the palaces of the nobility of Persia, such luxurious floor coverings were soon regarded by the European upper classes as the fashionable 'oriental' essential for the large town or country house.

This initially elitist demand filtered down to the general populace of Europe and America, so that over the last two hundred years many thousands of bales of Persian knotted carpets have been loaded on to camel trains, carried to the borders and shipped to the West. The influence of so long and grand a trade in textiles, quite unprecedented in the history of man's inter-cultural trade in craft goods, has had a profound effect on both village and town weavers, and to a lesser extent and more indirectly on the nomads of the region.

The constant demand and sheer volume of this trade led to the establishment of a sophisticated network of middlemen and dealers, in both Persia and the destination markets. This varied and colourful group of businessmen, who have won for the title 'carpet dealer' its perverse innuendo, has ensured that all the particular requirements for specific sizes and colours demanded by the Western consumer have been met.

Despite this intimate and more than two-hundred-year-old trade association, few Persian kilims had been introduced to the consumers of Europe and America until recently. Kilims tended to be derided as unsophisticated in materials, construction and patterning, and were consequently neglected by the knotted carpet dealers. It was only the curiosity and enthusiasm of a small number of enlightened Western collectors and dealers that led to the importation of Persian kilims in the 1950s and 1960s, and even then kilims were only shown in minority-interest 'art' and ethnographic exhibitions. Not surprisingly, it was the powerful colours and graphic quality of the Qashqai and Luri kilims of the south and south-west of Persia that stimulated many of the pioneer enthusiasts. Rather than

344 *A Shahsavan bag face from the central Mogan plain.*

viewing the kilims merely as floor rugs, many saw their potential as large hangings bursting with the drama of strong colour and colour interrelation. From these beginnings, as 'art' objects, it has taken only a short time for kilims to become appreciated by a wider audience who at last have started to recognize the richness of the Persian flatweavers' creative capabilities, and within the past fifteen years many varied examples of the full and diverse range of Persian kilims have been imported in quantity.

This new surge of interest does, however, create difficulties for the historian, collector and connoisseur, for many of the old, antique and distinguished kilims have disappeared into private collections. In addition to this, the changes wrought within the lands of the weavers over the past sixty years have disturbed and destroyed much of the inspiration behind the continuing creation of the 'traditional' flatweave. Reinforcing this trend is the new and large-scale trade in more recently made kilims; demand from the West, rather than domestic need, has determined the style and type of kilims produced. Commission work and the prolific reproduction of popular compositions have served to break down yet further both the necessity and the desire to weave in previously established tribal, nomadic, village or town styles. It is the recent and continuing loss of this legacy

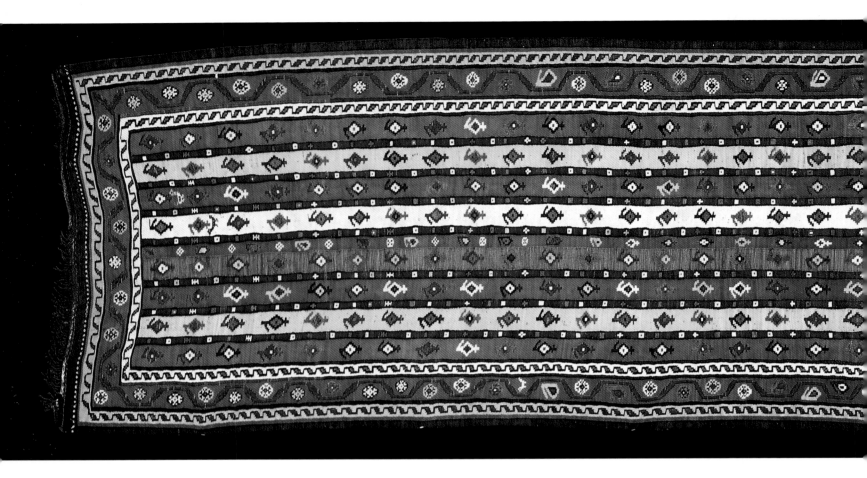

345   Bakhtiari of Chahar Mahal
(3.12 × 0.91 m, 10′3″ × 3′)
*A striking, unusually clear and colourful rug
from the Chahar Mahal district. The stripes of
vegetable-dyed wool contain evenly spaced stylized*
boteh *motifs, and are separated by narrow
stripes of black containing little squares and
crosses. The middle border reflects the* boteh
motif between two borders of running design.

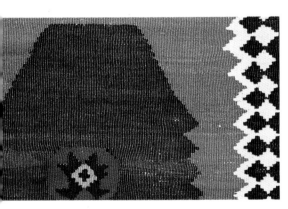

346   Qashqai
This small flatweave was made as a soufreh,
*eating cloth, or as a cover. Nomadic people such
as the Qashqai have had little contact with
commercial merchandise, and therefore weave
utility textiles according to their need. (Detail)*

that makes any attempt to ascertain the provenance of an old Persian kilim so problematic.

The kilims from Persia vary enormously, very much more so than those from Turkey or North Africa, lands that are demographically relatively homogeneous. By contrast, the population of modern-day Iran comprises very many different tribes of varied and far-flung origins, and it is only through some awareness of the history of these clans, groups, tribes and empires that any deeper understanding of the art of the Persian kilim can be gleaned.

Some of the earliest recorded indigens of Iran, the Kurds and the Lurs, continue to participate actively as tribal groups in the affairs of the region; their recent contributions are not associated, however, with their considerable flatweaving skills. The Kurds are long-time inhabitants of the northern land and it is within the crescent of the south Anatolian plateau and the western Zagros Mountains around the sources and tributaries of the Tigris and Euphrates rivers that their ancestors first lived, from the Palaeolithic period onwards. The numerous caves and natural shelters of the region, many still in use today, display clear signs of ancient habitation, and Jarmo, in the Chamchamal valley, may indeed be one of the sites where cereals were first farmed. There is also evidence that the area was one of the first to develop the art of weaving floor coverings in a form that is recognized today as kilim weave.

The Guti tribe, who pastoralized these valleys, were raiding Babylonia around 2200 BC, and by 1200 BC various tribes of Iranian extraction had moved into the Zagros Mountains, including the Medes whose kingdom enclosed eastern Kurdistan. By conquering the Medes in 550 BC, Cyrus the Great (d. ?529 BC)

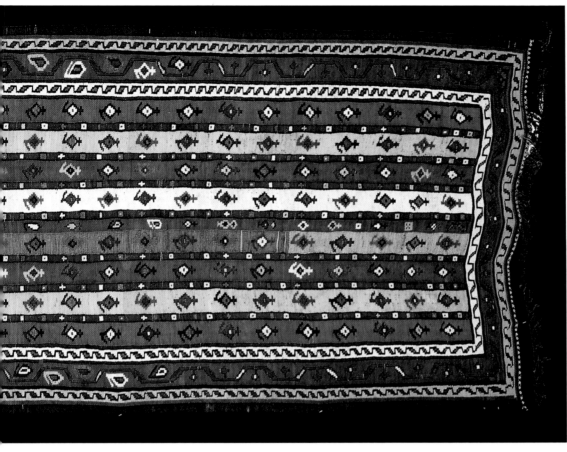

347   Kurds of Bijar
*The deep indigo blue of this kilim is expensive
to produce; indeed, the deeper the blue the
greater the cost. (Detail)*

348   Lurs (below)
$(2.18 \times 1.51\,\text{m},\ 7'2'' \times 5')$
*The weaver has cleverly divided the background
field into bands of colour, scattering motifs at
random. She has surrounded it with a border of
remarkable chequerboard design. The motif in
the centre of each medallion is of Turkic origins,
and is found in many kilims.*

349 *A bag face from the north-west, displaying a complex pattern made up of many traditional Turkic motifs.*

Opposite:

350 Kurds of Bijar
(1.44 × 1.05 m, 4'9" × 3'5")
Kurdistan is a harsh area of steep bare mountains, but it does support grazing for large flocks of sheep that produce some of the finest wool in the world. This kilim, bought in Bijar, has the soft feel of good hand-spun wool, and has been expertly finished by a village craftswoman.

established the great Achaemenid Persian Empire that continued under his successors for two hundred years. Persepolis, the capital, was built and ornamented by artisans from all over western Asia, the Middle East, the Mediterranean and eastern Europe. A culture compounded from Greek, Assyrian and Persian ideas developed within the tenets of the state religion of Zoroastrianism, founded by Zoroaster the Bactrian (?628–?551 BC). The Achaemenid Empire came to a sudden and dramatic end at the hand of Alexander the Great who defeated the last Achaemenid king, Darius III, in 330 BC.

The Macedonian Empire was inherited on Alexander's death in 323 BC by his general Seleucus, founding the Seleucid dynasty. The Parthians, a war-like group of mounted nomads, succeeded the visitors from the Mediterranean Basin, who in turn were defeated by Ardashir I, the founder of the Sassanian Empire in 224 BC. By warring with the Byzantine Empire to the west and the newly emergent Turks of the south Siberian wastes to the north-east, the Sassanian Empire was weakened and its lengthy reign was terminated in an abrupt fashion by the forces of a young world religion, Islam. The Islamic religious code outlined a way of life that was more stable than that associated with the religions of Zoroastrianism, Buddhism and Nestorian Christianity, and the invading Arabs found ready converts after their invasion in AD 636; the last Sassanian fortress of Merv was finally overcome in 651.

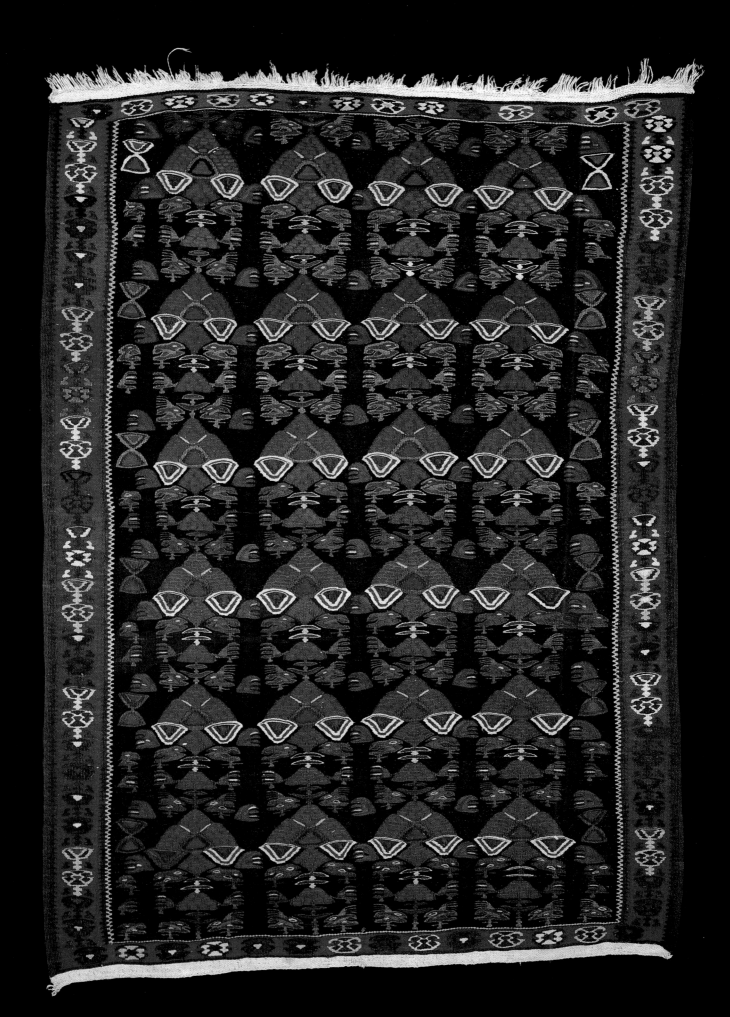

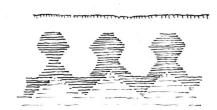

353 *A laleh abrassi* motif from the border *of a kilim woven by the Shahsavan.*

355 *The more elaborate* laleh abrassi *motif from a kilim woven by the Qashqai.*

Opposite:

351 Qashqai
(2.48 × 1.45 m, 8′2″ × 4′9″)
The small motifs in the central medallion of this kilim are simplified, and the zig-zag pattern is exaggerated by the narrow bands of white wool. Woven in quite finely spun wool in slitweave, it is finished in easily recognizable southern Iranian techniques. The thick coloured wool wrapping the selvedge and the three narrow bands of reversible weft float on the end panels are typical of Qashqai kilims.

352 Shahsavan of Saveh
(1.21 × 0.80 m, 4′ × 2′8″)
A very small kilim of a peculiar size, which suggests a particular yet unknown use. The strong design of coloured diamonds, each outlined with weft wrapping, is worked in twill weave and has been expertly drawn in a complete and even pattern to the ends. The seemingly random use of colour is carefully and symmetrically arranged around the centre line of the rug, shown by the red diamonds in the white side border.

354 Qashqai (right)
(3.44 × 1.82 m, 11′3″ × 6′)
The colourful nomadic lifestyle of the Qashqai is reflected in this kilim. The clear bright colours are all derived from vegetable dyes. As with many Qashqai kilims, the freely drawn field patterning seems to have been taken from a much larger design, as it has no definite start or finish. It radiates outwards from two central diamond medallions to form large-scale zig-zags against the borders.

356, 357 Kuba
(3.10 × 2.15 m, 10′2″ × 7′)
The creator of this complex design has woven a
spectacular kilim, although it would seem that
some mistakes were made in two unfinished
square motifs on the right-hand side of the
central medallions. The detail has been retained
in both the border and the ends, which unusually
incorporate animal motifs into part of the skirt
design. (Detail 357)

Successive invasions continued to engulf Persia. A branch of the Turkic tribe of the Oghuz, the Seljuks, left their lands near the source of the Syr Darya and moved south, converting to Islam and ruling over Persia and much of Asia Minor. At Rum, the Seljuks established their sultanate, modelling the city on Rome; it later became the root of the Ottoman Empire, and is now present-day Konya. The arts of Islam duly blended with and finally came to dominate the arts and crafts of the Turkic peoples, the cultural leaders of the region, together with those of indigenous groups such as the Kurds and the Lurs. By the mid-thirteenth century Ardebil, on the west shore of the Caspian Sea, had become the religious centre for zealots of a new Islamic cult, Sufism. This had a lasting influence on intellectual beliefs and ideals, which was then reflected in the kilims and their compositions (see Chapter Three, p. 59). Other long-term influences include the establishment of tribal confederations, organized by the Seljuk central government in the tenth century, to create a feudal system of semi-autonomous territories headed by a tribal leader, or khan. By this means, the government was guaranteed payment of taxes and forces for the army in return for benefits for the khan that included land and irrigation schemes, grazing rights and access to local taxation.

Two hundred years of peace under Seljuk rule was dashed aside in the thirteenth century by yet another group from Central Asia, the notorious Mongol hordes. Destruction and carnage have become synonymous with their name: it is thought that upwards of five million people perished at their hands in Turkestan and Persia alone. The devastation wrought, however, created a vacuum into which were drawn new influences, and the arts of the region received a wealth of fresh and stimulating creative imports, predominantly from China.

As Genghis Khan (?1162–1227) raped and pillaged, so agriculture declined and the people fled into the mountains to escape the heavy taxes and barbarous treatment. Town life atrophied and large-scale nomadism began; indeed, it was because of this Mongol campaign and the effects of the many other invasions, not as is generally thought, through climatic conditions, that so much of the population of Persia became nomadic. Another erstwhile robber, Timur Lenk, or Tamerlane (?1336–1405), the son of a Turkish emir, continued the central Asian domination of the region. By 1405 Tamerlane's empire stretched from the Indus to the Mediterranean. The obvious domination of many of the Timurid forms and ornaments in the traditional arts and crafts of Persia still persists today, along with the Sunni religious fervour that emerged from his capital, Samarkand.

The first native dynasty since the Islamic invasion to rule over the lands of Persia were the Safavids, whose ascension was assisted by the Turkomen. At the end of the rule of the Timurid khans, Persia was divided into small territories, and

358, 359 Shirvan
(3.20 × 1.84 m, 10′5″ × 6′)
A beautiful, classical Shirvan kilim, both in design and colouring, finely woven in slitweave on natural brown wool warps, with narrow bands highlighted in weft-twining technique. The zig-zag pattern separating the bands filled with larger motifs gives movement to an otherwise static design. (Detail 358)

360 *Typical Turkic hooked motifs are derived from the eight-pointed star. The light orange/red colour of the field, traditional to the Hashtrud region, is brought to life with lines of* abrash. *(Detail of 397)*

361 Kerman
Heavy weft-wrapping techinque and distinctive border designs are characteristic of kilims from this province of southern Iran. (Detail)

to the north-east two Turkoman tribes, the Kara Qoyonlu ('Black Sheep') and the Ak Qoyonlu ('White Sheep'), were brawling incessantly from the middle of the thirteenth century onwards. The Ak Qoyonlu eventually gained supremacy, and it was under their regime, in the thirteenth century, that the Sheikh Safi ad Din (1252–1334), from whom the name Safavid is derived, established a dervish order, and the remarkable Sufi school at Ardebil on the west shore of the Caspian Sea. By the end of the fifteenth century, within a strict military structure, the dervishes had become Shi'a and were titled Kyzylbash ('Redheads'), after the complex red felt turban headdresses that had been designed for them by the sheikh of the time and main architect of the Kyzylbash movement, Heidar (r. 1470–88). Eventually killed in battle, Heidar was succeeded by his young son Ismail; the Kyzylbash ensured the safety of the seven-year-old, who became the first Safavid shah, defeating the Ak Qoyonlu and taking Tabriz for his capital in 1501. A most important early objective of the Safavids was to unify the country, which they did by establishing the Kyzylbash as provincial leaders over a Shi'a kingdom. In this way the previously eminent Sunni lands of Central Asia were placed at the periphery of the Islamic world.

The Safavid dynasty ruled from 1500 to 1736, and had a significant influence on the culture of the land as well as its demographic make-up. The infamous Shah Abbas had his subjects shuttled, willing or unwilling, from one borderland to another as defenders of the kingdom. In his time many Kurds from the north-west were moved to the eastern province of Khorassan to form a demographic bulwark against the last great Turkic power in Turkestan, the raiding Uzbeks. It was not the Uzbeks, however, but Ghilzai Afghans who instigated the downfall of the Safavid Empire when in 1722, the Afghan invaders, led by Mahmud, a Moghul leader from Kandahar, captured Shah Abbas's great city of Isfahan. It was, however, a Turkoman, Nadir, who finally drove the Afghans out in several successful campaigns, subsequently becoming shah over a kingdom that now stretched from Iraq to Delhi, and from Uzbekistan to Makran. The new empire burned bright with success, dominated by the character of Nadir, but soon disintegrated at his death. Thenceforth the Turkish Qajars took over, ruling until the *coup d'état* of Reza Shah in 1921.

Most of the extant old Persian kilims were woven in the nineteenth and early twentieth centuries. With the repressive Pahlavi regime of Reza Shah (1878–1944), established in 1925, came the rapid changes brought by the tidal wave of direct Western influence and the ease and swiftness of modern transportation and communication methods. Yet despite these dramatic influences and the exponential growth in export demand for knotted carpets that established the large town and village workshops of Persia, kilims were still woven without change, for traditional family and domestic purposes, until relatively recently.

The policies of the Pahlavi regime were directly aimed at reducing the power of the regional tribes of Persia. Tribal leaders were disarmed and imprisoned, and nomadic groups suffered greatly, forced to settle on marginal lands that could not support them or their flocks. For a short period after the overthrow of Reza Shah in 1941, the tribespeople enjoyed a return to self-government and traditional lifestyles, but since 1956 the last Shah and the succeeding republican governments of Iran have continued with a tribal settlement programme in an attempt to create a homogeneous Iranian society.

For many centuries successive empires, monarchs and governments have wrought havoc, by conquest, raiding and internal demographic manipulation, on the distribution of the indigens and the settled immigrants, some from such far-flung places as Mongolia and Greece. The confusion caused by the ensuing cultural amalgamation, combined with the free movement of nomadic tribes across national and international borders, has meant that the origins of certain groups have become difficult to determine, and that the exact provenance of some kilims can only be accurately ascertained by buying directly from the weaver. The correct attribution of a flatweave is made more problematic by bazaar-dealers' stories and their imprecise use of familiar place names. A kilim can either be attributed to the tribe that wove the rug, the town where it was woven or found, or to the style used in the design, according to which is most pertinent. Although many groups of weavings will be identified by their traditional tribal name, others that originate from the diverse towns, villages and regions where there is a more recent 'tradition' of weaving will adopt the name of their place of manufacture: the weavers will have intermingled and intermarried, so that they have no single and definable tribal origin. The economic interdependence and ties of kinship which exist between the town-dwellers and the nomads further confuse the issue. Preconceptions of the nomadic lifestyle vary from a romantic fantasy of freedom, open spaces and an uncluttered existence close to nature, to the notion that nomads are disorganized, uneducated wanderers with no discipline or wealth. Neither is true. The nomadic life is very harsh, a ceaseless cycle of work in an inhospitable climate following the traditional patterns and rhythms perfected by their ancestors, and requires order and organization, and considerable wealth in the form of livestock. The migration of people is more than the compulsory observance of the dictates of nature and the seasonal ebb and flow of animal pastures, it is also a hereditary ritualistic, symbolic and mystical act.

Nomad, farmer, sedentary villager and city dweller may all belong to the same tribal sub-group (*taifeh*) and yet have very different lifestyles, depending on their economic circumstances. They will have opposing priorities regarding the acquisition and use of domestic tools and other household items, and a different understanding of the seasons and their natural surroundings. It is possible, however, because of family ties, for a wealthy and materialistic town-dwelling merchant to join the summer migration in the higher pastures in his new imported car. Ever-changing factors of this kind make the work of the tribal-weaving historian an increasingly complex task.

Given all the aforementioned issues that contrive to complicate any systematic survey of Persian kilims, this chapter attempts just such a task, journeying anti-clockwise through the tribal lands of Iran, from the north-western border to the frontiers with West Turkestan. The towns and villages that have served as a repository for various tribal migrations and resettlements, subsequently developing a weaving style of their own, will be described at the chapter's close.

The Kurds

As befits one of the oldest indigenous groups of the lands of modern Iran, the early history of the Kurds is wreathed in folklore. One such story tells of King

362   Harsin
The abrash *in the field gives life and vitality to this kilim from north Kurdistan. (Detail)*

363   Kurds of Khorassan
The very fine soft wool of this kilim is produced in the lush valleys of the 'Granary of Khorassan'. (Detail)

364 Veramin (right)
(2.48 × 1.37 m, 8′2″ × 4′6″)
The motifs in the field design are similar to 389, a Shahsavan kilim. The very dark brown wool used in the reciprocal border and unusual fingers projecting into the field suggest it was woven by Kurdish people in Veramin.

365 Iraqi Kurd
(3.58 × 1.14 m, 11′9″ × 3′9″)
This kilim was bought in Dezful, a town on the Iran-Iraq border in Khuzestan to the north of Shustar. It is woven in slitweave, every slit closed with weft wrapping, in coarse and very long stapled wool. The colours are harsh.

Solomon, who had five hundred *jinn* as his slaves. (A *jinn* is a supernatural being in Arabian mythology who lives in a world between spirits and mortals. *Jinns* are above the laws of nature, but man can control them by means of talismans.) The King sent them west to find five hundred beautiful virgins to add to his harem. Unfortunately Solomon died before the *jinns* returned, and so each married one of the maidens, settled in the green hills of the Zagros Mountains and raised the founders of the Kurdish nation. Such is the legendary origin of the group of people who mainly inhabit the area known as Kurdistan, an area that has no political existence and is not clearly defined on any side by natural topographical features.

The name 'Kurd' was first given to the local tribes and confederations in west Persia in A D 640, and this loose title encompassed most of the people of the vast area from Armenia down to the Zagros Mountains – that is, from the Euphrates to Isfahan. The pressure to convert to Sunni, the rise and fall of the governing empires of the region and the redrawing of international frontiers have progressively isolated the Kurds as a people and Kurdistan as an area. As victims of political manoeuvring the Kurds have for centuries been subjected to enforced migrations. The shahs deported thousands in the seventeenth and eighteenth centuries to the eastern borders of Persia. Not surprisingly, the Kurds have never united to form an autonomous nation or state, although in the twelfth century they established a tribal capital at Bahar, near Hamadan. They have invariably been beset by problems arising from rigid tribal organization under individual leaders or chiefs.

Fluctuations in international frontiers that divided Kurdistan continued into the nineteenth century. Britain and Russia attempted to preserve order in the buffer zone between their respective Asiatic empires, which included Kurdistan, but continuing border disputes further fragmented the Kurdish people. Prior to the First World War both Turkey and Persia reformed their administrative control of Kurdistan and their other remote territories, which resulted in further unrest, particularly a bloody clash between Armenians and Kurds in 1894 near Lake Van. The inter-war years saw little change for the Kurds, still without a political homeland and subject to the various central governments' desires to control and contain. Reza Shah restored Tehran's power over many of the tribal people of Iran, including the Kurds, by ruthless repression, banning seasonal migration and suppressing regional culture.

Immediately after the Second World War the Kurds of Iran came closest to creating an independent state. The Soviet Union, looking covetously to the Gulf and its convenient warm-water ports, at first backed a tribal coalition that included the Kurds of Iraq. Their tribal ideals, however, came to be regarded by the Soviets as nationalistic rather than Communistic, and therefore counterproductive to their aims, so they withdrew their support before the reoccupation by the Iranian army. In recent decades the Kurds, straddling the international boundaries of three countries, have become well known for their tragic role as pawns in every political and national struggle in the Near and Middle East.

Ethnically the Kurds are Iranian people, like the Persians, the Pushtuns and the Balouch. One thousand years of intermarriage, deportation and enforced interaction have assimilated the ancient Kurds into a group of peoples of differing nationalities and beliefs. But it is the Kurdish language in its many various dialects that distinguishes its people from other groups. Kurdish is related to modern Persian and other west Iranian languages of the Indo-European family.

The demographic spread of the Kurdish people within Iran reflects their history. The majority of Kurds live within the Iranian provinces of Kurdistan and Kermanseh. There are large Kurdish tribes in the far north-east of Iran, in the

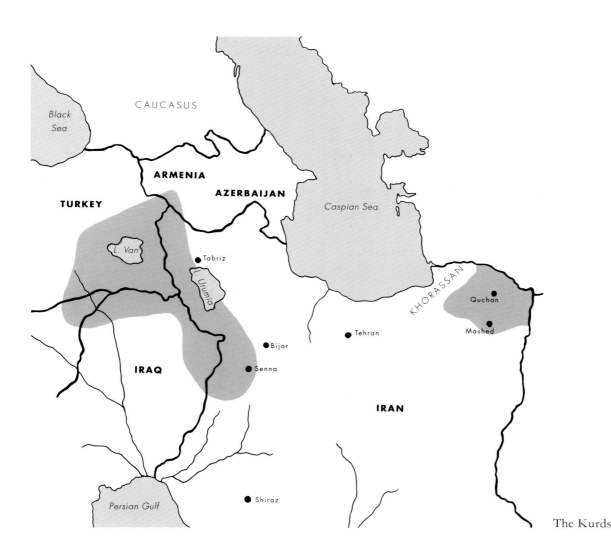

The Kurds

366 *Detail of 631.*

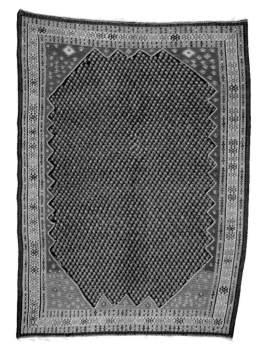

367 Kurds of Senna
(3.46 × 2.35 m, 11'4" × 7'8")
This kilim probably originated outside the urban workshops of Senna, for there is a nomadic and tribal feel and look about this rug. Most kilims woven in this region are much smaller, and large examples such as this are seldom seen. The border design is more typical of the Shahsavan, and the irregular zig-zag shape of the field is characteristic of Kurdish weaving in Bijar, as is the soft madder tone in the corners of the field.

Kopet Dagh range of Khorassan, a few in West Turkestan, and a few in the south-east of Iran, amongst the Balouch. Beyond the present frontiers of Iran there are groups in the Jeziri region of Syria, but the main concentration of Kurds is found along the Turco-Iranian border and around the towns of Bitlis, Erzinjan, Diyarbakir, eastern Antalolia, north-east Iraq and within Armenia.

As the Kurds are so widely dispersed, it is hardly surprising that they weave a disparate range of kilims. Types of Kurdish kilim differ from each other in every respect – design, structure, materials, size and colours. They vary from the sophisticated workshop-made kilims of Senna, with their silken, smooth appearance, resembling a traditional formal Persian carpet or fine tapestry, to highly individual tribal rugs, woven on rough ground looms from coarsely spun wool, that are alive with the traditions and expectations of the woman weaver, the family and the group. Imagery may range from the delicate Safavidesque floral motifs of carnations or roses from the town workshops, to striking and accurate representations of animals and humans woven in the villages and hamlets.

Kurds of Senna		367–8, 631
DESIGN	Field: Endless repeat of floral pattern over whole field/ Floral pattern within central medallion Borders: Multiple and floral	
SIZE AND SHAPE	Usually small and rectangular/Some large and square	
MATERIALS	Cotton warps, very fine soft wool wefts	
STRUCTURE	Very fine slitweave, extra weft inserts, curved wefts	
COLOURS	Predominately blue, red and ivory palette	
FRINGE	Grouped/Knotted into web	
SELVEDGE	Plain	
Remarks	One of the few Persian groups to weave prayer rugs	

The Kurds of Senna

The most well known of all Kurdish kilims originate from Senna, now called Sanandaj, and its environs. Senna is the present capital of Kurdistan and has been, since at least the Safavid era, a town with a sophisticated urban demand for workshop carpets and kilims. The influence of this can easily be seen in Senna kilims that have survived from the eighteenth, nineteenth and early twentieth centuries. Many designs, especially those of the Sanjabi and Jaff tribes, have been inspired by floral patterns of Safavid embroidery and brocade hangings that were, in turn, influenced by Indian design work. This legacy is also evident in the unique technical features of the knotted rugs from Senna that show similarities to those of Moghul rugs, suggesting that Senna weavers directly copied Indian textiles. Floral vines in stripes, highly popular in the Kashmiri textiles of the nineteenth century, are also found in Senna work.

Senna kilims are totally different both technically and aesthetically to the bold tribal and nomadic kilims woven by Kurdish people elsewhere. They display a

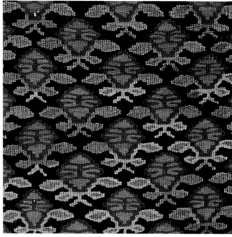

368, 369   Senna
(1.98 × 0.99 m, 6'6" × 3'3")
A modern kilim from the urban weavers of
Senna. The decline in standards of workmanship
and the use of synthetic dyes are evident here.
The wool is coarse, with cotton warps, and the
slitweave is loose. The field of flowers is reflected
in the border, a traditional Senna feature.
(Detail 369)

certain virtuosity in their flatweave technique, and are more closely associated visually with the knotted workshop carpets of Persia than with other kilims. In general, there are three types of composition:

a) An endless repeat of a floral pattern, or a floral pattern hanging from a grid or trellis that is surrounded by a narrow border or series of two or three borders. Motifs include leaf, vine, stem and flower.

b) Similar to the above and distinguished by a field of tiny floral motifs contained in a distinctive medallion in the centre. This type is similar to the formal knotted carpet design frequently known to the bazaar dealers of Tehran as the *herati* pattern. The intricate motifs in the field depict small flowers, *boteh* and beehives, often thought to represent a garden.

c) Most unusually for Iran, a prayer rug design, especially distinctive because of its bulbous *mihrab*.

Senna kilims are usually small in size, but occasionally large kilims are woven in a relatively square format. They are basically slitwoven, although the Senna weavers have refined the weaving of extra weft inserts and curved wefts not usually found in other Kurdish kilims. This permits the curvilinear outline of the design or motif to flow without steps or interruption. Colours are predominantly blue, red and white, and metal thread is sometimes used. Warps are usually cotton: wool warps are seldom used, as wool spun to the necessary fineness is too brittle. The wefts are often of fine long-stapled wool, or occasionally metal or silk, and more recently polychrome silk. The fringe (if it survives, for on a finely spun and woven kilim it is easily damaged and worn away) is of warps bunched together and knotted; if the warps are long enough, these are knotted again to form a web or net. The selvedges are usually left without extra weft reinforcements.

The craftsmanship and technical skill involved in spinning and weaving this group of kilims is more important to the weaver than the overall impact of the design, and indeed, Senna kilims are notorious for their lack of boldness. But in close proximity, the intricacy of the extra weft inserts, matched by the fineness and softness of the wool, more than compensates. Some very brash, yet finely constructed 'reproduction' kilims have been woven in the last ten years.

Woven for and kept in an urban environment, many fine early nineteenth-century examples have survived in good condition both in their land of origin as well as in the West. Senna kilims are said to have been used, presumably as hangings and covers, by ladies in the *hamam*, the bath house, where each hoped to display the finest weave. Senna kilims were one distinctive group whose worth was recognized by early collectors in the 1950s and 1960s, as well as by the auction houses.

The Kurds of Bijar

Bijar (meaning 'mixing of people') is a market town on the edge of Kurdistan. The flatweaves known collectively as 'Bijar' originate from the town itself and the forty or more surrounding villages. A good deal of the output comprises naive copies of Senna kilims made with coarse wool and harsh colours. There is, however, a large quantity of most individual and distinctive kilims produced by the Kurds of this area, usually slitwoven in wool with cotton warps. Bijar kilims may easily be confused with the abundant and very similar kilims of closely related origins from the west and north-west, such as those of the Shahsavan. A typical Bijar kilim is long and narrow, with bold patterning of medallions made up of triangles or diamonds of colour in the central field. They usually have two border patterns, of which the outer shows the reciprocal *laleh abrassi* motif (*laleh* means 'tulip'). One distinctive and charming feature of a range of kilims woven by the Kurdish people of the Bijar region is the appearance in the field, and sometimes the border, of small animal or human figures. Such figures, often woven on each side of the rug, depict men and women dressed in their tribal clothing; the man is placed to the left side of the rug and the woman on the right. Kilims decorated in such fashion are thought to be woven for weddings by young brides, to depict the newly married couple. Animal figures portray the importance of owning a herd of sheep and goats, a form of transportable wealth.

370   Kurds of Bijar
(1.44 × 0.91 m, 4'9" × 3')
This kilim and 350 are both small flatweaves typical of Kurdish work from the towns of Senna and Bijar, and the many small villages between. The weaver's ability to curve the weft threads and insert small areas of extra wefts results in her being able to create flowing lines, zoomorphic figures and floral designs. The wefts are of very finely spun wool, and the warps are of cotton. (Detail 377)

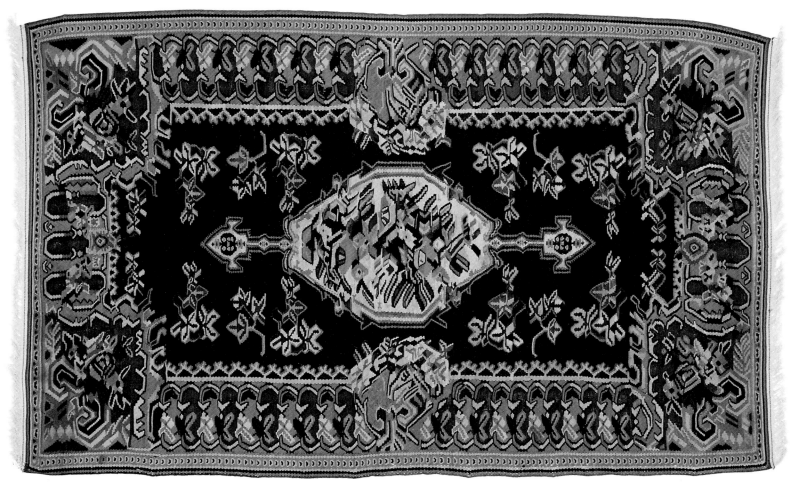

The horse blankets and bags of Bijar are woven in weft-wrapping technique. Such trappings are very difficult to distinguish from those of other tribal groups in the area: the way the wool has been spun, the weft wrapping, the details and finishes, and the style of selvedge are all very similar to that of Shahsavan work from the region. The two-headed animal motif and medallion of latchwork are, however, renowned examples of the finest of Kurdish decorative designs found on bag faces.

371 Kurds of Bijar
(2.13 × 1.14 m, 7′ × 3′9″)
An extraordinary late nineteenth-century kilim full of European baroque and rococo designs. Many characteristics of this rug are typical of Bijar craftsmanship. However, the border design, disproportionate with the rest of the rug, appears to have been copied from European work. (Detail 375)

Kurds of Bijar

350, 370–1, 373

DESIGN	Field: Bold geometric medallions on plain ground Borders: Narrow
SIZE AND SHAPE	Long and narrow
MATERIALS	Coarse wool/Sometimes cotton warps
STRUCTURE	Slitweave
COLOURS	Varied range of strong colours
FRINGE	All types
SELVEDGE	Plain/Parallel wrapping
Remarks	Woven representations of figures and animals

Opposite:

372   Kurds of Bijar
(4.49 × 0.83 m, 14′9″ × 2′9″)
Bijar is the weaving centre for many tribal groups who have intermixed, and this kilim could be attributed to the Shahsavan or to many other tribes from north-west Iran, although a certain colour and character defines it as being primarily Kurdish.

373   Kurds of Bijar
(3.27 × 1.44 m, 10′9″ × 4′9″)
The wool of this kilim is thickly and coarsely spun, dyed in the popular rose-pink colour derived from madder root and buttermilk. The human and animal representations on each side of the field are typical of Kurdish weavings from this region, and are said in the bazaars to represent bride and groom at their wedding, and their hopes of prosperity.

374   Kurds of Bijar
(4.26 × 1.21 m, 14′ × 4′)
The single central medallion has been elongated, to accommodate the long format of the rug, and filled with motifs typical of north-west Iran. The weaver has crenellated part of the inner guard border, and the pointed ends of the medallion, but along the sides she has changed to a most unusual design of small squares.

Details:

375   *Detail of 371.*

377   *Detail of 370.*

378   Saveh
This kilim has the same colouring and texture as 379, and most probably comes from the same village. Many of the small running designs can be found in weft-float flatweaves from north-east Iran, and north-west Afghanistan and Balouchistan. However, its light appearance places it in a category of its own.

376   Qazvin (right)
(4.26 × 1.06 m, 14′ × 3′6″)
This kilim, woven by semi-nomadic Rashwan Kurds from the Qazvin area to the north-west of Tehran, is full of powerful imagery. Its field is composed of bands of Turkic motifs separated by narrow bands of different reciprocal patterns. The centre of the field is filled with an unusual organic motif, the ends of which pierce the side borders. Note the two men depicted in traditional costume with their dogs.

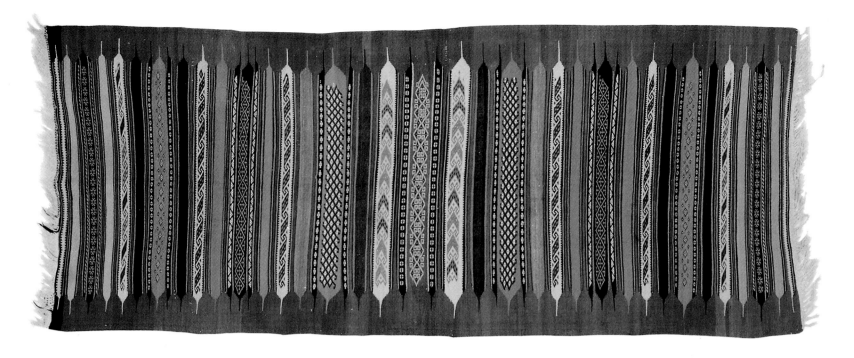

379 Saveh
(3.42 × 1.42 m, 11′3″ × 4′8″)
A remarkable piece that has the appearance of a saf *multiple prayer-arch kilim from Anatolia, although it originates from the area between Saveh and Qazvin, to the west of Tehran. Very heavily woven in a weft-floating technique, its thick cotton warps have the feel of Kurdish wool.*

Other Kurdish Groups of North-West Iran

Several Kurdish families living near the town of Qazvin are mainly Rashwan Kurds, thought to be the remnants of those that originally migrated from Turkey and Karabakh in the Caucasus to Khorassan. The Mafi group, closely related to the people of Kermanshah in south Kurdistan and north Luristan, are weavers of fine and distinctive weft-wrapped *khorjin* (donkey bags) embellished with a lattice pattern or a two-headed animal motif.

More Kurds live in the Elburz Mountains, the necklace of snow-covered peaks seen from the city of Tehran that forms a barrier to the Caspian Sea. Amongst these are the Khajavand Kurds of Kalardasht. The town of Akulisi, on the Caspian shore, has been renowned for its breeding of silk worms in mulberry groves. It is believed that Akulisi silk was transported to Senna in the seventeenth century for the production of the town's fine urban knotted carpets and kilims. Further north, a small group of Kurds dwell in the Talish Mountains close to the southern Caucasus, and Mahabad in southern Azerbaijan has long been a Kurdish centre and gathering point, as well as a marketplace for rugs and kilims. The Mahabad Kurds have close associations with the Kurds of Turkey and Iraq.

The Kurds of Khorassan

'Khorassan' means 'Land of the Rising Sun'. Its fertile valleys known as 'the Granary of Khorassan' are rich in crops and pasture, and large flocks of sheep and goats are raised here. The region also formed a gateway for the interchange of Persian and Turkic cultures, and here occurred the great revival of learning in the early Islamic era; the cities of Toos and Neisabur became centres of calligraphy, poetry, philosophy and science. Mashed, the ancient city of mosques and narrow, labyrinthine bazaar streets, is situated on the crossroads of caravan traffic on the Silk Route to China. The Kurds of Khorassan are derived from two tribal groups and now number some fifteen thousand people. One of the groups originally migrated from the Elazig district of central Anatolia and the other came from Karabakh. Both groups fled to Persia to escape persecution by the Ottoman

Turks in the sixteenth century. Some settled near Qazvin on the southern slopes of the Taleghan Mountains, and are the probable forefathers of the Rashwan Kurds who live there today. The remainder pressed on to Veramin on the edge of the vast Dasht-i-Kavir Desert, and were renamed the Chamishqazak.

In 1602 Shah Abbas moved this group again, to defend the north-eastern borders of Persia against the Uzbeks who were raiding his remote provinces from Central Asia. These Kurds are now divided into two confederations, the Shadlu and the Zafaranlu, that are then sub-divided into numerous tribes, all living semi-nomadic lives around the towns of Quchan, Shirvan, and Bujnurd to the north-west of the holy city of Mashed. Others live close to the border of West Turkestan, near Dareh Gaz and Kalat. Quchan is the main collecting point for their textiles and, as so often happens, has given its name to the many flatweaves of the semi-nomadic sub-tribes of the area and of the weavers in surrounding villages.

The Kurds of Khorassan weave in a wide and rich variety of designs, techniques and colours. It is possible to trace elements in their motifs back to their Caucasian and even their Anatolian ancestors. As many other tribal groups of quite different ethnic origins also live in this area – the Afshar of Kalat, the Turkomen and the Balouch, for instance – there is much inter-tribal copying of styles so that compositions, patterns and motifs become very mixed.

The flatweaves are usually weft-wrapped, and often loosely worked with colours that tend to be dark and perhaps a little dull, and the wool lacks the lustre and shine found in Kurdish weavings of north-west Iran. Many *soufreh* (eating cloths) are woven, and some are extremely long, having a soft natural brown plain field with black 'backgammon'-style fingers and finely woven weft-wrapped borders at each end. These *soufreh* are known as 'bridal path', a clear indication of their importance in the dowry and in the ceremony of the wedding feast. Many of the motifs are similar to those in Balouch weavings, although they are often more colourful and have a larger scale of pattern; they also bear a similarity to the kilims from Qala-i-Nau in north-west Afghanistan. The area is well known for its prolific production of bags, such as *maffrash* and the salt bags woven with the traditional Kurdish composition of a lattice jewelled with hooked lozenges.

Kurds of Khorassan	363, 380–1, 383
DESIGN	Field: Many different designs, relating to Caucasian motifs and those of neighbouring tribes
SIZE AND SHAPE	All sizes
MATERIALS	Wool warps, soft wool wefts
STRUCTURE	Weft-faced patterning, weft wrapping
COLOURS	Varied palette of dull and dark colours, with light brown, pale orange
FRINGE	All types
SELVEDGE	Usually plain/Parallel wrapping
Remarks	Bags, trappings and *soufreh* also woven

380 Kurds of Khorassan
(1.29 × 0.76 m, 4′ 3″ × 2′ 6″)
The Kurds of Khorassan weave many soufreh *or eating cloths such as this.*

382 Khorassan
(0.91 × 0.61 m, 3 × 2′)
This small chanteh *storage bag is beautifully woven in a floating weft technique that produces tight bands of patterning.*

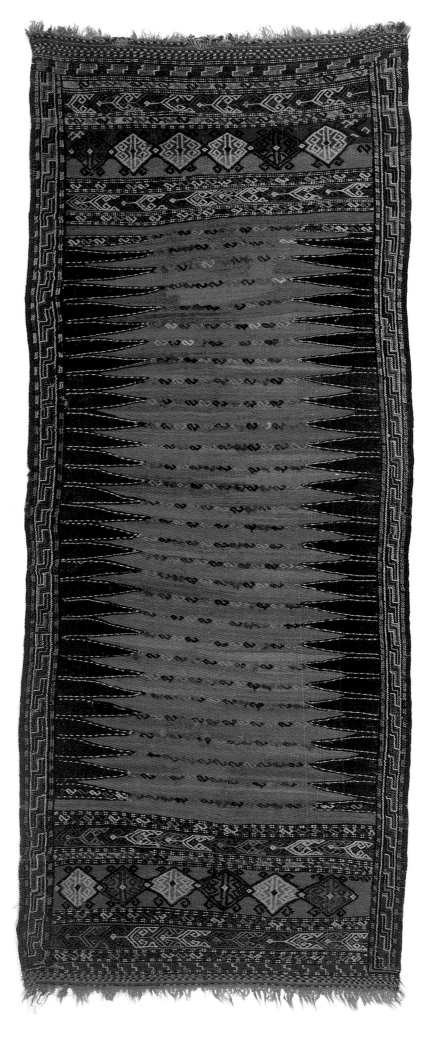

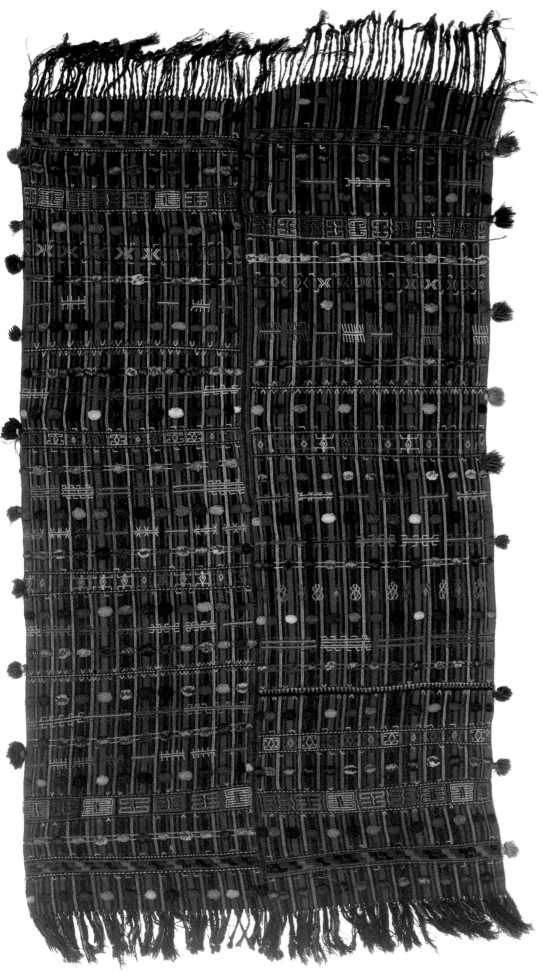

Opposite, right:

381   Kurds of Khorassan
(2.28 × 0.98 m, 7′6″ × 3′2″)
A long soufreh. On the traditional light brown field is an 'S' design in extra wefts. The dark 'fingers' are outlined with weft twining. The end panels are typically ornately patterned, and the narrow borders are weft-wrapped.

384   Kurds of Khorassan
An antique fragment of weaving that originated in north Iran, woven either by the Kurds of Khorassan or Balouch of Sistan. (Detail)

383   Kurds of Khorassan
(2.21 × 1.14 m, 7′3″ × 3′9″)
A cover from the Quchan/Bujnurd region north-west of Mashed. Woven in two pieces, this late nineteenth-century bedding cover is worked with extra weft patterning and supplementary wefts on a plainweave ground. Added ornaments are the long fringes and decorative tassels on the sides and in rows running right across.

The Shahsavan

The most famous confederation of north-west Iran are the Shahsavan, of whom the majority are a Turkic tribe. The remainder are of Kurdish, Tadjic and Georgian origin. 'Shahsavan' means 'those who are loyal to the shah' and the group was created by Shah Abbas to counter the powers of the Shi'a armies, the Kyzylbash: as the power of the Kyzylbash increased from shah to shah, there ensued an insidious spread of cupidity that eventually corrupted the entire political structure of the Safavid dynasty. Shah Abbas created a new volunteer army, loyal to himself, who, roused by the *Shahsavani* rallying call, successfully disbanded the Kyzylbash chiefs.

Many tribes from north-west Persia joined the Shahsavan, and non-Muslims such as Georgians, Circassians and Armenians were also employed; there was no cultural or tribal link at first, other than a common Turkic language. Tadjic peasants were then taken on as soldiers to create a balance between the Turkic and Farsi speakers. A large group of migrating tribes was also empowered to join and expand the newly formed confederate tribe; these nomads had been oppressed by the Ottoman sultans, but were now given land near Ardebil and incorporated in the Shahsavan group. Subsequently some migrated to Khorassan.

The Shahsavan's power declined with that of the Safavids, and its members soon reverted to tribal and nomadic conformations. Their tribal homeland in the Safavid period was Transcaucasia (the area of the Caucasus to the south of the main mountain range), a region attached to Persia that suffered the occasional incursions of Ottoman Turks. In the nineteenth century, however, the Transcaucasus was ceded to Russia and a border was established in 1884. Many Shahsavan tribal groups fled from the Russians and joined others further south, and so the Shahsavan were confined by this new international border to a small area to the south of the Arras River, and lost their traditional migratory route to their winter quarters in the Mogan plain to the north. The Shahsavan, depleted in numbers, became outlaws. Angered at the loss of two thirds of their territory, they attempted repeatedly to migrate back to the Mogan pastures. On one disastrous occasion the Russians ambushed the caravan, stripped all the nomads of their possessions and livestock and distributed them amongst local Persian government officials. This event is sacred in the history of the Shahsavan people, and all tribal events are placed historically before or after 'the distribution'. Reza Shah furthered the destruction of the Shahsavan and their nomadic way of life by banning all migration, forcing people to settle in villages and to wear Western clothes. After Reza Shah's abdication in 1941, the Shahsavan reverted to their pastoralist existence.

The various clans of the Shahsavan are now spread across north-west Iran. Some have settled amongst the Bakhtiari tribes, some in the Khamseh region of Fars, and others, who have totally integrated with the people of Khorassan, have been absorbed into groups as far east as Kashmir. The Shahsavan produce a large quantity of kilims, as these are their most common floor coverings. They are very traditional people, so their kilims are relatively limited in design and composition. Similar designs and compositions are used by all the Shahsavan groups, and yet there are subtle differences to be found mainly in the coloration, the weave and the finishing that distinguish the work of each sub-tribe.

385 Shahsavan
(3.20 × 1.24 m, 10'7" × 4')
This kilim is typical of the fine work of this semi-nomadic people. Horizontal bands contain Turkic motifs of eight-pointed stars, and the wool has a lustrous sheen.

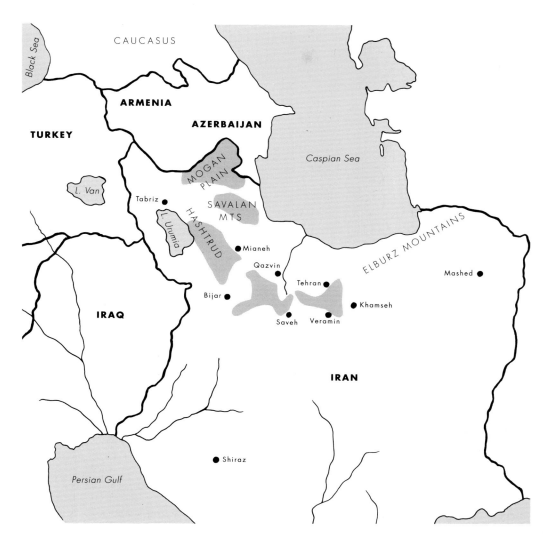

The Shahsavan

The compositions are commonly of large and striking motifs, running across the kilim in rows separated by narrow bands of finer patterning and more complicated weft-patterned weaving. The large motifs, up to four in each band, usually feature a star design. The star ranges from a simple symbol made up of eight pointed triangular shapes, dictated by the structure of the weave, to a more complex, but most characteristic crab shape of hooked lozenges, which is found in many Turkic weavings from Central Asia to Anatolia. This star can also be built up out of small triangles of different colours to make a diamond shape and sunburst, or the weave and colours crenellated to form a comb pattern. Between the bands of large motifs are contrasting rows of weft twining and narrow stripes of smaller star motifs, often simplified, or bands of motifs derived from the 'S' form. This 'S' form is either simplified from, or developed into, a much more complex dragon motif found on bags and *maffrash* in weft-wrapping technique.

The Shahsavan are prolific weavers of bags and *maffrash*, which are used as furniture in daily nomadic life. Such *maffrash* are woven by all Persian tribes except the Turkomen and Balouch from the eastern borders. Shahsavan bags are most frequently woven in a weft-wrapping technique with distinctive but complex animal, bird and flower motifs as well as the traditional star; alternatively they are sometimes constructed in slitweave and bear motifs similar to those found on the kilims. Their *khorjin*, or donkey bags, are invariably small, but very finely woven, constructed and finished. The Shahsavan also weave *namakdan* (salt bags).

386   Shahsavan or Azerbaijani
(3.18 × 1.74 m, 10'5" × 5'8")
This kilim may have been woven by the Shahsavan, or else have originated in the Shirvan area of Azerbaijan, for the banded format and the star motif contained within the hexagonal forms is typical of both. The diamond-shaped medallion with hooked arms is unusual, as is the one narrow band with a floral design. The other narrow bands feature a zig-zag pattern frequently found in Shirvan kilims.

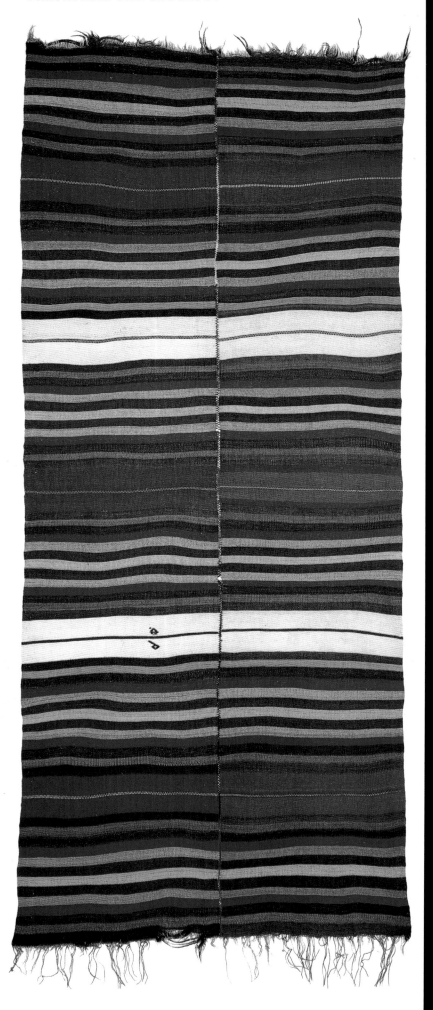

Opposite:

387 Shahsavan of Mogan
(3.20 × 1.21 m, 10′7″ × 4′)
This cover has been woven in two pieces and roughly sewn together. The plainweave is decorated by very narrow bands of weft float, in black and white or black and red wool. It is difficult to decipher the small weft-wrapped motif in black wool. It is neither a recognizable Persian numeral nor a letter of the alphabet.

388 Shahsavan of Bijar
(2.97 × 1.06 m, 9′9″ × 3′6″)
It is the weaver's artistry in the deployment of colour, reminiscent of the work of many twentieth-century painters, that is the predominant feature of this kilim, woven in weft-faced plainweave, with slitweave crenellations and zig-zags on the border. The black rectangle outlining one of the wide bands lifts the whole design and focuses attention on the rhythm of the different bands.

389 Shahsavan of Mianeh (left)
(1.37 × 1.06 m, 4′6″ × 3′6″)
The interlocking motifs of flame-like palmettes produce an unusual and powerful design. It has been attributed to the Shahsavan of Mianeh, despite the fact that this design can be found in Veramin. It is also an unusually small kilim for north-west Iran, and the border of barber-pole design in weft wrapping is certainly not typical.

390 Shahsavan of Veramin
A large diamond medallion made up from small stepped triangles. (Detail)

The Shahsavan use stripwoven *jajim* and panelled *verneh* on their floors as well as regular kilims. The *jajim* are made in the floating-warp technique practised in most Islamic countries, which produces lightweight weave used for covers. Narrow strips are sewn together to form the size and shape required for the *jajim's* intended function. The Shahsavan use *jajim* for bedding covers, blankets and in a square format as *rukorssi*. It is very difficult to determine where, within the different Shahsavan groups, particular *jajim* are woven.

Many *verneh* are large, and are used as rugs, backed by felt to make them more durable and softer under foot. Smaller examples are used as blankets, *soufreh*, *rukorssi* and horse blankets. Woven almost exclusively by the Shahsavan of Mogan, the *verneh* has a distinctive structure of extra-weft wrapping on plainweave, with a plain coloured ground that is usually woven in two or four strips.

The sub-tribes of the Shahsavan are identified regionally. The Persian textiles scholar Parvis Tanavoli, in his book devoted to the weavings of the Shahsavan, usefully categorizes its people into the following regional divisions: Mogan, Hashtrud, Mianeh, Khamseh, Bijar, Qazvin, Saveh and Veramin.

391 Shahsavan
The Shahsavan weave distinctive verneh *in extra weft wrapping on a plainweave ground, usually white. Small* verneh*, up to about 1.80 m (6′) square, are made from two or four panels sewn together, and used as* rukorssi, *or as horse or camel covers. Large pieces woven in four panels are backed with felt and put on the floor. (Detail)*

The Shahsavan of Mogan

This is the largest group of Shahsavan, for whom the Mogan plain is the original homeland and winter quarters (the *qeshlar*). In June, when the verdant pastures of the winter quarters dry up, the dry wind blows from the east and the temperature soars, they migrate about ninety miles from Mogan, close to the Caspian Sea, to the upper slopes of Mount Savalan. Despite the short distance, this is an important migration, as Mount Savalan is not only the summer quarters (the *yeilaq*), but also the repository of mystical and folkloric traditions. The Shahsavan hold the belief that the biblical city of Sodom was buried under the volcanic cone of Savalan. It is also said that Zoroaster was buried under a rock ledge next to a lake close to the summit, and that a few strands of the Prophet Mohammed's hair rest at the bottom of the lake. Another, less frequented summer pasture is found on the shores of Lake Neor in the Bagrow Mountains to the north of the Talish range. The Mogan plain provides ideal conditions for the Shahsavan pastoralists; however, the annexation of large tracts of their traditional territory by the Russians and enforced and repeated transmigration has encroached upon their lifestyle and depleted their numbers.

Mogan Shahsavan flatweaves are considered to be the most traditional of all kilims in design. There is both quality and harmony in the design, composition, colour and texture, successfully uniting practicality with decoration. Invariably woven in slitweave technique, the kilims are long and narrow, and made in two halves loosely sewn together. The colours are clear and bright, but limited in range, and undyed ivory-white or brown wool is used for the warps. The traditional bold horizontal bands of Turkic motifs are often bordered with a row of weft twining in one or two colours. These borders are narrow and bear the *laleh abrassi* design. Some kilims are composed of plainweave stripes of colour with no border.

Shahsavan of Mogan	387
DESIGN	Field: Wide horizontal bands of Turkic motifs, with narrow bands of geometric motifs between Borders: Narrow
SIZE AND SHAPE	Long and narrow
MATERIALS	Warps of natural brown wool, wefts of soft wool
STRUCTURE	Tight slitweave, rows of weft twining between bands
COLOURS	Dark crimson, green, brown, ivory white
FRINGE	Net/Plain/Sometimes backward diagonal plainweave
SELVEDGE	Plain/Extra cord wrapping
Remarks	Large Turkic star and spider motifs often distinguishing features

The Shahsavan of Hashtrud

These Shahsavan winter in and around the town of Hashtrud, and then migrate north in the summer to the slopes of the Sahand and Bosqush mountains. The majority of the Hashtrud Shahsavan migrated from Mogan in the eighteenth and nineteenth centuries and have become settled farmers. Hashtrud means 'eight rivers', a reference to the eight tributaries of the Qezel Owzan River, where fertile valleys and pastures are highly suitable for raising large flocks of sheep and goats. The coarse texture of the wool used in the warps and wefts and its loose weave help to distinguish Hashtrud kilims from those of other Shahsavan groups. The dyes used are paler; pastel shades of pink and green are particularly favoured, with only the occasional use of dark blue and brown. The finishes are usually simple. Their weaving has been much influenced by their Kurdish neighbours.

392　Shahsavan of Mogan
(2.05 × 1.01 m, 6'9" × 3'4")
A verneh cover. Its small rectangular format suggests that it was made as a horse cover, and the rows of horses decorating each end would seem to confirm this.

Shahsavan of Hashtrud　　　　394, 397

DESIGN	Field: Wide horizontal bands of Turkic motifs, with narrow bands of geometric motifs between Borders: Narrow
SIZE AND SHAPE	Long and narrow
MATERIALS	Warps of thick loose wool, wefts of coarse wool
STRUCTURE	Loose slitweave
COLOURS	Pastel colours, including pale pink and green, dark blue, brown
FRINGE	Simple/Knotted/Hemmed/Diagonal plainweave
SELVEDGE	Plain/Extra cord wrapping
Remarks	Weavings influenced by the Kurdish neighbours

Shahsavan of Mianeh　　　　389

DESIGN	Field: Shahsavan banded design/Large crenellated medallions Borders: Narrow
SIZE AND SHAPE	Large and rectangular
MATERIALS	Warps usually of wool, occasionally cotton, wefts of wool and cotton
STRUCTURE	Fine slitweave with weft-wrapped contour lines
COLOURS	Bright and clear cherry red, orange, yellow, light blue
FRINGE	All types
SELVEDGE	All types, often with parallel wrapping

The Shahsavan of Mianeh

Mianeh lies very close to Hashtrud, and although the Shahsavan of Mianeh moved to this district at the same time as the Shahsavan of Hashtrud, and are intermingled and share the same migratory path and pastures, there remain some differences in

393　Shahsavan
A Hashtrud kilim features a large central medallion and motifs scattered in the field.
(Detail of 397)

394 Shahsavan of Hashtrud
(3.20 × 1.95 m, 10′6″ × 6′3″)
The two large medallions contain a typical Turkic motif used by the Shahsavan. This is repeated as a loosely drawn line around each medallion.

395 Shahsavan of Khamseh
(2.20 × 0.55 m, 7′2″ × 1′10″)
A fragment from a striking kilim woven in the nineteenth century. There is an unusually wide palette of natural colours, the wool has a fine sheen and the traditional design is full of life and character.

their flatweaves. Mianeh Shahsavan kilims are both longer and wider than those from Hashtrud and the traditional banded design or large crenellated medallions are scattered with motifs. The warps are usually of wool, occasionally cotton, and undyed white cotton is evident in the field. Slitweave technique is used, with weft-wrapped contour lines in a contrasting colour to separate motifs from the field. Compared with weavings from the Mogan plain, a wider palette of colours is evident, including yellow, orange, cherry red, light blue and light brown. The finishes are good, often with parallel wrapping on the selvedge.

396, 398   Shahsavan
(1.27 × 1.14 m, 4′2″ × 3′9″)
*This small piece of very fine weave possibly came
from a large bag face, even though the ends are
not cut. It was woven in slitweave in two halves.
Although it has been attributed to the
Shahsavan weavers of north-west Iran, it may
originate in east Anatolia. (Detail 398)*

397   Shahsavan of Hashtrud (right)
(3.45 × 1.52 m, 11′4″ × 5′)
*The design of this kilim is similar to 394, and
is from the same area, even though the two small
figures woven into the field are more typical of
Bijar. The hook motif on the large medallions,
which is also used in a smaller scale on the
medallions down the sides of the field, can be
found on Turkish Kurd and other Anatolian
weavings. (Details 360, 393)*

399 Shahsavan of Bijar
(3.40 × 1.48 m, 11′2″ × 4′10″)
A minimal design in which the abrash *plays an important part. The field is outlined by a border of natural white and black wool. This kilim was woven near Bijar by semi-nomadic Shahsavan people.*

The Shahsavan of Bijar

This group of Shahsavan separated from the Mogan in the eighteenth century and settled as farmers in villages between Zanjan and Qazvin, and in an area close to Bijar and to the north of Hamadan. They are very active weavers of kilims, covers and bags in a large variety of forms, colours and designs. Within the area of Bijar live many tribal groups, the majority of whom are Kurds. There has been much cross-cultural influence between the groups, but the Shashavan retain their individuality by holding on to their original Turkish language. Many of the features found in Bijar Shahsavan kilims come from other areas, so it is often very difficult to be precise about their origins. Wool and cotton warps are used with slitweave technique, although there are a number of kilims decorated with rows of weft-faced patterning and ornamental rows of weft twining.

Shahsavan of Bijar	388, 399
DESIGN	Field: Very similar to Mogan kilims
SIZE AND SHAPE	Usually long and narrow
MATERIALS	Wool/Occasionally cotton warps
STRUCTURE	Slitweave/Occasionally weft-faced patterning with weft twining
COLOURS	Bright and clear orange, yellow, light brown, blue, pink
FRINGE	All types
SELVEDGE	Usually plain

Shahsavan of Khamseh	395
DESIGN	Field: Very similar to Mogan kilims
SIZE AND SHAPE	Usually long and narrow
MATERIALS	Coarse wool, tightly woven/Occasionally cotton warps
STRUCTURE	Fine slitweave/Occasionally dovetail
COLOURS	Darker and duller than other Shahsavan kilims, including dark brown, blue, dull red
FRINGE	All types
SELVEDGE	Usually plain

400 Shahsavan of Saveh
(3.00 × 1.05 m, 9′10″ × 3′5″)
Horizontal bands of Turkic motifs are typical of many Shahsavan kilims. The motifs have been outlined in white wool, lightening the appearance of the whole rug.

The Shahsavan of Khamseh

Not to be confused with the Khamsa tribe in the province of Fars, Khamseh (meaning 'five') is a region that encompasses the five former districts of Zanjan, each named after one of the five rivers of the region. Most of the people are settled in villages, but some families do migrate in the summer to the upper tributaries of the Qezel Owzan River. Intermingling with close neighbouring tribes has diluted the original Shahsavan group and has made identifying their flatweaves difficult. The most important tribe in the area, the Afshar, moved to near the town of Zanjan in the eighteenth century. Believed to be descendants of Azerbaijani Afshar, they are known as Afshar Shahsavan. Their kilims are generally fine, and tightly woven in slitweave and dovetail technique. Colours are dull and dark, blue, dull red and dark brown being popular.

The Shahsavan of Qazvin

Many of the people who occupied this area, originally known as Khalajestan, became devotees of Shah Abbas and joined the Shahsavan group during the Safavid era, with others following later. Now there is only a very small group of Shahsavan people in this area who have remained aloof from the influence of the Kurds and the other groups who have settled around Qazvin. This is a prolific kilim-weaving area and little differentiates Shahsavan work from other types. There is, however, a small group of flatweaves that are distinctive in that although they are similar in structure and design to Khamseh kilims, they have a more obvious use of turmeric yellow in their colouring.

401 Qazvin
(3.81×1.14 m, $12'6'' \times 3'9''$)
The field design of this kilim is made up of diamonds of random colours. The end border of reciprocal wave pattern returns down the side borders in an unusual ram's-horn pattern, more commonly found on Anatolian kilims.

Shahsavan of Qazvin	401
DESIGN	Field: Widely influenced by other tribes/Some designs similar to Mogan and Khamseh
SIZE AND SHAPE	Long and narrow
MATERIALS	Wool warps, coarse wool wefts/Occasionally cotton warps
STRUCTURE	Fine slitweave, dovetail
COLOURS	Usually dull, apart from a distinctive turmeric yellow
FRINGE	All types
SELVEDGE	Usually plain

Shahsavan of Saveh	352, 400, 404
DESIGN	Field: Very widely influenced by other tribes
SIZE AND SHAPE	Long and narrow
MATERIALS	Cotton warps, coarse wool wefts
STRUCTURE	Coarse and stiff slitweave, dovetail
COLOURS	Limited and rather dull
FRINGE	Backward diagonal plainweave/Knotted into groups
SELVEDGE	Extra cord reinforcement

402 *Detail of 404.*

403   Shahsavan of Veramin
The fine and lustrous wool, type of weave and palette of colours all indicate that this kilim was woven by Shahsavan people in Veramin. The weaver has scattered diamond motifs over the field, exaggerating some with white wool. (Detail)

404   Shahsavan of Saveh
(2.95 × 1.37 m, 9′8″ × 4′6″)
A nomadic kilim woven in the region of Saveh. The five medallions are each composed of different combinations of seven colours, and some are outlined in a contrasting colour to add depth and create the effect of shadow. The motif in the centre of each medallion, two triangles touching points, is reflected along the ends. The small stick-figure in the corner is waving or pointing. (Detail 402)

The Shahsavan of Saveh

The group of Shahsavan who live close to the town of Saveh and the Kharaqan Mountains still maintains a closely knit tribal and semi-tribal lifestyle. Some of the original Shahsavan people migrated to Baghdad at the end of the Safavid era, but were brought back during the eighteenth century by Nadir Shah and housed in Shiraz; they were subsequently relocated close to Saveh in 1792. Shahsavan weavings from this area have retained many of their distinctive design characteristics. Cotton warps are commonly used and both slitweave and dovetail techniques produce a stiff and coarse texture. The work is well finished, but the colours are dull.

The Shahsavan of Veramin

Veramin is one of the leading centres of flatweaving in Iran, producing a wide variety of textiles. Various tribal groups, including the Shahsavan, Afshar, Lurs and Kurds, live in the area, and there is an obvious overlapping of styles, especially between the Turkish-speaking Afshar and the Shahsavan. Because of these disparate influences a wide range of diverse compositions is woven by the Veramin Shahsavan in addition to their 'traditional' banded and diagonal compositions. Weaving techniques, in addition to slitweave and dovetailing, include weft-faced patterning, to create rows of decorative rosettes or 'S' patterns typical of the local Afshar and Kurdish kilims. The kilims are more rectangular in format than many of the other weaves from north-west Iran, and are well finished, often with a distinctive fringe knotted into groups of four.

Shahsavan of Veramin	403
DESIGN	Field: Varied/Traditional north-west Persian banded design
SIZE AND SHAPE	Rectangular
MATERIALS	Wool/Occasionally cotton warps
STRUCTURE	Fine slitweave, dovetail, rows of weft-faced patterning, weft twining, wide end panels of plainweave
COLOURS	Varied range
FRINGE	Knotted into groups of four
SELVEDGE	Extra cord reinforcement

The Lurs

The modern-day Lurs are heirs to an extremely ancient culture, which produced the famous Luristan bronzes of the sixth and fifth centuries BC. They are one of the few ethnic groups to have lived in their native land of Iran for at least three thousand years, and so can be called, along with the Kurds, one of the original Iranian people. The Luri tribes are widely dispersed, from the Iran–Iraq border and the town of Kermanshah in north Luristan and south Kurdistan, across the Zagros Mountains, to the Gulf plateau near Shiraz. The more southerly Lurs include the sub-tribes of the Mamasanni and Boyer Ahmadi.

Very little is known about the history of the Luri tribes apart from the fact that a very strong and artistic culture must have existed at the time of the manufacture of the Luristan bronzes. With the exception of the Bakhtiari, a sub-tribe of the Lurs, they have kept a low profile, pursuing a traditional lifestyle as nomads and pastoralist farmers, migrating annually, having little involvement in power and politics, and inhabiting what has been, until very recently, a remote and undiscovered part of Asia. The rugged terrain of stark rocky mountains that characterizes the area has served over the centuries to keep armies and inquisitive tax collectors at bay.

During the nineteenth century the Luri population was quite considerable, totalling about half a million people. The independence of Luristan has been steadily eroded for the last two hundred years, although it managed to remain an autonomous region well into the twentieth century. It was their neighbours, the Qashqai, who undermined much of Luri power, landownership and collection of taxes in the eighteenth and nineteenth centuries, and now in the twentieth century the increase in the wealth of the surrounding peoples, the discovery of oil and enhanced efficiency in communication and transport systems are doing much to damage the traditional and almost secretive ways of the Luri people, including the sub-tribes of Luristan and the Boyer Ahmadi in the province of Fars. Their

405 Lurs
(2.43 × 1.21 m, 8' × 4')
The sub-tribe of Boyer Ahmadi from north Fars province weave kilims with a large rhomboid design on a plain field. The weaver of this kilim has, by accident or by design, increased the size of the rhomboids as her work progressed. She has designed the first two corners of the border skilfully and successfully, but has been unable to repeat this in the final corners.

406 Lurs
(3.04 × 1.14 m, 10' × 3'9")
Here are curious contrasts of colour, pattern and scale. The simple red central field, with the small white cross at one end as a talisman and small black zig-zag fingers pointing inwards, could be compared with an eating cloth, or soufreh. The motif in the white inside border has obvious connections with ancient Luri/ Bakhtiari symbolism. There is then a dramatic change in scale with large interlocking triangles of colour, contrasting with a fine reciprocal laleh abrassi border.

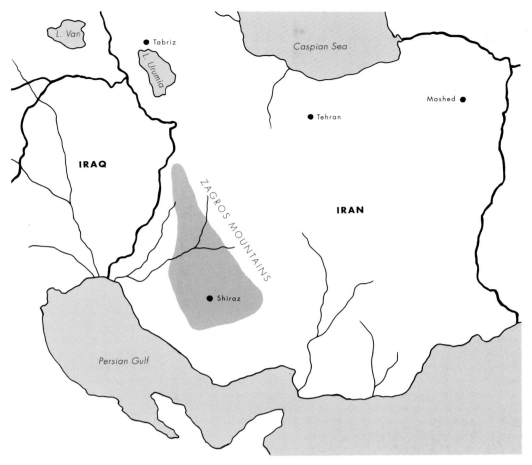

The Lurs

Opposite:

407 Lurs
(2.79 × 1.29 m, 9′2″ × 4′3″)
This panel design is said by some to have been derived from Persian knotted-pile carpet patterning of the eighteenth century, which represented gardens or fields. It is also thought to represent the box in which the holy Koran is kept, and the so-called 'comb design', seen here on the sides of each square, is supposed to have totemistic value as an image of cleanliness before daily prayers. It is difficult to imagine the weaver considering any of this proposed symbology when creating this abstract and naive work of art.

408 Lurs
(1.52 × 1.11 m, 5′ × 3′8″)
The freedom with which this kilim is drawn is remarkable. The zig-zag lines of colour in crenellated slitweave leave large triangles of plainweave next to each border. The simple small triangle pattern on the side and end borders and the rather sombre colours point to Luri origin, although the vitality of the design closely resembles Qashqai work.

409 Lurs
(2.66 × 1.44 m, 8′9″ × 4′9″)
There are certain kilims that are difficult to attribute to one tribe; it is particularly hard to differentiate between Qashqai and Luri work (see 354). The wool in this kilim is relatively coarse, and lacks the sheen and lustre found in the finer variety used by the Qashqai. The colours are duller, with greater use of pale yellow and brown. The warps are of brown wool, finished with horse or goat hair at the fringes, whereas the Qashqai invariably use white cotton warps. The outside border is similar to that of 354, but simplified, lacking the small coloured square in the laleh abrassi *side-border motif.*

independence finally ended with Reza Shah's enforced settlement programme in the 1930s.

Until very recently the weavings of the Luri tribes have been mistaken for the work of other peoples from the southern regions. Only in the last two decades has it been realized that many of the kilims attributed to the Qashqai were in fact Luri, and the belief that the Lurs were merely unimportant copyists of the flamboyant Qashqai weavers has had to be reversed. In fact, the Lurs probably had a major influence on Qashqai designs, for the Luri tradition of weaving is believed to stretch far back into history.

Lurs	405, 407–9
DESIGN	Field: Complex patterns/Medallions Borders: Simple and traditional
SIZE AND SHAPE	Rectangular
MATERIALS	Coarse brown wool warps, wool wefts
STRUCTURE	Slitweave
COLOURS	Dull and limited palette
FRINGE	Plain
SELVEDGE	Plain/Occasional extra-weft reinforcement
Remarks	Similar, but less colourful and ornate than Qashqai

410 Bakhtiari of Chahar Mahal
(1.14 × 0.91 m, 3'9" × 3')
This is half of a double storage bag, similar to
568. The face is finely worked in weft-wrapping
technique. The centre of this piece, which would
have been the fold at the bottom of the completed
bag, is heavily reinforced against wear and
abrasion with thick knotted-pile work. The
back of the bag is plainwoven in stripes with a
square panel of weft wrapping reflecting the
designs on the front. This feature is typical of
these bags.

Opposite, above:

411 Bakhtiari of Chahar Mahal
(2.29 × 1.21 m, 7'6" × 4')
The coarse wool, loose but heavy weave and
irregular finish suggest a rug of nomadic origin.
The double-interlock technique generally produces
unsatisfactory results, leaving an indistinct
outline around the intricate motifs and images
scattered on the field. The colours, design and
weave are typical of Bakhtiari people, but the
inclusion of human and domestic animal figures
is more common in Kurdish weavings.

412 Bakhtiari of Shushtar
(2.36 × 1.27 m, 7'9" × 4'2")
The colouring of this kilim is characteristically
Bakhtiari, and also indicative of their Luri
origins; the golden yellow and rich red are
favourites of the Bakhtiari.

A large group of most individual flatweaves and pile carpets is now attributed to the Lurs. Their designs are quite different from those of the Turkic tribes, and indeed any other Persian kilim. Scholars have suggested that their compositions were originally spawned from the culture and design work that produced the famous Luristan bronzes. However, as Luri and Qashqai kilims are often confused, it is as well to be fully aware of their differences. The wool of Luri work is much coarser in texture, more loosely spun and thicker in feel, and brown wool is used for warps (the Qashqai usually use white cotton). The colours are much duller and more limited in range than the wide palette of the Qashqai. The compositions of the Luri rugs, although indeed similar and the reason for much of the confusion and wrongful attribution, are less complex in form. The field is bold and uncluttered, with areas outside the main patterning left unadorned, and it has far simpler borders. The Luri *laleh abrassi* border is seldom woven in more than two colours, usually missing the small coloured square in each 'tulip' and the multiple zig-zag borders used by the Qashqai.

Those kilims woven by the Boyer Ahmadi tribe from around the town of Behbehan in northern Fars frequently have large rhomboid medallions in their field without any further elaboration or addition of small motifs in the area around them. The finishes are simpler, of long plainweave ends with an unsophisticated fringe. The selvedges are plain or simply reinforced with extra wefts, although sometimes they have distinctive coloured bunches of wool sewn into them.

The Bakhtiari

The Bakhtiari live in an area that until recently had no roads or modern means of communication. They weave a surprising variety of different and original designs, which have a definite identity and an unusual purity. Of late, however, it has become difficult to distinguish between some Luri and Bakhtiari work, owing to the proximity of the tribes and intermarriage. The Bakhtiari are a sub-tribe of the Lurs; the two have been linked throughout history, and family trees cross and recross many times since the fourteenth century. Much of their history is vague, however, and was possibly invented for political reasons. As with the Luri work, the Bakhtiari flatweaves have remained largely unrecognized or mistaken for other types. The Bakhtiari have no history of commercial textile production, weaving cloth only for domestic use, so their flatweaves are very functional, and are used as floor coverings, for storage and for transportation. Most kilims and the bags they make for carrying produce and possessions are in daily use, until they wear out and are replaced. Fine and prized examples are kept within the family, stored and used only on special occasions. Only in the past decade or so have the flatweaves of the Bakhtiari been sold in any quantity, in the bazaars of Isfahan, Shiraz, Shushtar and Tehran.

The ancestry of the present-day Bakhtiari tribes is confused and difficult to trace – they are supposed to be one of thirty tribal groups that migrated from Syria to Persia in the fourteenth century. A romantic folk tale set in the time of Shah Abbas tells of a certain Haydur Kur, the son of a Papi Lur khan, who left home after a family quarrel and became a shepherd to a khan of the Duraki (one of the regional groups of the Bakhtiari). The shepherd's lineage was, in time, exposed, and in true fairytale fashion he married one of the khan's daughters, and eventually became

413 Bakhtiari of Chahar Mahal
(1.67 × 1.06 m, 5'6" × 3'6")
Although the status and power of the Bakhtiari have changed over the years, they are still a wealthy group who keep close cultural ties with their ancestral past. This small and distinctive late nineteenth-century kilim has obvious tribal and nomadic origins.

leader of the Duraki. This story is typical of those related for political gain, and was probably invented during the nineteenth century to help the Duraki khans become the dominant force within a united Bakhtiari tribe.

The Bakhtiari probably evolved into a named tribe during the Safavid period, when the title 'Bakhtiari' was used to describe a region of administration within Luristan that later became the province of Isfahan, a large area straddling the Zagros Mountains. The wealthy khans of the area established themselves as landowners in the Chahar Mahal valley, between the Zagros range and Isfahan. A tribal grouping was therefore formed by political manoeuvring to acquire land and gather taxes, later assuming the name 'Bakhtiari' itself. The Bakhtiari khans grew in strength during the instability at the end of the Safavid dynasty, and the complex social and political structure of the tribe developed at this time into a pyramidal form of command capped by the Haft Lang and the Chahar Lang moieties. These titles were most probably derived from the form of tax paid by all the tribal confederations. The Bakhtiari paid in mules, the Qashqai in sheep and the Shahsavan in camels. *Haft lang* means 'seven legs', *chahar lang* 'four legs', and so out of every three mules given as tax, one and three-quarter animals (seven legs) was paid by the Haft Lang, one animal (four legs) by the Chahar Lang, and the remaining one leg by families in sub-groups not attached to either moiety. As with other tribal groups, internal disputes and fighting resulted inevitably in enforced migration, and ten thousand Bakhtiari families were forced to Khorassan during Nadir Shah's reign. The majority returned two or three years later, after his assassination.

During the nineteenth century, the Bakhtiari, along with other tribal groups – the Qashqai, Shahsavan and Kurds of Khorassan – were formed into a tribal confederation, and the power of the Bakhtiari people, and in particular their khans, waxed and waned over the years. Many of the tribespeople left their tents and settled in villages, occasionally making the long annual trek across the Zagros Mountains more as a spiritual pilgrimage than a pastoralist migration. When oil was discovered at the beginning of the twentieth century, enormous wealth and international power came to the landowners around Shushtar, the centre of the winter grazing. Reza Shah tried to repress the Bakhtiari, and yet their pattern of migration continues to this day; from their winter quarters on the fertile plains of Khuzestan and Luristan and around Dezful, Gatuard and Shushtar, they cross the Zagros Mountains to the Chahar Mahal valley. The remote valleys of the Zagros are speckled in the summer months with the triangular black tents of the Bakhtiari. It is inevitable, however, that as the onset of modern development reaches outlying villages, bringing with it clinics and schools, increasing numbers of nomads will settle into new agrarian developments.

Shiraz, the main bazaar and market town of the south-western region, has for a long time given its name to the pile rugs and flatweaves of the area; kilims have only been attributed specifically to particular tribes since about 1960, and even more recently to particular regions within the tribal areas. The main feature of Bakhtiari kilims is their weave: double-interlock technique is used, often throughout, a peculiarity of the Bakhtiari shared by few other flatweavers save the Uzbek Tartari of Afghanistan. The double-interlock technique creates very crisp divisions of colour and composition, and results in a strong, solid weave, without slits, that is not reversible. There is still very little known about the nomadic tribal

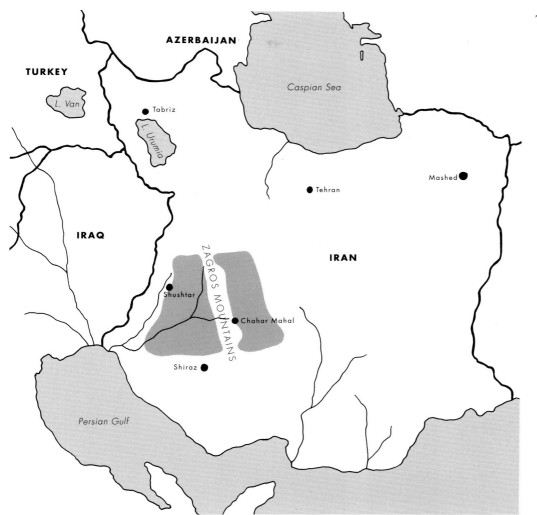

The Bakhtiari

rugs of the Bakhtiari, and many urban kilims have been incorrectly attributed to the nomadic people, usually those that have been poorly constructed and designed – such defects are excused by dealers as a byproduct of weaving whilst on the move. In fact, many nomadic 'Bakhtiari' kilims have great appeal, displaying an individual flair in design and inevitable amusing idiosyncrasies in the weave.

There are some kilims of unknown origin within the Bakhtiari tribes that have come on to the market quite recently. They are constructed using weft-wrapped work of coarsely spun wool throughout, with a distinctive border of arrow designs beset with a muddle of motifs and other designs in an invariably rose-red field, many apparently copied from pile rugs or weft-wrapped bags.

The Bakhtiari are renowned for their elaborate bags, such as their *khorjin* and salt bags. Essential items for the storage and transportation of household articles, bedding and clothing, bags are very finely woven in weft-wrapping technique, and bear motifs depicting what are perhaps the original and unsullied designs of the ancient Persians, akin to the animal heads seen on the Luristan bronzes.

Despite the confusion surrounding 'new' and wrongly attributed rugs, within the Bakhtiari group there is a distinct difference between the compositions woven in the region around the winter quarter market town of Shushtar and those from the valleys around the summer pastures of the Chahar Mahal.

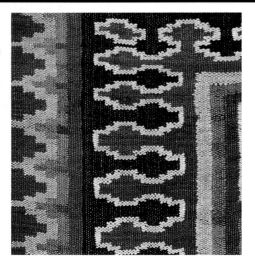

The Bakhtiari of Shushtar

The Shushtar kilims are quite different in composition to all other Persian kilims. Covering the field is either a series of medallions of varying sizes, or an all-over rhomboid pattern enclosed in a number of borders of different widths with a pattern of unusually complex geometric shapes pointing inwards. Outside these borders is an area of monochrome plainweave. Such a disposition gives the impression that the central design is floating on a plain backdrop, in a similar manner to an illuminated page from a Persian Islamic manuscript.

The warps of the Shushtar flatweaves are brown wool or camel hair, the wefts wool, camel hair or cotton, usually left undyed to emphasize the patterning but (and this is peculiar to Shushtar) sometimes dyed light blue. The weave is very dense and stiff, almost board-like, the wool is poor in quality, brittle and lacking the lustre frequently found in Qashqai kilims. The colours, as with those found on

Luri tribal weavings, are rather dull. Shushtar kilims are finished with a simple cut fringe and selvedges decorated with extra cord wrapping in barber-pole design.

Bakhtiari of Shushtar   412, 414–15

DESIGN	Field: Medallions/Rhomboids Borders: Complex and geometric, with outer border of plain-coloured weave
SIZE AND SHAPE	Long and rectangular
MATERIALS	Coarse wool warps, wool wefts/Occasionally cotton warps/Camel hair
STRUCTURE	Very stiff and hard double interlock
COLOURS	Limited and dull, including camel-hair brown, white, blue, deep rose red, yellow
FRINGE	Plain
SELVEDGE	Extra cord reinforcement in barber-pole design
Remarks	Many bags woven in weft-wrapping technique

The Bakhtiari of Chahar Mahal

The kilims of the Chahar Mahal valley have conventional borders showing a random series of wide and narrow patterned bands around a field of numerous different geometric motifs. The use of double-interlock technique makes it possible to weave in straight vertical lines. This technique is found in all Bakhtiari kilims, both in small ornamentations in the field and in the long edges of the borders. The texture of the weave is hard, similar to that of Shushtar kilims. Other features include end panels of plainweave with narrow bands of floating weft-patterning, and selvedges ornamented with coarse wool extra-weft reinforcement, often in two colours, to give a barber-pole effect.

Bakhtiari of Chahar Mahal   345, 411, 413, 417

DESIGN	Field: Numerous geometric motifs Borders: Small-scale motifs
SIZE AND SHAPE	Long and rectangular
MATERIALS	Coarse wool warps, wool wefts
STRUCTURE	Double interlock
COLOURS	Deep red, yellow, blue, white, brown
FRINGE	Plain
SELVEDGE	Extra cord reinforcement in barber-pole design
Remarks	Some bags and trappings

Opposite:

414   Bakhtiari of Shushtar
(1.96 × 1.21 m, 6′5″ × 4′)
By using double-interlock technique, the weaver has been able to draw long vertical lines in the pattern and change the colour without leaving a slit or needing to step the design. This technique, although uncommon in Iran generally, is used extensively by the Bakhtiari, and can thus be an obvious guide to the origin of a rug. Double interlock does, however, blur the edge of the patterning. This design is typical of Shushtar, but it is unusual to find such a large area of unadorned white.

415, 416   Bakhtiari of Shushtar
(1.82 × 1.11 m, 6′ × 3′8″)
This kilim displays many of the distinguishing characteristics of Shushtar designs. The whole composition, including the outer borders, seems to be floating on a field of unicolour plainweave in a manner similar to an illuminated page in an Islamic manuscript. (Detail 416)

417   Bakhtiari of Chahar Mahal
(2.44 × 1.22 m, 8′ × 4′)
A Bakhtiari kilim of an unusual design that was bought in Shiraz shortly after Iran opened up after twelve years of internal and external conflict.

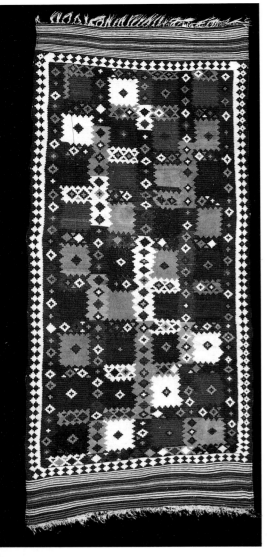

418 Qashqai
(2.94 × 1.44 m, 9′8″ × 4′9″)
The design of this kilim does not satisfy the eye in the way most Qashqai flatweaves do. There is a lack of organization in the patterning and the vertical and horizontal bands do not satisfactorily contain the rectangles.

Qashqai

418–23

DESIGN	Field: Geometric medallions and scattered motifs on square grid pattern/Horizontal bands of motifs Borders: Ornate and geometric
SIZE AND SHAPE	Rectangular
MATERIALS	Brown wool warps, fine wool wefts/Cotton warps
STRUCTURE	Slitweave
COLOURS	Strong, vibrant and varied palette
FRINGE	Knotted/Plaited
SELVEDGE	Usually extra cord reinforcement
Remarks	Many bags and trappings also woven

The Qashqai

As ever, there has been a lot of confusion over the tribal rugs of southern Iran, and in the nineteenth and early twentieth centuries most rugs from the region were called 'Shiraz', a favourite generic description amongst both Western and Persian dealers. The name derives from the principal town in the area, which was renowned for its weaving in the seventeenth and eighteenth centuries. Little work has been done there since then, however, until very recently, when a number of government-sponsored workshops were set up. A short time ago the rugs were given the new name of 'Fars' (or sometimes, even more generally, 'South-West Persia'), by traders and dealers, which conveniently encompasses many tribal groups, both sedentary and nomadic. Obviously, many of the rugs' original names and identities have been lost through this wide grouping.

Of all the southern tribes, the Qashqai have become most renowned for their colourful qualities of leadership; indeed, their history connects them with the most notorious ruler of Asia, Genghis Khan. The Qashqai regard their original homeland as Kashgar, in the remote corner of Central Asia close to China, and believe that they came westwards and south with Genghis Khan. It is most likely, however, that their name is derived from a pre-eminent tribal leader of the Safavid era, Jani Agha Qashqai, who was given authority over the tribes of the Fars region of southern Persia by Shah Abbas. The Qashqai are also possibly linked with the Khalaj or Qalach. The Khalaj were remnants of the Hephthalites, the White Huns, who in the fifth century threatened the north-eastern frontiers of the Persian Empire and founded the Khalaj Empire in northern India. The Khalaj were close allies of the Oghuz, ancestors of the Oghuz Turks, later the Turkomen, and were one of the first tribes to cross the Amu Darya (Oxus) River into the steppe bordered by the Hindu Kush. From these Afghan Khalaj were descended the Khalaj sultans of Delhi and the Ghilzai Afghans of Kandahar, who overthrew the Safavid dynasty in 1722. The migration of these people took place in several waves – none of which pre-dated the fourteenth century. Whatever the true origin of the Qashqai may be, it remains undisputed that some are descendants of the

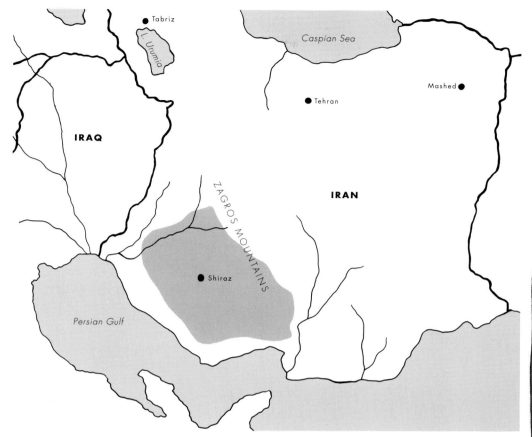

The Qashqai

Turkomen who invaded Azerbaijan in the early eleventh century, and it is clear that parts of their language are closely related to Azerbaijani Turkish.

Like so many of the tribes of Persia, such as the Bakhtiari and the Lurs, the Qashqai were forced to settle and prevented from undertaking their traditional migration by Reza Shah, and this misguided enforcement and attempt to 'Westernize' these nomadic people did untold damage to their cultures. The Darreshuri sub-tribe of the Qashqai confederation, famous throughout Asia as horse breeders, lost nearly all of their thousands of horses when forced, by the ban on migration, to winter in the cold mountains.

The rich and varied stories of the Qashqai's origin are most fitting to their tribal standing. They are probably the most famous and the wealthiest of all Persian tribes. The women are dominating and open, untrammelled by Islamic purdah. They stride forth in bright and full lurex-decorated skirts and colourful shawls, decked in jewelry. The migration of the Qashqai nomads is perhaps the most famous of all, and undoubtedly the longest, stretching about three hundred miles from their winter quarters (garmsir) near the Persian Gulf to the cooler summer pastures (sarhad) of the southern Zagros Mountains. The spring and autumn journeys are highly organized, taking traditional routes (il rah) with prearranged pastures for feeding their stock. Along the migration routes there are also, as often found in Asia, specific centres and villages where special items are made, manufactured, sold and bought. Up to twenty thousand Qashqai families take these byways to the hills each year. Their train includes all their animals – the cows, camels, horses, donkeys, hens and dogs, as well as their main source of wealth, sheep and goats. The towns in their summer quarters, Kazerun and Firuzabad (the traditional Qashqai summer capital), provide most of the nomads'

419   Qashqai
(3.12 × 1.44 m, 10'3" × 4'9")
Compare the design of this kilim with 487 and 495 woven by Ersari Turkoman people in Labijar, north Afghanistan, and 407, of Luri origin. There are similarities here that cannot be ignored and must relate to the common ancient Turkic ancestry of these two tribes. The exact origin of this rug could be either Qashqai or a close neighbouring Luri tribe, possibly the Doshman Ziari. It is a beautifully made kilim; the zig-zag borders are evenly drawn around all four sides, and the white motifs on the horizontal and vertical bands meet with precision.

420 Qashqai
(2.28 × 1.21 m, 7′6″ × 4′)
The weaver of this kilim has clearly taken pleasure in the interplay of shapes and lines, and has added extra visual amusement with the zigzag row of little cross motifs, on the right.

421 Qashqai
(2.43 × 1.21 m, 8′ × 4′)
Horizontal bands of motifs are divided by a reciprocal and interlocking wave pattern. These motifs also appear on many Turkic flatweaves, and betray the Qashqai's ethnic origins. The two traditional borders, found on most Qashqai kilims, are set elegantly side by side. Weavers always seem to have difficulty in returning the borders at the top and bottom corners, often introducing idiosyncrasies into the design at these points.

requirements. Tobacco, tea, sugar, clothing, utensils are all bartered for with carpets, kilims, and wool; only very rarely, when times are very hard, do they sell any of their livestock. In their winter quarters, the towns of Ababeh and Shahreza serve the same purpose.

Most of the time it is impossible to distinguish the nomads from the rest of the Qashqai population, and in both the summer and winter quarters there are village agriculturalists of Qashqai, Luri and Arab origins who own land and farm cereals. There are also many sedentary Qashqai farmers, and some of the nomads own land and will hire a farmer to maintain it at the times of migration.

The Qashqai women do all the spinning, dyeing and weaving, and as they have a high standing in the family, they exert a strong influence in the home, and even in tribal political decisions. Women form the central core of the Qashqai culture, have command over tribal identity, marriage ties, customs and aesthetics. Within a system where the activities of women have been traditionally suppressed, evidence of their undoubted artistic gifts is manifested in their kilim-making skills: the freedom and commanding presence of the women is reflected in the boldness and energy of their work.

Little weaving is done on the migratory journey, and the time of greatest weaving activity is in the summer months, in the cool higher altitudes of the southern Zagros Mountains. The Qashqai weave with the strong, glossy, long-stapled wool of the fat-tailed sheep, a breed that is very well suited to travelling long distances with the migratory caravan. Unusually, they shear their sheep only once a year, in May and June, after the animals have arrived at the summer pastures and have been washed in the rivers.

Qashqai kilims are perhaps the best known of all Persian flatweaves, for there is a freedom and boldness in the way the pattern is drawn that is not found elsewhere. Very often their use of small motifs betray the Turkic origins of the tribe, and certain similarities to Shahsavan kilims are noticeable, but at times their

422   Qashqai
(2.59 × 1.40 m, 8'6" × 4'7")
The drama of this design is suppressed to some extent by its drabness and limited range of colour. This is unusual for Qashqai weavers, who enjoy using a vibrant, clear and varied palette.

423   Qashqai
(2.43 × 1.21 m, 8' × 4')
Green is an uncommon colour for kilims further east than Anatolia. It is a difficult colour to achieve with any clarity. This particular green was probably derived by over-dyeing a yellow with a light indigo blue. This beautifully finished kilim is woven by the Amaleh sub-tribe.

219

424 Qashqai
(2.51 × 1.60 m, 8′3″ × 5′3″)
The wefts of this kilim are of finely spun wool shorn from the fat-tailed sheep kept by the Qashqai nomads. It is a breed that is well suited to travelling long distances with the migratory caravan. The warps are of quite coarsely spun white cotton, which shows through in places as the weft has not been heavily beaten down. The fringes have been plaited into a flat braid, and the wool weft wrapping at each end has been plaited and tasselled in each corner.

425 Qashqai
The end panels of rows of weft patterning on this kilim are characteristic of the Qashqai. (Detail)

aesthetically pleasing geometry, the fineness of their wool and their clear, strong colours combine to ensure their reputation as superlative examples of textile art. The Qashqai kilims are woven in slitweave, sometimes with cotton warps, and sometimes with natural brown wool. There are, broadly speaking, two different Qashqai compositions:

a) Kilims with horizontal bands of patterns: This composition is usually associated with the kilims made by tribal groups of the same Turkic origin as the Qashqai from north-west Iran; however, it is a style favoured and frequently used by the Qashqai themselves. The field, of horizontal banded patterns and motifs with narrow bands of running hook designs between, can be either contained within a border or simply run off the edge of the rug. The motifs used in the bands are so similar to those used by Shahsavan that it is in some cases very easy to confuse them. The border and end panels can usually provide the determining factor, for the Qashqai weave borders of elaborate and finely drawn *laleh* (tulip) motifs, frequently linked to a zig-zag inner border. The detail with which the design is drawn distinguishes a Qashqai weave from other work from southern Iran – the border on a Luri kilim, for example, is much simpler.

b) A central field within borders: The borders of fine *laleh* are similar to those of the above, and within the field lie two or three diamond medallions, or else a square grid pattern. Occasionally the field is plain, woven with undyed camel-hair wefts. This variety is usually large, therefore probably intended as *soufreh* for the all-important wedding ceremony.

As the Qashqai people are mainly nomadic, a large variety of storage bags are woven, and the different sizes and shapes indicate their use. These bags are most important; much time and skill have been invested in their making, and they represent a large part of the family wealth. Goods and chattels, food and bedding must all be transported in woven bags on the backs of the camels and donkeys during migration, and at the encampment the bags serve as furniture in the tent. The finishes and fastenings are elaborate, heavily embellished with brocade and brocade-decorated work, and knotted pile or extra-weft brocading and knotted pile reinforcement often give additional strength in places where the bag would rub against the animal.

The Khamsa

In Farsi, *khamsa* means 'five', and has thus become the name of a political grouping of five southern tribes created in 1862 by a powerful family of Shiraz, the Qavam, to counterbalance the increasing power of the Qashqai. The Qavam were traders who originated in Qazvin, who when they needed protection for their merchandise routed to and from the ports of the Persian Gulf, used the Khamsa as a buffer. The five tribes incorporate the Ainallu and Baharlu, which are Turkic-speaking, and the Arabic Sheibari, Jabbareh and Bassiri. After Reza Shah was deposed in 1941 the tribes that had been forcibly settled were free to choose between a sedentary or nomadic lifestyle. The Qashqai resumed their twice-yearly migration, whereas many of the Khamsa people, remained settled.

The finest weavers amongst the Khamsa are the Baharlu, who were originally part of the Kyzylbash in Azerbaijan; it is not known why they came south to Fars

The Khamsa

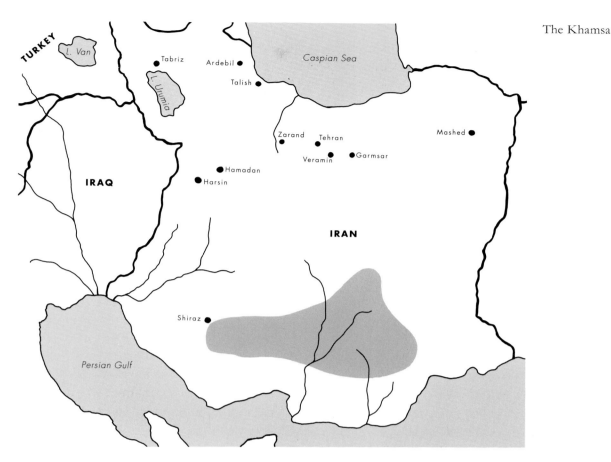

in the thirteenth century. The Ainallu were most probably related to the Shahsavan living in Qazvin in the eighteenth century, and the Bassiri have a very mixed ancestry, strongly Arab-influenced, and speak a dialect that is a mixture of Arabic and Farsi.

Khamsa	426
DESIGN	Field: Various, influenced by neighbouring groups
SIZE AND SHAPE	Small and rectangular/Large and rectangular
MATERIALS	Cotton/Sometimes wool wefts
STRUCTURE	Slitweave/Double interlock
COLOURS	Dull and limited palette
FRINGE	Various
SELVEDGE	Extra cord reinforcement
Remarks	Many bags and trappings also woven

The central market town and bazaar of the Khamsa is Shiraz, one of the great and ancient cities of Iran – craftsmen from the town helped to build Persepolis, the capital of ancient Persia, in 550 BC.

The dealers of Shiraz loosely attribute flatweaves and pile carpets to Shiraz, Fars and south-west Persia with little or no knowledge of their exact origin, complicating the task of identifying Khamsa kilims. No attempt has been made to

426 Khamsa
(1.37 × 1.14 m, 4′6″ × 3′9″)
Although this small tribal flatweave shows indications that it is Afshar in origin, it was bought in one of the villages close to Shiraz and attributed by the dealer to the Khamsa tribe.

427 Afshar of Sirjan
(1.01 × 1.01 m, 3′4″ × 3′4″)
The Afshar of the harsh southern regions of Iran are prolific weavers of bags, rukorssi and soufreh, *the essential textile furniture of nomadic people. This* soufreh, *or eating cloth, contains all the life and energy that can be put into a utility flatweave through the relaxed and natural freedom of drawing and subtle use of colours.*

distinguish subtle differences in weave, colour and finish, or to identify weaves at the time of collection or purchase from a particular village or encampment. The situation is further compounded by the fact that there is usually very little difference between the Qashqai and Khamsa weavings. It does seem, however, that the Afshar have had an important influence on the Khamsa compositions, which are often copied from the work of other peoples, as these invariably show remarkable similarities to those of the Afshar. Most kilims that can be attributed to the Khamsa with certainty are woven in slitweave or double interlock, with cotton warps. Sometimes white cotton is used in the field in unusually large areas, with patterning applied in coloured wool weft inserts. Various stylized domestic animals are woven into the design especially the *murgi* (chicken), and the *boteh* (paisley) design is popular. Bags and trappings of all sizes are woven, usually in weft-wrapping technique.

The Afshar

The origins of the Afshar (or Awshar, as they were sometimes known) may be traced to a tribe of the Oghuz, or Ghuzz Turkic peoples, who migrated from the Turkestan plains of Qibchaq. Initially an insignificant tribe that settled in Khuzestan near the Zagros Mountains, they were little known or heard of except in a violent period during the rule of Shumla (1148–1174).

It was not until the end of the fifteenth century, when, as one of the seven tribes of the Kyzylbash federation, they brought the first Safavid king, the boy Shah Ismail I, to power, with the subsequent rise of the Safavids, that they came to play a significant role in the history of Persia. By that time the tribe had expanded and dispersed, with a large section living near Lake Urumia in the north-west. The power and wealth of the Afshar steadily increased, and they were given lands west of Lake Riza'iyya by Shah Abbas, whence they spread eastwards. The Afshar leader, however, murdered the Shah's mother and brother in an attempt to gain more power. The young and deeply sensitive Shah then dissolved the Kyzylbash and created the new confederation – the Shahsavan – to which some of the Afshar allied themselves, but most were driven south, as rebels, to Kerman, where there are still nomadic groups, although most have settled in villages and lost their tribal identity.

The Afshar, one of the main Persian tribes, are among the most scattered of the Turkic peoples, and there are still recognizable groups of Afshar in Azerbaijan and Khamseh in the north-west, Khorassan in the north-east, Kerman in the south, and still within their ancient homelands of Khuzestan. The Afshar of Khamseh, however, who live in Zanjan, Hamadan, and the surrounding areas of north-west Iran, are a settled people who have intermingled with other Turkic tribes to such an extent that they have lost most of their identity. Their kilims, for example, are commercial copies of designs from other tribes. The other main tribes of Iran such as the Qashqai and Shahsavan, although dispersed, weave distinct and easily identifiable kilims with a uniformity of tribal designs. The Afshar have adapted to their local environments by integrating with the people, adopting many distinctive features of their rugs so that they are easily confused, although there is a dense and heavy feel to Afshar kilims other types lack.

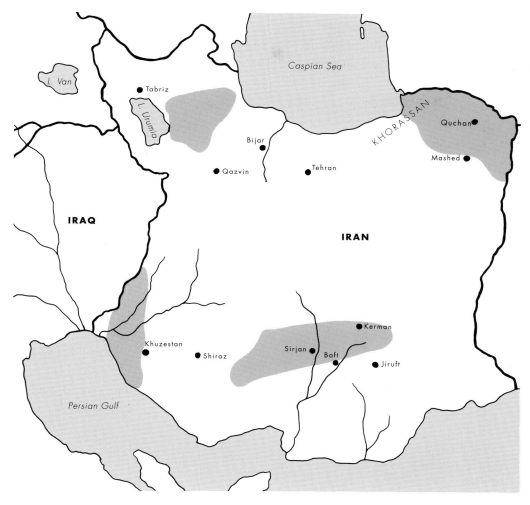

428   Afshar of Khuzestan
(0.61 × 0.61 m, 2′ × 2′)
Rock salt is of great value to shepherds living in continental Asia, far from the sea. As in Western cultures, the spillage of salt is considered bad luck, as well as a waste of a precious resource. Salt bags traditionally have narrow necks to prevent the salt from spilling.

The Afshar

The Afshar of Khuzestan

Khuzestan, in south-west Iran, was the earliest home of the Afshar, who settled in the Shushtar area around the Gargav River after mass migration in the twelfth century. Their kilims are similar in both design and weaving technique to neighbouring Luri work, and are often mistakenly classified as 'Luri/Bakhtiari'.

Afshar of Khuzestan	428
DESIGN	Field: Two or three medallions on a plain ground Borders: Narrow
SIZE AND SHAPE	Often small and rectangular
MATERIALS	Cotton warps, coarse wool wefts
STRUCTURE	Slitweave/Occasionally double interlock
COLOURS	Limited and dull palette
FRINGE	Thickly plaited
SELVEDGE	Extra cord reinforcement
Remarks	Very similar to Luri/Bakhtiari weavings

429   Afshar
This eating cloth is bordered by a distinctive zig-zag design. (Detail)

The Afshar of Azerbaijan

It is possible that there were some Afshar people living in Azerbaijan before the influx of Mongol and Turkic peoples in the twelfth century. There are still significant numbers of Afshar settled close to Lake Urumia, and others migrate as nomads between Mount Sahand and their winter quarters on the east shore of Lake Urumia. It is the Azerbaijani Afshar who are settled in villages, however, that weave kilims.

Afshar of Azerbaijan	432
DESIGN	Field: Large medallions on a plain ground Borders: Narrow
SIZE AND SHAPE	Long and rectangular/Occasionally small
MATERIALS	Cotton warps, wool wefts
STRUCTURE	Usually slitweave/Occasionally double interlock
COLOURS	Deep red, blue, white
FRINGE	Plaited
SELVEDGE	Extra cord reinforcement
Remarks	Very similar to other north-west Persian weavings

Afshar of Khorassan	430–1, 433
DESIGN	Field: Small detailed motifs in banded design/Small detailed motifs round a geometric medallion
SIZE AND SHAPE	Small and rectangular/Long runners
MATERIALS	Cotton warps, wool wefts
STRUCTURE	Slitweave, double interlock, weft wrapping, weft-faced patterning
COLOURS	Deep red, blue, camel brown, ivory white
FRINGE	Plain/Plaited
SELVEDGE	Extra cord reinforcement/Sometimes simple double warps
Remarks	Kilims are generally referred to as 'Kalat'/Very similar to other weavings from the area/Many bags and trappings also woven

The Afshar of Khorassan

The Afshar of Khorassan were forced to migrate from Azerbaijan and Kurdistan by Shah Abbas to act as a buffer against the Turkomen and Uzbeks. The largest group were the Chamishgazak tribe of Kurdistan who came from around Quchan, Shirvan and Bujnurd. The Azerbaijani tribe settled at the same time around Dara-

Opposite:

430   Afshar of Khorassan
(1.14 × 1.14 m, 3′9″ × 3′9″)
The drama of the dynamic design is largely the result of mistakes made by the weaver. She has created a design of four rows of zig-zags made up of small coloured squares interlocked together, but she has not been able to return the pattern at the corners. The tiny white rosettes are typical of Afshar weaving.

431   Afshar of Khorassan
(2.97 × 0.76 m, 9′6″ × 2′6″)
A long soufreh. Sometimes they can exceed 4.5 m (15′) in length and are known as 'bridal path', a clear indication of their importance in the ceremonial wedding feast. In one corner there is a small red diamond brocaded into the weave, possibly indicating the place for an honoured guest.

432   Afshar of Azerbaijan
(3.05 × 1.30 m, 10′2″ × 4′3″)
The medallions in the field contain complex motifs drawn with flowing lines. These are outlined and separated by a deep red line which makes the overall appearance less formal and organized. The rows of narrow borders are typical of flatweaves from north-west Iran.

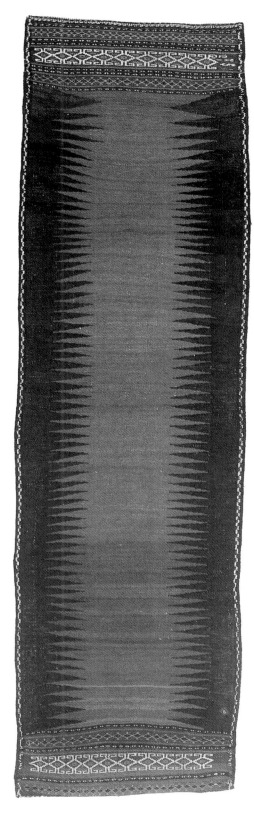

Gaz and Abivard, and since the Russian incursion into north-east Persia at the end of the nineteenth century the Khorassan Afshar have been concentrated around Dara-Gaz and Kalat Naderi. Their weavings are usually referred to as 'Kalat', and are often mistaken for Balouch and Khorassan Kurdish work, as they are very similar and the tribes often copy each other. Many bags and other small items are made as well as long runners with fine weft-faced patterning and supplementary wefts.

433   Afshar of Khorassan
(0.91 × 0.91 m, 3′ × 3′)
The zig-zag fingers down two borders have been echoed in the central design to give an impression of rows of zig-zags down the sides. The two diamond shapes add focus as they cut into or lay over the darker blue-green weave.

The Afshar of Kerman

This is the most important and largest group of Afshar, who were sent to Kerman in the sixteenth century as a reprisal for their rising against the Safavid shah. Their mountainous habitat provides good summer pastures, and they spend their winters in warm encampments on the shores of the Persian Gulf. There are many Turkic-speaking tribes living in this area of Iran who are unrelated to the Afshar, such as the Abdoughi, Reza Khani, Hasan Khani, Balouch and Lak, but within this great mix a certain amount of individualism and sense of identity and tradition still prevail, probably because the communities of pasturalists have to remain tightly knit in order to survive the harsh conditions of their migratory life. Although it produces a large number of knotted carpets, the area is also important for kilims and the rugs of Kerman are perhaps the most varied and diverse of all Persian tribal weavings. Afshar kilims feature many different motifs and designs, some reminiscent of Indian textiles, which have influenced the weavers of this region.

434   Afshar of Kerman
(2.06 × 1.65 m, 6′9″ × 5′5″)
Afshar flatweaves from Kerman province, are perhaps the easiest to recognize, despite their many varied designs. This kilim from Sirjan is densely woven in double-interlock technique. The field of intricate Turkic motifs is surrounded by a wide border and there is a barber-pole selvedge and plain fringe giving the finishing touch. The rug is scattered throughout with small white rosettes in extra-weft technique.

Afshar of Kerman   434

DESIGN	Field and borders: Many diverse and varied patterns, often scattered with small white flower motifs
SIZE AND SHAPE	Often small and rectangular
MATERIALS	Thick cotton warps, coarse wool wefts
STRUCTURE	Slitweave, double interlock, weft wrapping
COLOURS	Deep red, blue, yellow, white, occasionally green
FRINGE	Many different finishes
SELVEDGE	Often thick extra cord reinforcement with barber-pole design
Remarks	Bags and trappings also woven

Afshar of Sirjan   427

DESIGN	Field and borders: Many different patterns, with small rosettes in white cotton
SIZE AND SHAPE	Small and rectangular/Large and rectangular
MATERIALS	Cotton warps, wool wefts
STRUCTURE	Dovetail, double interlock
COLOURS	Dark red, blue, green, white cotton
FRINGE	Long and plaited, tied with coloured wool
SELVEDGE	Extra cord reinforcement with barber-pole design
Remarks	*Soufreh*, *rukorssi* and bags also woven

435, 436 Kerman
(2.84 × 1.54 m, 9′4″ × 5′1″)
The clear dark colours and comprehensive palette add to the richness of this kilim. The weaver has decorated the field with stylized camels and national flags, and bordered each side with similarly stylized plants or trees. (Detail 436)

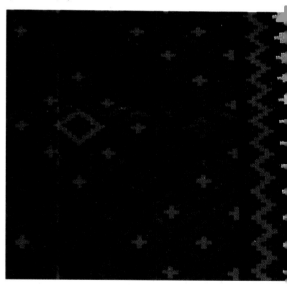

437 Afshar of Sirjan
The weaver of this rug from the Sirjan region has produced a design on two scales. When viewed close to, the stepped diamond shape with a central cross forms the dominant patterning. Viewed from a distance a larger interlocking 'V' pattern in dark colours appears. (Detail)

The Afshar of Sirjan

Sirjan is the principal market town of the Kerman region. Finely woven in a dovetail or double-interlock technique, Sirjan kilims have a neat selvedge and extra cord reinforcement, often in two colours – gold and blue – to give the barber-pole effect. The ends of the rugs are carefully finished with the cotton warp plaited into long fringes, and with a coloured wool binding to prevent unravelling. Colours are usually dark in tone and limited in range, and are mainly red, blue and green. As with many Afshar flatweaves, their distinguishing feature is the small rosette in white cotton that is usually integrated into the design, especially in the borders, rather than being scattered at random as in Garmsar, Veramin and Balouch kilims. Another border design consists of a zig-zag made up of small white rosettes. Many *soufreh* and *rukorssi* are woven here.

438   Afshar of Jiruft
(2.92 × 1.21 m, 9'7" × 4')
Usually there is little to distinguish Afshar weavings from those of the people they have integrated with. The design of this kilim is very similar to Bakhtiari work from Shushtar 415; there is, however, a border that runs right round the very edge of the rug. (Detail)

439   Afshar of Baft
(2.72 × 1.85 m, 8'11" × 6')
There are many motifs hidden in this complex pattern, including the familiar laleh abrassi, *and rows of running motifs, some Turkic, some identical to Balouch floating weft designs. Archaic symbols include the stylized swastika.*

The Afshar of Jiruft

Jiruft is an area of steep and fertile valleys through which runs the Halil River and its tributaries, near the town of Jiruft (modern Sabzevaran). The kilim compositions are very similar to those of the Bakhtiari, especially those found near Shushtar, six hundred miles to the west, the other side of Zagros Mountains. The inner border of pyramid shapes points towards the central field, which usually bears three medallions on a deep red background. The outer border of *laleh abrassi* tulip motifs is more elaborate than the crenellated version of this familiar pattern from southern Iran. Woven in double interlock, creating a very hard and thick weave, the kilims are well finished with barber-pole weft-wrapped reinforced selvedges, short striped end panels and a variety of fringe details.

Afshar of Jiruft		438
DESIGN	Field: Linked medallions Borders: Crenellated inner, complex geometric outer	
SIZE AND SHAPE	Small and rectangular/Large and rectangular	
MATERIALS	Cotton warps, thick coarse wool wefts	
STRUCTURE	Double interlock	
COLOURS	Deep red field, with yellow, blue, ivory white	
FRINGE	Varied	
SELVEDGE	Extra cord reinforcement with barber-pole design	
Remarks	Very occasionally bags and trappings are woven	

The Afshar of Baft

Weaving in Baft is very similar to that of neighbouring Jiruft, but the central field is usually divided into wide bands of Turkic or abstract motifs and narrow bands of rosettes in floating weft and weft twining.

Afshar of Baft		439
DESIGN	Field: Wide bands of Turkic motifs Borders: Narrow and geometric	
SIZE AND SHAPE	Small and rectangular/Medium and rectangular	
MATERIALS	Cotton warps, thick wool wefts	
STRUCTURE	Double interlock, weft twining	
COLOURS	Dull and limited palette of deep red, blue	
FRINGE	Various	
SELVEDGE	Extra cord reinforcement with barber-pole design	
Remarks	Very similar to weavings from Jiruft	

Regional Weaving

Kerman

This southern district of Iran can be regarded as an area of political confinement for unruly and especially 'unpatriotic' groups of largely Turkic people, although indeed the same could be said about most of the Iranian borderlands. The southern desert region of Kerman was first occupied by the Sassanid king Ardashir I, and became prosperous after being invaded by Turks and Mongols. The exquisite fourteenth-century architecture of Kerman was renovated by the Safavids in the sixteenth century, but the city was destroyed by an earthquake in 1794. Its famous Friday Mosque, however, has survived to this day. The province of Kerman is one of the least known areas in Iran, and its textiles are again mostly attributed to Shiraz and Sirjan, the collecting bazaars for the nomads and sedentary villagers exchanging kilims, pile carpets and wool for consumer goods and provisions.

440   Kerman
In the nineteenth century Kerman imported many ideas from Indian woven and printed textiles, such as floral designs. There is a menagerie of domestic and wild animals woven into this kilim, intertwined with floral motifs and vines. (Detail)

Kerman	435, 440–1
DESIGN	Field: Horizontal bands/Three medallions/Many designs from neighbouring tribes Borders: Interlocking and reciprocal arrow shapes
SIZE AND SHAPE	Various
MATERIALS	Cotton warps, loose wool wefts
STRUCTURE	Weft wrapped
COLOURS	Limited and dark, frequently red, blue
FRINGE	Plaited tassels
SELVEDGE	Thick extra cord reinforcement
Remarks	Influenced by the Afshar, Qashqai and Luri tribes

The Afshar, who were exiled to Kerman in the sixteenth century by Shah Abbas, are the largest and most important group in this region. The Buchaqchis, or Borchargchi Afshar are an unruly group from Zanjan in north Kurdistan, who were moved to Fars and then to Kerman by Nadir Shah. The Shuls came here from Luristan in the thirteenth century, and the Suleymen arrived from Fars in the seventeenth century. They are said to be the richest sheep and goat owners in southern Iran. The Qutlus and Qara'is are both important Turkic tribes who migrated to Kerman and to the Khorassan borders in the north-east and along the east side of the central Persian desert.

Many Kerman flatweaves are strongly influenced by Afshar, Qashqai and Luri work. Some of their individual design influences have come from the nineteenth-century textiles that made the town of Kerman famous, which were in turn infused with features imported from Indian textiles, such as *boteh* and floral leaf designs.

There is one design type peculiar to Kerman that is ironically often attributed by bazaar dealers to the Bakhtiari. This has an all-over weft-wrapped construction in coarse and loosely spun wool with cotton warps. The field is divided into bands,

441   Kerman
(1.52 × 0.91 m, 5′ × 3′)
A small flatweave that was possibly a prayer rug. Even though it does not have an arch shape in its design, there is an eccentricity in the field pattern – the row of cross shapes – that orientates the rug. A devout follower prays to Mecca five times a day on a rug or cloth.

or decorated with two or three central medallions. Motifs can be abstract, or feature *boteh* or domestic animals with interlacing floral designs. The border is of interlocking and reciprocal arrow shapes in white and either dark red or dark blue. The palette is limited and invariably dark in tone, and the fringes are plaited into chunky flat tassels.

Veramin and Garmsar

A great number of tribes have been moved or have migrated to these two oasis towns close to Tehran that straddle the old trading and migration route linking east and west Iran, continuing on to the Silk Route. Both Veramin and Garmsar (which means 'winter pastures') are generic titles given to weavings from the area around the two towns and their neighbouring villages, and also to kilims of similar designs woven elsewhere. Most of the more familiar tribal groups have settled here, such as the Kurds, Lurs, Afshar, Shahsavan, Qashqai, Turkomen and the Arabs, and there are also a significant number of people living here who have lost their tribal identity, but who weave individual and distinctive kilims that combine a mixture of design motifs and techniques from all the traditional weaving areas of Persia. Consequently, it is most difficult to identify with any certainty the precise origins of a rug from the area. Nevertheless, Garmsar and Veramin have a long tradition of producing large, well-made kilims and very fine trappings, and some very fine tribal rugs are still woven.

442   Veramin
(2.66 × 1.44 m, 8'9" × 4'9")
'Eye-dazzler' kilim designs are found throughout much of Iran and are woven by many different tribal groups, but they are usually attributed to Veramin, where the design could originally have been brought by Turkic weavers from Luristan in the south. The serrated edge motif that makes up this design can be combined into interlocking motifs of similar or different colours that are repeated horizontally, vertically, or diagonally, as in this case. The diagonal lines of motifs form two medallions on a larger scale, and the overall design appears to be part of a larger composition. (Detail 444)

443   Garmsar
(3.50 × 1.37 m, 11'6" × 4'6")
*The design here is associated with Garmsar and
is either woven by Luri or, more probably, by
Shahsavan people. Diagonal bands of Turkic
motifs fill the whole field. (Detail 445)*

Veramin   An ancient city full of mosques and shrines, Veramin was a central
bazaar town for Kurdish and Shahsavan people, who have now become totally
absorbed and lost their tribal identity. Nowadays only a few of the town's district
names recall the old tribal habitation. Most probably, the Kurds of Veramin
originated as the Pazuki from Erzurum in east Turkey and from amongst the
Chemisqazak Kurds who transmigrated via Veramin to Khorassan. The
Shahsavan may be the descendants of a Baghdadi tribe from Saveh. Despite the
confused lineage of its inhabitants, it is still possible to discover the tribal history
of Veramin kilims, for although they are characteristic of this region, they do
contain recognizable elements of their tribal ancestry.

The well-known 'eye-dazzler' kilims are woven throughout the area but are
usually attributed just to Veramin by traders. The design may have been carried
north by the Turkic weavers of Luristan who came to Veramin in the fourteenth
century when it became an important Mongol centre. The 'eye-dazzler' is woven
by the Qashqai but, to confuse the issue, the bazaar traders in Tehran and Veramin
call the work 'Shiraz', after the major city and market place for Qashqai and Luri
rugs.

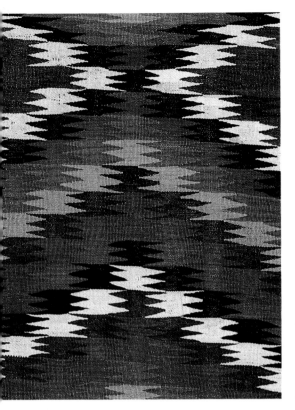

444   *Detail of* 442.

The decorative repertoire of the rugs is rich and varied, featuring either reciprocal patterns or narrow bands of pattern with repeating motifs. A composition peculiar to Veramin is occasionally found wherein the border appears at the top and bottom only. These kilims are woven in hard-wearing, tightly packed wool, sometimes with cotton warps, and the old examples have a fine lustre. Decorative techniques include slitweave, with motifs outlined in weft-wrapping technique and contour bands in contrasting colours. Although older weavings are usually rich and clear, more recent attempts can be exceedingly dull. Narrow bands of weft-faced patterning may be evident, either between wider bands of motifs or at the ends of the rug. End finishes are simple, carried to a plain fringe, with little or no end panel. The selvedges can provide a useful means of identifying Veramin kilims, for the multiple warps are twisted together at the edges for extra cord reinforcement with extra weft-wrapped decoration.

The Kurds of Khorassan lived for a time in Veramin after fleeing Ottoman persecution in Anatolia and the Caucasus in the sixteenth century, and the influence of Kurdish weaving can still be easily recognized. Small Kurdish-style details are discernible, such as extra-weft outlining that is used to add definition to a motif or medallion. The designs, patterns and motifs tend to be simpler than the originals, of which they are often a very pleasing abbreviation or précis, with less cluttered fields and fewer, narrower borders – an example, perhaps, of the stylization and diminution of the atavistic motifs following tribal migration and settlement.

Veramin		442, 563
DESIGN	Field: Many and varied/Distinctive 'eye-dazzler' designs	
SIZE AND SHAPE	Usually large and rectangular	
MATERIALS	Wool/Sometimes cotton warps	
STRUCTURE	Slitweave, with contour bands round motifs	
COLOURS	Rich palette of light blue, red, yellow, green, pale orange	
FRINGE	Plain	
SELVEDGE	Extra cord reinforcement/Weft-wrapped decoration	
Remarks	*Soufreh*, *rukorssi* and bags also woven, usually in weft-wrapping technique	

Garmsar   Kilims from this area are tightly woven in relatively coarse wool that is spun in medium ply. The warps are cotton, or – very unusually for Persian kilims – natural brown wool. A distinctive natural dark brown wool is used in the weft, along with vivid colours, which tend to be brighter and more intense than those woven in their original tribal areas, possibly because of the quality of the wool and the way it takes up the dye. Slitweave is practised, woven at an acute angle so that the slits are so small they hardly show. The fields are often of

445   *Detail of* 443.

horizontal or diagonal bands of lozenges, stars and hexagons, with very narrow borders. The motifs are outlined in contrasting coloured-wool contour bands and the border is sometimes divided from the field by a vertical row of weft wrapping in dark red or brown wool.

One distinctive feature often visible in Garmsar end panels is a very narrow band of weft-faced patterning, perhaps using as few as four weft strands, producing a tiny daisy-chain pattern, or joined 'S' shapes. This technique is found extensively on Balouch kilims and the daisy or rosette pattern also appears scattered at random over the field of the rug in ivory white wool – a charming idiosyncracy. Selvedges are heavy, with extra cord reinforcement in dark red wool.

Garmsar		443
DESIGN	Field: Diagonal bands of lozenge shapes Borders: Narrow and geometric	
SIZE AND SHAPE	Large and rectangular	
MATERIALS	Wool/Sometimes cotton warps	
STRUCTURE	Slitweave with occasional use of contour bands round motifs	
COLOURS	Deep red, blue, yellow, brown, ivory white	
FRINGE	Long and plain/Occasionally diagonally plaited	
SELVEDGE	Extra cord reinforcement in dark red wool	

Harsin and Hamadan

The towns of Hamadan and Harsin in north Kurdistan are centres of a prolific weaving industry. Hamadan was the ancient summer capital of Cyrus the Great, and many historic sites survive from his reign of wealth and artistic achievement, such as treasure mounds. At Harsin, the discovery of the Luristan bronzes was made, otherwise this is an unremarkable, drab and dusty town. Close by is the ancient village of Lalajin, which has an ancient and venerable pottery industry.

Harsin and Hamadan		446, 448
DESIGN	Field: Two or three linked medallions Borders: Narrow	
SIZE AND SHAPE	Long and rectangular	
MATERIALS	Wool warps, loose wool wefts	
STRUCTURE	Slitweave, extra weft inserts and curved wefts	
COLOURS	Deep pink, red, yellow, white	
FRINGE	Plain	
SELVEDGE	Plain, occasionally with extra cord reinforcement	

Page 234:

446   Harsin
(2.66 × 1.27 m, 8'9" × 4'2")
Kilims from Harsin are very similar to each other. Made of coarse wool coloured from deep pink to a soft or rich red, with medium to dark blues and white, they are invariably woven in small stepped slitweave, with curved wefts to produce small boteh, bird and 'beehive' motifs. The field usually has two or three medallions outlined in blue, yellow and white, and narrow borders holding rows of simple motifs.

447   Zarand
(3.55 × 1.14 m, 11'8" × 3'9")
The long format, soft colours and fine weave clearly point to the origin of this kilim. The rows of small 'flower bud' motifs, typical of Kurdish weavings from Senna and Bijar as well as Zarand, have been carefully arranged diagonally to form diamond medallions in the field, and are bordered by three rows of familiar motifs.

448   Harsin
(2.89 × 1.37 m, 9'6" × 4'6")
This kilim is a little different and more lively than those normally found in this area. Still using the traditional colours of deep red, blue and white, the weaver has drawn joined medallions with looping zig-zag lines. The wide border of three rows of running motifs returns across the ends and changes only slightly to accommodate the narrower bands.

449   Zarand
(3.50 × 1.14 m, 11'6" × 3'9")
Zarand is the generic name given to the rugs from the prolific weaving area around the market town of Zarand, west of Tehran. The kilims are invariably long and narrow and finely woven in small stepped slitweave, with running intertwined leaf borders. Curved wefts and weft inserts are used to produce field patterns that include floral or palmette designs.

Captions for 446–9 on page 233.

234

Captions for 450–3 on page 236.

235

The kilims of the two towns are most distinctive and are woven with wool warps and very loosely spun coarse wool wefts. Their fields range from a deep pink to a soft or rich red colour, and bear a design of two or three medallions with long stepped sides. The medallions and the spaces around them are filled with small *boteh*, or bird-like motifs in blue, yellow and black. These are similar to the motifs found on Senna and Bijar kilims. The rugs sometimes have many narrow borders, with rows of motifs running between contrasting white crenellated, or 'tooth', borders, on all four sides, and there are no end panels. Selvedges and fringes are simple.

Zarand, Saveh and Qazvin

Zarand is a village lying to the south-west of Tehran between the Kharaghan, Zagros and Elburz Mountains, within a region known for its prolific production of flatweaves. The populace is derived from settled Shahsavan nomads, Kurds and Persian-speaking farmers. 'Zarand' is a generic bazaar title given not only to the textiles of Zarand itself, but also of Qazvin and Saveh to the north.

Zarand kilims are long and narrow, and finely woven with cotton warps and heavy woollen wefts. Their small stepped slitweave, curved wefts and weft inserts are all used to produce designs of fine, floral, intertwined leaves, with running trefoil and vines in the narrow borders. The floral designs in the field often group to form a diamond grid pattern, or two or three medallions. The colours are traditionally muted blues, golden yellows and browns, but in more recent years vibrant and raw chemical colours have been used. There is no reinforcement on the selvedge other than the doubling up and plying of the outermost warps. The fringes are left long, in a knotted or net finish.

Zarand, Saveh and Qazvin	376, 379, 447, 449
DESIGN	Field: Floral patterns/Medallions of small stepped triangles Borders: Narrow
SIZE AND SHAPE	Very long and narrow
MATERIALS	Cotton warps, wool wefts
STRUCTURE	Slitweave with curved wefts and weft inserts
COLOURS	Varied palette, including vivid chemical dyes and soft brown, orange
FRINGE	Usually plain/Long and knotted
SELVEDGE	Plain

Ardebil

Ardebil is a large town that has in the past two decades become a centre for heavy industry. Many kilims are woven here and in the surrounding villages by the Turkic people. The weavers copy many styles and designs from north-west Iran, commercially, for the home market. They are generally thickly woven for durability, but colours are either drab or day-glow in effect from poor-quality fugitive chemical dyes. A decorative pattern is formed in slitweave in coarse machine-spun wool with cotton warps.

Ardebil 450

DESIGN	Field: Many and varied, copied from neighbouring groups
SIZE AND SHAPE	Usually medium and rectangular/Large and rectangular
MATERIALS	Cotton warps, coarse wool wefts
STRUCTURE	Slitweave
COLOURS	Dull/Day-glow poor-quality dyes
FRINGE	Usually plain
SELVEDGE	Plain with a little reinforcement

Talish

A mountainous area, overlooking the west shores of the Caspian Sea, Talish lies between Ashtara and Rasht. The people are mainly Turkish, and display an obvious Caucasian influence in their weaving. The rugs are known for their wide range of clear, bright colours and are woven in slitweave, with a field ornamentation made up of crenellated diamond shapes. Borders are narrow and are patterned with interlocking designs or motifs. The warps are of undyed brown wool with a simple knotted or plaited fringe.

Talish 452–3

DESIGN	Field: Medallions of stepped diamond shapes Borders: Narrow and geometric
SIZE AND SHAPE	Long and rectangular
MATERIALS	Natural brown wool warps, quite fine wool wefts
STRUCTURE	Slitweave
COLOURS	Varied palette of strong clear colours
FRINGE	Knotted/Plaited
SELVEDGE	Usually simple reinforcement

454   *A Qashqai camel girth.*

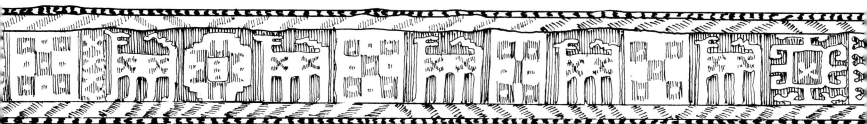

455   *Detail of* 474.

456   *Detail of* 457.

The Caucasus

Of all the rugs of the Oriental world, it is the work of the Caucasian weavers that has been most revered since ancient times. The superlative wool of these weaves was said to have inspired Jason to seek the Golden Fleece within the Caucasus, his destination Colchis in Georgia, where a special type of merino sheep was found that produced a superb coat. Collectors since that time have coveted the region's rugs not only for the quality of the wool but also for the weaver's creative deployment of bright and clear dyes, and the range of well-executed weaving techniques.

Situated south of Russia, with Turkey and Iran forming its other borders, this mountainous region forms both a bulwark and a corridor between East and West, and has thus provided a thoroughfare for many voyagers, who have each bequeathed fragments of their culture. It is no wonder, therefore, that the Caucasus is peopled by many different ethnic groups – there are some three hundred and fifty tribes, and more than ninety different languages and dialects spoken. As a consequence of this demographic traffic the Caucasus knew almost relentless devastation until the last century. Early warring factions included the Mongol Tartars in the thirteenth century, followed in the late fourteenth century by the armies of Tamerlane. These were succeeded by the Safavid Persians and the Ottoman Turks, who squabbled over the territory during the fifteenth century. Constant warfare resulted in the long-term destruction of the economy and the ruin of the people and their culture. Not surprisingly, few rugs survive from this period.

By the seventeenth century, eastern Transcaucasia had become a nominal part of the Persian Empire, although it remained mainly independent and was forced only to pay tributes and to provide troops on demand. In the first half of the nineteenth century there was much social and political change; the expansive Russian Empire sent administrators to the Caucasus, and many people moved out of the country to Turkey and Russia. The Russian administration established railways, roads and sea ports, which resulted in the increased import and export of merchandise, and this era subsequently proved a golden age for the production of woven goods. During this period of Russian supervision, the administrators received dues (according to their rank) in the form of money or goods, and woven artifacts were popular. The quantity of textiles produced greatly increased to meet this demand. The dealing in foreign merchandise ensured that towards the end of the nineteenth century chemical dyes were rapidly introduced into the area and these gained instant popularity because of their convenience; it was not discovered until years later that many were fugitive and faded rapidly. By that time the old and skilled use of well-processed natural colours, for which the region was so well known, had virtually become extinct.

Weaving is an integral part of Caucasian culture. It was practised mainly by women, although men wove rugs in urban areas, and was very much a part of the Caucasian social tradition. A girl would learn the art at an early age, slowly becoming familiar with the designs and techniques taught her by her mother, in order that she might weave rugs for her dowry. Women were generally held in high regard in Caucasian societies, particularly mothers, and in many regions the

main pillar of the house was carved with astral signs and known as the 'Mother Pillar'. Kilims had many purposes – floor coverings, curtains, wall hangings (many Caucasian kilims are found with cotton loops sewn to one of the selvedges), covers for seating areas and awnings for ox carts. Flatweaving is particularly suitable for the construction of storage bags of all sizes, woven for grain, food and domestic items, and *maffrash* for clothing and bedding.

Caucasian flatweaves are known for their dominant geometric compositions, which prevail in all regions apart from the Georgia and the Nagorny Karabakh areas, where floral patterning is often used. The geometric compositions and designs have been handed down from previous generations and include many ancient pre-Christian motifs and symbols as well as folkloric charms. Human figures, domestic and working animals, and mythological creatures such as dragons and fantastic birds, regularly appear. The banded design compositions of the Shirvan kilims may take their inspiration from the tale of the Maiden's Tower in Baku. The story tells of an early khan of Baku who had a beautiful daughter with whom he fell deeply in love. His daughter was greatly distressed by his incestuous desire, yet said she would yield to him if he built her a tower. The tower was built with haste, but the daughter, in anticipation of her fate, requested that it be built higher and higher, floor upon floor, until it became the tallest building in Baku; when completed the girl insisted on furnishing the tower. The khan became increasingly impatient; she asked him to grant her just one more request, a first

457   Kuba
(2.94 × 1.86 m, 9'7" × 6'1")
This finely slitwoven kilim features a well-drawn example of a Kuba design. The deep blue field accentuates the central medallions and adds depth to the pattern. The white pronged motifs are also seen on Azerbaijani knotted-pile rugs. Note the curiously shaped motif that appears in the four corners of the field. (Detail 456)

The Caucasus

look at the view from the top; and having climbed to the highest window with her entourage, she flung herself from the tower to the sea below.

The Caucasus spreads through four of the states of what was once the USSR, namely Azerbaijan, Daghestan, Armenia and Georgia. The complex ethnic mix of the Caucasus compels any regional analysis of its weaving traditions and production to be on the basis of religious enclaves rather than of ethnic groups.

458 Azerbaijani dragon *soumak*
A weft-wrapping technique rug, depicting an 'S' form representing a dragon, with the eyes at the top and the tail at the lower end. (Detail)

Caucasian soumak	458–61
DESIGN	Field: Frequently three central medallions, with many small filler motifs Borders: Multiple
SIZE AND SHAPE	Medium and rectangular/Large and rectangular
MATERIALS	Wool
STRUCTURE	Weft wrapping
COLOURS	Madder red, pink, blue, green, yellow, brown, white
FRINGE	Often plaited
SELVEDGE	Plain, with thicker outer warps
Remarks	Often found with hook motif as an outside border pattern

Azerbaijan

Of the four countries that make up the Caucasus, Azerbaijan produces the most kilims, and the land has a long history of weaving. The nomadic tribes wove kilims and carpets as well as a wide range of storage bags and sacks, such as

maffrash, *khurgin* and *chula*, and donkey and horse trappings. Smaller bags for salt, utensils and other items are also common. Not only are the Azerbaijani weavers prolific, they also employ many techniques at the loom. These include slitweave – known locally by the word *kilim*, warp-faced patterning (*jajim*), supplementary weft (*zili*), weft wrapping (popularly known as *soumak*) and extra weft wrapping (*verneh*). Furthermore, flatweaves are defined by regional names such as *palas* and *shadda*, so it is possible to ascribe a variety of weaving names to particular provenances as follows: *soumaks* are made in Kuba, *palas* and kilims in Hajikabul, *zili* in Khizy, *verneh* and *zili* in Kazakh, *shadda*, *verneh* and *zili* in Barda, *jajim* in Agjabedi, and *palas* and kilims in Jabrail.

Kuba

Kuba kilims are often decorated with large abstract indented medallions arranged in a well-organized format, and this composition appears from the number of such kilims to have been popular with the weavers. Others have large, central, hooked medallions which run down the centre, the full length of the rug. Such compositions are usually completed by a border of repeated motifs, and few areas of the rug are left undecorated. Kuba kilims in general have a greater diversity of composition than other Caucasian kilims and their colours vary from a dark to a softer palette. Slitweave technique is employed as a rule.

459   Azerbaijani *soumak*
(3.22 × 1.98 m, 10′6″ × 6′5″)
This kilim was possibly woven in the Kusary region. The motifs below the cruciform shape at the bottom make an animal face with somewhat comic features. The motifs are repeated in the same place above and below each medallion, but do not so clearly produce faces.

460   Azerbaijani *soumak*
(3.42 × 2.48 m, 11′2″ × 8′1″)
There is so much detail in this kilim woven in the Kusary region that the overall effect appears crowded. Note the small humanoid figures at the top and bottom of the central medallions.

241

461 Azerbaijani *soumak*
(3.12 × 2.53 m, 10′2″ × 8′3″)
Possibly woven in the Divichi area. The soft colouring mutes the bold pattern, which is generally referred to as a 'dragon soumak'. The numerous filler motifs are characteristic of weft-wrapped rugs, as are the hook motifs forming the outer border.

Opposite:

462 Kuba
(2.93 × 1.76 m, 9′7″ × 5′9″)
The deep blue ground creates the impression that the medallions are floating, an illusion emphasized by the saw-toothed surround. In contrast to the centre the side borders look heavy because of the oversized pattern. The small reciprocal design in the secondary borders is reminiscent of the kilims of southern Iran.

463 Kuba
(3.10 × 1.76 m, 10′2″ × 5′9″)
The white outlining design around the central medallions is well drawn and creates an illusion of perspective. Also interesting is the oval-shaped reciprocal design that separates the borders and the field. This design is found in kilims from the Senna area of Iran. The main border pattern is typically Kuba.

464 Kuba
(3.08 × 1.73 m, 10′ × 5′8″)
At one end the red field narrows, suggesting a prayer niche, although the weaver was probably experimenting with the overall design and subsequently changed her mind. The medallions and motifs appearing in the central panel are typical of this area, although here they are crudely drawn, as is the leaf and vine border pattern.

465 Kuba
(3.26 × 2.09 m, 10′8″ × 6′10″)
Bold and busy, the hooked medallions, border designs and filler motifs are characteristically Kuba. Kilims from this region normally have a great variety of motifs, most of which are intricate patterns used as individual forms.

Kuba		356, 457, 462–6, 629
DESIGN	Field: Repeat hooked diamond-shaped medallions/ Rectangular hooked medallions Borders: Decorated, narrow	
SIZE AND SHAPE	Large and rectangular/Some medium and rectangular	
MATERIALS	Fine wool	
STRUCTURE	Fine slitweave	
COLOURS	Burgundy and madder red, indigo blue, green, yellow, brown, black, white/More modern kilims include orange and chemical colours	
FRINGE	Often plaited	
SELVEDGE	Plain, with thicker outer warps	
REMARKS	Kuba kilims are easily recognizable by the two main types of medallion design used	

466 Kuba
(2.98 × 1.87 m, 9'9" × 6'1")
The indented medallion has a squarer formation than usual. The central chequered pattern is also used as a main motif in Georgian kilims.

467 Shirvan
The pinnacled border of this kilim is seen in some examples as short lengths of filler motif at the sides of the field, rather than as a continuous line. (Detail) Compare 470.

Shirvan

The compositions of Shirvan kilims appear to fall into two main categories, the first consisting of banded-format kilims without borders. The wider bands have hexagonal motifs of either a stepped or crenellated form, and small filler motifs of a diamond or triangular shape. Some of the narrow bands feature zig-zag patterns, and others a smaller version of the same diamond or triangular forms. On some examples of this composition, at the edge of the wider bands, a distinctive pinnacled zig-zag pattern is found, and although it does not necessarily appear in each of the wide bands, it is a characteristic pattern of these kilims. Some banded kilims only feature medallions and triangular motifs of the crenellated type, others the stepped medallion, which has a central crab motif very similar to those found in Shahsavan weavings from Khamseh and Bijar. Other kilims have both types of medallions in alternating wide bands.

The other main design is of a small motif, such as a star, that is arranged in rows over the field of the kilim, with narrow borders. Both these patterns have repetitive motifs, so that for maximum effect, the weaver has to rely on inspired colour combinations. Both dark and light palettes are used in Shirvan kilims, and the principal colours are red and blue combined with some green, yellow, brown and black. As with other Caucasian kilims, the wool is finely spun and the quality of slitweave is excellent.

Shirvan

359, 469–70, 473–4, 637

DESIGN	Field: Diamond-shaped medallions arranged in rows Borders: Usually plain
SIZE AND SHAPE	Large and rectangular
MATERIALS	Fine wool
STRUCTURE	Fine slitweave, with occasional details in supplementary weft wrapping
COLOURS	Red, dark and light blue, green, yellow, brown, black, white
FRINGE	Plaited
SELVEDGE	Plain, with thicker outer warps
Remarks	Zig-zag design often seen at sides

468 Shirvan
This kilim appears from its design to belong to the Shirvan family, but it has an unusually wide border and large dividing bands. The crenellated motifs are also found in Anatolian kilims. (Detail)

469 Shirvan
(3.20 × 1.89 m, 10′5″ × 6′2″)
The hexagonal motifs in this and other Shirvan kilims are also frequently found in Shahsavan slitwoven kilims and maffrash *bags woven in Iran. Small filler motifs seen at the sides of this kilim are characteristically Shirvan.*

470   Shirvan
(2.80 × 1.78 m, 9′2″ × 5′9″)
Without the clever use of colour this kilim, dated 1301 (1900), would be of little interest, but note how the diagonal colouring of the motifs creates the illusion of a diamond medallion design. The finely drawn zig-zag pattern that joins the border and main field is typically Shirvan, more so than the other elements of the design.

471   Daghestan
(5.17 × 1.24 m, 16′11″ × 4′)
A truly dynamic kilim typical of this area both in colouring and design. The main field emblem is supposed to represent dragons, a favoured theme in Caucasian rugs and kilims. Woven as a wall hanging, it still retains its loops. These kilims are sometimes known as Avar kilims. Avars were mainly found in the Balkan Peninsula, but the word 'avar' means 'from unknown origin'.
(Detail 475)

472   Daghestan
(3.16×1.59 m, $10'4'' \times 5'2''$)
Here trees and humanoid figures embellish the field, and in the border simplified dragon or fighting-cock motifs appear. (Detail 476)

473   Shirvan
(2.64×1.86 m, $8'7'' \times 6'1''$)
Another kilim where the main hexagonal motif is not unique to the area, but is used also by the Shahsavan people, and in Anatolian kilims.

474   Shirvan
(2.84×1.56 m, $9'3'' \times 5'1''$)
The carefully drawn design and fine slitweave of this kilim are complemented by its soft colours. 637 has the same format on a larger scale. (Detail 455)

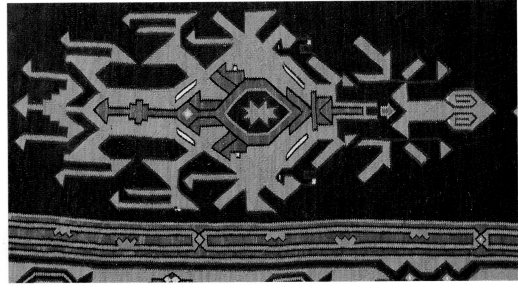

475 Detail of 471.

476 Detail of 472.

Opposite:

477 Daghestan
(2.25 × 1.50 m, 7′4″ × 4′11″)
Use of contrasting colour – especially yellow – and strong design make this a powerful kilim. Note the double 'Z' column motif contained within the main emblems, reminiscent of a dragon motif. Natural dyes have been used, with the exception of small amounts of fuchsin, which has faded to a greyish-pink.

	Daghestan	471–2, 477
DESIGN	Field: Large dominant medallions Borders: Simple and dark red	
SIZE AND SHAPE	Long and narrow	
MATERIALS	Tight thick wool	
STRUCTURE	Slitweave, giving surface texture ridged effect	
COLOURS	Dark blue ground, with medium blue, occasional dark green, brown, orange and a little white	
FRINGE	Twisted	
SELVEDGE	Plain	
Remarks	Woven as wall tapestries/The main motif is called *rukzal*, said to represent a dragon, a popular theme often used in Caucasian rugs	

Daghestan

Since the Middle Ages the villagers of Daghestan have been renowned for their expert craftsmanship, with different areas specializing in particular artifacts. Accordingly their weaving skills are particularly well developed, and as both good quality wool and the natural elements necessary for synthesizing colourful dyes were readily available, a masterly collection of textiles was created. Kilims are known locally as *davaghins*, many of which are of similar composition, size and colour. These flatweaves are very powerful both in design and colour combination, and were often used as wall hangings, many retaining their loops. The large abstract geometric motifs are known as *rukzals* and are thought to represent dragons. Another design that again features dragons, in this instance as a border motif, is heavily decorated with trees of life, birds, and often human figures. This composition has a softer colour palette, and is shorter in length. Both types are called 'Avar' by the rug traders of today. The Avar people are of undetermined origin but are known to have inhabited parts of the Caucasus in the

478 Karabakh
(3.37 × 1.74 m, 11′ × 5′8″)
The central medallion is a little 'thin', particularly in comparison with the heavily decorated border. However, the overall colour composition and design of this kilim are very complementary. The central motifs are reminiscent of Azerbaijani knotted-carpet designs, and the floral border, of Eastern European flatweaves.

middle of the sixth century. The Avar language is spoken in western and central Daghestan. Colouring is predominantly red and blue, and kilims are runner-like in shape. *Davaghins* have a different look to other Caucasian kilims because of the texture of their wool, which appears to be more intertwined.

Armenia

The Armenians are a nation of traders and weavers who adopted Christianity at the beginning of the third century, so it is not surprising that the cross is often incorporated into designs, or appears as a filler motif. Many Armenian artifacts bear signatures, dates and inscriptions relating to a particular event, and kilims are no exception. During the nineteenth century many kilims were made by Kurdish people living near Erivan, and around Mount Aragats. *Shadda* and *zili* were also made in the Armenian villages near Nagorny Karabakh. Armenians call kilims *karpets*, and they are also known by the Kurdish name of *yamani*. These became very popular in other areas of the Caucasus.

Georgia

Kilims known as *paradaghis*, as well as some knotted rugs, were woven in Georgia, and were most popular in the highlands. They were used as wall hangings and furniture covers, so the compositions tend to work best when laid out in a landscape format. Every family had their own particular design, and as kilims were not woven for sale, many still remain in their original homes. The use of colours in the textiles was limited, however, and many of the Georgian kilims are rather sombre. Designs vary quite considerably. Floral as well as geometric compositions are found, sometimes both incorporated into the one kilim but nevertheless generally simple.

Chapter Seven

Afghanistan and Central Asia

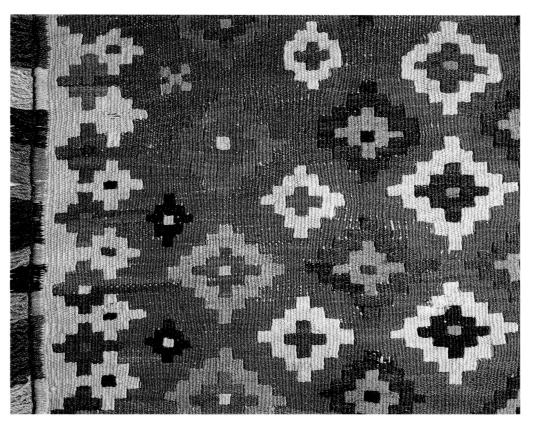

479   *Good quality natural dyes were used in north Afghanistan up until the middle of the twentieth century. This kilim, woven in Maimana, dates from the 1920s. (Detail)*

The Turkomen · Labijar · The Uzbeks
Sari-i-Pul · The Kazakhs · Maimana
The Aimaq · The Mushwani · The Balouch
The Mukkur Kutchi

480 Uzbek Tartari
This eight-pointed star motif and fine zig-zag border are typical of Tartari weaving. (Detail)

481 Labijar Uzbek
This composition features diamonds of apparently randomly chosen colours. (Detail)

A LAND-LOCKED COUNTRY OF STRONGLY CONTRASTING DESERT AND mountain terrain, Afghanistan has held a particular attraction for both travellers and conquerors since ancient times. Lying at the central crossroads of Asia, the country has undergone invasion by expansionist regimes from all over the world, which have met with the dogged and spirited resistance of the indigens, but which have each left in their wake their own cultural legacy. Alexander the Great came to Afghanistan in the fourth century BC following his rout of the Persian Empire, bringing with him a Mediterranean culture and establishing self-governing Greek colonies. Alexander was succeeded by his general Seleucus, and the Seleucid Empire continued to flourish, embracing, as it did, the crossing point of trade routes from Cathay and India to Europe and the Mediterranean basin. The country later formed part of the Parthian and Sassanian empires and was, at various times, subjugated by the Persians, Mongols and Moghuls, converting to Islam in the process. It has also been divided amongst smaller, native dynasties, the most notable being the Ghazni of the twelfth century. The history of Afghanistan, therefore, concerns itself with the interaction, development and influence of separate tribal groups, remnants of invading parties and nomadic peoples, which have resulted in a tumult of political and strategic intrigues.

A certain stability was achieved in the eighteenth century when there arose an independent kingdom centred on Kandahar in the south, which expanded over a hundred-year period to include the Persian borderlands and areas of the Punjab. This kingdom was beset by civil unrest and tribal back-stabbing in its later years, out of which emerged Dost Mohammed in 1823 as the self-styled Emir. The expansionist ambitions of Russia caused the British to interfere in the struggles over the throne in the First Afghan War (1839–42). The British twice more fought Afghanistan over alleged Russian infiltration and anti-British feeling, and after a further confrontation in 1919, Britain formally recognized Afghan independence. The boundaries of the newly emergent Afghanistan were drawn up to be expedient to the political and military requirements of the major powers, ignoring the pattern of indigenous tribal territories. The consequence of such ethnographic divisions and the importance of Afghanistan's central position have led to a never-ending conflict of interests that has of late culminated in long-threatened open conflict, bringing misery to millions of civilians.

More than a decade of sporadic guerilla warfare has had considerable effect on the lives of the village people and the nomads. Very little domestic weaving has taken place, although Afghan looms had previously been producing a remarkable variety and quantity of domestic textiles for many hundreds of years; indeed, the region of north Afghanistan and Central Asia is possibly one of the original loom-weaving centres in the world, and its textiles display hardly any outside influence. These ancient flatweaving skills have been largely overlooked by scholars and historians; very little has been written concerning the origins and use of the kilims and trappings. This directly reflects the preoccupation of 'oriental' carpet-dealers with Turkish and Persian production, the happy result of which has been, until recently, the ready and inexpensive availability of a great variety of original and old Afghan weavings.

Until the arrival of the trans-Asian travellers of the 1960s and 1970s, the flatweavers of the region were exclusively occupied with the production of kilims

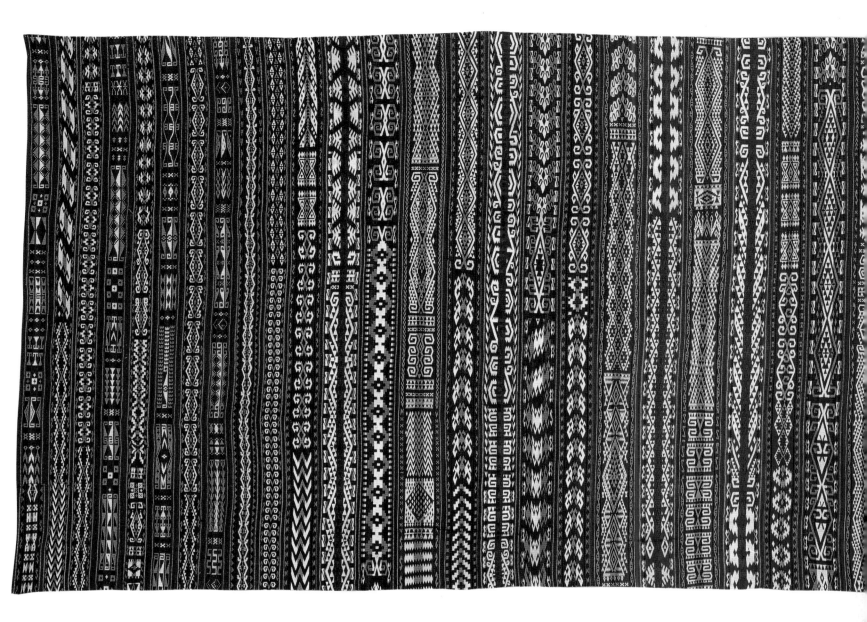

and trappings for their own use or for local sale. Depending on the cost of the materials, either vegetable or chemical dyes were used. From the dark and banded kilims of the Balouch nomads to the vivacious geometric patterns of the rugs of the Uzbek village people, the range of compositions was as varied as their tribal origins. The diversity of peoples, high proportion of nomads and preponderance of different languages – Pushtu, Farsi and all manner of local dialects – have all contributed to the difficulty of discovering the origin of a flatwoven textile. Names become duplicated or confused, and any other facts which may emerge have then to be jockeyed into some sort of 'logic'. Moreover, such information is commonly provided by dealers who are usually more eager to please than to adopt the role of textile historian. As with Persian kilims, which are also woven by intermingled tribal groups, the kilims of Afghanistan are usually identified by the name of the predominant tribe or principal market town or village in the area where they are woven; and from the Mongol and Turkoman peoples of the lands of the great steppes of Russia and China to the desert dwellers of the Balouch, the flatweavers of Afghanistan are to be found living amongst some of the most dramatic landscapes of the world, north and west of the Hindu Kush.

482, 483　Uzbek *ghudjeri*
(2.43 × 1.44 m, 8' × 4'9")
This kilim is representative of the very fine detail and wide range of colour used by Uzbek weavers. The strips of warp-faced patterning are less than 10 cm (4") wide and demonstrate the wide variety of traditional motifs and patterns available to the weaver. (Detail 483)

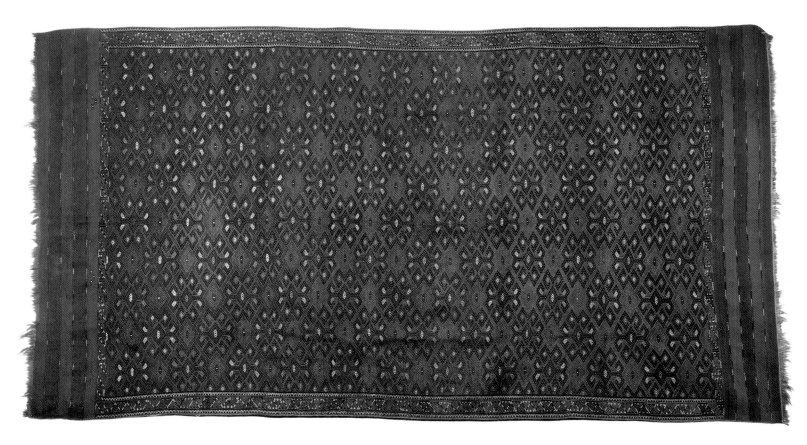

484   Yomut Turkoman
(3.66 × 1.32 m, 12′ × 4′4″)
Kilims from the Yomut tribe of Turkoman people, from the eastern corner of the Caspian sea, are invariably large and rectangular, with a madder-red background and the traditional Turkoman gul in black and blue.

485   Yomut Turkoman
The end panels of Yomut kilims are decorated with brocaded amulet motifs. (Detail)

The Turkomen

For so large and famous a group of Central Asian people it is a reflection of their turbulent, busy and migratory past that they have no surviving records of their own tribal history; all such information is derived from an oral tradition of local folktales and disseminated from the writings of others. The legend of the origin of the Oghuz (Ghuzz in Turkish), the ancestors of the Turkomen, is a suitably colourful tale, related by one Rashidal-Din writing in the fourteenth century. Oghuz Khan, so the story goes, was the great-grandson of Noah's son Japhet; when the prophet divided the earth amongst his sons, Japhet received the east; thus he is thought of as the father of all Turks and Mongols. When Oghuz Khan was born he refused his mother's milk because he saw her as a pagan and so, after three days she changed her beliefs so that Oghuz could suckle. Later, Oghuz did not consummate his first two marriages because he believed his wives were also pagan; his third wife, however, bore him seven sons. On hearing of the rejection of the first two wives, Oghuz's father was enraged and resolved to fight his son; such a battle gave Oghuz a thirst for fighting. Thereafter Oghuz fought a battle for every year of his life, losing none, and establishing a precedent for the belligerent Turkoman people.

The Oghuz were first described by Byzantine chroniclers as being loosely linked to a Mongolian tribe, the T'uchueh, who split into two, with one branch establishing itself in present-day Sinkiang, south Kazakhstan, and in Kirghistan. In the tenth century their descendants, by that time known as the Oghuz, had settled as pastoralists and farmers in the region to the south and east of the Aral Sea. The name Turkoman or Turkman was not itself adopted until the tenth or eleventh century by Oghuz tribes who appeared from out of the high desert

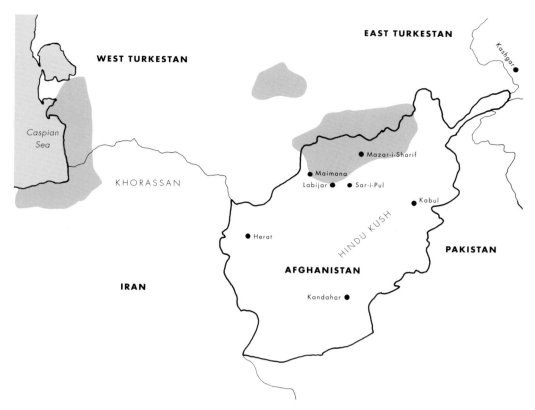

EAST TURKESTAN

WEST TURKESTAN

The Turkomen

Caspian Sea

KHORASSAN

• Mazar-i-Sharif

• Maimana
Labijar • • Sar-i-Pul

• Kabul

• Herat

PAKISTAN

AFGHANISTAN

IRAN

Kandahar •

486, 487   Labijar
(3.35 × 1.75 m, 11′ × 5′9″)
The weaver of this kilim has, within the rigorous requirements of traditional design, created a masterpiece through understatement and simplicity. The rectangles of red, yellow and blue step diagonally across the field and are linked by simple reciprocal arch shapes, which are reflected in the border. The motif in the centre of each rectangle is an abbreviation of a complex predecessor, the hour-glass motif, also frequently found on central Anatolian kilims, symbolizing light and energy. (Detail 486)

steppes, close by the Takla Makan Desert and the Tien Shan mountain range, to forge westwards across the Amu Darya (Oxus) River, invading and influencing the development of so many of the peoples of Asia, Asia Minor and the Middle East. From this massive invading migration, and the subsequent settling of some of the Oghuz Turks, is founded the early history of many of the Turkic tribes inhabiting the lands beyond Central Asia.

488 Yomut Turkoman
(0.91 × 0.68 m, 3′ × 2′3″)
This juval*, tent bag, features colours and motifs
that are typical of the Yomut.* Juval *are
usually woven in pairs, although not joined. The
reverse is plainwoven with narrow stripes of
weft-float pattern in ivory white.*

489 *Detail of* 490.

The Turkomen continued their incursions far afield, and in doing so established
two of the ruling houses of Persia: the short-lived dynasty of the Afsharids, whose
founder, the celebrated Nadir Shah (r. 1736–47), has been called 'the last great
Asiatic conqueror', and the dynasty of the Qajars, which lasted from the end of the
eighteenth century until Reza Khan's *coup d'état* in 1921. Reza Shah Pahlavi
reigned from 1925 to 1941, and was largely responsible for the modernization of
Persia.

Within their Persian homeland, however, the internal feuding between the nine
or ten Turkoman tribes, and clashes with the neighbouring people of Central
Asia, such as the Kazakhs, Kirghiz and Uzbeks, perpetuated a state of warfare.
Different cultures evolved and cities were built only to fall to marauding tribes.
This coincided with dramatic changes in climate, plagues and the disintegration of
irrigation systems. Such instability had great bearing on the fortunes of the
bazaars along the silk roads, the ancient trading routes between the East and West
which ran through the Turkoman territories.

The settled Turkoman people, mostly Sunni Muslims, have remained within
the area bounded by the Caspian Sea, the Amu Darya River, the Karakoram
Mountains and the Kara Kum Desert, spreading into the steppes of northern Iran
and Afghanistan to the north of the Hindu Kush. A few groups are also living
further north, close to the Aral Sea. There was no formal barrier between Persia,
Afghanistan and west Turkestan until the late nineteenth century, so the tribes
were therefore free to follow their centuries-old patterns of migration; a large-
scale and one-way movement of their peoples occurred during the early part of the
twentieth century, away from Bolshevik suppression, settlement and Commu-
nism to the borderland within Persia and Afghanistan. Although most Turkomen
are now sedentary farmers there still exists a number of bands of nomads, and all
Turkomen live up to the reputation of being tough horsemen and traders who
vigorously preserve a traditional lifestyle. This is particularly evident in their
weaving practices.

The Turkoman people are famed the world over as prolific weavers of fine
knotted carpets. So well established is this reputation that their social and tribal
background and lifestyle have been thoroughly researched and documented.
Their pile rugs, and the designs, motifs and symbolism found therein, have been
detailed, drawn, and analysed perhaps more than any other group of textiles. Little
of this work has, however, been related to the flatweaves of the Turkoman people.
What is certain, though, is that despite the fact that the Turkomen are descended
from the Oghuz, fellow ancestors to the Turkic tribes of Iran, there are no
similarities in the structure or design of the weavings of the two groups.
Turkoman flatweaves are large in size and brocaded with very little diversity in
composition, motifs or colouring, quite the opposite of the colourful slitweaves
from north Iran.

The cultural continuity of the Turkoman group has been greatly disturbed in
the twentieth century; there has been much intermarriage between the Turkomen
and the many various Turkic peoples who have settled in Uzbekistan, and a
general loss of immediate clan and tribal identity, especially in the last fifty years.
Demand from Western buyers, especially for knotted carpets, has dominated their
weaving activities. It is particularly unfortunate, therefore, that there is so little
known about the extent of manufacture and the use of flatweaves amongst the

Turkoman tribes prior to these changes. The Yomut people are the only Turkoman tribe from West Turkestan and Iran who continue to weave kilims. Within north Afghanistan, the large group of Ersari Turkomen weave kilims and bags. And, indeed, it is the bags rather than kilims that are most strongly associated with the weaving craft of the Turkomen. As an integral part of their nomadic and semi-nomadic way of life, a wealth of very traditional bags, tent and animal trappings are flatwoven, or partly flatwoven, by many of the Turkoman tribes, especially the Turkestan Tekke, and the Salor, from west Afghanistan and West Turkestan.

The Yomut Turkomen

The Yomut are to be found in north-east Iran, and across the border in west Turkestan close by the Caspian Sea. There is also a group to the north of the Kara Kum Desert and a hundred or so families living in Herat in west Afghanistan. The Yomut kilims of north-east Iran and the Caspian Sea area are large, rectangular and woven in one piece. The overall coloration is a distinct deep madder red through to a rich pink, with brocaded *guls* patterning the whole field in colours of dark brown, blue and turquoise with highlighting details in ivory-white wool. The *gul* is the predominant motif characteristic of Turkoman weaves, almost to the exclusion of any other design. *Gul* is the Persian word for flower; however, through the extended activity of knotting and weaving, the flower has become so stylized as to become unrecognizable as a figurative representation. All the major Turkoman tribes have their own stylized form of *gul*, and these are featured extensively in pile carpets and bags of all kinds. They are considered to be a form of tribal standard, important in the identification of the tribal group. The *gul* is displayed on camel bags, and it is often prominently exhibited at the nomadic encampment.

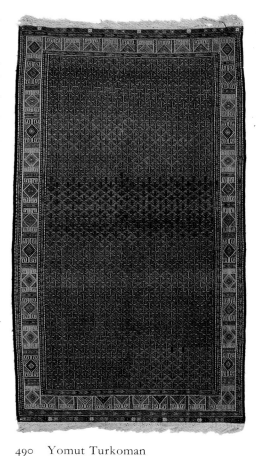

490   Yomut Turkoman
(2.28 × 1.21 m, 7′6″ × 4′)
The abrash in the field detracts from the more interesting aspects of this Yomut kilim woven in north-west Afghanistan. Its border features an ancient motif found on the felted roofs and door flaps of the Turkoman yurt. The motif in the field is more usually found along the top edge and reverse side of large juval and jallar, storage bags. (Detail 489)

Yomut Turkoman	484, 490–3, 496
DESIGN	Field: Repeating brocaded *guls* Borders: Narrow
SIZE AND SHAPE	Large and rectangular
MATERIALS	Warps of ivory-white/brown wool, with added goat or horse hair, wool wefts
STRUCTURE	Weft-faced patterning
COLOURS	Soft pink to deep madder-red ground, with brown, blue, turquoise and ivory-white brocading
FRINGE	Plain/Knotted/Net
SELVEDGE	Extra cord reinforcement/Parallel wrapping
Remarks	Many bags, animal trappings and tent bands woven

Yomut kilims are well finished, with either plain, knotted or long net fringes, and wide undecorated end panels in the traditional Turkoman red, often with intriguing and amusing motifs brocaded at random; the corners of the rugs are

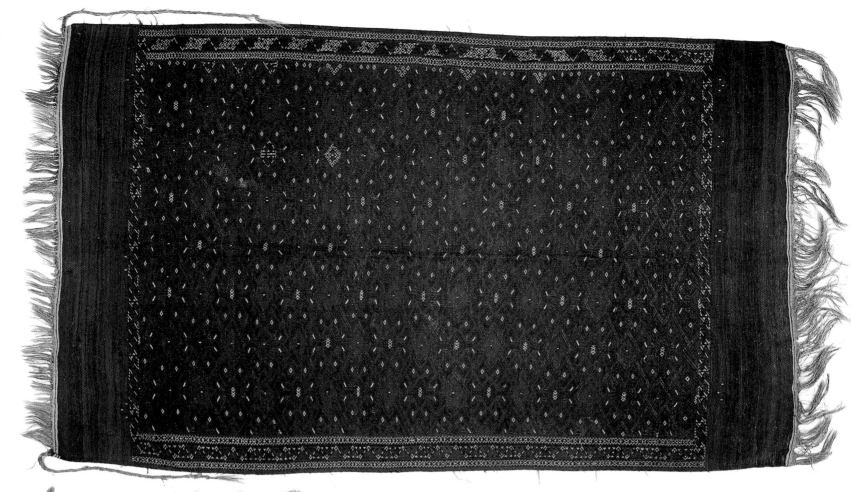

491 Yomut Turkoman (above)
(4.03 × 2.21 m, 13'3" × 7'3")
This kilim is not very old and is made with poor wool and cheap dyes. The field is a complex pattern of linked guls typical of most Turkoman kilims. This particular example is the bastani gul. *The narrow borders and wide plainweave end panels are typical; very often the weaver will brocade small motifs in the end panels.*

493 Yomut Turkoman (left)
(2.43 × 1.21 m, 8' × 4')
This kilim is tightly woven in a very unusual floating weft patterning technique. The large motifs at the ends of the field effectively change its proportions, and the small motifs in diagonal bands are positive and negative forms of the same pattern. The colour of the field is derived from dye concocted from madder root and pomegranate skin, well contrasted by the natural white wool in the border.

sometimes finished with short 'tails', or 'ropes' of weave, and these are used for pegging the kilim down on the ground outside for a festival or special occasion.

The Yomut people of Herat produce modern brocaded kilims. Although this group are largely diluted through intermarriage with the Ersari Turkomen of north Afghanistan, they vehemently consider themselves to be Yomut and their kilims still retain the traditional vivid red appearance of Turkoman pile carpets; unfortunately they are lustreless and woven to a very loose standard of brocade work, with large-scale imitations of the traditional *gul* or the *bastani* motif, a distinctive hooked star motif set in a lozenge or diamond grid pattern.

The Kashgari Turkomen

Kashgar, the principal town of East (Chinese) Turkestan, lies at a remote meeting point of several important trading routes on the ancient silk roads. As a fortified town it has enjoyed considerable strategical, commercial and social importance throughout the history of Central Asia.

The kilims woven there are extremely fine, soft and light, and can only really serve as covers, for which use they were originally intended. The compositions of these textiles are very similar in appearance to the Uzbek Tartari *safid* kilims from Sar-i-Pul and Samangan, although they can be distinguished by the quality of their wool and the tightness of their weave. On a background of fine ivory-coloured wool, the pattern is created by the rust red of the horizontal striping, broken by tiny chevrons of moss green and soft yellow. Kilims of this type are also made by the Turkoman people to the north of Kunduz in north-east Afghanistan.

494 Kashgari Turkoman
(2.23 × 1.01 m, 7′4″ × 3′4″)
The extremely fine wool of this kilim is so soft that it could be mistaken for a shawl. The motif in bands across the field is commonly used in the borders of small rugs or ensi, *door hangings.*

Kashgari Turkoman		494
DESIGN	Field: Bands of colour, narrow bands of chevrons Borders: None	
SIZE AND SHAPE	Long and very narrow	
MATERIALS	Very fine wool warps, fine wool wefts	
STRUCTURE	Plain weft-faced weave, extra-weft brocading	
COLOURS	Ivory white, rust red, moss green, yellow	
FRINGE	Usually long and knotted	
SELVEDGE	Plain, with double warps	
Remarks	One of the few types of white kilim	

Labijar

Labijar means 'next to the canal/small river'. This well-irrigated area encompassing four villages near the Darya Safidi River, close to Sherberghan, was deeply influenced by the occupation and colonization of Alexander the Great and the subsequent Seleucid Empire.

Opposite, far left:

492 Turkoman
(1.75 × 1.14 m, 5′9″ × 3′9″)
The powerful pattern is exaggerated by the extensive use of white wool. Many of the motifs found on small Turkoman kilims are similar to those on purdah, *suggesting that these were intended for the same use.*

Influx groups newer to the region include the Ersari and Saltuq Turkomen, who initially moved to Labijar from the north in the fourteenth century and were followed by many of their compatriots escaping from the Soviets at the end of the nineteenth century. The Ersari weave the most traditional kilims from this area, which are very easy to recognize. These flatweaves are rectangular and often very large, with a composition that comprises 30 cm (12″) to 38 cm (15″) squares or panels within the field, known as the *khesti gul*, each with an ancient Islamic motif in its centre. The most common is the double arrowhead design, said to bring good luck in hunting. Others include the hour-glass motif that gives light and energy, and an 'S' motif, also for good luck. The squares themselves are in contrasting colours of deep madder red, indigo and golden yellow, and are outlined with small, white diamonds. This patterning is also found in Turkoman carpets, and may represent the *bazubandi*, the metal box that the Koran is kept in.

The Labijar flatweaves have narrow borders comprising two or three coloured zig-zag patterns completed with wide plain-coloured ends. The selvedges are broad rows of extra-weft reinforcement, often taking in five or six warps reinforced with brown wool and goat hair. Overall, the Labijar kilims are substantially made, with thick wool warps, occasionally twined with horse hair and dense, almost board-like wefts; all the patterning is worked in slitweave or double-interlock weave. The Uzbeks of the Sherberghan area have in the past twenty years copied Ersari kilims, in a very much abbreviated and simplified fashion that changes the scale of the rectangles and motifs, often using wool shorn from slaughtered sheep in combination with poor dyes that give little lustre and abrash.

Labijar Ersari Turkoman		487, 495
DESIGN	Field: Squares with double arrowhead motifs Borders: Narrow zig-zags	
SIZE AND SHAPE	Usually very large and rectangular	
MATERIALS	Thick wool warps, wool wefts	
STRUCTURE	Very tightly woven slitweave/Double interlock	
COLOURS	Deep madder red, indigo, yellow, white	
FRINGE	Plain/Knotted	
SELVEDGE	Wide extra weft reinforcement/Parallel wrapped	
Remarks	Many copies of this design woven by the Uzbeks of Sherberghan	

The *bagh-i-chinar* poplar-leaf design is woven by the Uzbeks in Labijar, but, rather confusingly, it has been copied in large quantities for the export market during the last twenty years by the Hazaras of Sar-i-Pul and Mazar-i-Sharif. The *bagh-i-chinar* has, unfortunately, been dubbed the 'Christmas tree' by dealers and traders, an article that is totally alien to the weavers of north Afghanistan. The original Uzbek kilims are relatively fine, made of soft wool in soft colours. The Hazara copies, however, make much use of orange, and in most recent times there has been a strong fashion for dull purple. Those from Mazar are distinctively finished, featuring a 7 cm (3″) brown wool border with outlined diamond shapes in a weft brocade. Finishes are cheap and simple.

The Uzbeks have also woven very fine, simple kilims in Labijar in the past. Horizontal bands of undecorated weave are found in natural light brown and ivory-white wool tones, with bands coloured in pale golden yellow, light indigo blue and a brown madder red. Random stripes of lozenge, chevron or arrowhead shapes run across the width of the kilim and there are no borders; these flatweaves are well constructed with reinforced selvedges and horse hair spun into the plain-coloured warps.

Labijar Uzbek	497, 512
DESIGN	Field: Crenellated interlocking poplar-leaf design/ Bands of plainweave between bands of large chevrons Borders: Narrow
SIZE AND SHAPE	Various
MATERIALS	Soft wool warps, wool wefts
STRUCTURE	Tightly woven slitweave/Double interlock
COLOURS	Soft red, blue, brown, ivory white
FRINGE	Plain/Knotted
SELVEDGE	Plain/Reinforced with extra warps/Sometimes parallel wrapped
Remarks	Simplified copies are woven by the Hazara people

The Uzbeks

These are Turkic people, who are reputed to be of Uigur extraction: the Uigui are, historically, a Mongolian tribe, now absorbed by the surrounding Mongol, Chinese and Tartar populations. In the sixth century the Uigui settled in Kashgaria, Sin-Kiang Province, East Turkestan, as Buddhist monks, but soon after were converted to Christianity by Nestorian missionaries. The Uigur language, still current in Kashgaria, is a very pure and somewhat archaic form of Turki.

On the steppes of Central Asia, during the tempestuous years of the fourteenth century, the Uzbeks, at this time a sub-tribe of the Uigui, became political refugees and migrated to West Turkestan, close to the territory occupied by the Turkomen. Under the leadership of Uzbek Khan they abandoned their pagan, shamanistic and Christian beliefs and embraced Islam. Unlike the Turkomen, reputed nomadic plunderers and slave traders, the Uzbeks settled in the Kyzyl Kum Desert, around the great Muslim cultural centre of Bokhara, and in north Afghanistan, where they maintained their independence from Bokhara, Persia and the Russians.

Page 262:

495 Labijar Ersari Turkoman
(3.88 × 1.82 m, 12′9″ × 6′)
A large, carefully constructed and drawn kilim woven by the Ersari Turkomen. It features a very traditional design that has recently been copied by the Uzbek people. The ancient motif of a double arrowhead symbolizes successful hunting, and the zig-zags at the ends are said to be for good luck.

496 Turkoman
(2.55 × 1.21 m, 8′4″ × 4′)
An unusual kilim woven by the Yomut or Ersari Turkomen of north Afghanistan. There are definite Uzbek influences in the design, such as the bands of small chevron patterns, but the weave, the wool and the finish are Turkoman. The small flowers brocaded on to the large chevron patterns are called 'candlestick' motifs by Western dealers and traders, otherwise known as kuş, the Turkoman word for 'bird'. These motifs are usually seen on knotted-pile purdah from north Afghanistan, but there is nothing to indicate that this rug is a purdah screen as there are no loops on the corners or fringe attached to a long edge.

497 Labijar Uzbek
(3.32 × 1.37 m, 11′ × 4′6″)
The zig-zag design on Labijar kilims is usually restricted to narrow bands across the field. The weaver of this example has used the whole field on a dramatic scale, and enhanced the appearance with end panels patterned in a smaller scale. The muted colours are lifted by the pale line, which exaggerates the pattern.

Captions for 495–7 on page 261.

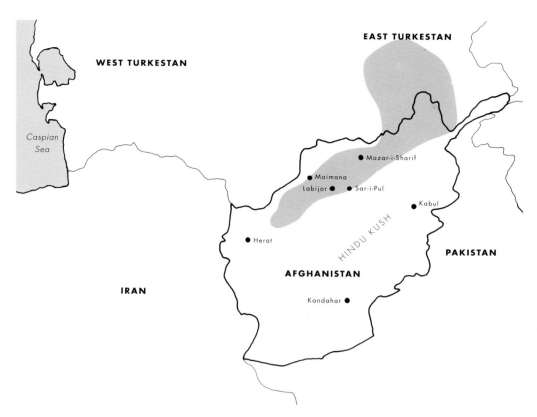

498   Uzbek
(1.75 × 0.91 m, 5′9″ × 3′)
A prayer rug found in Maimana of remarkable simplicity and naivity. It is not old nor are the colours of the border and prayer arch good, but it has the feel of the practical, utilitarian, uncluttered side of peasant life.

The Uzbeks have, however, always been a political rather than an ethnic group. There has been much intermarriage, resulting in a confusion of sub-tribe names, such as Naiman and Kipchack, which are also used by the Kirghiz. Uzbeks also live amongst the Turkomen and Karakalpaks, with cross-cultural influences from the Arabs and Tadjiks. Most Uzbeks are settled farmers although, more recently, some are employed in the service and transport industries. They have had a great influence over the weaving traditions of former Soviet Central Asia and north Afghanistan.

Samangan, also known as Aibak, is a traditional and prolific weaving centre for the Uzbeks in north Afghanistan. Samangan is a most ancient city, and Upper Palaeolithic sites as well as an important Buddhist stupa, known locally as Takht-i-Rustam (Rustam's Throne), dating from the fourth to the fifth century, have been

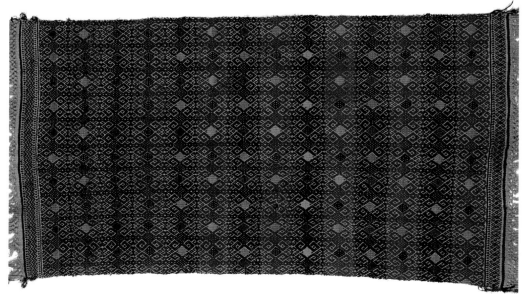

499   Arabi
(2.43 × 1.16 m, 8′ × 3′10″)
The Arabi, a scattered tribe of original Arab stock, have little tradition of kilim-weaving. This brocaded rug of coloured wool on plainweave cotton warps and wefts was found in Samangan. They have used a traditional Turkoman motif, and filled the spaces in the design with brocaded weave, adding spots of bright yellow in the centre of the motif.

unearthed in its vicinity. Early Arab geographers list 'Siminhan' as one of the largest cities in Central Asia, and before the destruction wrought by Ghenghis Khan, it extended over ten miles, right to the foot of the Hindu Kush. Tamerlane's chroniclers reported that through the fourteenth century, it remained in ruins, but due to its strategic position near a pass over the Hindu Kush and the rich soil of the steppes close by, the site was assured of revival, and Samangan again became a prominent caravan depot in the nineteenth century.

The Uzbek Tartari *safid* kilims found in Sar-i-Pul (see p. 268) are also woven in the Samangan area, but with a few subtle differences. There is a pronounced use of cherry red and bright yellow, in chevron and zig-zag patterns across the rug, and fewer large areas of undecorated white weave. Distinctive stripes of black wool are highlighted with small dotted lines of white running between the wider bands of patterning.

Uzbek *Ghudjeri*   504–5, 507

DESIGN	Field: Horizontal bands of tight and ornate patterning
SIZE AND SHAPE	Various
MATERIALS	Fine wool
STRUCTURE	Warp-faced patterning in narrow bands
COLOURS	Varied palette of strong colours, predominately red, blue, yellow
FRINGE	None
SELVEDGE	Cut ends bound with cloth/Cut ends turned under and stitched
Remarks	Made from long lengths of narrow bands cut and sewn together/Often used as covers or horse blankets

Uzbek *Kilim Suzani*   506, 508

DESIGN	Field: Narrow bands of plainweave over-embroidered with Central Asian motifs
SIZE AND SHAPE	Various
MATERIALS	Wool, cotton, wool embroidery
STRUCTURE	Balanced plainweave
COLOURS	Ivory-white ground, red, blue, black over-embroidery
FRINGE	None
SELVEDGE	Cut ends bound with cloth/Cut ends turned under and stitched
Remarks	Made from long lengths of narrow bands cut, sewn together and embroidered

The Uzbeks also make warp-faced patterned rugs, known locally as *ghudjeri*. On narrow tripod looms, they weave very long strips some 8 cm (3″) to 23 cm (9″) wide. The finished strips, packed with a multitude of complex, ancient motifs, are cut into equal lengths and sewn, selvedge to selvedge, creating a textile to whatever dimension is required. This time-consuming technique of manufacture produces kilims that are very finely patterned. These *ghudjeri* are traditionally woven in the Uzbek villages to the west of Mazar-i-Sharif, near Balkh and Aq Chah, but are also produced in most Uzbek communities. The Arabi people from Mazar-i-Sharif also weave *ghudjeri* that are more limited in pattern and colour, used as small eating cloths and horse blankets.

Another type of Uzbek flatweave is the *kilim suzani*, constructed of narrow bands of plainweave ivory-white wool, or sometimes cotton, sewn together and then over-embroidered with loosely sewn, brightly coloured wool in patterns that resemble those on felt *namads* – the floor rugs, door and roof covers of the traditional Uzbek tent, the *yurt*. The work on these *kilim suzani* is so similar to that found on the long tent bands that hold the parts of the *yurt* together and bind loads on pack animals, that they must be a recent adaptation, made to meet market demands.

500–503 *Details of 505, 508, 507, 506.*

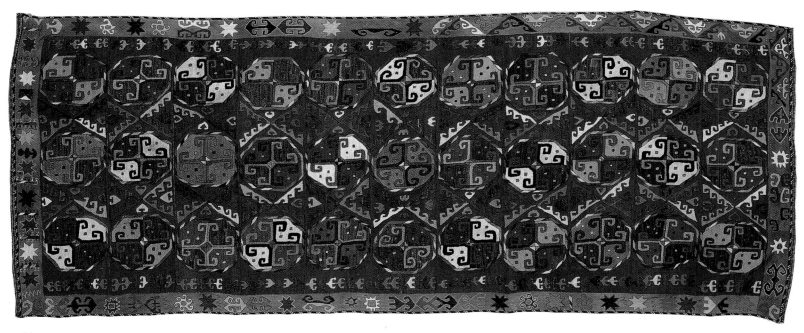

507 Uzbek *ghudjeri* (left)
(3.65 × 1.21 m, 12′ × 4′)
Narrow strips of plainwoven cotton are sewn together and then overembroidered with wool. This kilim would have been used as a purdah *or cover. (Detail 502)*

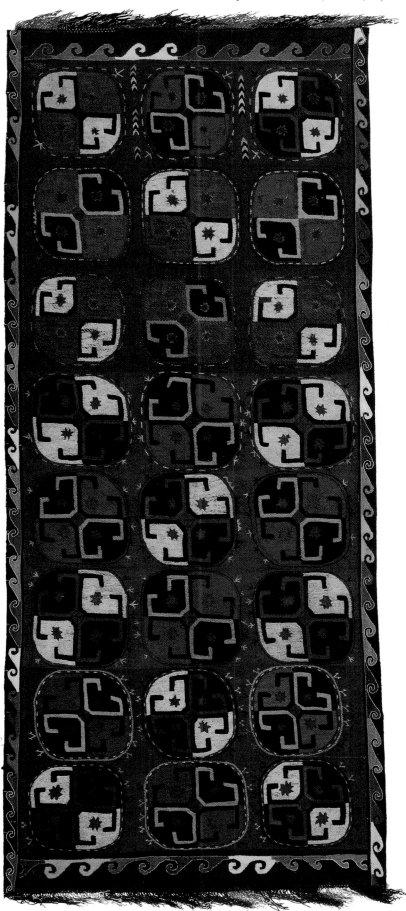

504 Uzbek *ghudjeri* (opposite, above left)
(3.04 × 1.37 m, 10′ × 4′6″)
An Uzbek ghudjeri *is a kilim made up of narrow strips of warp-faced patterning, cut and sewn together. Weaving in this technique can only be successfully done in narrow strips to avoid problems with the tension of the weave. The weaver will make strips up to 9 m (30′) long.*

505 Uzbek *ghudjeri* (opposite, above right)
(2.43 × 1.32 m, 8′ × 4′4″)
The dramatic appearance of this kilim is achieved using only three colours, bright red, dark blue and white. The weaver has used white warps down the centre of each strip, and woven and reversed the colour in the motifs from blue to red over the white background. (Detail 500)

506 Uzbek (opposite, below)
(2.75 × 1.06 m, 9′ × 3′6″)
This kilim was made as a cover for bedding, the embroidery being too fragile for a rug. The octagonal motifs have been carefully formed, and the triangular motifs with hook patterns and the borders have been drawn with a freedom and naivity that is very rarely found. (Detail 503)

508 Uzbek (right)
(2.74 × 1.14 m, 9′ × 3′9″)
This kilim suzani *has been put together in the style and manner of Uzbek felt rugs, or* namad. *It was made close to the town of Aq Chah in north Afghanistan. The pattern, an ancient symbol found on felts used for tent roofs and door covers, is embroidered on to plainwoven madder-red strips. The end and side borders are loosely sewn on. (Detail 501)*

509   Sar-i-Pul
(1.44 × 0.83 m, 4′9″ × 2′9″)
A small prayer rug woven by the Hazara people in Sar-i-Pul. The wool is typically poor. The weaver has used dovetail technique on the remarkable motif in the centre, resulting in a design with a fuzzy edge. She has used a familiar Central Asian hook design, with a modern lab-i-mazar *border motif.*

Sar-i-Pul

A small town set close by a river in the northern foothills of the Tibandi Turkestan range of mountains, Sar-i-Pul is surrounded by orchards of fruit and nut trees, and silk moths are cultivated within its mulberry groves. Situated about thirty miles south of the regional capital, Sherberghan, Sar-i-Pul is home to a wide diversity of people such as the Uzbeks, Hazara, Pushtuns, Arabi, Turkomen and Aimaq – an ethnic mix typical of many of the towns and villages in north Afghanistan. It is the Hazara women who do most of the weaving.

The Hazaras are reputed to be direct descendants of a military force left by Ghengis Khan to maintain the peace in central Afghanistan, who migrated to Sar-i-Pul late in the nineteenth century. Their looks betray their ancestry, for their faces are round and hairless, their eyes Mongolian. The Hazara are an impoverished people, even by Afghani standards, and are mainly peasant arable farmers, growing basic crops on poor, terraced and unirrigated land in the steep valleys of the Hindu Kush. Their poverty precludes their owning large numbers of sheep and goats. One and a half thousand years ago, this part of Afghanistan strongly adhered to the Buddhist faith, and there still exist vivid reminders of this in the form of ruined monasteries and stupas lost within the hills and valleys. Today, as befits their status, the Hazara are followers of the Shi'a sect of Islam.

Hazara kilims are often simplified copies of other compositions from adjacent areas and tribes in north Afghanistan – a particular favourite is the Turkoman *bagh-i-chinar* poplar-leaf design from Labijar. The best flatweaves come from the Hazara village of Charbagh, on the road between Sar-i-Pul and Sherberghan, where every house has at least one loom, kept either indoors or in a *yurt* set up close by. Although the wool used is the very best karaqul, the dyes are cheap and of poor quality, giving the kilims an uninteresting and lustreless look and feel. Nowadays it has become virtually impossible to attribute new kilims to any particular village, as inter-tribal and village copying is so widespread, from the people of Sar-i-Pul to Mazar-i-Sharif in the north and down across the Koh-i-Baba Mountains to Markazi Bihsud in central Hazarajat.

The kilims that come from the many villages of north Afghanistan, near to Mazar-i-Sharif, are generally of better quality and tighter weave than those from the remote, barren valleys of Hazarajat. These latter rugs are woven in large quantities, quickly and cheaply for the home market, using poor Hazaragi wool and garish, cheap dyes. The kilims for export are usually of superior quality, but remain loosely woven, with simple designs and plain brown wool borders replacing the traditional crenellations framing the field associated with the Bihsud area. Despite the fact that these kilims are made of good Ghilzai wool, they are not particularly attractive because of the over-simplified designs and crude colours.

The Uzbek inhabitants of Sar-i-Pul are collectively called 'Tartari', taking their name from the Tartars, the original Mongolo-Turkic tribes from the valleys of the In-Shan range who spread across Central Asia to the Middle East and include the Mongol-looking, Turkic-speaking people of Central Asia – the Uzbeks, Kazan Tartars, Turkomen, Kipchaks and Kirghiz. The Uzbek Tartari kilims fall into two categories. The first is the *safid* (*safid* means white). This is a very unusual style of soft woollen kilim with a creamy white field and little or no border-work. The field is patterned with horizontal bands of bright red zig-zags or narrow stripes of weave in red or yellow, and punctuated with small brocaded dashes of colour. Long and narrow in format, these flatweaves are sometimes found with a plain cream or ivory-white area in the centre of the rug, which suggests that it may be used as a *dashterkhan* (eating cloth). The end panels, usually finely woven, are wide bands of red weave, occasionally with double-interlock patterns of zig-zags and chevrons finished with long knotted fringes.

Uzbek Tartari *Safid*   511

DESIGN	Field: Narrow horizontal bands of colour on white field, sometimes with plain central area Borders: Small/None
SIZE AND SHAPE	Long and narrow
MATERIALS	Fine white or brown wool warps, wool wefts
STRUCTURE	Weft-faced plainweave, weft-faced patterning
COLOURS	Predominately ivory white or cream, narrow red, yellow and blue bands, small brocaded dashes
FRINGE	Plain/Knotted/Net
SELVEDGE	Plain/Simple reinforcement
Remarks	Woven in the Samangan area as well as in Sar-i-Pul/ Similar but not as fine as Kashgari Turkoman flatweaves

Uzbek Tartari *Ranghi*   510

DESIGN	Field: Overall grid of diamonds, each containing a Turkic star or spider motif Borders: Narrow zig-zags
SIZE AND SHAPE	Large and rectangular/Long
MATERIALS	Soft brown wool warps, wool wefts
STRUCTURE	Double interlock
COLOURS	Deep red and blue, green, yellow, white
FRINGE	Long and knotted/Net
SELVEDGE	Simple reinforcement
Remarks	*Khorjin* also woven with single star motif on each face

The other type of Uzbek Tartari kilim is the *ranghi* (*ranghi* means red). These are large kilims, usually about a double square in shape, and are always woven in double-interlock technique, one of the few types of Central Asian kilims to be woven thus. The wool is fine and soft, coloured deep red and blue, with occasional use of green, yellow and white. The compositions feature an overall grid of diamond shapes outlined in ivory white and containing a Turkic-style eight-

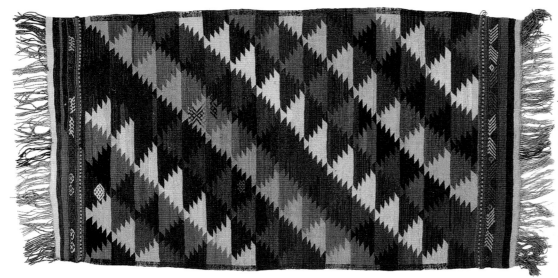

512 Labijar Uzbek
(2.13 × 1.21 m, 7′ × 4′)
Although this design is woven by the Uzbeks in Labijar, it has been copied by the Hazara people for selling both in the home market and for export. It has consequently become very difficult to distinguish between the different origins of rugs woven in this style within the last thirty years. The Uzbek weavers usually use better quality materials, finish the ends and reinforce the selvedge. The Hazara weavers use a simple border design in natural dark wool.

513 Uzbek Tartari *ranghi*
Although the colour of this kilim from Sar-i-Pul is unusual, the field pattern and border are typical. (Detail)

pointed star, or spider, motif. The borders are narrow and often feature tight zig-zag patterns of two or three colours. These kilims are beautifully constructed with a tight weave, and well finished with a simple selvedge and long, dark brown wool fringes. *Khorjin* and various small bags are woven in a similar style by the Uzbeks.

The Kazakhs

These are Turko-Mongol people who inhabit Kazakhstan, the adjacent areas of the Sinkiang region of China and north Afghanistan. First evolving in the fifteenth century, the Kazakh were initially a union of Turkic tribes who entered Transoxiana around the eighth century, and Mongols who migrated to the area in the thirteenth century as remnants of the Naiman tribes who were routed by Genghis Khan's armies. The subsequent Mongol conquest of Middle Asia and Kazakhstan resulted in the large-scale mingling, disintegration and consolidation of different tribes. The Norgai Horde and the Uzbek khanate, which in the mid-fifteenth century arose out of the ruins of the eastern sector of the Golden Horde, comprised various Turkic-speaking tribes as well as some Mongol tribes that had been assimilated by the native Turkic population. The term 'Kazakh' began to be applied ethnically in the early sixteenth century to all the steppe peoples who had inhabited this Uzbek khanate and the regions to the east. Collectively they were called the Uzbek Kazakhs, and it was not until the seventeenth century, with populations on the move due to the disintegration of the Hordes, that the Uzbeks and Kazakhs finally separated and became individual tribal groups.

The Kazakhs believe themselves to be descended from a progenitor whose three sons established the main divisions of the Kazakhs known as the Great, Middle and Little Hordes (Ordas), who occupied the eastern, central and western parts of what is now known as Kazakhstan. The Kazakhs speak the Turkic language but are Mongoloid in appearance and were originally nomads who bred valuable horses; wealthy khans owned herds numbering many thousands. Sheep and goats constitute their more everyday livestock.

The nomadic life of the Kazakhs was gradually curtailed by encroachment on their wide-ranging grazing lands. In the nineteenth century an increasing number

Opposite:

510 Uzbek Tartari *ranghi*
(4.13 × 1.70 m, 13′7″ × 5′7″)
The long narrow kilims from the prolific and diverse Uzbek weavers of Sar-i-Pul are easily recognizable. The colours are invariably red, yellow and blue, the weave double-interlock technique and the design an overall grid pattern of diamond shapes containing a Turkic eight-pointed star or spider motif.

511 Uzbek Tartari *safid*
(4.13 × 1.70 m, 13′7″ × 5′7″)
Safid means white, and these kilims have unusually large areas of white or ivory plainweave, often with small dashes of colour brocaded in the field. There are also narrow horizontal bands of red or yellow plainweave, and zig-zag patterning, in double-interlock technique.

514   *Detail of 515.*

of Kazakhs settled along the borders of their territory and planted cereal crops, and following the Russian Revolution in 1917, many wealthy Kazakhs fled with their herds into neighbouring Sinkiang and north Afghanistan. The remaining nomads were settled on collective farms so that by 1934 there was only one recorded nomadic group remaining in Kazakhstan. The majority of those remaining in Sinkiang dispersed in incredible hardship in the 1970s to Kashmir, and a smaller group fled to a new pastoralist life in eastern Turkey.

The Kazakhs are primarily felt-makers, and are not known for their flatweaves or knotted pile rugs. Indeed, in their traditional homeland of Kazakhstan virtually no traditional weaving is carried out, for the Communist ideal of collective farming has prevailed for most of the twentieth century. The Kazakhs in north Afghanistan are now closely intermingled with the Uzbeks, and weaving work uncompromised or uninfluenced by other tribes is rarely found.

The most distinctive kilims that can be attributed to Kazakh are the heavy weft-wrapped rugs woven in loosely spun, coarse wool, known as *lakai*. The background colour is invariably of a deep red to cherry pink, with a field divided into rectangles, each containing a star motif of obvious Central Asian origin, surrounded by a hooked design in black wool. The narrow border is a thin band of tiny triangles on a white background running either side of a wider band of small inverted motifs. These flatweaves are woven close to Kunduz, in north-east Afghanistan. Slitwoven kilims are rare, but a motif that distinguishes them from the other weavings of north Afghanistan and former Soviet Central Asia is a small angular reciprocal wave pattern, usually woven in black wool, outlining horizontal bands of typical motifs and stripes of plainweave in yellow and red.

Kazakh	514–17

DESIGN	Field: Rectangles each containing a large star motif, often with geometric border design continued round each rectangle
SIZE AND SHAPE	Various
MATERIALS	Very coarse thick wool
STRUCTURE	Weft wrapping
COLOURS	Cherry pink to deep madder red, black, white
FRINGE	Long and plain/Knotted
SELVEDGE	Simple reinforcement/Parallel wrapping
Remarks	Very heavy rugs with long unfinished ends of wool on the reverse

The Kirghiz   Another group from the Steppes who do not weave many kilims original to their tribe are the Kirghiz. They have similar origins to the Kazakhs, having been shunted into the eastern divide of the Transoxiana/Turkoman territories at the time of the Russian Revolution and the subsequent annexation of the Central Asian states. They do, however, merit an inclusion as prolific felt-

515 Kazakh
(1.14 × 0.83 m, 3'9" × 2'9")
This is an unusual small kilim woven by the Kazakh or Kirghiz people of former Soviet Central Asia. It is alive with movement in the design and border, and full of clear colour despite the limited use of madder red, yellow and natural wool. (Detail 514)

517 Kazakh
This bag features a distinctive Central Asian medallion with a star motif. (Detail)

516 Kazakh *lakai*
(2.80 × 1.82 m, 9'2" × 6')
Woven in very heavy weft-wrapping technique, these kilims are known in the bazaars as lakai, *and invariably have a rich red background, and a rectangular medallion design that features an unmistakably Central Asian hooked motif around a star pattern.*

makers, and as a strongly individual tribe, who used to be great horsemen, and were highly nomadic.

Maimana

This is the capital and market town of Faryab province, whose typical dusty Afghan bazaar is complete with rows of low shops, and houses that look so forbidding from the outside, and yet are so welcoming beyond the entrance door that leads to the traditional Muslim internal courtyard. Poplar trees stand sentinel along the irrigation canals, and the outskirts of Maimana are patchworked with groves of almonds, mulberries, and pistachios.

Maimana has been a settlement from ancient times; Palaeolithic graves and the evidence of early cave dwellings lie close by. According to the thirteenth-century Arab geographer, Yakut, the city was first settled by Israelites sent there from Jerusalem by Nebuchadnezzar. The town has always served as a market and resting place on the fringes of the great silk routes. Maimana prospered within the orbit of Samanid renaissance as one of the many flourishing towns that studded the plains from Herat to the mountains of Badakhshan before the Mongol invasions engulfed the area. Ravaged by the hordes, most of the cities were levelled forever, only a few, like Maimana, revived.

The Oghuz Turkomen have inhabited this area of north Afghanistan since the thirteenth century, mainly as semi-nomads. The Uzbeks drifted to Maimana district gradually, settling in the small villages and towns as farmers and traders, and they are now the largest group of people living in north Afghanistan. By the end of the nineteenth century Maimana had become a khanate of northern Afghanistan, along with Gurziwan, Darzab, Andkhoi, Sherberghan, Sar-i-Pul, Aqcha, Balkh, Kunduz, Khulm and Badakhshan. These khanates varied in size from year to year and ruler to ruler, mirroring the personal strength and influence of each khan, but Maimana always remained among the largest, and at one time even Balkh, known as 'the mother of all cities' since the time of Alexander the Great, came into its orbit. Sometimes independent, at other times in alliance, the dominant Uzbek khans constantly jockeyed for power amongst themselves, all the while playing clever games of politics with both Bokhara and Kabul by professing allegiance first to one and then the other. During the eighteenth century the Durrani khan gave the city to a friend and soldier of fortune; peace was maintained until his death in 1846, after which Maimana was weakened by fratricidal wars and complex internal affairs.

Unusually for a West Turkestan town, Maimana has no strong tradition of pile-carpet manufacture, not even by the Turkomen or the Uzbeks. It is, however, the Uzbeks who are the prolific kilim weavers. Although mainly woven by the Uzbek women, the flatweaves attributed to Maimana are also made by the many other tribes who live in the area, including the Hazaras, Tadjiks, Aimaqs and Turkomen who have adopted very similar weaving techniques and copied the 'traditional' designs and colours. Kilims are woven in all sizes, but large rectangular kilims are particularly common; smaller sizes have also been woven for many years to meet the demand in Kabul and for export. They are invariably constructed in slitweave or double-interlock technique, and the compositions are simple but strong, predominantly of large geometric shapes such as diamonds and triangles within the field, with a wide, geometrically patterned border incorporating many traditional designs. Such border designs include several that are found on Turkic kilims in Iran and Turkey, such as the *laleh abrassi* tulip design, which is simplified and woven in a large scale on the borders of most old Maimana kilims, and referred to in Pushtu and Farsi as *darakht* ('tree design'). The latchhook or bird's head design is also prevalent, again woven in an enlarged scale and called *daryaa* ('river design').

These kilims are also boldly coloured with the original strong and clear vegetable dyes that are known as 'wood colours' – reds, blues, oranges, rusty browns and yellows. More recently the bright chemical dyes imported from Germany have meant that the kilim colours have become much harsher, a particularly violent orange being fashionable in the late 1960s and 1970s, succeeded by a dull purple in the 1980s. Maimana kilims are simply finished, with a plain selvedge and a brown and white wool knotted fringe. The wool, usually from Hazaragi and Ghilzai sheep, is loosely spun and rather coarse.

Whereas 'Maimana' has been the generic name in the bazaars for all kilims woven by the Uzbeks from this area, it has been realized recently that a much more exact attribution can be made by paying close attention to the subtle variations in composition and texture.

518   Maimana
This small nomadic prayer rug is full of idiosyncrasies and character. (Detail)

Maimana	518, 520, 638
DESIGN	Field: Geometric patterns of diamonds and triangles Borders: Several, wide and geometric
SIZE AND SHAPE	Various, but can be very large
MATERIALS	Brown wool warps, wool wefts
STRUCTURE	Slitweave/Double interlock
COLOURS	Clear, strong palette of brown, yellow, orange, blue/ Bright chemical dyes used more recently
FRINGE	Plain/Knotted
SELVEDGE	Plain
Remarks	The most common kilims from north Afghanistan

Almar   A new classification was evolved lately after a dealer in Kabul referred to a particular design on some kilims as 'Ghalmari'. Poring over a map of north Afghanistan, repeating the name over and over in his Anglo-Pushtu accent (the 'i' suffix is the Pushtu means of describing the people of a place), he finally pinpointed the village of Almar and further research proved that this was indeed the original source of the style in question. Almar is a large village populated by Uzbeks, a few Tadjiks and Pushtuns on the arid, flat plain to the west of Maimana. It achieved renown for the peach-tinted marble found there, much sought after by Tehran city dwellers in the mid-nineteenth century, who carved from it ornate vases.

519 Almar
(2.89 × 1.98 m, 9′6″ × 6′6″)
*A distinguishing feature of this kilim is its
reciprocal hook design around the medallion and
in the narrow minor border.*

520 Maimana
(1.82 × 0.91 m, 6′ × 3′)
*This kilim was woven in the mid-1970s; its
colours are poor and lacklustre, and the design is
abbreviated and simplified so it bears little
relationship to its ancestors. It has been
commercially produced to provide a cheap ethnic
floor covering, but has no feel for its tribal
heritage.*

521 Serhadi
(3.04 × 1.82 m, 10′ × 6′)
*This kilim has cotton warps and soft, finely
spun wool wefts. The design is similar to
Maimana, but the workmanship and the finish
are superior. It is woven with limited colours in
slitweave technique.*

276

The Almar flatweaves are very similar in texture and feel to Maimana kilims, but with a large diamond design in the centre of the field formed from small squares of colour, woven in the interlock technique. These central diamonds spread out over the field with bands of 'hook' designs running perpendicular to them. The borders are usually woven on a smaller scale than those of the Maimana, but retaining the format of several rows of different motifs lining the four sides of the rug. The colours are predominantly a dull madder red and blue, with brown, yellow and small amounts of white.

Captions for 522–24 on page 278.

Almar
519

DESIGN	Field: Central diamond medallion with hooked pattern Borders: Geometric
SIZE AND SHAPE	Medium and rectangular/Large and rectangular
MATERIALS	Brown wool warps, wool wefts
STRUCTURE	Interlock/Slitweave
COLOURS	Dull madder red, blue, yellow, brown, white
FRINGE	Plain/Knotted
SELVEDGE	Simple/Double warp reinforcement
Remarks	Very similar to Maimana kilims

Serhadi Another Maimana kilim to be reclassified recently is the newly named Serhadi. These kilims have a much finer weave than the rather coarse wool used in Maimana, and the warps are sometimes of cotton, whereas the weft is invariably of very finely spun wool; indeed, these Serhadi kilims have a texture that is halfway between a wool kilim and a cotton *sutrangi*. Although the designs and motifs are similar to those used on Maimana kilims, the colours are soft and create a completely different appearance. The finish of the rugs is more complete, with

Page 277:

522 Serhadi
The weaver of this rug has used a limited palette of colours – red and soft yellow, natural white and black – and yet she has created a worthy design. The field patterning is of simple diamonds made up from small squares. Their size and crenellation is dictated by the short slits in the weave. Larger diamond patterns are drawn by using different colours. There are idiosyncrasies in the side borders, which add to the appeal of this rug. (Detail)

523 Serhadi
With such a mixture of characteristics from most of the traditional flatweaving areas of north Afghanistan, it is hard to point to the exact origins of this kilim. The structure is of slitweave and dovetailing, both used extensively in north Afghanistan. The field design is Maimana Uzbek, the colours are Serhadi and Maimana. It has the feel of a Serhadi kilim, yet it is woven with brown wool warps, not cotton. The borders are Turkoman from Labijar. (Detail)

524 Maimana *sutrangi*
(3.10 × 1.45 m, 10'3" × 4'9")
A large modern sutrangi. *Woven tightly with cotton warps and wefts, the rug is heavy and hard-wearing. The colours are all bright and chemically produced, but will probably fade rapidly in sunlight.*

warp-reinforced selvedges, and neatly knotted fringes with a row or two of weft twining on the end panels.

Serhadi		521–3
DESIGN	Field: Geometric shapes made up from diamonds and triangles Borders: Several, geometric	
SIZE AND SHAPE	Various but usually large	
MATERIALS	Cotton warps, fine wool wefts	
STRUCTURE	Double interlock, dovetail	
COLOURS	Soft red, pale blue, yellow, white	
FRINGE	Knotted/Net	
SELVEDGE	Double warp reinforcement	
Remarks	Similar to Maimana kilims, except for finer texture and weave	

Sutrangi   These flatweaves are made entirely from cotton, which is grown in quantity by the settled Turkoman farmers on Afghanistan's northern borders near Andkhoi and Aqcha. As with the *dhurrie*, its counterpart from the Indian subcontinent, the *sutrangi* is woven by prison inmates. Afghani *sutrangi* are made at Maimana jail, and more recently at Mazar-i-Sharif as well as other provincial jails. Some of the *sutrangi* are enormous, up to 18 sq.m (200 sq.ft) in area, and they have in the past been used as undercarpets, lying between the mud floor and the knotted carpets or kilims that were often donated to mosques. Smaller sizes of *sutrangi* and prayer mats are now woven for sale in the cities of Afghanistan. The colours of *sutrangi* are pastel shades of green, blue, pink and red, woven in tight slitweave in designs of simple triangles and diamonds.

Maimana *Sutrangi*		524, 599
DESIGN	Field: Diamonds, triangles and squares Borders: Geometric	
SIZE AND SHAPE	Can be very large	
MATERIALS	Cotton	
STRUCTURE	Tight slitweave	
COLOURS	Varied palette of pale and pastel colours	
FRINGE	Knotted/Net	
SELVEDGE	Double warp reinforcement	
Remarks	Woven by prison inmates	

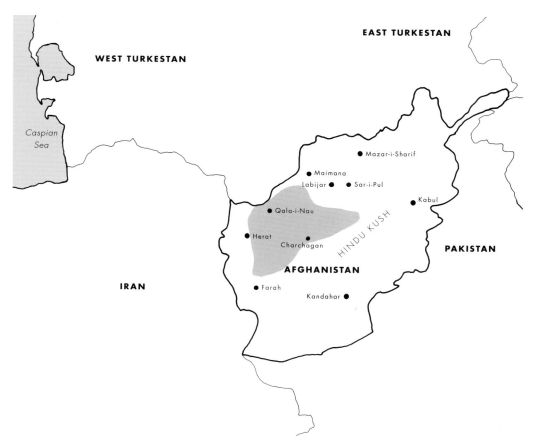

The Chahar Aimaq

525   Taimani Aimaq of Charchagan
(3.04 × 2.03 m, 10′ × 6′8″)
Kilims of this design, the work of the largest clan of the Chahar Aimaq, the Taimani, in the region around Charchagan in west-central Afghanistan, are comparatively rare, as none have been woven since the 1960s. They are unusually large and heavy, considering they are woven on ground looms. Many of the motifs in the weft-faced patterned bands are similar to those found on kilims from the north Afghan and Iran borders. It is the attention to detail and finish that is important in the final attribution of origin. (Detail 528)

The Aimaq

Known collectively as the Chahar Aimaq (*chahar* means 'four' and *aimaq* is a Mongolian word for nomad), these four tribes – the Taimani, the Firozkohi, Jamshidi, and the Qala-i-Nau Hazara – are all Farsi-speaking semi-nomadic or sedentary farmers and traders. Predictably the Aimaq have widely mixed origins. They are compulsive traders, exchanging goods such as clarified butter, other dairy products and woven materials for sugar, tea, rayon cloth and bazaar items unavailable in the distant central mountains. The Aimaqs have become rich traders through dealing in this manner with extended credit.

The Taimani Aimaq

The Taimani are by far the largest of the Chahar Aimaq group and there are about a dozen main clans and numerous sub-clans. They inhabit a vast area of west-central Afghanistan, especially around the market town of Charchagan in Ghor province. The landscape of this district has known recent and dramatic change. The steep-sided valleys of the Hari and Farah rivers were once thickly forested, but from the twelfth to the fourteenth century the small town of Ahrangaran ('the Blacksmith's'), became the fortified centre of a large armaments trade, supplying coats of mail, shields, cuirasses and swords to the Timurids, Mongols and Safavids, and the forests were cut down to furnish the forges with fuel. Charchagan stands on a now treeless plain on the south bank of the Hari river. It is a new town, built in 1959 as a grandiose homage to the future, anticipating the completion of the Asian Highway, a paved road stretching from Europe to the Far

526, 527 Taimani Aimaq of Farah
(1.62 × 1.11 m, 5′4″ × 3′8″)
*The Taimani Aimaq do not have a long history
of weaving weft-wrapped kilims like this, but
produce them nowadays with the hope of selling
them in the bazaars to a dealer who will export
them. Often taking motifs, colours and
techniques from neighbouring Balouch people and
from those found on Persian knotted carpets,
their designs are lively and figurative.*
(Detail 527)

East. Until this road is completed, it will still take two full days to travel some
three hundred miles from Herat. Charchagan holds a massive monthly market of
sheep and goats, which are exchanged and bartered for by the Aimaq and Durrani
nomads with the Kabul and Pushtun butchers; the animals will then be taken east
by the shepherds, a journey of about three months' duration.

Taimani Aimaq of Charchagan	525, 528
DESIGN	Field: Elaborate banded interlocking motifs Borders: None
SIZE AND SHAPE	Often large
MATERIALS	Soft wool
STRUCTURE	Very tight weft-faced patterning
COLOURS	Soft palette of brown, gold yellow, green, red, purple
FRINGE	Plain
SELVEDGE	Extra warp reinforcement/Parallel wrapping in red and white wool
Remarks	These kilims are very thick and heavy

The Taimani are semi-nomadic people, who move out of their mud-house villages after the spring planting in late March to take their flocks to the high summer pastures, and after returning briefly in May to plant melons, they go back to their summer encampment, the *yalaq*, until the September harvest begins. It is in these summer months that the women prepare the wool and do the weaving. The Taimani live in an encampment of distinctive square or rectangular felt-covered *yurts*, whereas the other Aimaq nomads are found in conventional, round and smaller-than-average Turkoman tents.

The kilims from the Charchagan region are very finely woven using soft Ghilzai wool, and the wefts are so densely compacted and beaten down on the loom that the kilims are very heavy and hard-wearing. This structural integrity is characteristic of their weft-faced patterning technique, and the compositions consist of banded designs of intricate interlocking motifs running across the rug in soft colours, such as browns, greens, gold, a gentle red and purple. There are no borders to these rugs, just a narrow band of extra-warp reinforcing the selvedge, often in loosely spun red and white wool, and the fringes are short and plain. The Charchagan Taimani kilims are unusually large for a rug woven in one piece, on a crude ground loom, in the complex technique of weft float. These kilims are also sometimes called *samani* or *sarmanid*, possibly derivatives of 'Samanid', the sophisticated dynasty who ruled from Bokhara, and claimed suzerainty over Ghor and large tracts of west Afghanistan, established the Ghaznavid dynasty and built the famous minaret of Jam in the twelfth century.

528   *Detail of 525.*

Taimani Aimaq of Farah		526, 529
DESIGN	Field: Varied, often representational and pictorial	
SIZE AND SHAPE	Usually small/Medium/Short runners	
MATERIALS	Wool	
STRUCTURE	Multi-techniques of knotted pile, weft wrapping, weft-faced weave	
COLOURS	Dark blue, red, black, with white details	
FRINGE	Plain/Knotted	
SELVEDGE	Plain/Parallel wrapping	
Remarks	Prayer rugs woven/Sometimes incorrectly termed Balouch	

Further west, down the Farah River, on the open plains between Tulak, Farsi and Herat, other Taimani people weave small weft-wrapped kilims. Though often incorrectly termed 'Balouch', these are in fact close copies of Balouchi work in both colouring and pattern. It is common to see rugs worked in a combination of weft-faced weave, weft wrapping and knotted pile; many are well designed and beautifully made for so complex a blend of techniques. These Taimani incorporate many representational figures of birds, people and animals into their weave, copied from illustrations of Persian carpets, and many of the modern rugs not only draw from traditional designs such as the *boteh*, but also feature representational

529   Taimani Aimaq of Farah
(2.18 × 1.05 m, 7'2" × 3'5")
Produced for the Western market, this complex pattern, probably from a modern Persian carpet, is woven in weft wrapping, weft-faced patterning and knotted work.

images of teapots, helicopters, tanks and even Kalashnikov rifles – folk art reflecting the turmoil of war. The sizes and compositions of these kilims are varied, but the colours are usually dark blue, black and dark red, with white detail designs in a floating-weft technique. As well as aping designs from the Balouch and figurative designs from Persia, the Taimani weave prayer rugs in a mixed technique of flatweave and pile, and narrow, short runners used in Herati houses as infill rugs round the main carpet.

The Firozkohi Aimaq

'Firozkohi' means 'mountain of turquoise'. These semi-nomadic Aimaq people are divided into two main groups; the Mahmud people, of very mixed origins, living to the west in the area between Herat and the north Afghanistan border, and the Firozkohi from the eastern part of Badghis province, around Qala-i-Nau and north of the Taimani Aimaq. These Firozkohi Aimaq live as semi-nomads in the wide fertile valleys close to the Murghab River and the sprawling, ancient, mud-domed village and caravanserai of Moghur. They are of obvious Mongolian descent and live in traditional small *yurts*. The cane walls of their *yurts*, called *chaparis* and brightly painted with ancient designs, are similar in every way to the elaborate reed screens, decorated with coloured wool, found on the sides of Kazakh and Kirghiz tents. The designs on these screens are so similar to each other, even though the tribes live up to a thousand miles apart, and are so close to Turkic kilim patterns, that there must be some historical association. It is possible that, like the traditional *gul* found on Turkoman knotted carpets and thought to be a standard for tribal recognition, the decoration on the sides of the *yurts* could be used as a declaration of ancestry by the clan or sub-tribe of each encampment.

Whilst many kilims, *torbah* (clothing bags) and *namakdan* (salt bags) are woven by the Firozkohi Aimaq in the style of other peoples, they weave for the domestic market, and for their own use, the *dashterkhan* eating cloths in an original design. These are made of loosely spun and woven flimsy plain brown karaqul wool, over-embroidered with geometric patterns and concentric diamond motifs, and their colours are soft pale brown, orange and green, white and cherry red. The *dashterkhan* are usually long and narrow, with simple plain fringes and selvedges.

Firozkohi Aimaq	534
DESIGN	Field: Embroidered geometric and diamond patterns Borders: Narrow
SIZE AND SHAPE	Usually long and narrow
MATERIALS	Loose, plain brown wool
STRUCTURE	Balanced plainweave
COLOURS	Brown, orange, cherry red, green, white
FRINGE	Plain
SELVEDGE	Plain
Remarks	Used as thin covers and eating cloths

The Jamshidi Aimaq

Similar work is done by the Jamshidi Aimaq, the third of the four Aimaq tribes. The Jamshidi, who are mainly sedentary people in Herat, are said to be of mixed Arab and Persian stock, diluted by considerable intermarrying with the Turkomen over the past century. The Jamshidi weave *suzani dashterkhan* – embroidered eating cloths – in a similar fashion to the Firozkohi. Little is known about their weaving.

Jamshidi Aimaq	530
DESIGN	Field: Embroidered geometric patterns, diamond motifs Borders: Narrow
SIZE AND SHAPE	Usually long and narrow/Some square
MATERIALS	Loose, plain brown wool
STRUCTURE	Balanced plainweave
COLOURS	Brown, orange, red
FRINGE	Plain
SELVEDGE	Plain
Remarks	Usually thin covers and eating cloths/Very similar to Firozkohi Aimaq

530   Jamshidi Aimaq
(3.00 × 0.48 m, 9'10" × 1'7")
The loosely woven cloth has been over-embroidered with brightly coloured wool to make a dashterkhan. *This textile is very thin and would be suitable only as a cover or meal cloth.*

Qala-i-Nau Hazara Aimaq	531, 533
DESIGN	Field: Narrow bands of intricate motifs and patterns Borders: Narrow/None
SIZE AND SHAPE	Medium and rectangular
MATERIALS	Fine wool warps, wool wefts
STRUCTURE	Weft-faced patterning, made in two halves
COLOURS	Varied palette including cherry red, gold
FRINGE	Knotted/Net
SELVEDGE	Extra cord reinforcement with barber-pole design
Remarks	Fine *khorjin* and bags also woven

The Qala-i-Nau Hazara Aimaq

The Qala-i-Nau Hazara are semi-nomadic people who live in the region of Qala-i-Nau ('New Castle'), the capital of Badghis province, and this Aimaq tribe are Sunni Muslims, quite different from the Shi'a Muslim Hazara from Hazarajat in central Afghanistan. They are descendants of the hordes who followed Ghenghis Khan through Central Asia, and it is not clear whether they settled in north Afghanistan at an early date or were forcibly moved there by Nadir Shah. The

531   Qala-i-Nau Hazara Aimaq
Such finely detailed designs are characteristic of the work of Qala-i-Nau weavers. (Detail)

532 Qala-i-Nau Hazara Aimaq
Although this wool-embroidered eating cloth is roughly made and finished, it has a distinctive composition and character. (Detail)

533 Qala-i-Nau Hazara Aimaq
(2.36 × 1.29 m, 7′9″ × 4′3″)
The design consists of ornate bands of pattern, a narrow border on all sides and long end panels woven in natural brown wool, with several rows of weft twining in coloured wool.

Persian word for a thousand is *hazar*, and a common folktale relates that Ghenghis Khan left one thousand troops in the area that is now central Afghanistan to maintain the peace, thus giving the descendants of the soldiers their tribal name.

Qala-i-Nau itself is a dismal town, but the surrounding hills are perfect for shepherds and their flocks, as the well-irrigated pastures stay green until late July. The Hazara Aimaq weave very fine kilims, small bags and *khorjin* in Qala-i-Nau and the neighbouring village of Laghari. Woven on narrow ground looms, often in two halves that are joined with neat multi-coloured embroidery stitches, these kilims are beautifully made and finished. Narrow bands of intricate patterns woven in the floating weft technique run across the rug, and the repeating motifs, of which there can be up to ten varieties on one rug, are similar to those used by the Balouch weavers of north-west Afghanistan and Iran, the Taimani Aimaq and also the Kurds from Kalat in Khorassan. Whether these motifs were copied from one group by another is not known. They may be a combination of ancient symbols, the meaning of which is long lost, or their similarity may be simply caused by common restraints of the weaving technique, as the Hazara Aimaq, Taimani, Balouch and Kurds of Khorassan all decorate their flatweaves in floating weft. Whatever the reason, the kilims of Qala-i-Nau are distinctive and individual and the weavers use a varied palette of colours, displaying a preference for cherry red and a rich golden yellow. The end panels of the kilims are of wide brown wool with several lines of weft twining, the fringes are knotted and selvedges finished with a barber-pole design of reinforcement.

The Mushwani

Of Pushtun ancestry, this widely scattered tribe is Persian-speaking, living as semi-nomads ranging across the hills south of the Amu Darya River in Herat and Badghis provinces, and in small communities of sedentary farmers and traders in the villages around Bona Qara in north-west Afghanistan. The kilims they weave are usually a combination of knotted pile, weft-wrapping and weft-faced techniques. Their production is commonly of small rugs and prayer mats, very similar to that of the Taimani Aimaq and the Balouch, who have taught the Pushtuns of this region of Afghanistan most of their kilim-weaving skills. The colours of their flatweaves are dark, usually black, dark blue and red, detailed with ivory-white motifs, and the rugs are finished with very long ivory-white fringes of karaqul wool.

534   Firozkohi Aimaq
(4.06 × 1.14 m, 13'4" × 3'9")
The work on this piece falls into the area between kilim-weaving and embroidery. A loosely spun, natural brown wool plainweave is over-embroidered with coloured wool. The patterning is not part of the structure but applied after weaving.

535   Mushwani
(0.83 × 0.68 m, 2'9" × 2'3")
An unusual prayer rug from north-west Afghanistan. At first sight it looks as if it was cut from a larger kilim, and the edges bound, with red wool tassels, although it was in fact woven to this size.

Mushwani		535
DESIGN	Field: Various designs	
SIZE AND SHAPE	Usually small/Medium	
MATERIALS	Coarse wool	
STRUCTURE	Multi-technique of knotted pile, weft-faced patterning, weft wrapping	
COLOURS	Black, dark blue, red, ivory-white details	
FRINGE	Plain/Knotted	
SELVEDGE	Simple reinforcement with parallel wrapping	
Remarks	Prayer rugs and bags woven/Many designs similar to Balouch	

536 Balouch
(2.79 × 1.67 m, 9′2″ × 5′6″)
It is difficult to detect exactly where this kilim originated within the Balouch tribal area. The side borders, finely woven in ivory-white wool, have a detailed pattern and motifs in one part that are typical of the Sarawan district, in eastern Balouchistan to the south of Quetta. The end borders of flower or star motifs are characteristic of southern Balouchistan, and yet the field is made up of patterns found in the north and north-east, with some bands of simple zig-zag pattern usually woven by Maldari Balouch.

The Balouch

Balouchistan is a sparsely populated area of arid deserts and mountains that is most inhospitable. The little rain that falls comes in torrents, and is quickly lost into the parched plains, and raging sandstorms spring up from nowhere; it is bitterly cold in winter and insufferably hot in the summer. In the west, 'the wind of 120 days' blows relentlessly, destroying any seasonal vegetation. The human occupation of this desert and scrubland region that straddles the borders of Pakistan, Afghanistan and Iran dates back to the fourth millenium BC, before which time the climate had precluded habitation.

The original tribal groups of the area were the Meds, fishermen living along the Makran coast, the Pathans, the original Afghan race, and the Jats, well-known agriculturalists from north India. Despite its isolation and geo-strategic insignificance, Balouchistan has been overrun by many nations. Alexander the Great travelled the southern route through the region in 325 BC, after his victories in India, and Buddhism flourished there under Parthian and later Kushan rule. Islam followed in the seventh century when the Arabs overthrew the Persian Empire and gradually annexed outlying provinces such as Balouchistan, ruling from Kunza in Jhalawan until the tenth century. When Persia regained its independence upon the gradual weakening of the caliphate, Balouchistan was returned to the Empire, but its chiefs were practically independent so long as they furnished military contingents when called upon.

From 1595 to 1638 the province of Balouchistan formed part of the Moghul Empire after Nadir Shah conquered north India, and his son, elected viceroy, became Khan of Khelat. Ruling with tyranny and licentiousness, he was murdered by his brother, who eventually created Balouchistan a confederation. The British became involved in the area in 1810 when they sent political missions to Sind and Balouchistan, which then covered the huge area from the Indus River to the Persian Great Desert, bounded by the Indian Ocean to the south and Afghanistan to the north. These missions were dispatched by the East India Company as an expansionist measure following the rise of Napoleon in Europe and overt threats by the French to lead an army into India. By the 1830s the British had set up a tenuous garrison, which closely followed the notorious fortunes of the British contingents further north in Kabul. Throughout the disastrous period of British control over Afghan foreign and internal affairs, the Khan of Khelat remained loyal to them, and fresh treaties of the 1890s drew Balouchistan closer to the Indian Empire. Balouchistan is now divided between the modern nation states of Pakistan, Iran and Afghanistan.

The Balouch, or Balouchi, are themselves comparatively recent arrivals to the region that now bears their name, appearing in the eleventh and twelfth centuries after being driven out of Persia by the Seljuks through Kerman and Sistan. They first conquered western Makran and the southern coastal area but failed to occupy the uplands of Kalat. The name itself means 'nomad', or 'wanderer', and tales of their ancestry suggest that they are derived from Arabi or Aleppo groups, but it is more probable that they originated as a separate people on the Persian plateau.

The western Balouch predominate in the Chagai Hills between Afghanistan and Pakistan, Makran and Sistan. The most important sub-tribes include the Nausherwani, closely related to the Tahuki tribe in Iranian Balouchistan; the

The Balouch

537 Balouch *Malaki*
(2.55 × 0.99 m, 8′4″ × 3′3″)
Many Balouch kilims, especially nomadic weavings, are produced on crude horizontal looms. The weaver sits on the warps to provide tension, weaving a width of a short arm span without shifting position, thus producing a narrow strip of weave. The two separately woven halves are sewn together to make a kilim.

Rukhshani, about whom there is very little known save that they are Farsi-speaking, having moved down from the Caspian Sea; the Boledi, who were once the ruling race of Makran; and the Gichki, who later ousted the Boledi from Makran.

The Rind are the main group in east Balouchistan, with the Mari and Bugti sub-tribes being the most numerous, occupying the southern buttresses of the Sulaiman Mountains on the edge of the Sind Desert. Their rivals, the Brahui, inhabit the highlands south of Quetta and Kalat, in the provinces of Sarawan and Jhalawan, with their sub-tribes living nomadic lives in Chagai and Karan on the Pakistan-Iran borders. The Brahui are a confederacy of tribes who rose to power in the seventeenth century under the chief Kambar, who overthrew the ruling Hindu rajas and introduced Sunni Muslim beliefs, and from whose name the title of the ruling dynasty, Kambarani, is derived. Speculation over their origins, however, has arisen from the fact that grafted on to their Muslims rites are social customs that are essentially Indian, and the Brahui speak a Dravidian language of the southern Indian peninsula. The Brahui are now settled farmers and semi-nomads living in the fertile and irrigated valleys along the Helmand River.

There has never been any large or enduring political union in this region and its weaving history is as confused. The flatwoven textiles of a wide variety of tribal and nomadic groups, including the Kurds from Khorassan and the Arabs of the Arabian Gulf plains, have been collectively labelled 'Balouch'. Many of the rug-weaving nomads and settled people from this vast area are referred to as Balouch even though many carry specific tribal names such as Taimani, Mushwani, Salar Khani, Jan Begi and Yacub Khani. This confusion has arisen because dealers and

538, 539 Balouch of Farah
(2.36 × 1.21 m, 7′9″ × 4′)
A typical 1970s Balouch kilim, woven in coarse wool, with a loosely weft-wrapped border and simple patterning in the field. The colours are a combination of plant dyes – madder red and indigo blue – and imported chemical dyes. This orange was very popular in the 1970s and 1980s. (Detail 539)

bazaar traders have grouped together all the flatweavings from western Afghanistan that are similar to each other in colour and weaving technique.

The issue becomes increasingly complex when one considers that the Balouch are viewed by many experts as random copyists of the designs of neighbouring tribes. Certainly they do take advantage of market trends and are often the first people to meet the demand for certain pile rugs and kilims for export, but they also have a long and most prolific flatweaving history of their own, perhaps one of the finest in all of Asia.

So little research has been conducted into the flatweavings of the Balouch that the distinguishing features of the weavings from the many sub-groups remain unknown. Any study of their weaving histories and attributes now initiated may already come too late, as the individuality, however subtle, of each sub-group and each area is being lost to commercialism, intermarriage and rapidly changing lifestyles. Nevertheless, in the dark and sombre colours of these flatweaves can be discerned a patina of tribal life and history, a reflection of the harshness of the landscape, climate and the traditional nomadic lifestyle. Usually, full appreciation of Balouchi work grows gradually, and frequently many collectors and enthusiasts progress towards it by first of all becoming familiar with the folk-story kilims of Anatolia, then the boldness and geometry of Persian kilims, before coming to recognize the subtlety of the pattern, texture and colour in Balouch flatweaving.

The traders of Iran, especially those from Tehran and Mashed, the two main collecting points for Persian Balouch kilims, categorize the rugs into three groups: those from Khorassan in the north-east, including the Kashmar and Mahualat families, those of the Baizidi tribe from Torbat-e-Haidari, and those of the Balouch living around Herat in Afghanistan, particularly the Timuri.

Balouch of North-East Iran

540–2

DESIGN	Field: Bands of complex interlocking motifs Borders: Narrow
SIZE AND SHAPE	Medium and rectangular/Large and rectangular
MATERIALS	Fine ivory-white or brown wool warps, wool wefts
STRUCTURE	Weft-faced patterning, weft wrapping, usually made in two halves
COLOURS	Fuller and brighter than other Balouch weavings, including turmeric yellow and green
FRINGE	Knotted/Net/Diagonally plaited
SELVEDGE	Extra cord reinforcement/Parallel wrapping
Remarks	Some bags and trappings woven

The Balouch of North-East Iran

The kilims from north Balouchistan, although sombre, have more colour than those from Afghanistan and further south, including a turmeric yellow and a

540   Balouch of North-East Iran
An unusually colourful runner woven in the 1970s. Some motifs are unique to the Balouch, but others are found on rugs from Anatolia, Iran and the Caucasus. (Detail)

541, 542   Balouch of North-East Iran
(0.83 × 0.83 m, 2′9″ × 2′9″)
This soufreh *eating cloth was bought from a Balouch family living in a village south of Mashed, in north-east Iran. The* soufreh *is a ceremonial centre cloth placed on the ground for meals. The food is placed on the cloth and the family and guests sit crosslegged around it eating from communal bowls. Note the talismanic 'eye' in the centre. (Detail 542)*

green obtained from overdyeing indigo blue with yellow. These flatweaves are usually weft-faced, woven in relatively wide bands across the field, up to 15 cm (6″) wide, with complex patterns, many similar to those found on local Kurdish weavings. Balouch kilims from further south are subdivided into Sistan, Bam and Zabul, from the area east of the Dasht-i-Lut in the remote eastern provinces of Kerman and Sistan.

The dealers in Afghanistan, hardly looking beyond their national boundaries, attribute north Balouch weavings to Herat, including in this all the weaves of the tribes living on the northern Afghanistan border, and often, mistakenly, Taimani weavings from the Chahar Aimaq people of Ghor province. These latter are almost identical to those of the Balouch people settled just across the border in Khorassan. Other Balouch weavings are attributed broadly to the Afghan Balouch and the Pakistani Balouch. Several subdivisions have been made, however.

The Balouch of Charaknasur

Charaknasur is a prolific weaving district in the south-west of the region, a flat hot desert area either side of the border near Zabul and Sistan inhabited by mainly nomadic people, whose migration route in the past took them up to the Afghan-Soviet border. These people weave what are considered to be the finest Balouch kilims with the darkest and richest colours, such as indigo blue and black, and deep madder red. Such colours are expensive, for the correct dye-yielding plants are difficult to find and time-consuming to process. The darker the indigo, the more valuable the textiles.

Balouch of Charaknasur	545, 555, 632
DESIGN	Field: Bands of complex interlocking motifs and patterns featuring turtle design Borders: Narrow
SIZE AND SHAPE	Medium and rectangular/Large and rectangular
MATERIALS	Very fine ivory-white wool warps, wool wefts
STRUCTURE	Weft-faced patterning, weft wrapping, usually made in two halves
COLOURS	Very dark palette, black, deep red, blue, small details in ivory white
FRINGE	Knotted/Net/Diagonally plaited
SELVEDGE	Extra cord reinforcement/Parallel wrapping
Remarks	Bags and trappings/Usually considered the finest of Balouch weavings

Charaknasur weaves, recognizable by the unlikely 'turtle' design, are finely woven on ivory-white wool warps with deeply coloured bands of motifs in weft-wrapping work and narrow bands of undecorated areas in between. Most large kilims are woven in two halves and joined together, although it has often proved

543   Balouch of Charaknasur
Typically Balouch weave and colours. (Detail)

difficult for the weavers to align the patterning across the rug; sometimes, in fact, the first half is packed away on the back of a camel. Charaknasur weavers frequently use spun goat hair to join the kilim halves, using a loose half-hitch knot. Their *soufreh*, *rukorssi* and bags all show a finesse and dedication to the art of weaving.

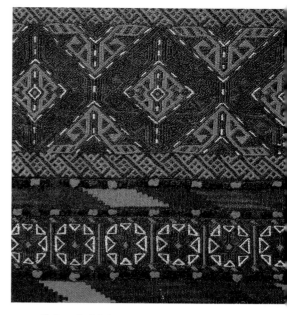

544   Balouch *Malaki*
The Balouch weavers often use narrow rows of tufted wool between horizontal bands of motifs. (Detail of 549)

Balouch of Farah

538, 551

DESIGN	Field: Bands of complex interlocking motifs and patterns Borders: Narrow
SIZE AND SHAPE	Medium and rectangular/Large and rectangular
MATERIALS	Fine ivory-white wool warps, wool wefts
STRUCTURE	Weft-faced patterning, weft wrapping, usually made in two halves
COLOURS	Very dark palette, black, dark red, blue
FRINGE	Long and knotted
SELVEDGE	Extra cord reinforcement/Parallel wrapping
Remarks	Bags, trappings and prayer rugs also woven

The Balouch of Farah

Farah used to be a well-known centre for Balouch kilims of exceptionally fine quality. It is a dusty, remote market town on the Farah River, which has for centuries been the site of the annual fair and sheep market for Balouch nomads from the mountains of west Afghanistan to the arid Dasht-i-Lut in Iran. The kilims, bags and tent trappings from the Farah district are very dark in colour, predominantly black, dark sombre blue and deep red. Virtually no white is used, except in the ivory-white warps which show on the long fringes. Very finely and densely made, the large kilims were usually woven by a young girl as part of her dowry, to enable her to demonstrate her skill in weaving and to add wealth to the family.

Balouch *Malaki*

Balouch *Malaki* weavings of the nomads who roam the desolate area around the Dasht-i-Margo ('Desert of Death') are similar in many ways to those of the Charaknasur nomads, but lack the lustre of the wool and detail in finish, although they do show an extensive use of white wool in the field pattern. Amongst their distinctive features is a row of weft twining between the bands of weft-wrapped patterns, usually ending in long freely hanging 'tails'. These were originally decorated with cowrie shells and small blue and white glass beads, traditionally made by the glass blowers in Herat; not surprisingly, these ornaments usually break off. The *Malaki* weavers also use multiple techniques in their weavings, such as a combination of weft-faced patterning, weft wrapping and knotted pile running in bands across the rug and down its borders, very often in a star pattern.

Page 292:

545   Balouch of Charaknasur
(3.15 × 1.42 m, 10'4" × 4'8")
This kilim is very tightly woven in a mixture of techniques: weft wrapping and floating weft to give the bands of ornate motifs, and interlock and slitweave for the simple narrow bands. There is a multitude of ancient symbols and motifs used in such kilims. Serious field research is urgently needed to identify these symbols before they are lost, along with their tribal identity and social history.

546   Balouch *Malaki*
The short tassels within the weave were originally threaded with glass beads and cowrie shells. (Detail of 547)

547   Balouch *Malaki*
(1.82 × 0.99 m, 6' × 3'3")
The weaver of this rug has used three completely different techniques: weft-faced patterning, weft wrapping and knotted pile. The kilim is woven in one piece, even though long slits have been left between the field and the knotted border, and the weave remains very flat considering the different tensions required by the various techniques. Originally the tassels in the field and on the border would have been decorated with white glass beads and small cowrie shells, a detail typical of Malaki *weavings.*

Captions for 545–7 on page 291.

548   Maldari Balouch
(2.25 × 1.00 m, 7′5″ × 3′7″)
*Simple rows of zig-zags are
woven between bands of
plainweave and narrow detailed
bands of weft-faced patterning.
The simple design, dark colours
and lack of borders are all
typical of Maldari Balouch
work.*

549   Balouch *Malaki*
(3.35 × 1.96 m, 11′ × 6′5″)
*A very typical example of
Balouch weaving: a large
rectangular format, woven in two
halves and sewn together with a
half-hitch knot in spun goat's
hair; rich but sombre colours –
deep red, dark blue and black –
with small startling motifs in
ivory-white wool; and tight weave
producing a very hard-wearing
and dense textile in a variety of
techniques. The overall design is
of horizontal bands of intricate
patterns and motifs, set within a
border on all four sides.*

550   Maldari Balouch
Simple horizontal bands of plainweave are woven between bands of motifs worked in weft-faced patterning technique. (Detail)

This mixed process certainly tests the skills of the weaver in keeping the tension even and the rug lying flat. Such skills are often exemplified in dowry textiles as a demonstration of a young girl's weaving prowess.

Balouch *Malaki*		547, 549, 553
DESIGN	Field: Bands of complex interlocking motifs Borders: Narrow	
SIZE AND SHAPE	Medium/Large and rectangular	
MATERIALS	Ivory-white wool warps, wool wefts	
STRUCTURE	Knotted pile, weft wrapping, weft-faced patterning, weft twining, usually made in two halves	
COLOURS	Black, ivory white or cream, dark red, blue	
FRINGE	Knotted	
SELVEDGE	Extra cord reinforcement/Parallel wrapping	
Remarks	Bags, trappings and prayer rugs also woven	

The Maldari Balouch

Maldari Balouch kilims are altogether simpler. *Maldar* means 'sheep owner' or 'goat owner', and the group is nomadic or semi-nomadic. Maldari kilims are composed of simple bands of plain-coloured weave, commonly in natural brown or black wool or else dyed with indigo or madder. Any patterning that exists is of ivory-white wool, often of the simple six-sided flower pattern, and the rugs are finished with little or no border.

551   Balouch of Farah
The weavers of southern and western Balouchistan nowadays weave many long and narrow soufreh *commercially for the home and export market. They have been adapted for use by house dwellers to fill in the spaces around the main carpet. This piece pre-dates this commercialization by several decades, and is a fine example of intricate Balouch weaving.*

Maldari Balouch		548
DESIGN	Field: Bands of plainweave and geometric motifs Borders: Narrow/None	
SIZE AND SHAPE	Medium and rectangular/Large and rectangular	
MATERIALS	Coarse wool warps, wool wefts	
STRUCTURE	Weft-faced plainweave, weft twining, weft wrapping, usually made in two halves	
COLOURS	Dull palette of black, ivory white, brown, deep red, blue	
FRINGE	Plain/Knotted	
SELVEDGE	Extra cord reinforcement/Parallel wrapping	
Remarks	Bags and trappings/Usually very simple weavings	

The Balouch of South-West Pakistan

Further south, within the Chagai province of Pakistan, and eastward to Kandahar and the edges of the Sind Desert, lies the western part of Balouchistan. This area has long produced fine nomadic flatweaves. The colour of the field is bright, of light madder red and orange created by overdyeing madder red with a concoction made from pomegranate skins or yoghurt. The finest are used as covers for bedding and clothing stacked at the back of the tent. These are the *shaffi*, recognizable by their very finely woven borders of white wool with rows of tiny motifs running into the plainweave bands of the field. The kilims of the Balouch of Chagai and Sind have similar motifs and colours, but flatweaves are thicker, very tightly woven and harder-wearing. The border designs are of a larger scale, and bands of intricate patterning in weft-float technique lie within the field.

552 Balouch of South-West Pakistan
(2.53 × 0.99 m, 8'4" × 3'3")
This kilim, made near Kandahar, although very similar to a shaffi *bedding cover, has been used as a floor rug. It is possible that the difference in use is determined by the border, here completely enclosing the field pattern. On the* shaffi *the bands of background colour run through the border design to the edge. However, the border motif that appears at one end is reminiscent of rugs which are hung vertically, the Turkoman* ensi *and* purdah.

Balouch of South-West Pakistan	552, 554
DESIGN	Field: Bands of intricate patterns, bands of plainweave Borders: Patterned with white motifs
SIZE AND SHAPE	Long and narrow
MATERIALS	Fine wool
STRUCTURE	Weft-faced patterning, weft twining, plainweave, occasionally made in two halves
COLOURS	Light madder red, orange, white
FRINGE	Plain/Knotted
SELVEDGE	Extra cord reinforcement
Remarks	Light covers also woven/Colours are brighter than other Balouch weavings, with distinctive white 'lace' patterning

(3.50 × 0.99 m, 11'6" × 3'3")
*The fine white lace-like patterning and mid-red background colour are
characteristic of bedding covers from Chagai province. Balouch homelands
extend widely but their kilims are easily recognizable.*

553 Balouch *Malaki* (above)
(1.53 × 0.91 m, 5' × 3')
*The Balouch are prolific weavers of prayer rugs, which are not usually made
in flatweave by other Afghan tribes. The star motif in the knotted-pile
borders and cross panels is frequently used by the nomads from the
Dasht-i-Margo area of south-west Afghanistan.*

555 Balouch of Charaknasur (right)
(0.91 × 0.91 m, 3' × 3')
A fine soufreh *from the Charaknasur region of Balouchistan. The deep red
rectangles on the inner border probably indicate place settings. The two rows
of zig-zag fingers pointing into the plain central field are traditional in
soufreh, although their significance has long been lost.*

Mukkur Kutchi

556, 558

DESIGN	Field: Diamond medallions with scattered motifs Borders: Crenellated
SIZE AND SHAPE	Very long and narrow
MATERIALS	Loose, coarse wool warps, wool wefts
STRUCTURE	Loose slitweave
COLOURS	Bright red and orange, yellow, brown, white
FRINGE	Long with large knots or tassels
SELVEDGE	Extra cord reinforcement
Remarks	Often embellished with metal and glass beads

556, 557 Mukkur
(2.63 × 1.21 m, 8'8" × 4')
The weaver of this kilim has had difficulty forming the three diamond-shaped medallions in the field, resulting in a charmingly idiosyncratic unevenness. She has included some synthetic yarn dyed vivid pink, highly regarded because of its rarity in an environment and lifestyle which is harsh and unadorned. (Detail 557, reverse)

The Mukkur Kutchi

This town on the long, hot road between Kabul and Kandahar in southern Afghanistan is not only an important caravanserai and *chaikhana* (literally 'tea house', or 'inn'), it also serves as the traditional gathering and market place for the Kutchi nomads of eastern and central Afghanistan. These are the Pushtu-speaking Kutchis, a colourful and memorable group who may be dubbed the gypsies of Central Asia. The Kutchi are wanderers rather than nomads, earning a livelihood as traders and tinkers. It is a romantic and captivating sight to see a caravan of Kutchi, with sometimes just two or three but more often dozens of camels, walking alongside a dusty road or trail. The train will incorporate fierce dogs, as well as the sheep, goats and children, and all possessions, along with the younger, less mobile animals and birds such as chickens, piled on the camels. In the spring

558, 559   Mukkur
(3.58 × 1.21 m, 11′9″ × 4′)
The colourful Kutchi gypsies weave equally colourful kilims. Made in loosely spun slitwoven wool with elaborate fringes decorating the ends, these highly decorative kilims are of a consistent format with medallions enclosed in a field by a three-coloured crenellated border, an outer border of motifs in squares, and a zig-zag pattern down the selvedges. (Detail 559)

and again in the autumn a large fair is held outside Mukkur, and the nomads and travellers come from hundreds of miles away to exchange goods, dairy produce and animals for consumer essentials from the bazaars. Whole hillsides are covered with encampments for several months of the year.

Curiously for a wandering group, the Kutchi do not weave many bags or tent and animal trappings. Those they do weave are usually large and rectangular, adorned with several huge woollen tassels, with the opening on the long side of the sack secured by three coloured and thickly plaited wool ties. The kilims of the Kutchi are invariably long and narrow in shape, woven in a loose slitweave, with quite coarsely spun wool. The field of diamond shapes and scattered motifs is usually enclosed within a crenellated border, outlined in white, a design copied from Turkic star motifs. The Kutchi embellish, decorate and embroider everything, wearing bright, full clothing, jangling jewelry, and garish embroidered shawls. The kilims are, not surprisingly, equally ornate, often with a finish of mirrored sequins, shells and brightly coloured beads sewn on to the fringes. Quite often a long kilim will be adapted to make a *purdah*, a screen to divide the women's part of the tent from the men's, through the addition of a fringe and tassels to a selvedge.

Chapter Eight

A Kilim Miscellany

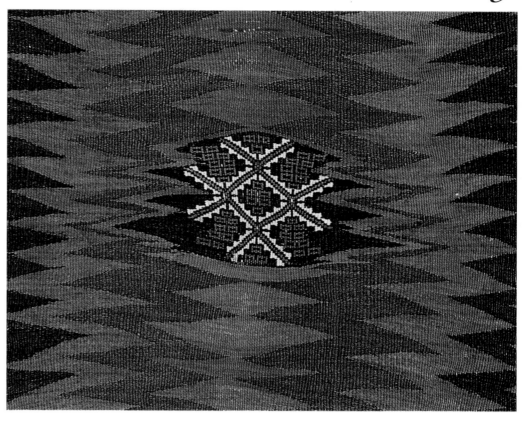

560 *This kilim, made by the Afshar tribe of Iran, features a Turkic motif at its centre. (Detail)*

Soufreh · *Rukorssi* · Bags
Tent Bands and Textiles
Animal Trappings
Other Textiles

561 Malatya *heybe*
Although the main design is different, the overall effect and the narrow bands of plainweave and patterning on this heybe, *or saddle bag, are the same as those found on 565. With use, the wefts that form the pattern disappear first. Repairs have been carried out in brightly coloured wool by the former owner and user of this bag. (Detail)*

562 Afshar
(1.22 × 1.22 m, 4' × 4')
The intricate border of brocading and many rows of simple weft wrapping contain a field of dramatic zig-zags, with a Turkic motif squeezed into the centre.

HE KILIM WEAVERS OF THE ISLAMIC WORLD ARE CONCERNED, FOR THE MOST part, with the production of rugs and covers for the floor, wall hangings and textiles that afford some comfort and decoration in the sleeping and seating areas of their homes. There are many groups, however, who have for many years woven a variety of other utilitarian and decorative textiles. The dowry of the nomad will not only consist of rugs, but also of flat-woven sacks or bags, so essential for storing and transporting food, and decorative covers for the horse or camel used in the wedding procession. For the village and city dweller, such woven dowry pieces or wedding gifts are of little use: their specialist production is more likely to consist of ceremonial textiles such as the eating cloths known as *soufreh*, although even most of these ceremonial items owe their origins to a nomadic or part-nomadic past.

Soufreh

These flatweaves are used primarily as eating cloths, spread on the floor to provide a clean surface on which food may be presented. The gathered company will then sit cross-legged around the *soufreh* to eat. *Soufreh* are commonly woven by the Kurds of Khorassan in north-east Iran as well as by the Balouch within the neighbouring areas of north Afghanistan. Other tribal groups do use eating cloths, and are known to weave *soufreh*, but to a lesser extent, being content to use printed cotton cloth not dissimilar to a table cloth.

Most extant examples of *soufreh* are usually not of a great age, for as they are in daily use they tend to wear quickly, although some wedding *soufreh* have been well preserved. Within each tribe or area, the *soufreh* cloths are usually woven to conform to a particular format and design composition.

The Balouch   Their *soufreh* are either about 1.15 m (3'6") square, or long and narrow (0.45 × 1.80 m/1'6" × 6"), containing a plain central field coloured in deep madder red or indigo with zig-zag fingers pointing into the centre of the textile and an elaborate border of floating weft weave or knotted pile. These zig-zags are often found on the sides in the field of *soufreh* of many different origins, but as yet their significance is not understood.

The Kurds and Afshar of Khorassan   More often than not, their cloths are long and narrow in shape, measuring about 90 cm (3') wide and from 1.80 m (6') to 3.65 m (12') or more in length. Those of extraordinary length are locally known as 'bridal path', indicating their use at wedding feasts. The field of these *soufreh* is of a natural light brown camel-hair colour with simple side borders of zig-zag fingers, usually in dark brown wool, complete with coloured outlining and elaborately designed end panels of floating weft in tight colourful bands of pattern. The centre of the field does sometimes contain motifs such as medallions that indicate the place intended for food dishes. *Soufreh* that are in square format – most often woven by the Afshar – feature a simple motif in the centre of a plain field.

The Kurds and Afshar of Central Iran   Their *soufreh* are usually square, coloured in rose pinks, reds, greens and light browns, and often have an acentric design in the field. They are also recognizable by their knotted pile borders on all four sides.

Other Tribes The Qashqai weave very large *soufreh*, some 3.65 × 1.80 m (12 × 6′) in size, which are used at weddings. These usually contain a plain field with perhaps a scattering of patterned areas that indicate the places for food dishes. The zig-zag fingers, so common in *soufreh* of many areas, run along two sides of the kilim and can be very small, so that they are almost indistinct amidst the traditional Qashqai border designs. *Soufreh* are also occasionally woven by the Chahar Aimaq of north Afghanistan and the Shahsavan of north-west Iran. In Turkey there is no widespread tradition of weaving *soufreh*, but some small, square kilims woven in the slitweave and *çiçim* techniques may have been used as eating cloths or table cloths. In North Africa, *soufreh* are not woven, but kilims and cloths are spread out for food and to welcome guests.

As with many traditional nomadic domestic weavings and utensils, the *soufreh* fulfil a variety of functions associated with food preparation; they are used, for instance, in several of the processes of bread-making, a crucial part of daily life in Western and Central Asia, especially amongst the Balouch. All are of the same scale and design as the square eating-cloth *soufreh*, and serve two or more uses.

Soufreh-i-nan Pazi (*pazi* means 'bake') The bread, in the form of long, flat unleavened loaves, is taken from the communal oven and put in the cloth. The four corners are then folded in to keep the bread fresh, warm and dust free.

Soufreh-i-Ghamir (*ghamir* means 'flour') The bread dough is mixed either directly on the cloth, or in a bowl on the cloth, after which it is left to 'rest' before baking.

Soufreh-i-Ard (*ard* is another word for 'flour') The cereal is milled and sieved over the cloth to make flour, and very often *soufreh* have flour engrained into the weave.

The traditional *soufreh* can easily be confused with the more recent production of small runners for the Balouch have woven many narrow rugs, on a commercial scale, in the past twenty years. Some are very fine, woven in a mixture of techniques such as knotted pile, weft wrap and weft float, which suggest their function as samplers prepared by a young girl to test her skill and the effect of certain colours and designs before she embarks on a large dowry kilim. These flatweaves are often about 0.45 × 1.80 m (1′6″ × 6′) in dimension and are frequently placed around the main carpet in the urban houses of their country of origin.

Rukorssi

The name of these cloths is shortened from the full title '*soufreh-i-ru-korssi*' ('cloth to cover oven'). In winter a felt or quilt is laid over a wooden or metal frame and a charcoal brazier or metal bowl containing hot coals is placed underneath. The family and guests sit around this brazier, with the felt tucked up to their shoulders,

563 Veramin *rukorssi*
(1.14 × 1.14 m, 3′9″ × 3′9″)
The 'cross with diamond' motif is found on many rukorssi *from the Veramin area. The weaver has filled the diamond in the centre with a complex spider, or star, motif, and used simpler star-derived motifs in the four satellite diamonds. The 'cross with diamond' motif has been cleverly scaled down and used as a running design around the border, producing a complete and interesting composition.*

564 Afshar *rukorssi*
(1.11 × 1.11 m, 3′8″ × 3′8″)
This rukorssi *seems to depict a garden. In the southern provinces of Iran, where it originated, the landscape is dry, mountainous desert, so the appeal of a green garden of flowers, trees and water is strong and is represented in many art forms.*

565 Malatya *heybe*
(0.98 × 0.49 m, 3′2″ × 1′7″)
The same weft-faced patterning technique as seen here also appears as bands of design on large kilims from this area. Much larger sizes were also made but are rarely seen.

566 Kurds of Khorassan *khorjin*
(0.99 × 0.61 m, 3′3″ × 2′)
The clear and vibrant colours are typical of Kurdish workmanship. Woven with extra weft decoration on an unusual balanced plainweave ground, this piece would be used for the everyday transportation of market produce and animal feed.

covering them up to the neck, to keep warm. The *rukorssi* is placed in the middle of the felt or quilt as a ceremonial and decorative centrepiece, away from any risk of damage from the hot coals. *Rukorssi* cloths are used by sedentary and urban people, for the nomads have no access to charcoal and use camel dung as well as dry scrub grass and thistles, all of which burn with a high flame. Townspeople have to buy in their fuel, and so a stove under a quilt and a *rukorssi* serves as an excellent form of localized and economic heating in the winter months. The *rukorssi* are very similar in size to the *soufreh*, but often a little larger, about 1.22 m (4′) to 1.40 m (4′6″) square, and they usually lack the *soufreh*'s characteristic zig-zag finger design. *Rukorssi* are woven by the same people and in the same areas as *soufreh*, such as north-east Iran, north-west Iran and Balouchistan, as well as around the town of Veramin, where there has been widespread intermarriage between various tribes such as the Shahsavan, Lurs, Kurds and Qashqai. Despite this tribal amalgamation, the Veramin *rukorssi* are distinctive and possess an individuality found more often on cloths of 'pure' tribal origins, having an impressive square and diamond design in the centre that is either brocaded or knotted on to a plain field.

Jajim Rukorssi

These warp-faced stripweaves are found in north-west Iran, Azerbaijan and the Khamseh region (east of Qazvin) as well as in the Fars region of Iran. Narrow bands of warp-faced patterning weave are cut and sewn together to make up the required size of cloth. *Jajim rukorssi* are often mistaken for horse blankets.

Bags

Nomadic people have developed many different types of bags for the storage and transportation of all of their possessions. Materials such as metal, wood and associated vegetable fibres for basket-weaving are very scarce, moreover expensive, in the lands occupied by nomads, and so bags are made from wool, a raw material that is readily available, washable, and malleable. The shape, fastenings and texture of these bags have been developed to suit a particular purpose, as indeed have those of the village and town dwellers, although to a lesser and diminishing degree. Having no furniture, the nomadic and semi-nomadic people have to store and transport all clothing, bedding, as well as household items, in bags. The wealth and thus status of a family is judged by the number of bags owned; this in turn leads to the provision of an impressive dowry for the daughters of the family. As a result of this symbolic importance attached to the storage bag, they are often extremely well woven and finely detailed.

Khorjin

(also known as *heybe* in Turkey and *khurgin*, or *keite*, in the Caucasus)
These are pannier bags that are also called saddle and donkey bags, found in use all over West and Central Asia and woven in weft-faced patterning. Their primary function is to carry goods on the back of an animal such as a donkey, horse, or camel. The size of the container sacks varies according to their use, from the smallest bags for carrying a shepherd's midday meal, or the newly born lambs.

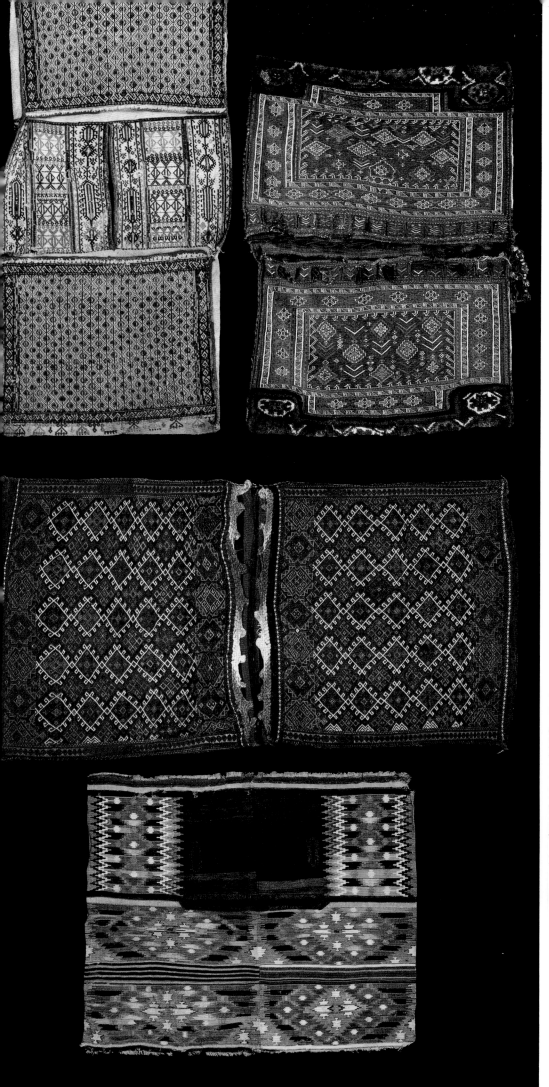

567   Konya *heybe*
(1.33 × 0.50 m, 4'4" × 1'7")
Many heybe *were woven with the middle as carefully decorated as the main part, and the slit in the centre is also a common feature. Normally the reverse is in plainweave, often with stripes of alternating colour, and occasionally small decorations appear.*

568   Bakhtiari *khorjin*
(1.14 × 106 m, 3'9" × 3'6")
A typical example of the individualistic work of the nomadic Bakhtiari people. A working bag or textile has as much love put into it as a large dowry weaving, and contains as many, if not more, elements important to tribal custom and culture. The bird's head motif stylized by the Bakhtiari weavers surrounds the central panel on each half of the bag.

569   Malatya *heybe*
(0.92 × 0.48 m, 3' × 1'7")
Woven in one piece, this nineteenth-century flatweave has two ends that are folded inward, and the selvedges are bound to create a double-ended bag. The end warps have been plaited and loops made so that the bag may be sealed. The use of different-coloured natural wool for the warps adds to the decorative effect. The natural dyes used are typical of the Malatya area.

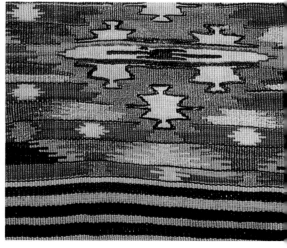

570, 571   Aleppo saddle bag
(1.08 × 1.23 m, 3'6" × 4')
Few bags or sacks of any kind have survived from this region; doubtless they were woven, but as flatweaving ceased in the early twentieth century, they are now very rare. (Detail 571)

572   Kars çuval (right)
(0.99 × 0.62 m, 3′3″ × 2′)
Çuval *are larger in size than* yastiks, *although
they can serve the same purpose. This fine
slitweave* çuval *was probably made for storing
clothing, and could have been used as a cushion,
as this filling is soft. The main pattern is
typical of Kars. Many more recently woven*
yastiks *feature similar designs, although their
colours — browns, orange and pinks — are more
modern.*

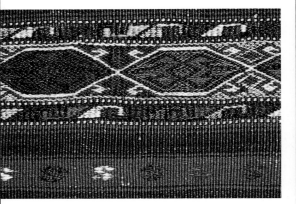

573, 574   Bergama çuval
(0.81 × 0.52 m, 2′8″ × 1′8″)
*The bottom corners and backs of bags are often
damaged, and sometimes the front part is all
that remains. However, the front side of
Bergama* çuval *is normally the only decorated
area, the reverse being woven in stripes of
alternating colours of plainweave. It is still
possible to find very finely woven examples of*
çuval *from this region. (Detail 573)*

575, 576   Adiyaman çuval
(0.79 × 0.74 m, 2′7″ × 2′5″)
*The horizontal zig-zag pattern, an adaptation
of an* elibelinde *motif, symbolizing fertility,
creates a three-dimensional effect on this
nineteenth-century* çuval. *Coloured wool is
normally used for the plainweave ground,
although sometimes natural brown wool is found.
(Detail 575)*

577　Hazara Aimaq *juval* (top left)
(1.21 × 1.14 m, 4′ × 3′9″)
The Hazara Aimaq people from north-west Afghanistan adorn their juval *bags with crocheted fringes. The elaborate work round this bag in natural brown wool also has coloured wool wrapped round the threads, a technique they use to decorate the reed side screens of their tents. A* juval *such as this from Qala-i-Nau is hung on the wall of a tent and used to store small items of clothing or cooking equipment.*

579　Shahsavan of Khamseh bag (left)
(0.60 × 0.53 m, 2′ × 1′9″)
The clear bright colours, soft wool and beautifully executed weave are all typical of Shahsavan work from the beginning of this century. A bag such as this would be in daily use, containing small household items such as a mirror, or perhaps other valuable personal objects.

581　Yomut Turkoman *jallar* (left)
(1.42 × 0.53 m, 4′8″ × 1′9″)
A Yomut Turkoman jallar *is tied to the side wall of the yurt to store small domestic items. It is invariably of a short and wide format, with decorative fringes and tassels along the bottom edge. This* jallar *has small areas of silk brocading in a traditional pattern on the face.*

578, 580, 582　Uzbek felt bags (right)
(0.86 × 0.38 m, 2′10″ × 1′3″)
Felt bags are used by the Uzbek nomads as horse panniers. Although the same size and shape as the flatwoven bags used to hold the ends of tent poles, they are not as strong. The truly ancient and atavistic motifs are beaten into the felt, appliquéd or embroidered. Similar motifs are found on the felt tent roofs and doorways, and were originally thought to be tribal flags or standards.

583 Uzbek *verneh*
(1.14 × 1.14 m, 3'9" × 3'9")
A simple donkey cover, woven by a peasant farming family in north Afghanistan. Such an essential and everyday textile still contains in the weave and design the essence of their culture and weaving history.

584 Shahsavan of Mogan *chanteh*
(0.91 × 0.61 m, 3' × 2')
This single bag has been opened along its sides. Most bags are woven in one long piece, so that the weaver has to take care to weave the outside face, the middle and the back sections in the right order, to the right dimensions and in the right orientation. The ends are folded together and the sides sewn up. The strong middle section then forms the area of most wear, the bottom edge.

Each half of a donkey bag is about 60 cm (2') square, and the large camel bags used for carrying feed, chaff and produce can measure as much as 1.20 m (4') square. *Khorjin* are usually woven in one long piece, the weaver taking care to work out how to weave the outside, middle and back sections of the textile to the right dimensions and in the right orientation. To make up the bag the ends are folded into the centre and the sides sewn up; this ensures that the bags have great strength, as there are no seams where the load is heaviest. *Khorjin* are woven in any of the weaving techniques, but are more often of a thick and strong, heavy technique such as weft-wrapping or floating weft, and represent some of the finest flatweaving. The inner side of these bags is usually less elaborately decorated, sometimes just of plainweave, at other times having lines of simple designs. The dimension of the area connecting the two bags varies from about 5 cm (2") up to about 30 cm (12"), according to function, and this part of the weave is usually decorated. The openings of the bags are generally fastened by a row of plaited wool loops that fit through slits in the top of the bag and interlock with each other, or alternatively by means of a long strand of multi-plied wool that passes through the loops.

Chanteh and Single Bags
(also known as *çanta* in Turkey, and *chanta* in the Caucasus; a *kese* is a Turkish money bag)
This type of bag has many different uses, and many contain anything from personal adornments, a mirror, sewing and mending materials, money, tobacco, writing materials and paper, to a Koran. Each bag has a different, and at times, definite function, and is often woven for a particular article. Money bags, by necessity, have to have an end that may be secured, usually by folding over and tying, and sometimes these money bags are rather large – as are those of tax collectors.

Kola-i-Chergh Tent-pole Bags
A most distinctive bag used as a sleeve for tent poles bundled together for transportation during migration. This is a particular speciality of the Ersari Turkomen and of other nomadic people who use *yurt*-type tents. Its cylindrical shape is closed at one end in a tapering fashion, and it is often highly decorated, tasselled and embroidered. Such a bag forms an important part of a nomadic girl's dowry.

Namakdan
(also known as *duz torbasy* in the Caucasus)
This is a salt bag. Rock salt is of great value to many of the people of Asia, living so far from the sea. Such a bag not only holds rock salt to be used by shepherds for their flocks, but is also needed in the tent to store cooking salt. As in Western cultures, the spillage of salt is considered an omen of bad luck, and so the *namakdan* is woven in a tight double interlock or weft-wrap technique, in a broad-based bottle-shape with a narrow neck-piece that folds down to close the bag and prevent the salt from spilling. The salt bags are woven by only a few tribes; the Balouch weave the greatest number, but they are also woven by the Uzbek Tartari, the Taimani and the Shahsavan.

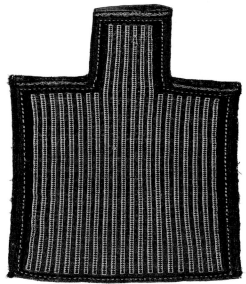

585   *A weft-wrapped* maffrash *panel made by the Shahsavan of Hashtrud.*

Maffrash

This bag is best thought of as a form of textile furniture with the same function as a chest. *Maffrash* are used by tent dwellers in most areas of Turkey but are only made by the Caucasian Turks in north-east Anatolia, in the weft-wrapped or slitweave technique. *Maffrash* are also found in Iran, with many being woven in Azerbaijan, but they are not made in Afghanistan or by the Central Asian nomads, for here the *juval* is used instead. The *maffrash* bags and chests remain in use in the villages, but have often been replaced in cities by cupboards and chests of drawers. *Maffrash* are used for storing clothing, materials and bedding, and it is essential for every girl to possess a pair of *maffrash* when she marries, to contain her very personal possessions. She will therefore weave these *maffrash* as early as she is able, often at the age of six or seven, assisted by her female relatives, with as much loving care and skill as possible. The *maffrash* bag is often mistaken in the trade for a cradle woven to be slung from a wooden frame or tripod.

586   Balouch *namakdan*
(0.53 × 0.68 m, 1′9″ × 2′3″)
The texture of this salt bag, woven in weft-float technique, is so dense and hard it is like a board.

Juval, jallar and torbah

(also known as *çuval*, or *torbah*, in Turkey)
These bags are hung on the side of the tent for the storage of clothes, bedding and household items such as pots and cooking utensils. They are most commonly found in north Iran and Afghanistan, woven by the Turkoman tribes, particularly the Tekke and Yomut, as well as the Uzbeks in the Maimana area, the Balouch from both west Afghanistan and north-east Iran, and the Kurds of Khorassan. The *çuval* is used for storing animal feed and grain in Turkey, and in Tunisia such a sack is known as *ghrara* and *makhla*.

The *juval* is the largest type of tent bag and is always woven in pairs up to 1.20 × 0.90 m (4 × 3′) in dimension. It was formerly used as a container to transport goods on the side of a camel. The *jallar* is a short wide bag fixed to the tent wall that invariably has a long wool fringe hanging from its bottom edge; it is used to store small household items and kitchen equipment. The *torbah* is the smallest of these tent bags, usually about 45 cm (1′6″) square. Another unusual type of bag originates from Hakkari region, near Van in eastern Turkey. It is triangular in shape and is used by the women to carry their babies on their backs.

Balisht

(also known as *yastik* in Turkey, *tatrayin* in Morocco, and *usada* in Algeria and Tunisia)
This is a large sack-sized bag that when stuffed with raw cotton is used by nomads and townsfolk alike as a floor cushion to rest against, for even city houses do not have much wooden furniture.

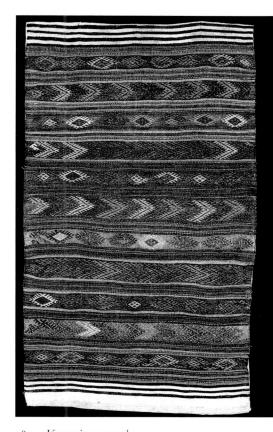

587   Karapinar *çuval*
(0.99 × 0.61 m, 3′3″ × 2′)
With the advent of modern packaging materials, the art of weaving beautiful storage bags such as this has been lost forever.

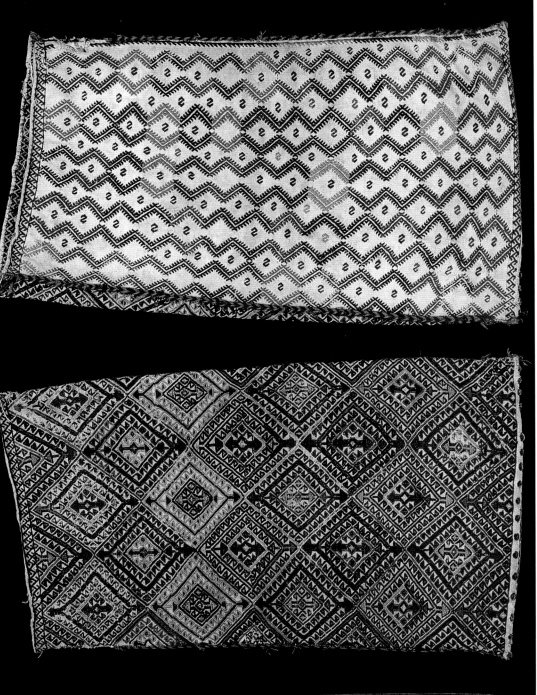

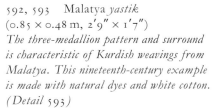

588–91   Konya *yastik*
(0.72 × 0.46 m, 2′4″ × 1′6″)
The weaver has put every effort into creating an equally decorative reverse side to this yastik. *The zig-zag pattern supposedly represents running water, which according to folkloric belief symbolizes the desire for life. (Details 589, 591)*

592, 593   Malatya *yastik*
(0.85 × 0.48 m, 2′9″ × 1′7″)
The three-medallion pattern and surround is characteristic of Kurdish weavings from Malatya. This nineteenth-century example is made with natural dyes and white cotton. (Detail 593)

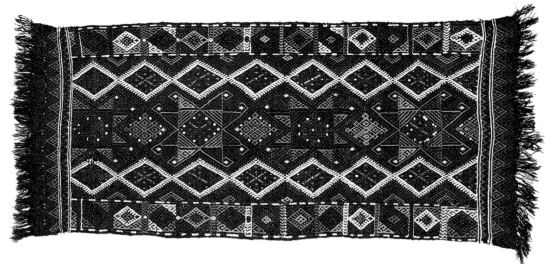

594   Konya *yastik*
(0.99 × 0.48 m, 3′3″ × 1′7″)
The fine work in this nineteenth-century weaving indicates that it was made more for decorative than utilitarian purposes. The structure is of weft-wrapping technique on plainweave, the white patterning is cotton, and natural dyes have been used.

595   Bakhtiari *verneh*
(2.13 × 1.67 m, 7′ × 5′6″)
This magnificent horse cover from south-west Iran demonstrates the love the Bakhtiari have for their animals. The elaborate black, white and red border wraps cleverly around the shape. The whole piece is woven in double-interlock technique, and is carefully finished.

597   Adiyaman cradle
(0.45 × 0.68 m, 1'6" × 2'3")
This weaving was made for carrying a baby on a mother's back. The shape is achieved by weaving an oblong, folding it in half, binding a side next to the fold, then folding back the 'wings' of the free corner. The long tassels create a very decorative effect; near the top they are bound with gold metallic thread.

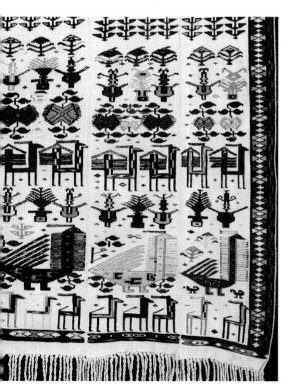

598   *Verneh*
The weaver of this delightful horse cover has depicted a wealth of interesting motifs – camels, dragons, human figures, dogs, trees, fruits, and even some chickens are all represented here.
(Detail)

Tent Bands and Textiles

It is surprising indeed that people who live an extremely hard life, often on the edge of poverty, in areas where the climate and environment require the whole family to work from dawn to dusk, have the time or desire to decorate their living quarters so energetically. Almost all nomadic and semi-nomadic tent dwellers weave textiles to decorate their tent, as well as bands to hold it up or secure it in strong winds. Many of the decorations are worked in knotted pile, whereas tent bands are flatwoven. These tent bands are also used as ties to strap baggage on an animal's back, and the bands are woven in long lengths, in a width that varies from 5 cm (2") up to 30 cm (12"), according to use. The wide bands have structural use, as they prevent the wall of the round *yurt* of the Turkoman, Uzbek and Kirghiz, or the *alachiq* tent of the Azerbaijani Shahsavan, from falling outwards. Narrower bands are used to lash the roofing poles, which vary from the hoops on barrel tents used by the Balouch to the upright poles on Qashqai, south-west Iranian and Bedouin tents. Tent bands are constructed in the warp-faced patterning technique, as well as often being decorated with brocade, embroidery and appliqué.

Purdah
(also known as *ensi* in Turkestan and *hatchlu* in Iran)
This textile is used within the tent to divide the women's quarters from the men's, and is found most frequently worked in the knotted pile technique, though sometimes in flatweave. As it is intended for hanging, the weave is often light in weight, adorned with a 'false' fringe along one long side, and loops are sewn at intervals along the opposite selvedge.

Animal Trappings

In Turkey the camel headdress is called *deve başlik* and is decorated with cowrie shells. For many of the people of Islamic North Africa and West and Central Asia, a pack animal is central to daily existence, and so the covers and harness for their horses and camels are sometimes more detailed and beautiful than any textile woven for themselves. The position that these pack animals hold in the cultural traditions of the people is also very important. They serve not only as a means of labour and transport, but also as a badge of wealth and a crucial part of the dowry. Of the animal trappings, the saddle cover or blanket for horses and camels is perhaps the most important, as it is the largest textile. The horse blanket has a most distinctive shape, composed of a square with an extension of two panels as fingers that are fastened together under the animal's neck. Covers such as these vary from simple plainweaves with a minimum of decoration, to elaborate weft-wrapped dowry pieces woven by girls of all the Persian nomadic tribes. Warp-faced *jajim*-work is commonly made into saddle covers. The camel trappings are often the most esoteric and unrecognizable pieces of small flatweaving, demonstrating the skill and finesse of painstaking workmanship. Neck bands have a long 'V' shape to carry a bell, and shorter, wider bands are used as girth padding to prevent the various bands and straps used to support the load from chafing. Such items are made by the Balouch, although the Turkomen and tribes from western Iran also weave blankets and trappings for camels.

Other Textiles

Namad

Felt is probably the oldest woollen textile made by man, thought to have originated in Central Asia and Mongolia, the native heartland of the Oghuz tribes who then migrated across Central Asia to Anatolia. The technique is simple: wool is wetted and compacted so the scaly surface of the fibres mats, and they become irreversibly tangled together. Felt is principally used as clothing: the *kepenek* worn by shepherds from eastern Anatolia, for example, are coats of felt so thick they stand up by themselves. Felt also makes good boots and hats, being naturally warm and partially waterproof, and is used by the nomadic and semi-nomadic people of Central Asia and north Afghanistan and many of the tent-dwelling people of Iran, Anatolia and North Africa, as the principal covering for the tent. The appliqué, patchwork and embroidered decorations on many of the felts are atavistic, and are probably some form of a tribal standard, perhaps derived from the oldest and original designs that were later to embellish kilims. The Uzbek and Kirghiz make felt rugs for the tent floor in wintertime; these are good for insulation but not very durable.

Sutrangi

These are cotton flatweaves that are woven in slitweave or interlock technique. See Chapter Seven, p. 278, for a full description.

Moj

Moj are woven by the Qashqai and Lurs. Because these textiles are not found in any other Turkic weaving area, it can be assumed that the Qashqai weavers picked up the technique from the Farsi-speaking Lurs after they moved to their present homelands. Superficially similar to *jajim*, these cloths have been both described as *jajim* in literature and attributed to the Qashqai as *jajim*. The *moj* are woven in balanced twill weave in two halves of the same size that are then sewn together; their construction takes place within the village workshops especially set up for the commercial weaving of these blankets and bedcovers, for resale in the bazaar. *Moj* means 'wave' in Farsi, and they are so called because of their quickly woven pattern of interlocking zig-zags which runs over stripes of colour along the warps. Many more complex and time-consuming compositions and patterns are woven, however, and these include rhomboid medallions, diagonal and rectangular lattices, and other work similar to slitwoven kilim patterns but restricted by the twill weaving technique. Luri *moj* are dull and limited in palette, as are their kilims, in comparison with the brightly coloured and precisely woven Qashqai pieces. The Lurs, however, are the more inventive and imaginative with their designs.

599 Afghan *sutrangi*
(1.37 × 0.83 m, 4'6" × 2'9")
Sutrangi *are woven with cotton warps and wefts. Originally very large* sutrangi *were used as an underlay for mosque carpets, but in recent years smaller pieces have been made by prisoners in Afghan jails to provide a meagre income for food.*

600 Luri *moj*
(2.13 × 1.52 m, 7′ × 5′)
Moj *are woven exclusively by the Qashqai and Luri village people in special workshops dedicated to their production for sale as blankets. Although the Luri weavers use duller colours and are perhaps less skilful that the Qashqai, their* moj *have more variety in pattern and are inspired in design.*

601 Qashqai *moj*
(2.13 × 1.52 m, 7′ × 5′)
Although moj *are very similar in appearance to* jajim, *they are invariably woven in a balanced twill weave technique in two separate halves and sewn together.* Jajim *are woven in a warp-faced technique in very long narrow strips then cut to the required length and sewn.* Moj *is a Farsi word for 'wave', and describes the typical patterning of zig-zags of alternating colours over an apparent background of coloured stripes.*

Jajim

These are closely woven warp-faced textiles made of narrow strips of 6 cm (2″) to 18 cm (6″) width, that are cut and sewn together along their selvedges. The narrowness of the strips is unavoidable as the warp-faced patterning technique cannot be woven to any width because of the difficulty of maintaining an even tension in the weave. *Jajim* are woven primarily by the Shahsavan and the Qashqai in Iran, but also to a lesser extent by all the other tribal groups. The Uzbek and Turkoman people call such work *ghudjeri*. Stripweaving is also practised in Anatolia in plainweave, so that the strips are wider, normally 30 cm (12″), and are then made up into covers with a maximum of five strips. These strips are made in multiple colours with patterns of extra weft floats and inlaid brocading. The *jajim* is, because of the nature of its construction, very versatile, and can be used as a blanket, bedding cover, horse cover or rug. *Jajim* weave is made up into *rukorssi*, provides the components of bags of various shapes, and is used as a very coarse wash-cloth. The Bakhtiari make long and unusual coats from this weave, worn by men, and more recently, the fine and long strands of vegetable-dyed wool dismantled from older weaves have been sought for carpet repair and construction in Iran.

Verneh

A floor covering used by the Shahsavan. Its most important characteristic is its weave of extra weft wrapping on a plainweave ground. The small *verneh*, about 1.80 m (6′) square, are made of two, four or six panels sewn together, and used as *rukorssi*, as well as horse or camel covers. Larger *verneh*, about 3.00 × 150 m (10 × 5′), woven in two or four panels, are used as floor covers when lined with felt.

Chapter Nine

New Kilims

602   *A superbly woven modern kilim made in Uşak, Anatolia. The weaver has successfully reproduced a*
traditional Sivrihisar design. (Detail)

Turkey

Iran

Afghanistan

603 *A new Turkish kilim of Sivrihisar design.*

Fᴿᴼᴹ ᴛʜᴇ ᴍᴏᴍᴇɴᴛ ᴛʜᴀᴛ ᴛʜᴇ ᴋɪʟɪᴍ-ᴘʀᴏᴅᴜᴄɪɴɢ ᴄᴏᴜɴᴛʀɪᴇs ғᴇʟʟ ᴠɪᴄᴛɪᴍ ᴛᴏ the allures and pressures of modernization, the painful transition from a backward agrarian to a more 'advanced' society was set inexorably in motion; this goal has often been pursued through grandiose plans and projects of strong central governments presiding over industrialization and collective farming, along with tight control of unruly transhumants. All such initiatives have led to the absolute decline of the 'traditional' lifestyle and the creative productivity of the rural and village peoples, the very tribal groups who weave most kilims and associated flatweaves.

This deterioration in the quality and originality of flatweaves has not affected the trade in new kilims. A cursory visit to a dealer, either in the flatweave-producing countries themselves or in the Western World, may show a bewildering array of kilims of all ages; but although it must be clearly stated that not all old and antique kilims are well-made or desirable artifacts, a comparison of pre-industrial examples and more recent work will generally reveal a decline in both compositional virtuosity and technical standards, as well as in colouring, that is all too evident. Until the late nineteenth century all the constituents intrinsic to the production of original, well-coloured and constructed kilims were readily available in the daily lives of the peoples of North Africa and West and Central Asia. Since the beginning of the twentieth century, the quality ingredients for superior flatweaving have either been denied or diluted.

The changes inflicted on the weavers have been dubbed 'the three d's', which stand for the prevalence of chemical dyes, the dichotomy between demand and supply, and the death of 'traditional' lifestyles. It was the introduction of the easy-to-use and cheap synthetic dyes that first drew Western collectors' attention to the decline in 'traditional' standards of knotted pile and flatweaving from the Orient and North Africa. Some of these colours ran at the slightest provocation, faded with alacrity, or faded unevenly – characteristics that have come to be seen as hallmarks of synthetic dyes. It was not only the dyes that offended the consumers and commentators in the West, however, but also the brutish matching of shades and tones. Freed from the constraints and limitations of the natural world's dye sources, many colourists seemed to delight in the jarring combination of brash and often fluorescent oranges, purples, yellows, pinks and violets – colours so easily attainable from a powder or as pre-dyed yarn from the merchant.

Although the cheap and ready supply of synthetic dyes had for many decades supplanted the use of natural colourants, with the emergence of mass tourism there was an upsurge of Western middle-class interest in flatweaves, as many intrepid travellers – the voracious consumers of the Western World – alighted on the 'oriental rug' as an ideal holiday souvenir as well as a decorative commodity for their homes. The traditional domestic consumption of flatweaves was, therefore, rapidly overtaken by profitable international trade, precipitating the dichotomy between demand and supply. Merchants were keen to meet the demand by the cheapest and most profitable means and weavers were delighted by the rewarding and steady stream of orders. The increase in consumption meant that economies had to be made in the supply process until the rugs cut from the village and town workshop looms became sorry replicas of glories past.

The near-death of a 'traditional' lifestyle – the third 'd' – has ensured that the wholly 'original' and 'naive' domestic weaving output of the previously nomadic

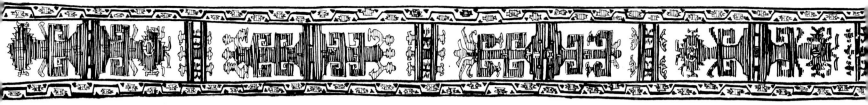

604   *An Uzbek tent band.*

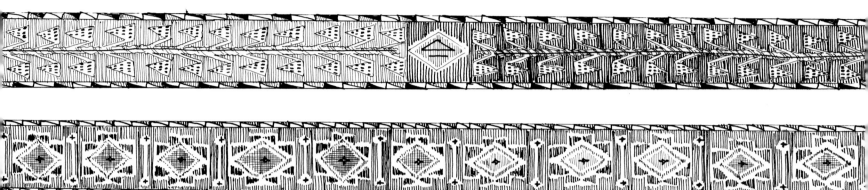

605, 606   *Turkoman tent bands.*

tribespeople, semi-nomadic groups and tribal villagers has suffered irrevocable damage. As the groups have settled, had their movements curtailed or have succumbed to the pleasures of a sedentary life, so the need for many of their bags, trappings and rugs has come to an end. It is impossible to reinvoke the now historic conditions that have led to the production of many of the finest nomadic kilims, woven by groups such as the Qashqai of Iran and the Turkomen of Central Asia. And indeed, it is not only the production of these utilitarian textiles that has been afflicted by the social and economic changes brought about by the quest for modernization. One of the key functions of fine textiles has been for centuries to form part of the dowry. Dowry textiles, beautifully and painstakingly worked by young girls and mothers bound by social and family duty, have been supplanted across the range of tribal groups by a preference for valuable commodities of the new age – televisions, motor bikes, refrigerators and other consumer durables. Weaving skills are now directed towards the commercial sector – with predictable results.

Faced with such a dirth of quality flatweaves, the dealers and merchants – primarily of the Western markets, but more recently within the countries of origin as well – have focused their interest on new rugs that return to the standards of production and integrity of patterning of the pre-industrial past.

Modern kilim production generally falls into three main categories. Some flatweaves continue to be made by the nomads and villagers of North Africa, Turkey, Iran and Afghanistan for domestic use that, despite their synthetic dyes and unusual raw material combinations, still reflect their tribal and family histories. Many more kilims are woven for commercial gain and these have tended, with the recent focus of Western consumer interest on the flatweave rug, to become tired imitators of patterns and styles from many areas beyond the weavers' homelands. Synthetic dyes and machine-spun wool are the least expensive components for such kilims, and may be purchased, in common with most mass-produced commodities, in low, medium and fine grades. Lastly, there

607 *Kilims and carpets are laid out to be sun-faded in the Doşme Alti region of southern Anatolia, near Antalya. This method of toning down the vivid colours favoured by the village weavers is widely practised and more successful than chemical washing. It normally takes about two months to achieve the desired hues.*

608 *Detail of 610.*

609 *Detail of 611.*

is the 'new antique' production that has set out to be market leader in high-quality kilims. Seeking to justify their high prices as well as attempting to achieve genuine colour-fading characteristics, weavers of these kilims have reintroduced vegetable dyes. It is ironic, however, that just as the market preference for the 'traditional' dyes has been catered for, careful and artistic dyers can produce results with synthetic dyes which are virtually indistinguishable from their natural counterparts! This can cast doubt on the authenticity of some supposedly naturally dyed textiles, especially as some of the dealers' claims can only be validated by a laboratory test. These new 'antiques' are also of varied quality, reflected in the complexity of the composition and the fineness of the weave.

The centre of ingenuity for this new kilim production is undoubtedly Turkey. Commissioned work with more atavistic design characteristics is becoming increasingly popular in Iran and certain very small projects have been established in Afghanistan as well as within the refugee camps on the Pakistan border. The tradition of weaving continues in North Africa, although to a lessening extent. The Berbers of Morocco are now weaving modern kilims in a 'Tunisian style' to sell to tourists, yet a number of recently woven traditional-design rugs can still be found in the bazaars. North African flatweaving has never been as prolific as in the Near and Middle East, and has now diminished to the scale of a minority folk art.

Turkey

In Turkey, the commercial production of new kilims was started in the early 1980s as a direct result of the new international demand for a constant supply of kilims of consistently useful sizes, colours and qualities tailored specifically for the Western market. Certainly, then as now, the villagers were continuing to make kilims to satisfy their own needs, but the quality, sizes and colours were not always suitable for trading purposes and the supply was distinctly irregular. In order to gain acceptance in both the international and home tourist markets, new commercially woven, competitively priced Turkish kilims of a certain standardized quality had to be available in quantity, and so it was necessary to implement changes in traditional weaving processes as well as to cut certain corners as far as the quality of raw materials was concerned. This new kilim production, although scoffed at by some purists, is very important, as these flatweaves will be the antiques of the future. The cheaper 'decorative' kilims made with machine-spun wool and chrome dyes will probably not stand the test of time very well; those made from the 'traditional' materials will endure and their appearance will improve with the years.

Sheep-shearing remains a male task, undertaken once or twice yearly, and whatever wool is surplus to domestic requirements is sold to the wool factory. On arrival at the factory, the fleeces are left out in the sun to dry and the light-coloured wool is then separated from the dark, as dark wool is used in its undyed state. The wool then goes through several combing processes to untangle the strands into a suitable state for spinning. Modern kilim production mainly uses machine-spun wool, which is inferior to the hand-spun variety, as during the combing process much of the natural lanolin is lost, and vegetable oil is added to the wool to counteract this, making it greasy. This grease does not come out in the dyeing process, despite the fact that the wool is heated to a high temperature in order for

610 Izmir
(1.78 × 1.14 m, 5′10″ × 3′9″)
A copy of a Thracian design, woven in the villages near Izmir. The quality of the workmanship is excellent, but the use of slitweave on such fine wool warps has resulted in a thin kilim that will not last very long if used as a rug. The abrash *in the green is overstated and has a striped effect. (Detail 608)*

611 Izmir
(1.82 × 1.24 m, 6′ × 4′)
The weaver of this kilim has excelled in her work; it is most unusual to see modern weaving as well accomplished. She has even included some curvilinear wefts in the slitweave. This kilim will stand the test of time: natural dyes have been used and the wool is hand-spun. It has a much stronger construction than 610. The design is from Aydin, which is not far from Izmir. (Detail 609)

612 Uşak
(1.83 × 1.18 m, 6' × 3'10")
The geometrized floral pattern derives from a long tradition of copied design. This version has been copied from a kilim woven in eastern Anatolia in about 1950 influenced by Caucasian and European designs, the latter in turn taking their inspiration from Islamic patterns.

the dyes to take. The oil remains even at the final washing stage, and as a result new carpets and kilims rapidly become dirty.

Once spun or double spun by machine into a continuous length, the woollen yarn is wound into hanks ready for dyeing, a process that is carried out in a different factory. Chrome dyes are widely used nowadays, and they are fast to washing if mordanted well, but in general tend to result in a 'flat' tone. Dye factories are usually archaic establishments, often makeshift buildings with corrugated-iron roofs, large steaming cauldrons, tins of commercial dyes and rinsing baths. The wool is dyed in minimum quantities of about 120 kg (265 lbs) for the sake of economy; in this way there is also a reduction in the possible colour variations that can easily occur in different dye lots. When the process of dyeing and drying is finished, the wool is delivered to the factor, who will distribute it to the far-flung villages, or else the weavers will collect the wool from his shop or warehouse.

The weaving of new kilims in Turkey is still carried out in time-proven manner, using a vertical loom, and most kilims are woven in slitweave or *çiçim*, a supplementary weft technique using thick yarn that produces a raised pattern. Fortunately in the Anatolian villages there is no such thing as a co-operative, and the women weave at home at their leisure when they have finished their more pressing household chores. The looms themselves are set up inside the houses, but in the south, in the summer months, they are often moved outside to a shady position.

New kilims are made in more practical sizes than were their antecedents, which were woven on narrow looms in two pieces and sewn together down the centre. Of the 'traditional' sizes, a 'medium' example (see p.22) was not very popular, the small kilims were used for prayer, and the larger rugs, used for seating and floor decoration, were abundant. Ironically it is the medium sizes, of least use for the Turkish consumers, that are most suited to the Western home.

Flatweave compositions are known to the weavers by heart, and if a new style is required, they will often directly copy designs from other kilims or photographs of kilims. In general the villagers and traders who organize the new production do not really understand the tastes of the foreign consumer and tend to make new kilims in the same colours and compositions as those found in museums, catalogues, books, or any photographs that they can acquire. These may be authentic, but for commercial purposes not entirely desirable, as new colours can never look as good as the effect derived from natural dyes that have had time to mature.

Unlike knotted carpet makers who copy designs from cartoons drawn on graph paper, kilim weavers in Anatolia do not seem to be able to understand a drawing of a kilim. Weaving a new design takes the weaver much longer than one she already knows, so it is not so easy to get her to accept a design that is complicated, and naturally she will ask a very much higher price for such work. As long as the designs form a geometrical pattern, the weaver will be able to attempt to replicate what is required, but to try to get her to weave a more abstract or representational composition is another matter altogether.

Once the work has been completed the kilim is taken off the loom, and the end warps are knotted to stop the fringe from unravelling. When making the smaller, 'rug-size' kilims, the weaver will often make an identical pair, as the composition

is fresh in her mind and the second one is therefore made more quickly and easily. For the larger kilims, it is common practice for more than one weaver to work at the loom, as a kilim that is, for example, 3.05 × 2.15 m (10′ × 7′) in dimension would take three women at least two months to complete. Often mother, daughter, cousin and neighbour will all contribute to the work.

When finished, the kilims are either collected from the villages, or if the factor lives nearby, the women will deliver their work themselves and collect their weaving fee. These new kilims are then prepared for the marketplace. Newly woven kilims are somewhat 'furry', and loose surface fibres are burnt off with a blow torch. This process leaves the surface much smoother and the composition is more clearly defined, although such finishing singes the kilim so that the flatweave must be washed with warm water. Many new knotted carpets often undergo heavy chemical washing; kilims, however, are not well suited to this: some may be washed to attain an antique-looking finish but although this tones down the colours, it leaves the warps looking rather yellow. After the washing process, the kilims are placed in a centrifugal spinner to extract the water, and hung on poles in a hot room to dry.

In Anatolia the main production areas for new kilims are in the west and west-central parts of the country, although the Kayseri region produces some new kilims of generally poor quality, noted for looser weave and garish colours. Some natural wool kilims of fine quality, and silk kilims, are also made in the area, however. New kilims also come from Malatya, and in the environs of Konya,

614 Konya
(1.65 × 1.25 m, 5′5″ × 4′1″)
*This kilim has been made using hand-spun wool
and natural dyes. The design has been adapted
from a far longer kilim that would have
featured many repeats of the hexagonal central
motif. Note the 'fingers' at the edges of the
central medallions.*

615 Konya
(1.93 × 1.24 m, 6′4″ × 4′)
*Konya has always been a prolific weaving area,
and the new kilims woven here are well made,
mostly with natural dyes. The wool is normally
coarsely hand-spun, resulting in a robust kilim
of thick warps. The design used here is typical
of the Konya/Obruk region.*

traditionally a prolific weaving area, many quality kilims are woven using hand-spun wool and predominantly natural colours. This admirable regard for the 'real' thing comes at a price not all can afford, and the capacity for production is not very large. In the far west, close to Izmir, some very fine weaving is taking place that copies authentic designs, and the use of natural colours is widespread. Most of the commercial production takes place around the towns of Denizli, Eşme and Uşak.

Although weavers can copy the designs of their ancestors, the meaning of the motifs and designs has usually long been lost, and consequently, to some degree, the new commercial kilims lack the character and originality of those woven purely for personal reasons. Very few kilims are being made with 'contemporary' compositions, as the trend has, to date, lent towards reproducing authentic designs in mainly authentic colours. While this is no bad thing, as traditions and heritage should be preserved, it nevertheless tends to discourage any creative impulse.

When new kilims first started to be made solely for commercial purposes the standard of weaving was very good; subsequently it has tended to deteriorate periodically and has yet to return to its first flush of quality-orientated zeal. The simple reason for this is that once a considerable demand has been established for a product, less care goes into the making, as production is spread amongst increasing numbers of weavers in order to produce the quantities required.

616 Uşak
(1.79 × 1.16 m, 5′10″ × 3′9″)
*A superbly woven kilim; every effort has been
made to create an authentic Sivrihisar design,
for the colouring, technique and pattern are all
perfect. The only inferior feature of this kilim is
its machine-spun wool, which although very fine
is nowhere near as good as hand-spun. This
design is known as a* bacali *or 'chimney' design,
and is often used on modern kilims.*

617, 618 Konya
(1.85 × 1.25 m, 6′ × 4′1″)
*This kilim uses traditional motifs to create a
plausibly authentic design, although the
patterning is not typical of the Konya area.*
(Detail 617)

619   Uşak
(1.66 × 1.08 m, 5′5″ × 3′6″)
This kilim was woven in about 1985. At that time the excellent weaving was defined as being of average quality; today it would be classed as fine. Because of market demand for new kilims the weavers complete their work as fast as possible; consequently, the quality regularly deteriorates. The design used here is reproduced from a Thracian kilim, although the white ground and borders give an unusual effect to a much copied pattern.

To improve the saleability of the new commercially produced kilims, many experiments have been made in colour and composition. The borrowing of decorative styles from other flatweaving cultures has been one idea that has met with mixed success, and it is interesting to note that a kilim woven in Turkey, for example, with an Indian *dhurrie* (cotton flatweave) composition complete with *dhurrie* colours simply does not work: the quality of weaving differs, and the basic character of a particular flatweaving style does not necessarily lend itself successfully to another. Meddling with colours and hues is the time-honoured prerogative of factors and merchants, and new kilims have been woven using bright aniline dyes with the specific intention of putting them in the sun to fade – indeed, this is often seen to be essential with the domestic or family village output of kilims. Unfortunately, however, the end product tends simply to look like a new but faded kilim. Again the Turkish merchants seem to misunderstand the international taste and demand for the ethnic flatweave, for the very allure of Anatolian kilims is their characteristic strength of colour, and even new-production kilims can look attractive when seemingly alarming combinations of the brightest colours are used.

Commercial kilim production has transformed the lives of many village families in Anatolia, bringing a new and regular source of income separate from farming. No matter how desirable it is for the merchants to procure a balanced output of kilims throughout the year, the rural lifestyle of the weavers ensures that the manufacture of kilims is a very seasonal affair. The work at the loom is predominantly carried out during the winter months in most villages, whereas during the summer the women are helping their menfolk tend the crops and gather the harvest.

The number of weavers in Anatolia is limited, as not all village women want to weave, or know how to weave. Although a Muslim country, it is progressive, and if a family is able, it will give its children the best education possible, so that even many girls will go to university rather than remaining in the villages learning a craft by which they will never improve their status or satisfy any aspiration that may lie beyond the horizon of parochial ruralism.

Even with the growing popularity of kilims, demand for Anatolian goods is certainly not assured; when new kilims started to be made, prices remained fairly stable. Nowadays, raging inflation, the monthly rise in cost of domestic raw materials, and the weavers' demands for more money for an often inferior item, all contribute to an escalation of prices. For the foreign traders, the exchange rates often work in their favour, ameliorating such domestic inflation, but if prices continue to climb the international buyers will be forced to turn to other countries to seek cheaper goods.

As old kilims have virtually ceased to exist in the market place, unless at an exorbitant price, it can only be hoped that the commercial production of new kilims will develop and improve, and that there is a widespread return to more traditional materials, such as good quality hand-spun wool and natural dyes. Of course the methods of preparing such materials are time-consuming, but the end results are well worth the extra effort and attention to detail, and will become, with the passage of time, the collectable pieces of the future.

Iran

Senna and Shiraz are the two main centres in Iran where new kilims are produced in any quantity. Although a considerable number of kilims are still made in most of the traditional weaving villages and regions, very few are of notable quality, but the nomadic and semi-nomadic people continue to weave good utilitarian textiles for their own use. Nevertheless, it would seem that contemporary weavers are unwilling to invest the time, enthusiasm and commitment, or the money for materials, needed to create a fine kilim, as the 'traditional' lifestyle of the villagers and nomads continues to come under pressure from central government and their own demands for personal Western-style advancement.

In both Senna and Shiraz the production of kilims in workshops for commercial sale is assisted by regional government weaving projects. All too often, however, as in Turkey, the requirements for the Western marketplace are misunderstood, and economy and quantity become a benchmark for flatweave production. The resulting kilims are practical in size but the colours are harsh and brash, the materials machine-finished and decidedly inferior. Their compositions and overall appearance lack the traditional character and freedom of line that can only be created within a life lived close to nature.

620 Senna
(1.52 × 0.95 m, 5′ × 3′3″)
The government in Iran made many efforts in the 1980s to establish and maintain commercial kilim-weaving workshops, but still on a minute scale compared with the huge industry manufacturing hand-knotted pile carpets. There are many well-made modern kilims woven in the traditional Senna design, but the materials are usually poor, and the colours very brash.

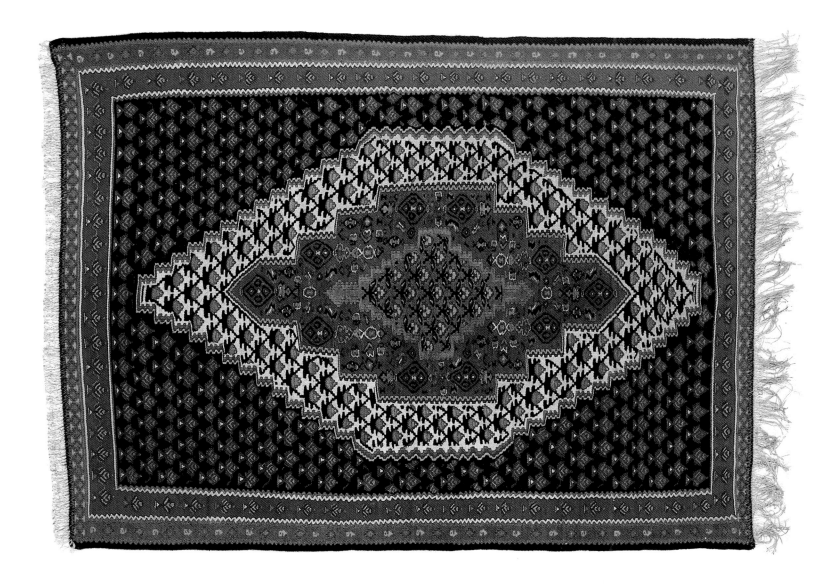

621 Afghan
(2.13 × 1.37 m, 7' × 4'6")
The Afghans who are refugees in the North-West Frontier Province have started to weave new kilims from imported wool. Turkoman and Uzbek weavers, now usually men, have here drawn a design in the traditional Maimana style from north Afghanistan. The chemical colours are over-bright, but may soften with age.

622 Afghan
The weaver has successfully copied a Persian Turkic kilim design, and produced a commercially attractive modern rug, woven in a temporary shelter in a semi-permanent refugee camp. (Detail)

Afghanistan

The prolonged war in Afghanistan, dating from 1979, has destroyed much of the country, its infrastructure and its culture, and several million of its people were driven to neighbouring countries as refugees. This destruction and the consequent desperate flight from the former security of the family home to an alien climate and environment all but halted the weaving of kilims and related flatweave textiles. The weavers' source of wool was removed when most of the sheep were destroyed or used for their meat.

Recently, however, various projects have been set up amongst the refugees in the North-West Frontier Province of Pakistan, and near Quetta in Balouchistan, whereby new kilims are woven from imported merino yarn. The wool is dyed locally using chemical dyes from eastern Europe, China and India, and most of the weavers are Turkomen and Uzbeks, although a few Pushtuns are learning the craft. Interestingly, it is mainly men who are doing the weaving, a change of role enforced by the lack of alternative remunerative occupations. The quality of weaving varies from poor to quite excellent, and the designs (such as Maimana compositions) come from north-west Afghanistan, together with some Turkic styles copied from Iranian kilims.

In the region of Iran around Mashed, a large number of Balouch people have arrived to escape from the bombing of their villages, and have settled in semi-permanent encampments, where they have integrated well. They weave traditional mixed-technique kilims that are weft wrapped and knotted, in a variety of sizes, using good materials and rich dark colours.

The recent rapid popular acceptance of kilims in the West as fashionable accessories for designed interiors has brought them to the attention of a wider audience. For the tradition of flatweaving to survive, however, a closer understanding and knowledge of the opposing cultures of East and West and their requirements is needed. To a Western buyer, a kilim is an exciting, unusual, ethnic floor covering that is practical whilst still meeting many differing interior design requirements. The traditional designs and motifs invoke romantic notions of atavistic origins and nomadic lifestyles; appealing images to many city dwellers. To the Eastern weaver, a regular income from selling her work to an exporter can bring freedom from the drudgery of peasant farming and wealth to spend in the local community.

Since it is the Western buyers who drive this trade, it is they who must demand the quality of craftsmanship to ensure that the tradition of flatweaving does not spiral down to the level of quick reproduction at minimum cost. A well-woven, well-coloured kilim will mature with age to become an interesting collectable antique in years to come. At the same time, the weaver needs to create a balance between commercial practicality and the craftsmanship of fine weaving, with a knowledge of the tradition of kilim designs and colours. If all these parameters are met, fine kilims will be made and the tradition of tribal flatweaving will be maintained.

Chapter Ten

Collecting Kilims

623   *Kilims from Reyhanli, Anatolia, are distinctive both in their weave and in their colour palette. As they are no longer woven, they are rare and highly sought after by collectors. (Detail)*

Unlike the knotted carpet, which has been held in high esteem for centuries, the kilim was of little interest to dealers until recently. As there was no market, the number of kilims that have survived the last hundred years is considerably less than that of knotted rugs. Initially, the significance of the kilim as a historical and ethnographic art form was only realized by a few discerning people. It was only as recently as the late 1970s and early 1980s that the existence of kilims has become known to a wider audience. Since that time a vast number of kilims of all types and ages have left their native countries for destinations all over the world. The growing public awareness and subsequent popularity of kilims over the last few years has resulted in a scarcity of old and antique examples available in the current market, which, even if they were available in any quantity, would probably still be too expensive for a person on an average income.

Old kilims were first procured from village houses and tribespeople, either bought or bartered for with new machine-made rugs or other commodities. When this supply was exhausted, many old kilims were acquired from mosques or swapped for new hand-made rugs. In this way, most of the older and more interesting kilims have ended up in the possession of the museums, dealers and collectors of the West, where at least their preservation is ensured.

Today's prospective collector will be comforted to know, however, that there are still many quality flatweaves available, and occasionally an extremely old and rare kilim may surface that may well have been overlooked before the market

624 *A Persian bag face from Veramin.*

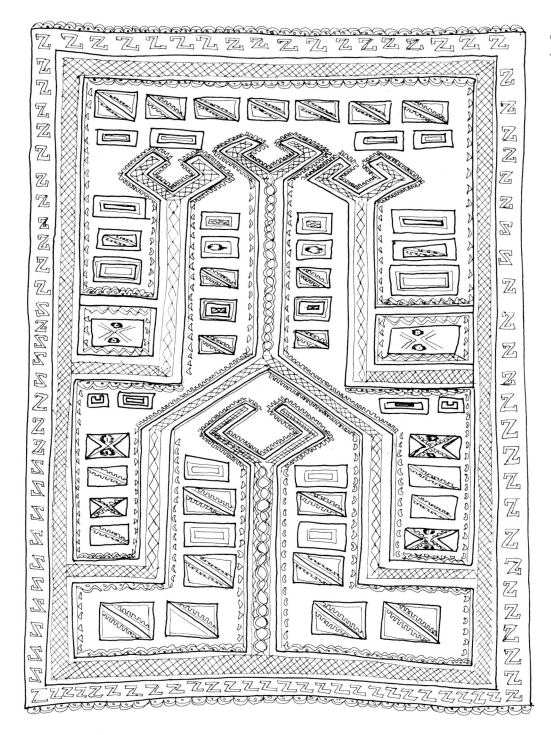

625 *A stylized Anatolian prayer rug from the Obruk area.*

explosion. The majority of these will appear in the West, for very few kilims of any worth remain within their countries of origin. The experienced dealers of the Orient will not only instantly recognize a good kilim, but will also be aware of its international market value, so it is very unlikely that a rare and valuable textile will pass unnoticed. The idea of buying in frenetic and crowded Eastern bazaars may have its allure, but in reality will probably prove expensive and disappointing. Even if, armed with a little knowledge, one manages to secure a deal at half the original sum, it is likely that the textile will still be overpriced. Bargaining is a skill that is learned by experience and extreme patience, as is shown from the following account, written over one hundred years ago, which demonstrates how little bargaining for textiles has changed since the times of the early travellers:

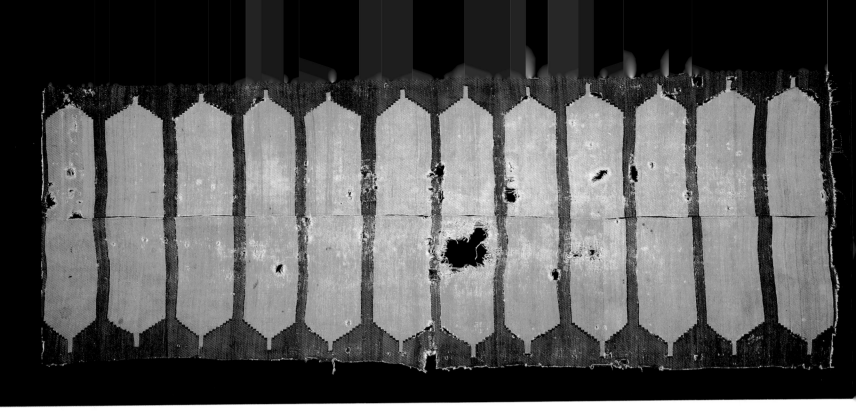

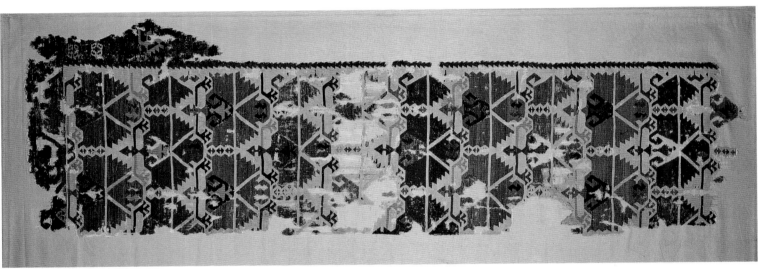

626   Sivas *saf*
(3.47 × 1.65 m, 11′4″ × 5′4″)
Saf, *or multiple prayer-arch*, *kilims are used for prayer and
for separating off the area of the mosque where the women pray.
This* saf, *woven in the nineteenth century, is unusual in that it
has only three colours and no decorative design.*

627   Konya
(2.92 × 0.90 m, 9′6″ × 2′11″)
*This design is known as an 'Ottoman Carnation', but according
to certain theories drawing parallels between neolithic
Anatolian symbols and kilim motifs, this design is in fact a
deity holding vultures.*

628   Bakhtiari of Chahar Mahal
(1.78 × 1.18 m, 5′10″ × 3′10″)
*A very fine horse cover. Rows of animals parade across the
weave. Note the unusual faces and figures at the top. Although
made in the mid-nineteenth century, it is in perfect condition
and has probably been used just once, in a bridal procession.*

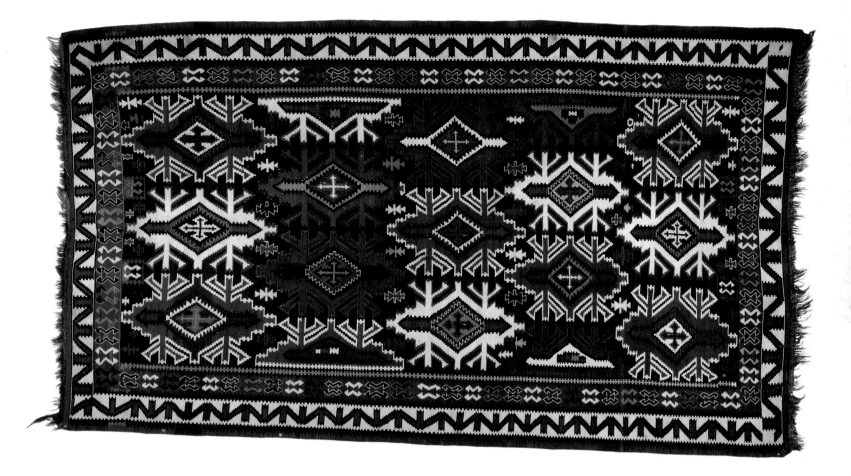

We had a very long piece of dirty paper between us, and a pencil, which latter, when not actually on the paper, [the Persian carpet seller] employed in alternately sucking and picking his ears. Bargaining would commence by his putting a fabulous price on the article, and then writing the price very imperfectly on the paper. This he then handed to me to make an offer in return. When I had done this he always argued some time, and would go down a little, repeating this process several times, while I, on my part, to his discomfort, continued firm in sticking to the original sum I had offered him. After a time he would descend no lower, but attempted, by a little jugglery, to get the better of me, by showing fresh articles, and endeavouring to persuade me to examine and bid for them, while his son replaced the others which we had been bargaining over with an inferior sort. The discovery of some such trick as this would put me in a rage, and, although it is not showing discretion to ever lose your temper with Orientals, I was compelled sometimes to apply very strong language to them, and go away with every expression of disgust. (*Oriental Carpets, How They Are Made And Conveyed To Europe – With A Narrative Of A Journey To The East In Search Of Them*, Herbert Coxon, 1884)

There are many other pitfalls of buying in the markets of Africa and Asia. Any information offered about the age, provenance or constituents of a particular example may well be invented. Most old rugs will have had some repairs made to them, which may not be visible to the untrained eye; and if a rug has been heavily repaired, this may create problems when it is washed: a rug that has been repaired in its country of origin may have been well restored, but the dyeing of the repair

629, 630   Kuba
(2.98 × 1.84 m, 9'9" × 6')
With use of a prominent design and powerful colouring, this nineteenth-century slitwoven kilim is strong in impact. The weaver has created an asymmetrical effect from an otherwise repetitive design by her artistic arrangement of colours in the medallions. The border pattern is often seen in this form, and may be a simplified version of a leaf and vine design. (Detail 630)

632, 633 Balouch of Charaknasur
(0.91 × 0.91 m, 3′ × 3′)
It is unusual to find an old example of a utility flatweave in reasonable condition; this very fine soufreh *must have been used and washed many times. As with many traditional nomadic household weavings, a* soufreh *can have a variety of associated functions. It is used in several of the processes of bread-making: as a cloth to catch the flour as it is ground and sieved; as a place to mix the dough and let it rest; and as a cover for the flat-baked loaf, to keep it fresh and dust-free. (Detail 633)*

631, 634 Kurds of Senna
(2.03 × 1.34 m, 6′8″ × 4′5″)
The kilim opposite demonstrates the pinnacle of urban workmanship achieved by the Kurdish weavers of Senna in the second half of the nineteenth century. The central medallion, similar to formal Herati knotted-carpet design, is surrounded by a field of tiny floral and zoomorphic patterns that is often thought to represent a garden. The borders are a tracery of interlocking flowers and vine leaves. The sophistication of its construction, slitwoven with curved wefts in a very fine soft wool, ensures such a kilim rarity and distinction. (Detail 634, see also 366)

wool is often hurriedly carried out, and may fade obtrusively when washed. If you are not fully aware of what the design should look like, check to see that you are not being sold half a kilim – many kilims have eccentric designs that end unexpectedly, so it is not easy to be sure. If the kilim has been cut, it will have a new end border of different-textured wool, even if the colours are accurately matched. Other market tricks include unravelling damaged kilims, washing and reweaving the original wool into a new rug that will then be passed for an old flatweave. The experienced buyer will know, by looking at the fringes, which will be obviously new, that something is not quite right about the rug even though the colours look well seasoned. Fringes are the first part of the rug to erode, however, and have often been replaced. If you are buying a rug that is a genuine antique, it is wise to check that you are permitted to export it. The vendor should be able to advise on such matters and obtain any necessary documents. Further costs, such as export and import tax, shipping, insurance, handling and postal charges, must also be explored.

Kilims may prove worthy investments, although they may take time to yield a return. The prices of old or antique flatweaves rise annually as the supply dwindles ever further; however, if a rug has been purchased in its country of origin, a devaluation of currency may iron out any profit. The kind of flatweave of an age and quality that is guaranteed to appreciate in value will not be cheap, and reselling necessitates seeking out a purchaser. There are no established market

635   *Detail of 636.*

prices, but general guidelines can be gleaned from magazines such as *Hali* and the *Oriental Rug Review*. Auction houses will make valuations, and many hold specialist rug sales. These are usually well attended by traders who will know the right price to pay. When buying at auction, do not bid against the dealers, as you will probably end up with an overpriced kilim.

Of course not everyone can afford to buy the best and oldest kilims, and there are a number of other options that are interesting, attractive and usable. Fragments of very old kilims, for instance, are of great historical and visual interest, although they will need to be mounted before they are hung. During the twentieth century, with the widespread use of chemical dyes, many kilims have been woven with entirely synthetically dyed yarn or with a mixture of dyes. Such kilims are decorative, practical and available at an affordable price. Many of these kilims have great charm and character, even though the purist may consider them inferior. Such pieces are not all commercially produced, and the quality of the

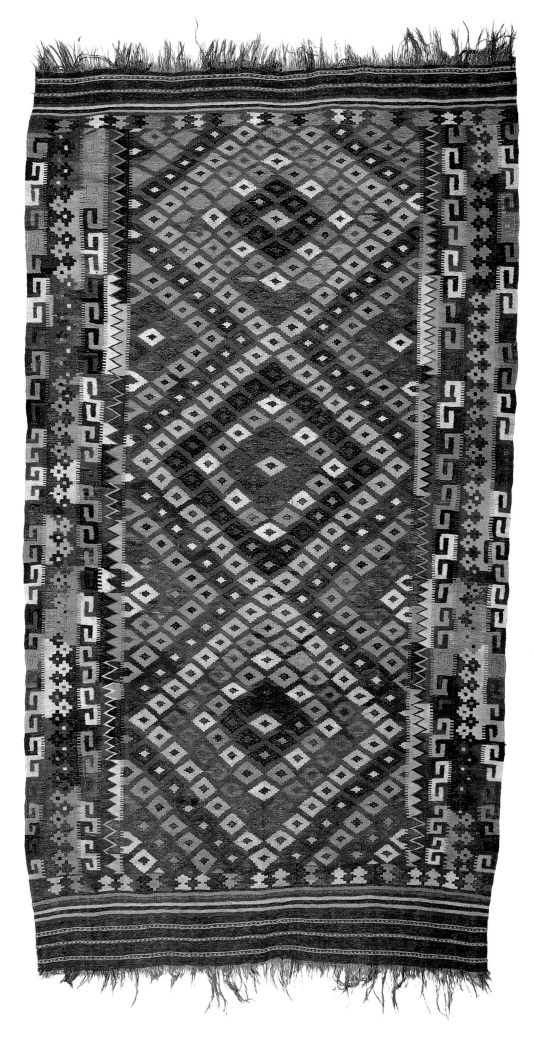

Opposite:

635, 636   Kurds of Bijar
(1.98 × 1.06 m, 6'6" × 3'6")
Although this kilim dates from the mid-nineteenth century, it has been locked away in a dowry chest for most of its life; indeed, its soft feel and lack of damage or wear both indicate that this kilim has never been used. It must have been highly prized by its owner for the vivacity of its design and the quality and warmth of the natural dyes. (Detail 635)

637   Shirvan
(3.10 × 2.00 m, 10'2" × 6'6")
Powerful vibrant colours are the chief characteristic of this nineteenth-century slitweave kilim, where shades of red, blue, green, yellow and white contrast in perfect harmony; the design, although typically Shirvan and well balanced, is secondary to the rich natural colouring. Motifs like those in this kilim are not exclusive to Caucasian kilims, as they are also found in Anatolian work. Motifs made by supplementary single wefts decorate the smaller dividing bands.

638, 639   Maimana
(4.01 × 2.05 m, 13'2" × 6'9")
Maimana is the market town in the centre of the most prolific weaving area in north Afghanistan. Woven with coarse wool in slitweave and dovetailing, this kilim has designs that comprise bold diagonal patterns made up of small squares. The side borders are wide, with up to five bands of reciprocal, mirrored or interlocking motifs. Old pieces, which are usually large, have a rich, warm palette of colours and a quality that was lost with the opening up of the country to tourism and export in the 1970s. (Detail 639)

333

640 Konya
(1.50 × 1.14 m, 4′11″ × 3′8″)
The main design of this kilim can easily be read as a turtle; according to ancient Turkish mythology, the turtle carries the world upon its back. Whether it shows a turtle or just a pattern, this small nineteenth-century kilim is a powerful work of woven art.

641 Sivas
(1.67 × 0.86 m, 5′6″ × 2′10″)
The design of the central panel of this nineteenth-century kilim is atypical, and seldom seen. The dark blue motifs extending from the centre are a simplified version of an elibelinde *mother-goddess motif, while the red and green motif on the white ground is a* bukagi *fetter or shackle motif which, according to folklore, represents family unity.*

wool is often high. Even these more recent kilims are now disappearing at a remarkable rate, however, for the demand for them is increasing as their decorative appeal gains momentum. Also, the need to weave some smaller items, such as bags, has now been removed by ubiquitous modern substitutes.

New kilims, unless made from good quality hand-spun wool and vegetable dyes, will not increase in value. Although rugs made in the authentic manner will undoubtedly become the antiques of the future, the standard of weaving in such kilims is far inferior to the craftsmanship of the last century. This is because these kilims are made for the commercial market, and the time required to weave a very fine kilim would raise its price to that of an antique one. Nevertheless, new kilims made from natural materials last longer, and their colours improve with time, so although they are significantly more expensive than those woven from machine-spun chemically dyed yarns, their higher cost is justified. The overridingly inferior characteristic of any new kilim, however, is that it lacks the 'soul' of its antecedents, which were woven purely for personal use.

Captions for 642 and 643 on page 336.

Page 335:

642 Qashqai
(2.89 × 0.91 m, 9′6″ × 3′)
*This kilim could easily be mistaken for a
flatweave of the Shahsavan of north-west Iran.
The lack of borders is most unusual in a kilim
from the south with a horizontal band design.
The motifs are typically Turkic, as in 421, and
the three narrow bands of complementary weft
weave at the ends are characteristic of the region.
The clear strong colours are another indication of
Qashqai origins (probably Amaleh or
Darashuri sub-tribe). The colours are natural,
as the kilim pre-dates the introduction of
chemical dyes in the late nineteenth century.
(Detail 645)*

643 Konya
(3.96 × 1.52 m, 13′ × 5′)
*This kilim was woven in the nineteenth century
by the Hotamiş tribe in the Konya area. The
form created by the coloured areas in the field is
rarely seen in kilim designs; the same is also
true of the pattern made by the brown and white
forms, which when viewed horizontally resembles
a Picasso-like figure. It has been thought that
the border motif, said to represent a double
bull's head, has a connection with neolithic
Anatolian symbology. Whether it is a bull's
head, ram's horn, or just a design, it frequently
appears in kilims.*

644 Erzurum
(1.73 × 1.23 m, 5′8″ × 4′)
*The weaver of this nineteenth-century kilim
showed great imagination in her arrangement of
motifs in the prayer niche. The indented circular
motifs that appear in the central panel represent
berries or many seeded fruits, said to symbolize
fertility.*

645 *Detail of 642.*

Buying and collecting kilims can become a serious addiction, and many collectors have subsequently become dealers. Many kilim dealers are the worst sufferers from this craving, and a telephone call to say a certain antique kilim has surfaced can result in a mad dash to view the rug before the news spreads further afield. A unique kilim spotted at auction becomes an irresistible temptation. The novice must remember, however, that rugs are not necessarily valuable because they are old; indeed many are very much past their prime. The most important thing is to like what you are buying. If you feel in need of advice, it is worthwhile consulting your local dealer, who should be in touch with market trends and supply shortages. In general, rug dealers will be happy to help and impart some of their expertise to the prospective buyer.

Chapter Eleven

Caring for Kilims

646   *A kilim and carpet merchant's shop in Konya, once a* hamam, *or Turkish bath, where both the rugs and the decor contribute to the alluring atmosphere.*

647   Qazvin
A date woven into the end border of a kilim in Arabic numerals. Converted into the Western calender, the year of weaving is 1938, which is relatively recent for such a fine kilim. (Detail)

Kilims, like other rugs and textiles, need some care and attention, such as occasional cleaning and restoration when any damage occurs. The Turkish word *sakat*, meaning 'unwell', is charmingly used to describe such problematic rugs. Hand-woven rugs will last for years if looked after properly.

Durability

The strength of a kilim will depend on the materials used, the tightness of its weave and its age. Obviously if the kilim is old and has already received a good deal of wear and tear, it should be kept away from busy areas of the home. The fineness of wool and weave is another important consideration. If a kilim is 'thin' but constructed from good-quality, fine hand-spun wool, its lifespan will be considerably longer than that of a machine-made carpet, and a loosely woven kilim, even if it is physically thicker, will not necessarily last longer than one that is finely woven from good-quality wool. In addition certain weave types tend to wear faster than others. The pattern of a weft-wrapping technique rug will erode more quickly than that of a kilim made in slitweave or plainweave technique because the wefts are 'floating' and therefore more vulnerable. Kilims can easily bear the weight of furniture, but constant friction is harmful and chair legs, for instance, can catch in the slits of the weave. Measures can be taken to prevent this such as placing cups under the legs, or attaching a piece of thick felt to their underside. It is a good policy to alternate the position of a kilim and turn the rug around occasionally, particularly if one side or one end receives a heavy flow of traffic or more exposure to natural light.

Rugs will disintegrate in continual damp conditions. Should you experience leaking radiators, flood, or other water-related problems, consult your insurance broker and local dealer who will, no doubt, assist with such problems.

Underlay

Rugs on smooth floors can be hazardous, and all rugs will 'walk' if laid on a fitted carpet with a deep pile. Such problems can be alleviated or eliminated by the use of an underlay. There are many different types available, serving varied functions, and your local rug dealer should be able to advise you as to what is suitable. Underlay helps to cushion a rug, and can entirely stop slipping or sliding; it also lessens any wear and tear. Any floor surface that is supposedly smooth will have uneven areas, and any bumps that are continuously walked over will eventually erode the weave and the rug will need to be restored. Underlay can allay this danger and it is considerably cheaper to replace the underlay than to have the rug restored. There are many different products available on the market, some of which are effective against movement problems, but tend to leave a sticky deposit on the floor surface and the underside of the rug. This is removable with white spirit, which should not damage either a polished floor or machine-made carpet; however, it is advisable to consult manufacturers before using any substances that might be potentially harmful. Many of the underlays on offer are ineffectual, and most are expensive; therefore, before any acquisitions are made, it is worthwhile asking advice of your local rug dealer, who will, no doubt, have experience of the particular problem in hand, and will be able to help. The conclusive way to stop rugs 'walking' on fitted pile is to have them sewn down on to the carpet. This is

648   *Peacocks, goats and dragons worked in weft-wrapping technique.*

not always practical, of course, particularly if the rug needs to be washed with any frequency.

Cleaning

When a rug begins to look dirty, it should be sent to be washed. Washing is beneficial to kilims and carpets, as dirt and grit will, with time, become ground into the weave and slowly destroy it. Hand-woven rugs should be washed regularly in any case, as this polishes the wool, gives life to the colours and helps with general wear and tear. New rugs can be dry-cleaned, but such treatment is not recommended for anything that is at all old. It is not advisable to wash rugs or kilims at home, as problems such as colour run or uneven shrinkage can arise. When a weave is wet, it is stiff and hard like cardboard, and colour seepage can occur if the rug is not dried in the correct manner.

Spills should be attended to immediately. Use absorbent paper, such as kitchen towel, to soak up the moisture, then sponge the weave with clean water, and re-absorb. Do not use salt for red wine, nor other corrosive substances on rugs. If any marks remain and the cause of the stain is known, it is easy for professionals to remove them with certain chemicals. Chemical treatments – 'Scotchguarding', for example – to prevent dirt or staining are not recommended for hand-woven rugs.

Storage

If it is necessary to store kilims for any length of time, certain precautions must be taken. Firstly, the rug should be washed, and preferably mothproofed – moths, as a general rule, like to breed in areas where air does not circulate. (It is not the moth itself that destroys the textile, but the larvae.) Before storing, any textile should be wrapped in airtight packaging, with moth balls, and it is preferable to store fabric of any type in rolls rather than folded up. If possible, acid-free paper should be placed between the folds or rolls of the textile, and moth balls should not actually touch the fabric. Stored kilims should be kept at a constant temperature to prevent any condensation occuring inside the airtight packages. It is also advisable to wash, or at least air the kilim when it comes out of storage, to discourage moths further, as they like to breed in undisturbed conditions. Other possible predators are mice and rats, which will only be deterred if they are denied access, so rugs and textiles should be stored in a suitable container. Please note that insurance policies to not cover any of the above possible hazards.

Repair

The well-known saying 'a stitch in time' is true of all repairs. It is advisable to consult a professional restorer or dealer before sending a rug for restoration or repair, as they will always give an estimate for any work that is necessary, and tell you whether it is worth the cost – at times, particularly if a rug is very old, the wool may have become so brittle (particularly if it has been neglected and unwashed for many years) that repair may not be financially viable. Restoration is a skilled art, and it will only cost more if bad repairs have been carried out and subsequently have to be removed before proper restoration is effected. Fringes will be the first part of the kilim to deteriorate, and vacuum cleaners are lethal. If the fringe disintegrates or is damaged, the actual weave of the rug will be next. Stopping fringes from unravelling is easily done; reweaving the ends can be very costly.

649 *Many kilim and carpet merchants start their business apprenticeship as restorers when they are still young.*

Glossary

For a more detailed exposition of the different weaving terms and techniques see pp. 43–54.

For the Turkish names of a variety of symbolic patterns and motifs see pp. 66–72.

See also pp. 22, 80, 241, 248–50, 301–312 for regional variations.

abrash   Variations in tone or intensity of colour.

Afshar   A tribal group from Iran.

Aimaq   A tribal group from Central Asia.

alizarin   The main colourant obtained from madder.

alum   Potassium aluminium sulphate, used as a mordant.

aniline   A synthetic dye derived from coal tar.

Arabi   A tribe of Arab origins; also a breed of sheep.

ashqar   A mordant used with indigo and madder.

awassi   A breed of sheep from the Middle East.

azo dye   A direct dye, which can be used without a mordant.

bagh-i-chinar   A design representing a poplar leaf.

Bakhtiari   A tribe from the Zagros Mountains in south-west Iran.

balisht   A large floor cushion, also known as *yastik*, *tatrayin* and *usada*.

Balouch   A tribal group inhabiting Iran, Afghanistan and Pakistan.

balouchi   A breed of sheep.

bastani gul   A motif found on Turkoman weavings.

beşik   A textile slung from a wooden frame to make a child's cradle.

bonçuk   Anatolian blue bead, often with an 'eye', said to protect against evil.

boteh   A curved motif, similar to the paisley pattern, derived from Indian and Persian flowers.

brocading   A term used for supplementary weft and extra weft weaving techniques, which usually result in a raised pattern.

caravanserai   A Central Asian inn, or overnight stopping place.

carding   The process of pulling wool through a spiked 'comb' to align the fibres before spinning.

Chahar Aimaq   A tribal group from north-west Afghanistan.

chanteh   A single bag used to hold domestic and small personal items. Also known as *canta* and *chanta*.

Chiadma   An Arabic tribal group from Morocco.

çiçim   A Turkish word for a kilim made using the supplementary weft technique.

compound weave   A weave comprising two or more sets of warps and/or wefts.

curved wefts   A weaving technique whereby the wefts are beaten down unevenly, enabling curvilinear shapes to be drawn.

dağlic   A breed of sheep from central and east Turkey.

damga   Anatolian tribal insignia.

dashterkhan   Afghan name for a *soufreh*, or eating cloth.

double interlock   A weaving technique whereby the wefts interlock with each other between the warps and on the reverse of the weave.

dovetailing   Also known as single interlock weave. A weaving technique whereby the wefts share the same warp when returning at the edge of adjacent colour blocks.

dye liquor   The liquid produced when a vat dye is brewed.

end panel   The part of a flatweave between the patterned end borders and the fringe. Usually woven in plainweave.

Ersari   One of the Turkoman tribal groups.

extra weft   A weaving technique whereby extra wefts are inserted into the weave to correct a non-aligned weft or to exaggerate a curved weft.

flatweave   A rug or textile woven without a pile.

gaadic   A breed of sheep from Balouchistan.

gabbeh   A losely woven and knotted rug from south Iran.

gelim   A Persian word for a kilim.

ghilzai   A breed of fat-tailed sheep from Central Asia.

ghudjeri   A Central Asian textile woven in warp-faced patterning. See *jajim*.

Glaoua   A Berber tribal group from the High Atlas.

gul   A small motif or medallion, most commonly Turkoman.

Hazara   A tribal group from north-central Afghanistan.

hazaragi   A breed of sheep from Afghanistan.

heddle rod   A rod attached to alternate warps by short threads, allowing the weaver to separate alternate sets of warps and pass the weft through the 'shed'.

herati   A repeat pattern found on Persian weavings; also a breed of sheep from the Herat area of Afghanistan.

horizontal loom   A ground loom used mostly by nomadic people.

ikat   A dye resist technique.

indigo   A natural dyestuff, used to produce blue. Chemical indigo is called by the same name.

jajim   The Persian name for narrow strips woven in warp-faced patterning, which can be sewn together to make larger pieces; or the name for these larger pieces themselves.

jallar   A short, wide bag used to store household items.

juval   Also known as *çuval*. A rectangular bag used to store and transport goods.

karaman   A breed of sheep from Turkey.

karaqul   A breed of sheep from north Afghanistan.

Kazakh   A tribal group from Central Asia.

kermes   A type of insect used to produce crimson dye. (From the Arabic word *qirmiz*.)

Khamsa   A tribal group from south Iran.

khorjin   Also known as *heybe* in Turkey. A double-pannier bag used to carry goods on the back of a donkey, horse or camel.

Kirghiz   A tribal group from Central Asia.

kiviçik   A breed of sheep from Turkey.

kola-i-chergh   A bag used to contain the ends of tent poles.

Kurds   A tribal group from Turkey, Iraq and Iran.

Kutchi   A nomadic group from Central Asia.

lab-i-mazar   A small white border design found on certain kilims from north Afghanistan.

laleh abrassi   The popular 'tulip' motif.

lazy lines   Dividing lines produced by the slit-weaving technique, breaking up large blocks of one colour into smaller areas.

Lurs   A tribal group from the Zagros mountains of Iran.

madder   A natural dyestuff used to produce red.

maffrash   A box-shaped storage 'chest' made from a flatwoven textile, used for storing bedding and clothing.

medallion   A decorative pattern usually found in the field of a rug.

merino   A breed of sheep from Australia.

mihrab   The prayer niche in a mosque, depicted in prayer rugs by a triangular, square or rounded form. The mihrab in a rug is always pointed towards Mecca for prayers.

moj   A distinctive flatwoven textile made by the Qashqai and the Lurs from south Iran.

mordant   A substance used to enable dye to penetrate yarn and adhere to it, and to make the colour fast. From the Latin *mordere*, to bite.

motif   A distinctive element or recurring feature of a pattern.

mouflon   A breed of small sheep found in Asia.

namad   A felt rug, or *yurt* cover.

namakdan   A salt bag, also known as *duz torbasy* in the Caucasus.

nazarlik   An Anatolian talisman.

Oulad Bou Sbaa   An Arabic tribal group from Morocco.

palas   A Caucasian word for a kilim.

plainweave   Also known as balanced plainweave. The simplest form of flatweaving.

ply   Two or more single threads twisted together. The ply is twisted in the opposite direction to the spin of the individual threads.

purdah   A cover, curtain or screen used to separate women from men.

Pushtuns   A tribal group from Central Asia.

Qashqai   A tribal group from south Iran.

ranghi   Red; an Uzbek Tartari kilim featuring red as the predominant colour.

rove   A bundle of washed fleece.

rukorssi   A square textile used to cover an oven or stove.

rukzal   A bold medallion found on Daghestan kilims.

runner   A long narrow rug, traditionally used as a 'filler' for the areas not covered by the main carpet. Nowadays a term used for corridor rugs.

saf   A multiple prayer arch kilim.

safid   White; an Uzbek Tartari kilim with a white field.

sajjada   An Arabic word for a prayer rug.

Salor   One of the Turkoman tribal groups.

scouring   Washing wool to remove some of the oils.

selvedge   The outside edge of a rug or textile.

Shahsavan   A tribal group from north-west Iran.

shed   The space between alternate sets of warp threads created by lifting the heddle rod.

shed rod   A rod that is inserted into the shed so that when the heddle rod is released the alternate set of warp threads is pushed below the freed set of warps, creating a counter shed.

shuttle   A stick notched at its ends to hold the weft thread.

single interlock   See dovetailing.

skirt   The end section of a rug. *See also* end panel.

slitweave   A weaving technique that leaves a vertical slit between two blocks of colour.

soufreh   An eating cloth on which meals are set out, or a square cloth used in the preparation of bread.

souk   Marketplace.

soumak   A term popularly used for weft wrapping and for Caucasian rugs made in weft-wrapping technique.

spindle   The tool attached to a strand of wool and spun to produce the yarn.

spinning   The process of twisting the raw wool fibres into long threads.

sun-fading   The practice of toning down the original colours of a rug by exposing it to strong sunlight.

supplementary weft   A weaving technique whereby additional wefts are added to a simple weave. See *çiçim*.

sutrangi   A flatwoven textile made of cotton in slitweave or interlock technique, from north Afghanistan.

suzani   A term generally used to describe embroidery work, derived from the Persian word for a needle.

synthetic dye   A dye produced by artificial chemical means.

tablet weaving   Also known as card weaving. A complex technique whereby narrow bands of flatweave are produced.

Tekke   One of the Turkoman tribal groups.

tent band   A woven strip used for securing the *yurt*, or for strapping loads on to pack animals.

torbah   A small rectangular bag used for domestic articles.

Turkomen   A tribal group spread over a wide area of Central Asia.

twill   A weaving technique whereby the warps and wefts are interlocked.

twist   A term used to describe the direction of spun yarn. 'S' indicates a clockwise twist and 'Z' an anti-clockwise twist.

Tyrian purple   Dye obtained from the mucous gland of the whelk.

urial   A breed of wild sheep. Most domesticated sheep come from ancestors of this animal.

Uzbeks   A tribal group from Central Asia.

verneh   A textile woven in strips of extra weft wrapping on a plain ground, from north-west Iran and the Caucasus.

vertical loom   An upright loom, usually fixed.

warps   Threads that run from the top to the bottom of a textile or rug, forming the basis of its structure. Their ends may be left free to form fringes.

warp-faced patterning   A weaving technique whereby the pattern of the textile is created by the warps. See *ghudjeri* and *jajim*.

warp-faced plainweave   A weaving technique wherein the warps conceal the wefts.

wasm   A Berber tribal insignia.

weft   The yarn that runs widthways across a rug or textile, over and under the warps to form the weave.

weft-faced patterning   Also known as weft-float patterning or floating weft technique. A weaving technique whereby a pattern is created with wefts which 'float' on the back of the weave when not in use.

weft-faced plainweave   A simple weaving technique whereby the wefts conceal the warps.

weft-float brocading   A weaving technique whereby a simple weave is decorated using supplementary wefts. See *zili*.

weft twining   A technique for adding extra decoration to a weave.

weft wrapping   Also known as *soumak*. A weaving technique where wefts are wrapped round the warps in a variety of combinations.

whorl   The weighted end of a spindle.

yastik   A cushion, or pillow.

Yomut   One of the Turkoman tribal groups.

Yörüks   Anatolian nomads

yurt   A nomadic tent, usually circular.

Zaiane   A Berber tribal group of the Middle Atlas.

Zemmour   The main kilim-weaving Berber tribal group of Morocco.

zili   A Turkish word for the weaving technique of supplementary weft wrapping.

Bibliography

Magazines and Journals

Hali, London.
Journal of the Guilds of Weavers, Spinners and Dyers, Taunton, Devon.
Journal of the International Hajji Baba Society, Washington DC.
National Geographic, Washington DC.
Oriental Art Magazine, Richmond, Surrey.
Oriental Rug Review, Meredith, New Hampshire.
Royal Central Asian Society Journal, Oxford.
'Spin-Off', The Magazine for Spinners, Loveland, Colorado.
Tehran Rug Society Journal, Tehran, Iran.
The Textile Museum Journal, Washington DC.

General Books on Kilims

Andrews, Peter and Saiwosch Azadi, *Mafrash: Woven Transport Packs as an Art Form among the Shahsavan and other Nomads in Persia*, Berlin, 1985.

Arseven, Celal Esad, *Les Arts Décoratifs Turcs*, Istanbul, 1950.

Azadi, Siawosch, *Turkomen Carpets*, Fishguard, Wales, 1975.

Babayan, Levon, *Romance of the Oriental Rug*, Toronto, 1925.

Bacharach, Jere L. and Irene A. Bierman, *The Warp and Weft of Islam: Oriental Rugs and Weavings from Pacific Northwest Collections*, Seattle, WA, 1978.

Barnard, Nicholas, *Living with Decorative Textiles*, London, 1989.

Barnard, Nicholas and Alastair Hull, *Living with Kilims*, London, 1988.

Bausback, F., *Alte Orientalische Flachgewebe*, Mannheim, 1977.

Beattie, May H., *Carpets of Central Persia*, World of Islam Festival Publishing Co., [Kent], 1976.

Beaumont, Roberts, *Carpets and Rugs*, London, 1924.

Bennett, Ian (ed.), *Complete Illustrated Rugs and Carpets of the World*, New York, 1977.

Bennett, Ian (ed.), *The Country Life Book of Carpets and Rugs of the World*, Feltham, Middlesex, 1977.

Beresneva, L. (ed.), *The Decorative and Applied Arts of the Turkmen*, Leningrad, 1976.

Bernadout, Raymond, *Nomadic Persian and Turkoman Weaving*, London, 1977.

Black, D., M. Francis and C. Loveless, *In Praise of Allah*, London, 1975.

Black, David and Clive Loveless, *The Undiscovered Kilim*, London, 1977.

Bogolyubov, Andrei, *Carpets of Central Asia*, Fishguard, Wales, 1973.

Burkett, M.E., *The Last of the Bedouin in Jordan*, Kendal, Cumbria, 1983. Abbot Hall Art Gallery exhibition catalogue.

Campana, Michele, *Oriental Carpets*, Feltham, Middlesex, 1969.

Coen, Lucien and Louise Duncan, *The Oriental Rug*, New York, 1978.

Cootner, Cathryn, *Flat-woven Textiles: The Arthur D. Jenkins Collection*, vol. 1, Washington DC, 1981.

De Calatchi, Robert, *Tapis d'Orient*, Paris, 1967.

Denny, Walter B., *Oriental Rugs*, Washington DC, 1979.

Dimand, Maurice S., *Peasant and Nomad Rugs of Asia*, New York, 1961.

Edwards, A.C., *The Persian Carpet*, London, (1953) 1975.

Ellis, Charles Grant, *The Flat-Woven Kilim of the East, Near Eastern Kilims*, Washington DC, 1965.

Erdmann, Kurt, *Seven Hundred Years of Oriental Carpets*, Berkeley, Los Angeles and London, 1966.

Eskenazi, John J., *Kilim*, Milan, 1980.

Francis, M. and Y. Petsopoulos, *Kilims: A Traditional Art* (forthcoming).

Gans-Ruedin, E., *Connoisseur's Guide to Oriental Carpets*, Rutland, VT, 1971.

Gluck, Jay and Sumi, *A Survey of Persian Handicrafts*, Tehran, 1977.

Harris, Nathaniel, *Rugs and Carpets of the Orient*, London, 1977.

Hawley, W.A., *Oriental Rugs: Antique and Modern*, (London, 1913), New York, 1970.

Hegenbart, Heinz, *Rare Oriental Woven Bags*, Munich, 1982.

Iten-Maritz, J., *Enzyklopädie des Orientteppichs*, Herford, Germany, 1977.

Justin, Valerie, *Flat Woven rugs of the World, Kilim, Soumak, Brocading*, New York, 1980.

Kay, Shirley, *The Bedouin*, Newton Abbot, Devon, 1978.

Landrau, A.N. and W.R. Pickering, *From the Bosphorus to Samarkand: Flat-Woven Rugs*, Washington DC, 1969.

May, C.J.D., *How to Identify Persian and Other Oriental Rugs*, London, 1969.

The Mysterious East: Puzzles of Origin, Authenticity and Function in Oriental Rugs and Embroidery, Canadian Museum of Carpets and Textiles, Toronto, 1977.

Petsopoulos, Yanni, *Kilims: The Art of Tapestry*

Weaving in Anatolia, The Caucasus and Persia, London, 1979, Essential reference book.

Pinner, Robert and Walter B. Denny *Oriental Carpet and Textile Studies* (4 vols) O.C.T.S. and Sotheby's, London.

Reinisch, Helmut, *Gabbeh*, Graz, 1986.

Tanavoli, Parvis, *Bread and Salt: Iranian Tribal Spreads and Salt Bags*, Tehran 1991.

Thompson, Jon, *Carpet Magic*, London, 1983.

Weir, Shelagh, *The Bedouin: Aspects of the Material Culture of the Bedouin of Jordan*, London, 1976.

Weir, Shelagh, *Spinning and Weaving in Palestine*, London, 1970.

History and Tribes

Abercrombie, Thomas J., 'Afghanistan: Crossroad of Conquerors', *National Geographic*, Washington DC, Sept. 1968, pp. 297–345.

Andrews, Peter A., 'Alacix and Kume, the Felt and Tent of Azerbaijan', *Ethnology and the Popular Tradition of Iran*, no. 3, pp. 19–45, Tehran, 1977–78.

Arfa H., *The Kurds*, London, 1966.

Barnes, Alexander, *Travels into Bokhara*, 3 vols, London, (1834) 1973.

Barth, Fredrik, *Nomads of South Persia: The Basseri Tribe of the Khamseh Confederacy*, Oslo, London and New York, 1964.

Barthold, V.V., 'A History of the Turkman People', *Four Studies of the History of Central Asia*, vol. 3, Leiden, 1962.

Bates, W.H., *Illustrated Travels: A Record of Discovery, Geography and Adventure*, London, 1869.

Bernadout, Raymond, *Catalogue of Turkoman Weaving including Beluch*, London, 1974.

Bird Bishop, Isabella L., *Journeys in Persia and Kurdistan*, New York, 1891.

Cahan, C., *Pre-Ottoman Turkey*, New York, 1978.

Caxon, Herbert, *Oriental Carpets*, London, 1884.

Chardin, Sir J., *Travels in Persia*, London, (1720, 1927) 1972.

The Country of the Turkomans, Royal Geographic Society, London, 1977.

Dickson, H.R.P., *The Arab of the Desert*, London, 1949.

Douglas, O., *Strange Lands and Friendly People*, New York, 1951.

Eagleton, W., Jr., *The Kurdish Republic of 1946*, London, 1946.

Edmonds, Cecil John, *Kurds, Turks and Arabs. Politics, Travel and Research in north-eastern Iraq, 1919–25*, London, 1957.

Faegre, Torvalid, *Tents: Architecture of the Nomads*, London, 1979.

Fodor's Guide to Turkey, London 1978–79.

Garnett, L.M., *Home Life in Turkey*, New York, 1909.

Grousset, R., *The Empire of the Steppes: A History of Central Asia*, New Brunswick, NJ, 1970.

Huart, C., 'Kizil Bash', *Encyclopaedia of Islam* (1st edn), vol. 2, pp. 1053–54, London and Leiden, 1913–38.

Irons, William, *The Yomut Turkmen: A Study of Kinship in a Pastoral Society*, Ann Arbor, MI, 1975.

Joghrafia-yi Moffasal-i Iran (An Extended Geography of Iran), vol. 2, Tehran, 1932.

The Koran, trans. N.J. Dagwood, London, 1975.

Lewis, Bernard, *The World of Islam*, London, (1976) 1992.

Lockhart, Laurence L., *The Fall of the Safavid Dynasty and the Afghan Occupation of Persia*, Cambridge, 1958.

Lockhart, Laurence L., *Nadir Shah. A Critical Study*, London, 1938.

Malcolm, Sir John, *The History of Persia, from the Most Early Period to the Present Time*, 2 vols, London, 1815.

Minorsky, Vladimir, E., 'Ak Koyunlu', *Encyclopaedia of Islam* (new edn), vol. 1, pp. 311–12, Leiden, 1960.

Morier, James, *A Journey Through Persia, Armenia and Asia Minor to Constantinople, in the Years 1808 and 1809*, London 1812.

Munshi, Iskander Beg, *Tarikh-i Alam-Ara-yi Abbasi*, 2 vols, Tehran, 1971.

Naderi, Nader Afshar, *Il e-Bahme'i* (Monograph on the Bahme'i Tribe), Tehran, 1968.

Oberling, P., *The Qashqa'i Nomads of Fars*, The Hague, 1974.

Rudenko, S.I., *Frozen Tombs of Siberia: The Pazyryk Burials of Iron-Age Horsemen*, Berkeley, CA, 1970.

Schneider, D., *The Travellers' Guide to Turkey*, London, 1975.

Weaving, Spinning, Materials, Dyes

Albers, Annie, *On Weaving*, Middletown, CT, 1965.

Baines, Patricia, *Spinning Wheels, Spinners and Spinning*, London, 1977.

Balpinar, Belkis, Belkis Acar and Eren Yayinlari, *Kilim – Çiçim – Zili – Sumak: Turkish Flatweaves*, Istanbul, 1983.

Beutlich, Tadek, *The Technique of Woven Tapestry*, London, (1967) 1982.

Bohmer, H. and W. Bruggemann, *Rugs of the Peasants and Nomads of Anatolia*, Munich, 1983. An excellent section on dyes.

Bridgewater, Alan and Gill, *Guide to Weaving*, London, 1986.

Brunello, F., *The Art of Dyeing in the History of Mankind*, Vicenza, 1973.

Burnham, Dorothy K., *A Textile Technology: Warp and Weft*, London, (1980) 1983.

Collingwood, Peter, *The Technique of Rug Weaving*, London, 1968. Detailed descriptions of techniques from a professional weaver.

Collingwood, Peter, *Textile and Weaving Structures: A Source Book for Makers and Designers*, London, 1987.

Collingwood, Peter and Ann Sutton, *The Craft of the Weaver: A Practical Guide to Spinning, Dyeing and Weaving*, London, 1982.

Emery, Irene, *The Primary Structure of Fabrics*, Washington DC, 1980. Essential classification of weaving techniques into groups and subgroups).

Hecht, Ann, *The Art of the Loom*, London, 1989. Weaving, spinning and dyeing across the world.

Ross, Mabel, *Encyclopaedia of Handspinning*, London, 1988.

Ross, Mabel, *Sheep and Wool for Handicraft Workers*, Edinburgh, 1978.

Design and Symbolism

Albarn, Keith *et al.*, *The Language of Pattern. An Enquiry Inspired by Islamic Decoration*, London and New York, 1974.

Ardalan, Nader and Laleh Bakhtiar, *The Sense of Unity: The Sufi Tradition in Persian Architecture*, Chicago and London, 1973.

Azadi, Siawosch, *Turkoman Carpets and the Ethnographic Significance of their Ornaments*, Fishguard, Wales, 1975.

Bakhtiar, Laleh, *Sufi: The Expression of the Mystic Quest*, London, 1976.

Balpinar, Belkis, Udo Hirsch and James Mellaart, *The Goddess from Anatolia*, 4 vols, Milan, 1989.

Donaldson, B.A., *The Wild Rue: A Study of Mohammedan Magic and Folklore in Iran*, London, 1973.

Flint, Bert, *Tapis, Tissages, Formes et Symboles dans les Arts du Maroc*, vol. 2, Tangier, 1974.

Ford, P.J.R., *Oriental Carpet Design*, London, (1981), 1992.

Kerimov, L. *Folk Designs from the Caucasus*, New York, 1974.

Mackenzie, D.A., *Migratiuon of Symbols*, London, 1926.

Rageth, Jurg, *Kilim: Primitive Symbols of Mythology*, Rome, 1986.

Revault, Jacques, *Designs and Patterns from North African Carpets and Textiles*, New York, 1973.

Westermarck, Edward A., *Ritual and Belief in Morocco*, 2 vols, New York, 1968.

Wuff, Hans E., *The Traditional Crafts of Persia: Their Development, Technology and Influence on Eastern and Western Civilizations*, Cambridge, MA, 1966.

North Africa

De Ucel, Jeanne, *Berber Art*, Norman, OK, 1932.

Fiske, Pickering and Yohe, *From the Far West: Carpets and Textiles of Morocco*, Washington DC, 1980. Study of Moroccan weavings.

Hainault, J. and H. Terrasse, *Les Arts Décoratifs au Maroc*, Paris, 1925.

Harmer, J., J.S. Hyde, M. Lorimer and W.R. Pickering, *Windows on the Maghrib: Tribal and Urban Weavings of Morocco*, Washington DC, 1991. Frank H. McClung Museum exhibition catalogue.

Kiewe, Heinz Edgar, *Ancient Berber Tapestries and Rugs and Ancient Moroccan Embroideries*, Maison Française, Oxford, 1952.

Prosper, Ricard, *Tapis de Haut Atlas et du Haouz de Marrakech*, vol. 3 of *Corpus des Tapis Marocains*, Paris, 1927.

Prosper, Ricard, *Tapis de Moyen Atlas*, vol. 2 of *Corpus des Tapis Marocains*, Paris, 1926.

Prosper, Ricard, *Tapis Marocains*, Paris, 1932.

Reswick, Irmtraud, *Traditional Textiles of Tunisia and Related North African Weavings*, Craft and Folk Art Museum, Los Angeles, 1985.

Sijelmassi, M., *Les Arts Traditionels au Maroc*, Paris, 1974.

Stanzer, Wilfried, *Berber: Stammesteppiche und Textilien aus dem Königreich Marokko* (Tribal Carpets and Weavings from the Kingdom of Morocco), Graz, 1992. Exhibition catalogue of Richard Hersberger's collection and detailed study of Berber weaving.

Anatolia

Acar, Belkis, *Kilim ve Duz Yaygilar*, Istanbul, 1975.
Acar, Belkis, 'Yuncu Nomadic Weaving in the Balikesir Region of Western Turkey', *The Nomadic Weaving Tradition of the Middle East*, Pittsburgh, PA, 1978.
Akatay, A., S.L. Schwartz and W.T. Ziemba, *Turkish Flat Weaves*, London, 1979. An easily readable introduction to kilims.
Balpinar, Belkis and Udo Hirsch, *Anatolian Kilims (Kilim Anatolici)*, Milan, 1984, Exhibition catalogue, insight into social and historical context of weavers.
Balpinar, Belkis and Udo Hirsch, *Flatweaves of the Vakiflar Museum, Istanbul*, Wesel, 1982. Catalogue for the Museum, depicting classic kilims.
Cootner, Cathryn and Garry Muse, *Anatolian Kilims: The Caroline & McCoy Jones Collection*, London, 1990.
Cootner, Cathryn *et al.*, *Flat-Woven Textiles: The Arthur D. Jenkins Collection*, Washington DC, 1981. Flatweaves and horse covers from the Textile Museum's collection.
Eagleton, William, *An Introduction to Kurdish Rugs and Other Weavings*, London, 1988. Collector and former diplomat's field research in Kurdistan.
Erbek, Guren, *Kilim: Catalogue No. 1*, [Turkey], 1988.
Fertig, Barbara C., *Turkish Rugs from Private Collections*, Washington DC, 1973.
Frauenknecht, Bertram, *Frühe Türkische Tapisserien (Early Turkish Tapestries)*, Nuremberg, 1984. Exhibition catalogue of tribal kilims, accompanied by James Mellaart's theory with regard to Neolithic weaving in Anatolia.
Gorgunay, N., *Dogu Yoresi Halilari*, Ankara, 1974.
Hirsch, Udo and Jurg Rageth, *Frühe Formen und Farben*, Basle, 1991. Exhibition catalogue of the first symposium held in Basle in 1990.
Iten-Maritz, J., *Turkish Carpets*, Tokyo and New York, 1977. Carpet weaving in Anatolia, some kilims.
Jones, H.M. and R.S. Yohe, *Turkish Rugs*, Washington DC, 1968.
Landreau, Anthony N. and Ralph S. Yohe (eds), *Flowers of the Yayla: Yörük Weaving of the Toros Mountains*, Washington DC, 1983. Exhibition catalogue from the Textile Museum.
Mackie, Louise W., *The Splendour of Turkish Weaving*, Washington DC, 1973.
Petsopoulos, Yanni, *From the Danube to the Euphrates: Kilims of the 18th and 19th Centuries*, Athens, 1990. Catalogue for the exhibition held at the Titanium Gallery.
Petsopoulos, Yanni and Belkis Balpinar, *One Hundred Kilims: Masterpieces from Anatolia*, London, 1991. Kilims from private collections.
Pinkwart, Doris and Elizabeth Steiner, *Bergama Cuvallari: Die Schmucksäcke der Yuruken Nordwestanatoliens* (Storage bags of the Yörük tribes of northwest Anatolia), Wesel, 1991.

Persia and the Caucasus

Black, David and Clive Loveless (eds), *Woven Gardens: Nomad and Village Rugs of the Province of Southern Persia*, London 1977.
Boralevi, Alberto, *Sumakh: Flat Woven Carpets of the Caucasus*, Florence, 1986. Essential reference.
De Francis, Amedeo and John H. Wertime, *Lori and Bakhtiyari Flatweaves*, Tehran, 1976.
Discoveries from Kurdish Looms, Mary and Leigh Block Gallery, Northwestern University, Illinois, 1983.
Ford, P.J.R. and H.E. Pohl-Schillings, *Persische Flachgewebe*, Cologne, 1987.
Frye, Richard Nelson, *The Golden Age of Persia: the Arabs in the East*, London and New York, 1975.
Frye, Richard Nelson, *Kilims from the Caucasus*, London, 1974.
Grigoliya, Tatyana *et al.*, *Rugs and Carpets from the Caucasus: The Russian Collections*, London, 1984.
Housego, Jenny, *Tribal Rugs: An Introduction to the Weavings of the Tribes of Iran*, London, 1978.
Kelims der Nomaden und Bauern Persiens, Galerie Neiriz, Berlin, 1990.
Oberling, Pierre, *The Qashqa'i Nomads of Fars*, Paris, 1974.
Opie, James, *Tribal Rugs of Southern Persia*, Portland, OR, 1981.
The Qashqa'i of Iran, Whitworth Art Gallery, Manchester, 1976. Exhibition catalogue.
Stanzer, Wilfred, *Kordi: Lives – Rugs – Flatweaves of Kurds in Khorassan*, Vienna, 1988.
Tanavoli, Parvis, *Shahsavan Iranian Rugs and Textiles*, New York, 1985.
Tanavoli, Parvis and John Wertime, *Tribal Animal Covers from Iran*, Tehran, 1975.

Central Asia

Andrews, Mugul and Peter *et al.*, *The Turcomen of Iran*, Kendal, Cumbria, 1971.
Bogolyubov, Andrei Andreyovich, *Carpets of Central Asia*, 2 vols, 1908 and 1909, Fishguard, Wales, 1973.
Boucher, Jeff W., *Balouchi Woven Treasures*, Alexandria, VA, 1989.
Boucher, Jeff W. and H. McCoy Jones, *Balouchi Rugs*, Washington DC, 1974
Boucher, Jeff W. and H. McCoy Jones, *Rugs of the Yomud Tribes*, Washington DC, 1976.
Eiland, Emmett and Maureen Shockley, *Tent Bands of the Steppes*, 1976
Franses, Jack, *Tribal Rugs from Afghanistan and Turkestan*, London, 1973.
Konieczny, M.G., *Textiles of Baluchistan*, London, 1979.
Knor, Thomas and David Lindahl (eds), *Uzbek*, Basle, 1975.
Lefevre & Partners, *Central Asian Carpets*, Fishguard, Wales, 1973.
Mackie, Louise and Thompson Jon, *Turkomen: Tribal Carpets and Traditions*, Washington DC, 1980.
Parsons, R.D., *Oriental Rugs Vol. 3: The Carpets of Afghanistan*, Woodbridge, Suffolk, 1990.
Rugs of the Wandering Baluchi, David Black Oriental Carpets, London, 1976.
Schurman, U., *Central Asian Rugs*, Verlag Österreich [Austria], 1969.
Tate, G.P., *The Frontiers of Baluchistan*, London, 1909. Weaving in Seistan.
Tschebull, Raoul, *Kazak*, New York, 1971.
Tzareva, Elena, *Rugs and Carpets from Central Asia: The Russian Collections*, London, 1984.
Zick-Nissen, Johanna, *Nomadenkunst aus Baluchistan*, Berlin, 1968.

Dealers, Sources and Services

In this section, the names and addresses of dealers from all over the world are listed, together with the services they offer (e.g. cleaning and repairing) and the kinds of artifacts stocked. Obviously it is not possible to list everybody, but we have tried to give details of well-established houses and traders, as well as some more unusual and specialist galleries and businesses. It is advisable to call before you visit a dealer or showroom – some are only available by appointment.

Key to services and types of artifacts stocked:
Imp. Importer
Ret. Retailer
W. Wholesaler
Manu. Manufacturer
Col. Collector
Rep. Repairs

A. Antique
O. Old
N. New

N Af. North Africa
Anat. Anatolia
Cauc. Caucasus
Pers. Persia/Iran
Afgh. Afghanistan

Australia

Alexandra and Leigh Copeland,
P.O. Box 2048,
West St Kilda; Victoria 3182
Tel: 3 9534 0606
Imp., Ret.; O., N.; Pers., Afgh.

Nazar Rug Galleries,
183 Military Road,
Mosman, New South Wales 2088
Tel: 2 9331 1505
Imp., Ret., W., Rep.; A., O., N., Anat., Cauc., Pers., Afgh.
Expert repairs and valuations.

Nomadic Rug Traders,
125 Harris Street,
Sydney-Pyrmont,
New South Wales 2009
Tel: 2 9660 3753
Imp., Ret., Col., Rep.; A., O., Cauc., Pers., Afgh.
Old and antique oriental rugs, kilims, textiles and tribal art. Government-approved valuer and member of the Australian Antique Dealers Association.

Austria

Herbert Bieler,
Sonnenfelsgasse 8,
A-1010 Vienna
Tel: 1 513 1321
Imp., Ret.; A., O.; N Af., Anat., Cauc., Pers., Afgh.

Kelimhaus Johannik,
Langegasse 27,
A-1080 Vienna
Tel: 1 406 2213
Email: kelimhaus@kelim.at
Website: www.kelim.at

343

M. Kirdok,
Backerstrasse 2,
A-1010 Vienna
Tel: 1 513 8291

Konzett,
Enge Gasse 1,
A-8010 Graz
Tel: 316 81 3500
Email: konzett@galerie-konzett.com
Website: www.galerie-konzett.com
Imp., Ret., Col.; A., O.; N Af., Anat.
As known from their publication *Gewebte Poesie,*
they still have outstanding early Anatolian kilims.
Since 1993 the focus has been on Moroccan Berber
weaving art, and they have the most exquisite tex-
tiles of this provenance.

Woven Gardens,
Salesianer Gasse 23,
A-1030 Vienna
Tel: 1 712 4699
Imp., Ret., W., Rep.; A., O., N.; Anat., Cauc., Pers.,
Afgh.

Belgium

Herman Vermeulen,
Kraanlei 3,
B-9000 Ghent
Tel: 9 224 3834
Imp., Ret., W., Rep.; A., O.; Anat., Cauc., Pers.
A stock of over 500 kilims, including old decorative
examples, new, naturally dyed kilims and a large
selection of 19th-century and earlier flatweaves.
More than twenty years' buying experience in the
Middle East.

Steppe & Oase,
Zeedijk 766,
B-8300 Knokke
Tel: 50 62 43 61
Imp., Ret.; A.; Anat. Cauc.

Brazil

Isfahan Import. Ltd.,
Av. Epitácio Pessoa 1772-Lagoa,
Rio de Janeiro, RJ 22471-000
Tel: 21 523 1141
Email: isfahan@openlink.com.br.
Website: www.isfahan.com.br/
Imp., W., Manu.; O., N.; Pers., Cauc.
Distributor of Borhani Qashqai, Shiraz and
Gabbeh kilims; 50–100-year-old Shirvan,
Daghestan and Qashqai kilims.

Canada

Design Resource,
Box 3424,
Smithers, British Columbia V0J 2N0
Tel: 250 847 1417
Fax: 250 847 1462
Email: djbrsrc@bulkey.net
Ret., W.; O., N.; Pers., Afgh.

The Oriental Carpet Gallery,
55 York Street,
Stratford, Ontario N5A 1A1
Tel: 519 273 3207
Fax: 519 273 4522
Imp., Rep., Ret.; O., N.; Anat., Cauc., Pers., Afgh.
New and old kilims and carpets.

Parrots 'n Parsnips,
99 King Street, King's Court,
Hwy 26 East,
Thornbury, Ontario N0H 2P0
Tel: 519 599 5153
Fax: 519 599 3648
Ret., N., O.; Pers., Afgh.

Rubaiyat,
722 17th Avenue SW,
Calgary, Alberta T2S 0B7
Tel: 403 228 7192/6549
Fax: 403 228 4756

Sharanel Inc.,
103 Woodview Drive,
Pickering, Ontario L1V 1L1
Tel: 905 509 4423
Fax: 905 509 4424
Email: sharanel@idirect.com
Imp., W., Col.; A., O., N.; Pers., Afgh.
Open by appointment. Owner Geoff Somes regu-
larly visits Afghanistan and Iran in search of kilims,
kilim bags, tent bands, *soufreh* and related kilim
accessories.

Woven Gardens,
4875A Sherbrooke Street West,
Montreal, Quebec H3Z 1G9
Tel: 514 488 0444
Ret.; O., N.
A wide selection of floor coverings, kilims, ethnic
and antique artifacts.

Denmark

Wiinstedt Orientapper & Kelim Gallery,
Strandvejen 201,
DK 2900 Hellerup,
Copenhagen
Tel: 39 62 4169
Imp., Ret., W., Rep.; A., O., N.; Anat., Cauc., Pers.,
Afgh.
Specialist in antique and old Persian and Caucasian
kilims and carpets; excellent restoration done.

France

Galerie Girard,
32 rue Auguste Comte,
69002 Lyons
Tel: 4 78 38 21 54
Email: info@galerie-girard.com
Website: www.galerie-girard.com
Ret., Coll., Rep.; A.; Anat., Cauc., Pers.
Sale and restoration workshop for antique kilims.

Galerie Sofreh,
23 rue de Lille,
75007 Paris
Tel: 1 40 20 44 69
Fax: 1 40 20 44 69
Ret.; A.; Anat., Cauc., Pers.

Galerie Triff,
35 rue Jacob,
75006 Paris
Tel: 1 42 60 22 60
Ret., W.; A., O., N.; Anat., Cauc., Pers.

Thanakra Gallery,
170 bis rue de Grenelle,
75007 Paris
Tel: 1 40 62 98 88
Email: hcrouzet@thanakra.com

Website: www.thanakra.com
Imp., Ret.; O., N.
Moroccan tribal textiles.

Germany

Frauenknecht Teppich und Textilkunst,
Steinsdorfstrasse 21,
D-80538 Munich
Tel: 89 295 259
Email: bertram-rugs@t-online.de
Imp., Ret., W.; A., O.; Anat., Cauc., Pers., Afgh.
Museum-quality fragments and early kilims, carpets
and textiles.

Galerie Arabesque,
Breitscheidstrasse 98,
D-70176 Stuttgart
Tel: 711 634 734
Fax: 711 649 1309
Ret.; A., O.; N Af., Anat., Cauc., Pers., Afgh.

Galerie Tursun,
Neumarkt 36–38,
D-5667 Cologne
Tel: 221 331 9238
Imp., Ret., Rep.; A., O., N.; Anat., Cauc., Pers.
Specialist in old kilims and restoration.

Kabul Galerie,
Wandsbeker Chaussee 114,
D-22089 Hamburg
Tel: 40 200 2062
Fax: 40 209 77883
Ret., W.; Afgh.

Kelim,
Büttnerstrasse 25,
D-97070 Würzburg
Tel: 931 15 942
Email: werner.braendl@kelim-art.de
Website: www.kelim-art.de
Imp., Ret., Col.; A., O., N.; Anat., Cauc., Pers.,
Afgh.
Several thematic exhibitions per year. Co-work
with the 'Bieber Project' for reviving the nearly lost
Anatolian textile culture.

Mohammad Tehrani,
Neue Groningerstrasse 10,
D-20457 Hamburg
Tel: 40 32 42 86
Fax: 40 32 23 39
Email: M.Tehrani@t-online.de
Imp., W.; A., O.; Anat., Pers., Afgh.
Nomadic and tribal rugs, kilims and small weavings
a speciality.

Zollanvari GmbH,
Kehrwieder 4,
D-20457 Hamburg
Tel: 40 37 500 570
Email: zollanvari@zollanvari.ch
Website: www.zollanvari@zollanvari.ch
Imp., W.; N Af., Anat., Cauc., Pers., Afgh.
Antique North African and old Anatolian kilims,
old and new Persian tribal flatweaves. Specialist in
top-quality tribal carpets and flatweaves from
southern Iran.

Greece

Galerie Dora Penga,
19, Prox. Koromila str.,
546 23 Thessaloniki

Tel: 31 286 482
Email: penga@magnet.gr
Website: www.penga.gr
Imp., W., Ret.; O., N.; Anat., Pers., Afgh.
Shops in Thessaloniki and Athens.

Ireland

Peter Linden,
15 Georges Avenue,
Blackrock, Co. Dublin
Tel: 1 288 5875
Email: lind@indigo.ie
Website: www.peterlinden.com
Imp., Ret.; A., O., N.; Anat., Pers., Afgh.
Old and antique kilims, also select modern kilims
with natural dyes.

Israel

Anatolia,
25 Simtat Chelouche,
Tel Aviv 66847
Tel: 3 510 8013
Email: tolia@internet-zahan.net
Ret.; A., O., N.; Anat., Cauc., Pers.

Marvadim,
Mitzpe Hila,
Galilee 24953
Tel: 4 997 4172
Email: marvadim@internet-sahav.net
Imp., Ret., Col.; A., O.; N Af., Anat., Cauc., Pers.,
Afgh.

Italy

Battilossi,
Tappeti d'Antiquariato,
Corso Cairoli 4,
10123 Turin
Tel: 11 88 25 76
Email: battisrl@tin.it
Ret., Rep.; A.; Anat.
Antique kilims. Mostly Turkish, before 1800.
Specialists in antique carpets, textiles and kilims;
restorers of antique textile art since 1960.

The Carpet Studio s.a.s. di Alberto Boralevi & Co.,
Torre degli Strozzi,
Via Monalda 15/R,
50123 Florence
Tel: 55 21 14 23
Fax: 55 26 50 560
Email: aborale@tin.it
Website: www.nonplusultra.com/gallerie/carpet-
studio
Specialist in antique oriental carpets and kilims,
also sells early examples and fragments.

Ekbatan S.N.C.,
Via della Pallotta 2b,
06124 Perugia
Tel: 75 31 980
Email: info@ekbatan.com
Website: www.ekbatan.com
Imp., Ret., W.; A., O.; Anat., Cauc., Pers., Afgh.

Eskenazi & C. Srl,
Via Borgonuovo 5,
20121 Milan
Tel: 2 86 46 48 83
Fax: 2 86 46 50 18
Email: john.eskenazi@john-eskenazi.com

Website: www.john-eskenazi.com
Ret.; A., O.; Anat., Cauc., Pers.
Specialists in old and antique weavings, they have
organized two exhibitions ('Kilim', 1980, and
'Anatolian Kilims', 1984), with catalogues. Also
published a book in four volumes on kilims: *The
Goddess from Anatolia, Balpinar, Hirsch* and *Mellaart*
(1989).

The Kilim Gallery,
Via di Panico 8,
00186 Rome
Tel: 6 68 68 963
Imp., Ret., Col.; A., O., N.; Anat., Cauc., Pers.,
Afgh.
Kilims and antique rare pile carpets.

Michail di David Sorgato,
Via S. Orsola 13,
20123 Milan
Tel: 2 86 45 49 01
Email: info@michail-david-sorgato.com and
michaildavid@iol.it
Website: www.michail-david-sorgato.com
Imp., Ret., Rep.; A., O.; Anat., Cauc., Pers.
19th-century kilims and carpets. Regular exhibi-
tions.

Misrachi Tappeti d'Arte,
Via Rovello 8,
21021 Milan
Tel: 2 86 20 79

Mohtashem di Mirco Cattai,
Via Manzoni, 40,
20121 Milan
Tel: 2 76 00 89 59
Email: mohtashem@iol.it

Ottoman Art,
Via della Sposa n.10. n.15,
06123 Perugia
Tel: 75 57 36 842
Email: Bozoglu@iol.it
Ret.; O., N.; Anat., Cauc., Pers.
Old kilims and new production vegetable-dyed,
hand-spun wool kilims.

Rodolfo Scognamiglio,
Porto Rafael,
07020 Palau (SS),
Sardinia
Tel: 07 89 70 60 16
Email: ro.do@tiscalinet.it
Ret.; A., O.; Anat., Cauc., Pers.
Old and antique kilims.

Sharon Antichita' di Baghai,
Via Bogino 10/E,
10123 Turin
Tel: 11 81 78 204/33 72 28 099
Email: sharonbs@tin.it
Ret., Rep.; A., O.; Anat., Cauc., Pers.
Antique and collectable kilims and tribal art. Highly
qualified restoration, valuations.

Ziya Bozoglu Textile Art,
Via Calderini 11,
06123 Perugia
Tel: 75 57 36 842
Email: Bozoglu@iol.it
Ret.; A.; Anat., Cauc., Pers.
Antique kilims and early fragments from Anatolia,
Persia, Caucasus, Central Asia.

Mexico

Anthony Foster,
Rio Nilo 54,
Col. Cuanhtoc
D.F. 06500
Tel: 5 207 7421
Email: AFRugs@aol.com
Imp., Ret., Rep.; A., O., N.; Anat., Cauc., Pers.,
Afgh.
Specialist in fine old European and Oriental
carpets and flatweaves. Excellent restoration studio.

Netherlands

DW Kinnebanian B.V.,
Heilegeweg 35,
1012 XN Amsterdam
Tel: 20 626 7019
Website: www.artonline/cat-antiek/cat-kinebanian/
Ret., Rep.; A., O.; Anat., Cauc., Pers., Afgh.
Antique and old kilims and carpets.

Toele,
Overtoom 430432,
1054 JV Amsterdam
Tel: 20 618 1179
Imp., Ret., Col., Rep.; A., O., N.; N Af., Anat.,
Cauc., Pers., Afgh.
Kilims from many origins, specialist in Balouch
kilims.

New Zealand

Mary Kelly Kilims,
44 Ranui Road,
Remuera, Auckland
Tel: 9 529 2090
Email: mkelly@xtra.co.nz
Imp., Ret., W., Col.; A., O., N.; Anat., Cauc., Pers.,
Afgh.

Portfolio,
52 George Street,
Port Chalmers,
Dunedin
Tel: 3 472 7856
Imp., Ret.; O., N.; N Af, Anat., Cauc.
Kilims, pile rugs and textiles.

Portugal

De Natura,
Rua da Rosa 162A,
1200-389 Lisbon
Tel: 1 34 66 081
Fax: 1 34 25 844
Website: www.guialisboa.pt
Imp., Ret.; A., O., N.; N Af., Anat., Afgh.
Handicrafts and articles for interior decoration.

Idilio,
Rua Camara Pestana,
Edificio Sintra No 10,
2710-546 Sintra
Tel: 1 92 44 533
Fax: 1 92 44 534
Email: idilio@mail.telepac.pt
Website: www.idilio.com

Spain

Lloyd Rowcroft,
Apartado de Correos 372,
San Pedro Alacantara,

29670 Malaga
Tel: 95 278 6083
Imp., Ret., Col., Rep.; A., O., N.; N Af., Anat.,
Cauc., Pers., Afgh.
Advice, cleaning, restoration, valuations and study
groups.

Sweden

HALI Rugs & Books,
Åkervägen 40,
181 41 Lidingö – Stockholm
Tel: 8 765 11 31
Email: info@hali.nu
Website: www.hali.nu
Ret.; A., O.; Anat., Cauc., Pers.
Antique and old kilims, flatweaves, rugs and other
peasant textile art. Books on kilims, oriental carpets
and textile art.

J.P. Willborg,
Sibyllegatan 35 & 41,
114 42 Stockholm
Tel: 8 783 02 65
Email: antiquerugs@jpwillborg.se
Website: www.jpwillborg.com
W., Ret., Rep.; A.; N Af., Anat., Cauc., Pers., Afgh.
Antique kilims, tribal rugs, Swedish folkweavings,
African art.

Switzerland

Ali Shirazi,
Zollfreilager Block 1,
Kabin 337,
Postfach 159,
CH-8043 Zurich
Tel: 1 493 1108
Imp., W.; A., O.; Pers., Afgh.
A collection of unusual and nomadic pieces.

Galerie Rageth,
Sieglinweg 10,
CH-4125 Riehen
Tel: 61 641 33 22
Email: galerie@rageth.com
Website: www.rageth.com
Leading authority and specialist in early kilims and
author of several books, the most recent on radio-
carbon dating of Anatolian kilims.

Nomadenschätze,
Kirchgasse 25,
CH-8001 Zurich
Tel: 1 252 55 00
Imp., Ret., Rep.; A., N.; Anat., Cauc., Pers., Afgh.
Long-established specialist kilim traders, antique
and new, naturally dyed, kilims.

Theo Haeberli,
Lindenstrasse 9,
CH-9062 Lustmühle
Tel./Fax: 71 333 29 55
Specializing in antique textiles, tribal carpets, kilims
and bags.

Werner Weber,
Freilagerstrasse 47,
CH-8043 Zurich
Tel: 1 492 4747
Fax: 1 491 2124
Email: info@-wernerweber.com
Website: www.wernerweber.com
Imp., W.; A., O.; Pers.

Specialist in Iranian kilims for 20 years.
Antique kilims (Shahsavan, Qashqai, Bakhtiari,
Luri) as well as new production.

Zollanvari Co.,
Freilagerstrasse 47,
8043 Zurich
Tel: 1 493 28 29
Email: zollanvari@zollanvari.ch
Website: www.zollanvari@zollanvari.ch
Imp., W.; N Af., Anat., Cauc., Pers., Afgh.
Antique North African and old Anatolian kilims,
old and new Persian tribal flatweaves. Specialist in
top-quality tribal carpets and flatweaves from
southern Iran.

UK

Aaron Nejad,
403–405 Edgware Road,
London NW2 6LN
Tel: 0208 830 5511
Fax: 0208 830 5522
Email: aaron@nejad.demon.co.uk
Website: www.antique-rugs.net

Alastair Hull,
The Old Mill, (correspondence)
4 The Green,
or 18A High Street, (gallery)
Haddenham,
Ely CB6 3TA
Tel: 01353 749 188
Fax: 01353 740 688
Email: kilimking@dial.pipex.com
Website: www.tribalartdirectory.com
Imp., Ret., W.; O., N.; Pers., Afgh.
Travels frequently to Afghanistan and Iran, buying
kilims to sell from his gallery and from exhibitions
in unusual venues around the UK.

Ambalo Ltd.,
OCC Building D,
105 Eade Road
London N4 1TJ
Tel 0208 880 1880
Email: ambalo@dial.pipex.com
Imp., W., Manu.; O., N.; Pers., Afgh.
Specialist importer and manufacturer of Afghan
kilims.

Ahwazian Ltd.,
OCC, Building A, 1st Floor,
105 Eade Road,
London N4 1TJ
Tel: 0208 802 9990
Email: ahwazian@aol.com
Website: www.i-i.net/ahwazian
Imp., W.; O., N.; Pers.
Old and new kilims and carpets.

Ananda,
24 Bond Street,
Brighton BN1 1RD
Tel: 01273 725 307
Fax: 01273 207 474
Email: ananda@fastnet.co.uk
Ret.; O., N.; Anat., Pers., Afgh.
Afghan, Balouch and Central Asian kilims and
associated textiles. Cushions, furniture, tribal art
and handicrafts. Indonesian ikats and other textiles.

Anthony Hazledine Antique Oriental Carpets,
High Street,

Fairford GL7 4AD
Tel: 01285 713 400
Imp., Ret., Rep.; A., O.; Anat., Cauc., Pers.
Specialist in antique kilims and tribal rugs. Cleaning
and valuations.

Axia,
121 Ledbury Road,
London W11 2AQ
Tel: 0207 727 9724
Email: axia@dircon.co.uk
Ret.; A., O.; Anat., Cauc., Pers.
Yanni Petsopoulos is the author of the first kilim
book: Kilims (Thames & Hudson 1979).

Behar Profex Ltd.,
The Alban Building,
St Albans Place, Upper Street,
London N1 0NX
Tel: 0207 226 0144
Email: Cleanse repair@compuserve.com
Website: www.behar.co.uk
Rep.
Well-established cleaners, conservators and restor-
ers of fine tapestries, carpets, rugs and kilims.

Chandni Chowk,
1 Harlequins,
Paul Street,
Exeter EX4 3TT
Tel: 01392 410 201
Fax: 01392 421 095
Email: chandni@bigfoot.com
Imp., Ret., Col., W.; A., O., N.; N Af., Anat., Pers.,
Afgh.
Wide range of new, old and antique folk and tribal
applied arts.

Clive Rogers Oriental Rugs,
Coach House Studios,
66 Staines Road,
Wraysbury, Berkshire
Correspondence: PO Box 234,
Staines TW19 5PE
Tel: 01784 481 177/00
Email: info@orient-rug.com
Website: www.orient-rug.com
Imp., Ret.; A., O.; Anat., Pers.
Specialist in historic and early pieces and frag-
ments, mostly Anatolian but also Central Asian and
Persian. European tapestries and Indian dhurries.

Coats Oriental Carpets,
4 Kensington Church Walk,
London W8 4NB
Tel: 0207 937 0983
Email: alex-coats@hotmail.com
Website: www.coatscarpets.co.uk
Ret., W., Rep.; A.; Anat., Cauc., Pers., Afgh.
Antique kilims and carpets.

David Black Oriental Carpets,
96 Portland Road,
London W11 4LN
Tel: 0207 727 2566
Email: davidblack@david-black.com
Website: www.david-black.com
Imp., Ret., Rep.; A., N.; Anat., Pers., Cauc.
Antique, new natural dye kilims, pile carpets and
dhurries. Cleaning, restoration and valuations.

Dennis Woodman,
105 North Road,
Kew TW9 4HJ

Tel: 0208 878 8182
Email: WoodmanKew@aol.com
Old and new kilims. Advises on repairs and restoration, all carried out on the premises.

Fairman Carpets Ltd.,
218 Westbourne Grove,
London Q11 2RH
Tel: 0207 229 2262
Email: fairman-carpets@ukonline.co.uk
Website: www.fairman-carpets.com
Ret., Rep.; A., N.; Anat., Cauc., Pers.
Valuations done. Antique kilims and modern nomadic tribal flatweaves.

Gordon Reece Gallery,
Finkle Street,
Knaresborough HG5 8AA
Tel: 01423 866 219
Fax: 01423 868 165
Imp., Ret., W., Rep.; A., O.; Anat., Cauc., Pers., Afgh.
Stocks over 1000 rugs, mostly old and antique pieces. Organizes nine specialist exhibitions a year. Permanent stock of antique Chinese, Japanese, Indian and Tibetan furniture, sculpture and ceramics.
Also at:
16 Clifford Street,
London W1X 1RG
Tel: 0207 439 0007
Fax: 0207 437 5715

Haliden Oriental Carpets,
98 Walcot Street,
Bath BA1 5BG
Tel: 01225 469 240
Email: enquiries@haliden.com
Website: www.haliden.com
Ret., Rep.; A., O., N.; Anat., Pers., Cauc.
Old and antique kilims, flatweaves and pile rugs. Trade enquiries welcome.

The Kilim Warehouse Ltd.,
28a Pickets Street,
London SW12 8QB
Tel: 0208 675 3122
Email: info@kilim-warehouse.co.uk
Website: www.kilim-warehouse.co.uk/kilim/
Imp., W., Ret., Manu., Rep.; A., O., N.; Anat., Cauc., Pers., Afgh.
Founded 1982 by José Luczyc-Wyhowska. Kilims of every origin and age. Own new production, both modern and traditional.

Joseph Lavian,
Building 'E', 105 Eade Road,
London N4 1TJ
Tel: 0208 800 0707
Email: Joseph.Lavian@btinternet.com
Website: www.btinternet.Com/~joseph.lavian
Imp., W.; A., O.; N Af., Anat., Cauc., Pers., Afgh.
Kilims, pile rugs, Aubussons, Savonneries, tapestries and textiles.

The Lenkoran Gallery,
21 Goldhurst Terrace,
London NW6 3HD
Tel: 0207 604 4116
Email: gb@lenkoran.co.uk
Website: www.lenkoran.co.uk
Imp., Ret.; A.; Anat., Pers., Cauc.
Specialist in Anatolian kilims pre-1850 and in 19th-century Caucasian and Persian flatweaves.

Liberty Plc.,
Regent Street,
London WIR 6AH
Tel: 0207 734 1234
Website: www.liberty-of-london.com
Imp., Ret.; A., O., N.; Anat., Cauc., Pers., Afgh.
North African and European kilims also stocked. Will source any kind of kilim required.

Nathan Azizollahoff,
Oriental Carpet Centre,
Top Floor, Building A,
105 Eade Road,
London N4 1TJ
Tel: 0208 802 0077
Email: nathan.co@ndirect.co.uk
Imp., W.; O.; Anat., Pers., Afgh.
Old kilims and carpets.

Orlando Dos Santos,
12 St Benedict's Close,
Church Lane,
London SW17 9NU
Tel: 0208 767 4646
Restoration of kilims and pile carpets.

Oriental Rug Gallery,
42 Verulam Road,
St Albans AL3 4DQ
Tel: 01727 841 046
Email: rugs@orientalruggallery.com
Website: www.orientalruggallery.com
Also at:
Eton, Berkshire
Tel: 01753 623000
and
Guildford, Surrey
Tel: 01483 457600
and
Oxford
Tel: 01865 316333
Imp., Ret., Manu., Rep.; O., N.; Anat., Cauc., Pers., Afgh.
Kilims and carpets from 12 different countries.

Out of the Nomad's Tent,
21 St Leonard's Lane,
Edinburgh EH8 9SH
Tel: 0131 662 1612
Fax: 0131 667 6107
Email: kilims@reade.co.uk
Imp., Ret., W.; A., O., N.; Anat., Iraq., Pers., Afgh.
Rufus Reade and Maggie Struckmeier collect most kilims at source, travelling widely to find interesting examples. Selling exhibitions are held all over the UK.

The Persian Carpet Studio,
The Old White Hart,
Long Melford,
Sudbury CO10 9HX
Tel: 01787 882 214
Fax: 01787 882 213
Website: www.persian-carpet-studio.net
Ret., Rep.; A.
Specialists in restoration and cleaning.

Persian Tribal Rugs,
28 Milton Road,
Cambridge CB4 1JY
Tel./Fax: 01223 311 970
Website: www.persiantribalrugs.uksw.com
Also at:
21 Burwash Manor Farm,

New Road,
Barton CB3 7AY
Tel./Fax: 01223 264 811
Ret., W.; O., N.; Pers.
Direct importers from Iran.

The Read Molteno Gallery,
North End Cottages,
Broughton,
Stockbridge SO20 8AN
Tel: 01794 301 606
Fax: 01794 301 603
Ret.; O., N.; Anat., Pers., Afgh.
Specializes in ethnic decorative artifacts, including kilims, textiles, carvings, furniture and jewelry.

Richard Purdon Antique Carpets,
158 The Hill,
Burford OX18 4QY
Tel: 01993 823 777
Email: antiquerugs@richardpurdon.demon.co.uk
Website: www.purdon.com
Imp., Ret., Rep.; A., O.; Anat., Pers., Cauc.
Also Balkan kilims and antique rugs.

Robert Stephenson Oriental Carpets,
1 Elystan Street,
Chelsea Green,
London SW3 3NT
Tel: 0207 225 2343
Imp., Ret., Manu., Rep.; A., O., N.; Anat., Pers., Cauc.
Specialist in old and antique East European kilims. Manufactures Bessarabian kilims in modern designs and natural dyes.

Sala Gallery,
The Works,
Bower Hinton,
Martock TA12 6LG
Tel: 01935 827 051
Fax: 01935 825 556
Email: sala@dial.pipex.com
Website: www.sala.uk.com
Ret.; A., O., N.; Anat., Pers., Afgh.
A wide selection of kilims, carpets, antique furniture, tribal art and fabrics.

Samarkand Galleries,
8 Brewery Yard,
Sheep Street,
Stow-on-the-Wold GL54 1AA
Tel: 01451 832 322
Email: mac@samarkand.co.uk
Website: www.samarkand.co.uk
Imp., Ret.; A., O.; Cauc., Pers., Afgh.

Sara & David Bamford,
The Workhouse,
Presteigne Industrial Estate,
Presteigne, Powys
Tel: 01544 267 849
Restoration and conservation specialists.

Thames Carpet Cleaners,
48–56 Reading Road,
Henley-on-Thames RG9 1AG
Tel: 01491 574 676
Website: www.thames-carpets.co.uk
Ret., Rep.; A., O., N.; Anat., Cauc., Pers., Afgh.
Specialists in cleaning and restoration of fine and rare oriental rugs, tapestries, Aubussons and silks.

Turkmen Gallery,
8 Eccleston Street,

London SW1W 9LT
Tel: 0207 730 8848
Imp., Ret.; A., O., N.; Anat., Cauc., Pers., Afgh.
Also rugs and textiles from Central Asia.

Woven Art,
67 Webb Road,
London SW11 6SD
Tel: 0207 924 3030
Fax: 0207 924 3300
Ret.; Anat., Cauc., Pers., Afgh.

USA

Atiyeh International Ltd.,
PO Box 3040,
Newberg, OR 97132
Tel: 503 538 7560
Email: rugs@atiyeh.com
Website: www.atiyeh.com

Berbere Imports,
144 South Robertson Boulevard,
Los Angeles, CA 90048
Tel: 213 274 7064
Fax: 310 205 7953
Email: Berbere@yahoo.com
Imp., Ret., W., Rep.; A., O., N.; Anat., Cauc., Pers.,
Afgh.
Importers of rugs and kilims, including large size.

Caravanserai Ltd.,
1435 Dragon Street,
Dallas, Texas 75207
Tel: 214 741 2131
Email: caravanserai@earthlink.net
Website: www.caravan-serai.net
Imp., Ret.; A., O.; Anat., Pers., Afgh.
19th- and 20th-century kilims from many sources,
both decorative and tribal.

Emmett Eiland's Oriental Rug Co.,
1326 9th Street,
Berkeley, CA 94710
Tel: 510 526 1087
Email: erugs@internetrugs.com
Website: www.internetrugs.com

Foothill Oriental Rugs,
1460 Foothill Drive,
Salt Lake City, UT 84108
Tel: 801 582 3500
Fax: 801 582 3501
Imp., Ret., W., Rep.; A., O., N.; Anat., Cauc., Pers.,
Afgh.
A comprehensive selection from all major rug-
producing countries except China. Specializes in
flatweaves and tribal rugs.

Fugio International,
1621 12th Avenue,
Seattle, WA 98122
Tel: 206 322 6677
Fax: 800 571 9590
Email: sales@fugioltd.com
Website: www.fugioltd.com
Imp., Ret.; O., N.; Pers., Afgh.
Tribal rugs, cushions, kilims and bags.

Hazara Gallery,
6042 College Avenue,
Oakland, CA 94618
Tel: 510 655 3511
Fax: 510 655 5223
Email: info@hazaragallery.com

Website: www.hazaragallery.com
Ret.; A., O.; Anat., Cauc., Pers., Afgh.
Specializes in tribal weavings such as carpets,
kilims, embroideries and trappings.

Istanbul Imports,
623½ Queen Anne N,
Seattle, WA 98109
Tel: 206 284 9954

Istanbul to Samarkand,
1101 West 34th Street,
Austin, Texas 78705
Tel: 512 451 8533
Email: dendres@flash.net
Imp., A., O.; Anat., Cauc., Pers., Afgh.
Direct importer specializing in old, antique collec-
table and decorative weavings from many sources.
Travels frequently to Turkey and the Caucasus for
interesting examples. Also Kutahya and Isnik
ceramics, pillows, bags and trappings. Annual exhi-
bition.

The James Blackmon Gallery,
2140 Bush Street # 1,
San Francisco, CA 94115
Tel: 415 922 1859
Fax: 415 922 0406
Email: blackmon@concentric.net
Website: www.artnetcom/jwblackmon
Imp., Ret., Rep.; A.; Anat., Pers.
Appraises, lectures on, cleans, conserves and sells
antique textiles.

John & Susan Wertime,
P.O. Box 16296,
Alexandria, VA 22302
Tel: 703 379 8528
Email: wertime@erols.com

Kilim,
150 Thompson Street,
New York, NY 10012
Tel: 212 533 1677
Fax: 212 533 0402
Imp., Ret.; A., O.; Anat., Cauc., Pers.
Specializes in old and antique kilims, saddle bags,
prayer kilims, runners and tribal kilims in all sizes.

The Pillowry, L.A.,
8270 Melrose Avenue,
Los Angeles, CA 90046
Tel: 323 651 5131
Email: vjvjggjgj@aol.com
Imp., W.; A., O.; N Af., Anat., Cauc., Pers., Afgh.
Antique and old kilims from Central Asia and
Eastern Europe; antique tapestry pillows.

The Pillowry, N.Y.,
P.O. Box 6902,
New York, NY 10128
Tel: 212 308 1630
Email: lawent@earthlink.net
Website: www.pillowry.com
Ret., W.; A., O.; N Af., Anat., Cauc., Pers., Afgh.
Specialist in pillows, with a world-wide collection
of antique and old textiles and kilims, tapestry,
Aubusson, silk and paisley.

Rudolph J. Geissmann,
PO Box 85,
Cardiff by the Sea, CA 92007
Tel: 760 944 7571
Email: sailor@cts.com
Website: www.antique-carpets.com

Imp., Ret., Rep.; A., O.; Anat., Pers., Cauc.
Antique and old kilims and carpets, expert repairs,
cleaning, valuations.

Santos Gallery,
521 S.W. 10th,
Portland, OR 97205
Tel: 503 227 6650
Fax: 503 234 1345
Website: www.santosgallery.com
Ret.; A.
Selection of antique kilims, vegetable-dyed and in
good condition.

Shaver Ramsey Oriental Galleries,
2414 East Third Avenue,
Denver, CO 80206
Tel: 303 320 6363
Email: shram@earthlink.net
Imp., Ret.; A., O., N.; Anat., Pers., Afgh.
Vast collection of kilims, from antique, classic and
collectable, to the more modern and decorative.

Silk Route Corp.,
3119 Fillmore Street,
San Francisco, CA 94123
Tel: 415 563 4936
Imp., Ret., W., Manu., Col., Rep.; A., O., N.; N Af.,
Anat., Cauc., Pers., Afgh.
More than 41 years of experience in the rug busi-
ness, both in the USA and Afghanistan.

Stephen Miller Gallery,
730 Santa Cruz Avenue,
Menlo Park, CA 94025
Tel: 888 566 8833
Website: www.stephenmillergallery.com
Ret., Rep.; A., O., N.; Anat., Cauc., Pers., Afgh.
Comprehensive selection in all sizes.

Sümer Nomadic Rugs,
Village at Wexford J7F,
Hilton Head, SC 29928
Imp., W.; Anat., Cauc.

Sun Bow Trading Co.,
108 4th Street NE,
Charlottesville, VA 22902
Tel: 804 293 8821
Fax: 804 293 8835
Website: www.sunbowtrading.com
Imp., Ret., W., Rep.; Anat., Pers., Afgh.
Source acquisition of tribal and nomadic textiles
and rugs from Konya to Kashgar.

Tamor Shah,
3219 Cains Hill Place NE,
Atlanta, GA 30305
Tel: 404 261 7259
Imp., Ret., W.; A., O.; Afgh.
Fine antique and semi-antique rugs, kilims, tapes-
tries, embroideries, costume and lace.

Trocadero Textile & Nomadic Art,
2313 Calvert Street at Connecticut Avenue NW,
Washington, DC 20008
Tel: 202 328 8440
Imp., Ret., W., Col., Rep.; A., O., N.; Anat., Cauc.,
Pers., Afgh.
Well-established firm renowned for their collection
of antique kilims, tribal weavings and ethnographic
furniture from the Swat Valley and Morocco.
Exceptional repair service available on rugs and
textiles. Pillows, kilims and carpet bags also avail-
able.

Turkana Gallery of Old and Antique Kilims,
125 Cedar Street, Penthouse,
New York, NY 10006
Tel: 212 732 0273
Fax: 212 349 6484
Email: Byramhouse@aol.com
Website: www.pdavies@tribal-kilims.com
Imp., Ret.; A., O.; Anat., N Af., Cauc., Pers., Afgh.
A pioneer in introducing the kilim to the USA.
Specialists in collectable Anatolian kilims. Large
selection of antique Caucasian kilims as well as
outstanding examples from other areas. Also tribal
bags, animal trappings, costumes and pillows.
Excellent washing, restoration and appraisal ser-
vices. By appointment.

Woven Legends Inc.,
4700 Wissahickon Avenue,
Philadelphia, PA 19144
Tel: 215 849 8344
Fax: 215 849 8354
Imp., Ret., Rep., W.; A., O., N.; Anat., Cauc., Pers.
Fine antique and modern kilims.

Yayla Tribal Rugs,
283 Broadway,
Cambridge, MA 02139
Tel: 617 576 3249
Email: yayla98@aol.com

Websites of interest

www.rugnotes.com Over 8300 pages of oriental
rug information, attribution, guides, book reviews,
and 4 discussion boards.

www.turkotek.com Non-commercial site devoted
to weaving where rug enthusiasts can meet.

www.hali.com Oriental rugs and textiles.

www.cloudband.com Oriental rugs and textiles.

www.nonplusultra.com Oriental rugs and textiles.

www.weavingartmuseum.com Online museum
with exhibitions and information.

Auction Houses

Australia

James R. Lawson Pty., Ltd.,
212 Cumberland Street,
Sydney, NSW 2026
Tel: 2 9241 3411
Email: lawsons@lawsons.com.au
Website: www.lawsons.com.au
Monthly auctions of oriental rugs and kilims. In
May and November there are specialist sales
devoted to fine and early examples.

Germany

Stuttgarter Kunstauktionshaus,
Adlerstrasse 31–33,
D-70199 Stuttgart,

P.O.B. 10 35 54,
D-70030 Stuttgart
Tel: 711 649 69-0

UK

Bonhams,
Montpelier Street,
London SW7 1HH
Tel: 0207 393 3900

Christie's,
8 King St,
St James,
London SW1Y 6QT
Tel: 0207 839 9060

Christie's (South Kensington) Ltd.,
85 Old Brompton Road,
London SW7 3LD
Tel: 0207 581 7611

Phillips,
101 New Bond Street,
London W1Y 0AS
Tel: 0207 629 6602

Rippon Boswell & Co.,
6 South Kensington Station Arcade,
London SW7 2NA
Tel: 0207 589 4242

Sotheby's,
34–35 New Bond Street,
London W1Y 9HB
Tel: 0207 493 8080

Woolley & Wallis,
56–61 Castle Street,
Salisbury,
Wiltshire SP1 3SU
Tel: 01722 424525

USA

Christie's,
502 Park Avenue,
New York, NY 10022
Tel: 212 546 1000

Rippon Boswell Inc.,
Suite 819, Windsor Tower,
5 Tudor City Place,
New York, NY 10017
Tel: 212 599 5650

Skinner Inc.,
63 Park Plaza,
Boston, MA 02116
Tel: 617 350 5400
and
357 Main Street,
Bolton, MA 01740
Tel: 508 779 6241

Sotheby's,
1334 York Avenue,
New York, NY 10021-4806
Tel: 212 606 7000

Switzerland

Rippon Boswell & Co. AG,
Kurbergstrasse 25,
CH-8049 Zurich
Tel: 1 341 7854

Sources of Illustrations

Herbert Bieler: 18, 19, 115, 229, 230, 231, 239, 259, 264, 301, 305, 342, 354, 579, 627.
David Black: 595.
Galerie Neiriz, Berlin: 218, 233, 241, 251, 252, 329, 345, 356, 374, 388, 389, 402, 404, 411, 414, 418, 452.
Hazara Oriental Rug Gallery: 566, 631, 634.
Alastair Hull: 100, 102, 105, 106, 110–113, 117, 118, 247, 343, 360–369, 375–385, 390, 393, 395, 397–400, 403, 410, 417, 424, 425, 428–437, 439–441, 446, 448, 450, 451, 453, 479–481, 484, 485, 488–490, 492–499, 509, 513–515, 517–519, 521–524, 529–532, 534–537, 540, 543, 552, 554, 555, 557, 578, 580–583, 599, 620–622, 628, 632, 633, 635, 636, 638, 639, 647.
Valerie Justin, The Pillowry, Los Angeles: 160, 165, 167–169, 173, 178, 181, 182, 184, 187, 189–194, 211, 276, 458.
Geert Keppens: 15, 199, 200, 215, 219, 225–227, 234, 237, 238, 246, 257, 258, 260, 266, 269, 287, 288, 321–323, 328, 331, 335, 337, 346, 391, 392, 394, 406, 412, 413, 415, 416, 419, 420, 426, 427, 438, 442, 444, 482, 483, 486, 487, 500–503, 505–508, 538, 539, 541, 542, 560–562, 564, 565, 568, 577, 586, 600, 601.
Koninklijk Instituut voor de Tropen: 25, 28–30, 32, 33, 45.
Marjorie Lawrence: 5, 8, 186, 188.
Robert Lawrence: 31.
Hugo Luczyc-Wyhowski: 236, 249, 267, 284, 310, 320, 359.
José Luczyc-Wyhowska: 4, 14, 26, 27, 35, 40, 42–44, 51, 163, 164, 172, 174, 176, 177, 179, 180, 185, 196, 207, 212, 213, 216, 217, 220, 221, 232, 235, 242, 245, 248, 254–256, 261, 262, 265, 273, 275, 277–282, 286, 290, 292, 294, 295, 304, 307, 309, 312, 314, 330, 332–334, 338, 340, 341, 367, 386, 457, 462–466, 469, 471–474, 477, 478, 597, 607, 611, 613–616, 618, 629, 637, 646, 649.
Mark Shilen Gallery: 13, 23.
Don Meier: 12.
James Merrell: 3, 7, 210, 214, 228, 243, 244, 250, 274, 293, 300, 319, 372, 373, 401, 409, 443, 445, 447, 449, 491, 504, 510–512, 516, 520, 525–528, 533, 553, 556, 558, 559, 584, 610.
Linda Miller: 283, 298, 339, 422, 459, 460, 461.
Jurg Rageth: 201, 203, 223, 240, 251, 252, 263, 270–272, 285, 289, 291, 302, 306, 315, 317, 318, 324–327, 336, 569, 574, 575, 587, 592, 594, 626, 640, 641, 643, 644.
Gordon Reece: 371.
Royal Geographical Society: 20.
Daniele Sevi: 222, 468, 642.
Mohammed Tehrani: 387, 396, 407, 423, 470, 563.
Turkana: 206, 224, 253, 350, 370, 467, 567, 571, 572, 588, 590.
Zollanvari: 348, 405, 408, 421.

Acknowledgments

A book such as this requires the co-operation and generosity of many people. We are extremely grateful to all those who have helped us with travelling, answering innumerable questions, translating, providing information, examples and photographs, and who have offered enthusiastic support.

Many of the wonderful kilims illustrated here have been expertly photographed for us from personal collections and stock by the following: Geert Keppens, Lokeren; David Black, London; James Merrell, London; Hazara Oriental Gallery, California; The Pillowry, California; Turkana, New York; Linda Miller, New York; Zollanvari AG, Zurich; Galerie Neiriz, Berlin; Mohammed Tehrani, Hamburg; Herbert Bieler, Enzerdorf; Daniele Sevi, Milan; Jurg Rageth, Basle. We would also like to thank Nicholas Barnard for sourcing many of the photographs; Jean Engel, for her advice on Moroccan kilims; Richard Tucker for the map illustrations; Don Medier, the intrepid traveller, and Robert Lawrence, for photographs taken in Afghanistan and Tunisia. Finally, thank you to all the unknown weavers, spinners and dyers who created these works of art.

Index